ENGAGING THE TIMES

The Witness of Thomism

THE AMERICAN MARITAIN ASSOCIATION
BOOK SERIES • VOLUME 27

AMERICAN MARITAIN ASSOCIATION BOOK SERIES

Since 1988, when the American Maritain Association's book series was founded by Anthony O. Simon, the association has published an annual collection of essays coming largely (although not exclusively) from papers presented at its international meetings. The many volumes of the series range over the entire span of themes and problems found not only in Maritain's writings but also in those of St. Thomas Aquinas, and are intended for specialists and non-specialists, alike. In Maritain we find a Thomist who is fully engaged with his times and an encouragement to do the same with our own. So encouraged, these volumes are offered in the same spirit of friendship for which Jacques and his wife, Raïssa, had so notable a genius.

ENGAGING THE TIMES

The Witness of Thomism

EDITED BY JOSHUA SCHULZ

AMERICAN MARITAIN ASSOCIATION

Distributed by

THE CATHOLIC UNIVERSITY
OF AMERICA PRESS
Washington, D.C.

Manufactured in the United States of America

Distributed by the Catholic Univesity of America Press
620 Michigan Avenue, N.E., 240 Leahy Hall
Washington, D.C. 20064

Library of Congress Cataloging-in-Publication Data
Names: Schulz, Joshua, editor.
Title: Engaging the times : the witness of Thomism /
edited by Joshua Schulz.
Description: Washington, DC : American Maritain Association, 2017. |
Series: Publications of the American Maritain Association
Identifiers: LCCN 2017020741 | ISBN 9780982711996
Subjects: LCSH: Maritain, Jacques, 1882–1973.
Classification: LCC B2430.M34 E54 2017 | DDC 194—dc23
LC record available at https://lccn.loc.gov/2017020741
ISBN 978-0-9827-1199-6

Dedicated to my wife, Christine

Contents

Acknowledgements

One does not edit a volume such as this on one's own, and many thanks are owed to many people who had a hand in this work. Michael D. Torre deserves credit as the president of the American Maritain Association in 2015 who organized an incredible conference of international Maritain scholars, and Giuseppe Butera's wise direction as the general editor of this series has been invaluable. I would like to thank the anonymous referees who helped select the works for this volume, as well as the many authors—some represented herein, and some who are not—whose excellent work continues to advance our understanding of Jacques and Raïssa Maritain and the world we share with them. Much thanks are also due to Stephen Loughlin, Brian Kane, and Karen Walton at DeSales University, who have encouraged and funded my travel to Maritain conferences for several years. Much thanks to Rebecca Schreiber of Kachergis Book Design for her help with the cover art depicting the story of St. Anthony of Padua and the mule. Brought to its knees by a Eucharistic miracle worked by St. Anthony, the mule represents the intellectual stubbornness of the workaday world and its uncomprehending dismissal of philosophical reflection and theological priorities. It is a classic and hopeful image of the Church's fruitful engagement with the world. Finally, I have the deepest gratitude for my wife of many years, Christine, for her companionship, her insight, her love, and her support.

JOSHUA SCHULZ

Introduction

Engaging the Times

THE PERIOD OF THE mid-1930s to 1940s marked something of a turning point in the career of French-Catholic Thomist Jacques Maritain. Already well-known for his metaphysical and epistemological work, Maritain responded to the worldwide social and political turmoil of his times with several works of moral and political philosophy. Books such as *Humanisme intégral* (1936) and *Les droits des homme et la loi naturelle* (1942) established the contours of his thought, which were further developed in *Christianisme et démocratie* (1943) and *Man and the State* (1949).

Maritain's approach to moral and political philosophy was at one and the same time both traditional and liberal. For instance, Maritain insisted on both the truth of the natural law tradition from which he worked as well as its compatibility with democratic and religious pluralism—positions which later found expression in documents of Vatican II, such as *Gaudium et Spes,* but which, at the time of their writing, made him several enemies on the right and left alike (though they made him influential in Latin America). For these reasons and others, in addition to the fact that both his wife and mother-in-law were Jewish, Maritain fled to the United States at the outbreak of World War II in 1939.

From his posts at Princeton and Columbia Universities, Maritain devoted some of his energies to the support of the Allied war effort, e.g., recording several radio broadcasts in support of Charles de Gaulle's Free French Forces and the French resistance movement, as well as writing essays for American audiences condemning anti-semitism and the political, cultural, and humanitarian stakes of the war. "If the Axis powers win the war," he wrote in "The Crisis of Civilization," "night will fall on the world and freedom will die for centuries—all freedoms, and honor, and the very possibility of living as men."

At the conclusion of the war Maritain was rewarded for his efforts with an appointment as French Ambassador to the Vatican, and was a key contributor to the United Nations Universal Declaration of Human Rights (1948). Indeed, one of our contributors argues that Maritain's November 1947 speech to the Second Session of the General Conference of UNESCO in Mexico City galvanized support for the Declaration, which was foundering on the shoals of disagreements about the theoretical foundations of human rights. His other contributions to the post-war world, direct and indirect, are many, and the opening essays in this volume focus on Maritain's engagement with the practical problem of his times.

The first essay in this volume, Michael D. Torre's "The Nobility of Jacques Maritain's Witness and Work in World War II," gives an overview of the post-war period of Maritian's life that forms the backdrop for this book. Torre outlines Maritain's "practical turn" in the 1930s, looking at the inspiration of *Integral Humanism,* Maritain's development of Christian humanism and the need for a "pluralistic but theocentric democracy," and his work as a public figure who voiced powerful critiques of Hitler, Mussolini, and the tragedy of the Spanish Civil War.

In "Maritain and the Possibilities for Cooperation in a Still Divided World," Richard Schenk focuses our attention on Maritain's suggestions about how to achieve the important right to religious freedom, his contributions to the work of UNESCO in 1947 and 1948, and his indirect involvement with the Second Vatican Council. First, Schenk discusses the context and importance of Maritain's claim—instrumental to the passing of the UN Declaration on Human Rights—that it was not necessary to achieve theoretical consensus about the justification of human rights in order to achieve the practical consensus necessary to pass the Declaration. Second, Schenk examines Maritain's indirect influence on the debates about religious freedom through works such as *Integral Humanism* and *Man and the State,* as well as four memoranda on the topic of religious freedom Maritain wrote in response to questions from Pope Paul VI about the Council's proceedings. Schenk ends his essay by reflecting on the importance of Maritain's "creative fidelity" to Aquinas as a model for contemporary Thomists engaging in social questions.

French Maritain scholar Florian Michel then examines Maritan's political positions as a young man, of which he held many. As Michel writes, Maritain was "a socialist, an anarchist, a revolutionary, a Dreyfusard, a feminist, a republican at times, a libertarian sometimes, a Péguyist in his own way, and a Proudhonian on occasion." Michel carefully traces Maritain's transition from a young, ardent socialist to the sophisticated defender of Thomistic democracy who never lost his early concerns for the poor and for liberty.

John Dunaway traces the impact of the work of Jacques and Raïssa Maritain on the American Civil Rights Movement. Dunaway shows that several leaders or actors in the movement, including John Howard Griffin and Saul Alinsky, drew on their personal and intellectual engagement with the Maritains as inspiration. Others, such as the Rev. Dr. Martin Luther King Jr. and Thomas Merton, were careful readers of Maritain.

Finally, Gregory Reichberg's article, "Jacques Maritain, Spain, and Holy War," examines the strategy adopted by Maritain when he argued against claims made during the Spanish Civil War that the Nationalists were waging a "holy war" in defense of Catholicism in Spain. His critique of this religious ideology was two-pronged. On the one hand he explained how the violent methods employed by the Nationalists were wholly incompatible with action that might be deemed "holy." Hence, to speak of a "holy war" in this context was an unacceptable oxymoron. On the other hand, setting his argumentation within a philosophy of history, Maritain elucidates that while the idea of holy war might have had a basis within the "sacral" conception of the temporal that was prevalent during the European Middle Ages, within the "secular" conception of the temporal that is characteristic of European modernity, this idea no longer enjoys any possible validity. Hence, appeals to "holy war" in the Spanish context of the 1930s reflected a dangerous anachronism that should henceforth be recognized as illegitimate within Christian discourse.

Taking Maritain's own interaction with modernity as their model, other essays in this volume display how a resurgent Thomism can engage with the pressing issues of our own day.

Part II of the volume presents several examples of how Thomistic principles can be applied to the analysis, critique, and improvement of modern culture and education.

In "Market Pressures, Outcomes Assessment, and Catholic Higher Education: At the Crossroads—Again," Noel Adams examines the vision of higher education Maritain sets forth in *Pour la justice,* one in which both faith and reason play essential roles in the search for truth. In this work Maritain also expressed his concerns about secular influences on this vision. Adams argues that market pressures, the outcomes assessment movement, and the increasing influence of anthropocentric humanism are in fact damaging Catholic higher education, facilitated by the educational implications of the G.I. Bill of 1944 and the 1971 Supreme Court case *Tilton v Richardson.* Although the Church reacted to these secular influences in *Gaudium et Spes* and *Ex Corde Ecclesiae,* they seem to have had little impact on Catholic universities. University educators are urged to rededicate themselves to the goal of educating for the spiritual and moral development of human beings.

Walter Schultz explains how this might be done in "Two Universal Principles of Education: Intuition and Love." Pedagogy, he argues, as the discipline concerned with teaching how to teach, is about discerning proper method in the teaching profession. Specifically, there are two universal principles which must be adhered to within the classroom and lecture hall: intuition and love. These principles are universal because they direct us to what *is* and what it is to be human; and it is Jacques Maritain who identifies these universal principles as primordial and the primary concern of education. This means that the teaching profession involves more than method and teaching itself. This is so because intuition and love designate the immediate, pre-conceptual apprehension of reality and the human person. The primary agency in the process of education is the natural inclination of the will toward reality through intuition and toward the person through love. The universality of these principles is exemplified when the classroom and lecture hall merge with other venues for education within the global forum, working toward establishing our humanity, avoiding the pitfalls of self-indulgent individualism and totalitarian control.

Taking a broader approach to modern culture, Stephen Chamberlain examines the structural underpinnings that make a philosopher's engagement with the world both possible and fruitful in "Interpreting the Times: The Philosopher's Understanding in Engaging the World." The essay undertakes a meta-analysis of the philosopher in relation to the particulars of his time; or, to put it another way, it considers the intentional structure and virtue of the philosopher insofar as he takes on the role of cultural critic. In doing this, Chamberlain shows how an Aristotelian-Thomistic philosophical psychology undergirds and explains the specific virtue or disposition (*habitus*) of the philosopher insofar as he interprets the times against the backdrop of universal values, principles, and causes. In undertaking this task, Chamberlain focuses on two central notions. First, he examines the intellectual virtue of understanding (*sunesis*) as discussed by Aristotle in Book VI of the *Nicomachean Ethics*. Aristotle's brief analysis suggests how *sunesis* can be considered a hybrid virtue that integrates qualities of both practical wisdom (*phronêsis*) and speculative wisdom (*epistēmē*). These qualities are essential for the cultural critic insofar as he offers a truthful analysis of the movements or trends of his day. Secondly, the author shows how the notion of understanding as an intellectual virtue can be developed and deepened through a Thomistic account of the cogitative power or particular reason (*ratio particularis*). It is through the cogitative faculty that intuitive reason, in its instrumental use of the internal sense power, is able to perceive and in turn interpret the particulars of one's age. Such perception is essential to the success or virtue of the philosopher as cultural critic.

In Part III we turn to issues in Thomistic Anthropology. Brian Kemple argues in "Jacques Maritain and *Ens ut Primum Cognitum*" that although St. Thomas' teaching that being is the first known was very often interpreted within realist philosophies to mean that *ens ut primum cognitum* is *ens reale*, this assumption carries a train of unfortunate consequences. Nevertheless, the ardor of Thomists for overcoming idealism does not diminish the great benefits to be found in their teachings on the development of human knowledge. Kemple proposes a substantial investigation of Jacques Maritain, especially his *Preface to Metaphysics* and *Degrees of Knowledge*. After discussing contributions to the Thomistic doctrines of abstraction, Kemple examines Maritain's account of the process of concept formation and the nature of the object of the concept, as well as the root of Maritain's philosophy of being in relation to his philosophy of knowledge. On this basis, Kemple suggests that we can develop our understanding of St. Thomas beyond what Maritain has given us.

In "Subjectivity and the *Prise de Conscience* in Jacques Maritain," Francisco Eduardo Plaza claims that, although Jacques Maritain was critical of the modern age, he was also able to recognize its positive contributions. Maritain stated that we are living in the "reflective" or "reflex" age, in which man is generally becoming more aware of and vested in his own subjectivity. He referred to this kind of self-awareness in various works as the *prise de conscience* (a beginning of awareness). While this modern development has born great fruit, it can also breed problems when divorced from the true good outside the human person. Karol Wojtyla (St. John Paul II) also noted this modern trend, and recognized it as a way of genuine advancement in human thought. Although both Wojtyla and Maritain took a somewhat different approach to the matter, it is interesting to note that they nevertheless reached roughly the same conclusions with respect to their view on the person and his subjectivity. Plaza focuses primarily on how Maritain presented subjectivity in the human person, and secondarily on the parallels between Maritain's thought and that of Wojtyla.

Gregory Kerr tackles contemporary philosophical naturalism in "Will the Real Agents Please Stand Up? Jacques Maritain and David Bently Hart on Science and Human Agency." Kerr argues that philosophical naturalism both misunderstands human beings *as objects* that we know and limits our very capacity to think in an authentically human way, as is evident in contemporary treatments of human agency and consciousness, in which human agency disappears. However, as Maritain argues in *Person and the Common Good* and *Education at the Crossroads*, the concept of a human being as a real agent, one who is freely intelligent and intelligently free, is central to issues of human dignity, rights, and political freedom. Kerr argues that the reason philosophical naturalism cannot account for agency is that human nature as such is simply not available to the sciences as they are practiced today. Kerr argues that this lacunae gives us good reason to reassess Maritain's thesis in *Degrees of Knowledge* that true epistemology would recognize a "diversity of dimensions" to reality rather than artificially flatten the world to a single dimension of being.

In "The Body's Justice: A Hylomorphic View of the Genesis of Virtue," Federico Tedesco examines the metaphyisical basis of justice within a hylemorphic anthropology. If the body is a part of the complete quiddity of man, he argues, then the somatic virtues inherent to his body must be a part of the total virtue (*hole arte*) whereby man gains perfect happiness. Tedesco discusses the Aristotelian roots of Aquinas's concept of a *complexion corporis*, showing that only in the human body can the elements combine according to a proportional equality, giving rise to a distributive justice, which is a necessary condition for the genesis of the other virtues. Finally, Tedesco provides a hylemorphic account of the instruments which generate the justice of the body in the cases in which one's *complexion corporis* is unbalanced by nature or because of the bad habits produced by his environment.

The final part of our volume engages with several problems in ethics and aesthetics. In a powerful essay, "The Corrosive Effect of Doubt on the Natural Law," James Jacobs deepens Maritian's analysis of the twentieth century's political crises as being due to a loss of a sense of human transcendence in the Enlightenment. Drawing on Richard Taylor and Josef Pieper, Jacobs argues that modern man lives in an atmosphere polluted by Cartesian doubt. Within a Thomistic framework, Jacobs argues that this atmostphere distorts the way modern man pursues the primary precepts of the natural law, and that this blind seeking after the human goods lies at the heart of our own civilizational crisis.

Anne Francis Ai Le, OP considers Maritain's understanding of the relation between religion and politics in "It is Right and Just: Ontological Poverty and the Duty of Religion." She argues that the recognition of our dependence on God as our greatest Benefactor, on Whom all things depend, calls forth the response of religion. For Maritain, such recognition of religion can benefit and should be allowed to have a role in the political arena. Following Maritain's example, Ai Le argues for the significance, stemming from man's ontological poverty, of the duty of religion in the Thomistic tradition against the popular claim that religion is but a matter of personal preference and thus should be relegated to the personal, subjective sphere.

In his 2004 allocution on "Life-Sustaining Treatments and the Vegetative State," Pope John Paul II characterized nutrition and hydration for patients in a persistent vegetative state (PVS) as obligatory and proportionate in principle. This has been characterized by a number of Roman Catholic ethicists as a significant departure from the Roman Catholic ethical tradition, which has normally included the weighing of potential benefits and burdens of a given medical procedure in order to determine whether it is ordinary (and thus obligatory) or extraordinary, optional care. In "Revisionism or Within the Roman Catholic Ethical Tradition? John Paul II on Assisted Nutrition and Hydration," Justin Gable, OP argues that Pope John Paul II's stance on PVS patient care cannot be read as a mere presumption in favor of nutrition and hydration, nor can it reasonably be construed , even on this stronger reading, as altering the ethical tradition of the Church, standing, on the contrary, firmly within it.

In "Art and Morality: Nuancing the Divide through Creative Intuition," Megan Furman examines Maritain's complex distinction between the realms of art and morality. While Maritain is aware that many good artists are not saints, and that many saints are not good artists, his treatment of the often *positive* relationship between art and morality is more ambiguous. By investigating Maritain's account of creative intuition, Furman analyzes the ways in which art can be both moral and amoral, using Dante as a paradigm case of a fruitful interaction between art and virtue.

In our final essay in the volume, "Mothers, Children, and their Common Good," Karen Chan explores contemporary attacks on traditional conceptions of the family, and specifically, the dignity of the vocation of motherhood. Utilizing a Maritainian understanding of the common good, she defends the notion of the common good of the family and the ways in which this common good flows back into its constituent parts. Chan uses this analysis to reject modern arguments which construe motherhood as unjustly limiting the freedom and development of women, arguing instead that motherhood is a unique and significant expression of the integral perfection of women.

I

MARITAIN ENGAGÉ

MICHAEL D. TORRE

The Nobility of Jacques Maritain's Witness and Work in World War II*

I. Introduction

IN 2014, THE American Maritain Association's annual conference focused on Jacques Maritain at his "beginning": as the former pupil—turned sometimes severe critic—of Henri Bergson in his first book, and the direction of his thought directly thereafter. In 2015, the focus now shifts to the man in his "prime," the man he had become after twenty years dedicated to advocating Thomistic philosophy and principles in Paris following World War I. In *Pour la justice,* which contains addresses and essays that Maritain gave in the United States during World War II, we also find addresses that manifest the practical direction his thought had taken in the years just before the outbreak of war, responding to the Nazi threat then menacing Western civilization.

II. His Witness

My intention in this essay is simply to recall those times and provide an outline of his portrait for us in these war years. As his first book amply attests, his first love was theoretical philosophy. Epistemology, metaphysics, and the relation of empirical science to the philosophy of nature all dominate his interest in the fifteen years following the first war. However, his thought took a "practical turn" in the early 1930s, no doubt in part due to

* For René and Dominique Mougel and *Le Cercle d'Etudes Jacques et Raïssa Maritain,* in gratitude.

the rise and importance of Communism, Fascism, and then National Socialism, and especially as galvanized by the Spanish Civil War—a practical turn amply captured in his *Integral Humanism*. He had not only become interested in offering a new political vision (of a "Christian humanism" and a "pluralist but theocentric democracy"), but he had also become a "man of action" and of political manifestos—responding to the rise of Hitler and his anti-Semitism, to Mussolini's invasion of Ethiopia, and especially to the anguish of the Spanish Civil War.[1] He had become more than a cultivated Catholic professor of Thomistic philosophy; he was now a "public figure," a Catholic layman who took provocative political stands and who was a figure of some controversy.[2]

Thus, Maritain found himself in the United States at the beginning of 1940, partly at the behest of the French Government,[3] whose office of Cul-

1. See *Pour le bien commun* (April, 1934), a Catholic response to French political extremists, especially of the Right; *Manifeste pour la justice et la paix* (October, 1935), responding to Mussolini's invasion of Ethiopia; and *Pour la peuple basque* (April, 1937), responding to Hitler's bombardment of Guernica. His *Lettre sur l'Independence* (December, 1935) staked out his own political position as independent of parties on the left or right, however much he might join with the former on a vital matter at issue. For a fuller discussion of this time of manifestos, and the influence of Maritain and the "circle of Meudon" in forming the political conscience of many French Catholics, see Bernard Doering, *Jacques Maritain and the French Catholic Intellectuals* (Notre Dame, Indiana: University of Notre Dame Press, 1983), 60–84.

2. His fifty page preface to Alfredo Mendizibal's 1937 book on the Spanish Civil War—*Aux origines d'une tragédie*, translated the following year as *The Martyrdom of Spain* (New York: Charles Scribner's Sons, 1938), 1–48—reaffirmed his unwillingness to side with the Left, yet he was just as adamant in refusing to side with Franco or endorse his holy war "crusade." In doing so, he made himself *persona non grata* with the Spanish bishops and many Spanish Catholics who felt that, in this time of civil war, one could not but side with Franco. (For a Spaniard who both well understood and presented the good and evil on *both* sides of the conflict, yet whose work evinced this position, see José Gironella's rightly renowned trilogy, *The Cypresses Believe in God, One Million Dead,* and *Peace is Breaking Out.*) Sins against *ius in bello*—on both sides—that Maritain and others decried need not determine the issue of *ius ad bello*. Yet surely Maritain was within his rights to argue that *he* was an "outsider," and thus positioned to plead for peace. For one of his most eloquent defenses of his position on Spain, see "An Interview with Jacques Maritain," in *Commonweal* 29 (February 3, 1939): 398–402. In works such as *L'Impossible Antisemitisme* (1937) and a discourse on "Les Juifs parmi les nations" (February, 1938), one that evoked controversy when given, receiving "cat-calls" from part of his audience, Maritain had shown himself to be the implacable opponent of Nazi racism, denouncing Anti-Semitism as un-Christian. (As a result of this, when the Gestapo reached Paris in June 1940, one of the first things it did was to go hunting for him, in Meudon.)

3. Jacques, Raïssa, and Vera left Marseille on the "Exocorda" on January 4, 1940, successfully crossed the Atlantic to Boston and took a train, reaching Toronto on January 15, 1940. See Jean-Luc Barré's *Jacques et Raïssa Maritain: Les Mendiants du Ciel* (Paris: Stock, 1995), 469–70, and *Raïssa's Journal*, preface by René Voillaume (Albany, New York: Magi, 1974), 286 and 289. The degree of

tural Affairs requested that he be in the New World at this time of growing crisis, as someone who could help represent its interests there.[4] Four months after his arrival, in mid-May, while still residing in a Manhattan hotel,[5] and as Germany turned the full force of its arms on France, he received a cablegram confirming his (admittedly undefined) "mission" to the United States, as a kind of semi-official representative of French intellectual life and culture.[6] Within a month, France had been forced to capitulate before the Nazi blitzkrieg.

In the black days of that month of late May and early June 1940, Europeans everywhere contemplated the seemingly inevitable descent into the

---

my indebtedness to Barré's account of these war years will quickly be apparent. I am even more in debt, as he himself was, to René Mougel, the first to deal with Maritain's years in New York. See "Les années de New York, 1940–1945," in *Cahiers Jacques Maritain*, nos. 16–17 (April, 1988): 7–18. For an account of their liner's arrival from Boston into New York on January 15, see *The Brooklyn Daily Eagle*, January 16, 1940: 18; www.bklyn.newspapers.com/image/52686538/. It appears Raïssa mis-identifies their port of debarkation as New York City in her *Journal*, for Jacques—in a note to Yves R. Simon from January 18, 1940—says that they "arrived via Boston" and it was thus that he had not had a chance to meet with Julie Kernan in New York City. See *Jacques Maritain-Yves Simon Correspondance, Tome I: Les années francaises* (1927–1940), edited and annotated by Florian Michel, with the collaboration of René Mougel and Anthony O. Simon, Introduction by Philippe Chenaux (Tours: Éditions CDL, 2008), 397. That also better fits with Raïssa saying they arrived in Toronto on January 15.

4. See Jean-Luc Barré's *Les Mendiants*, 467, citing Raïssa's journal note 281: entry for October, 14, 1939.

5. They moved from Canada (Toronto and then Montreal) to New York on March 2, 1940: see *Raïssa's Journal*, 290. In a letter to Simon, Maritain implies that they initially stayed for several weeks with Kernan (since he has Yves write him c/o her address); see *Correspondance I*, 405. After the three of them return from a visit to Chicago, he writes Simon from the Prince George Hotel in New York City on May 19 and 21, so they seem to have still been staying there: see *Correspondance I*, 411–12. Julie Kernan gives their hotel that "summer" as the Brevoort (11 5th Avenue); see her *Our Friend, Jacques Maritain: A Personal Memoir* (New York: Doubleday, 1975), 120. Possibly, then, they moved from the Prince George to the Brevoort sometime in May. Kernan remembers them chiefly as being in a hotel at a *hot* time (120), and the beginning of June (when they were in the Brevoort, if not the Prince George) was indeed stifling hot that year. However, on June 18th, Maritain writes Simon to say that they have just begun to "sublet an apartment" for three months; see *Correspondance I*, 415. For more on this apartment, see footnote no. 32.

6. Barré, *Les Mendiants*, 470. Jacques confirms as much; see *Raïssa's Journal*, 293 (note no. 7). As his *Carnet Noir* indicates, he cabled for instructions on May 16th, receiving them quite soon thereafter, on the 20th, the cable having been sent on the 18th. (My thanks to Florian Michel for letting me confirm these dates from Maritain's *Carnet Noir*, which will soon be published.) For a moving account of their anguish at that time—from May 15th to 19th—see Kernan, "A Day To Remember," in *Our Friend*, 11–13. The day in question seems to have been May 19th. That fits with Kernan saying he received his instructions "the next day." Guderian's panzers had blazed to the channel. On the 21st, Maritain writes Simon to say that his instructions to continue to stay in New York had been received by the day before (June 20th); see *Correspondance I*, 412.

night of Nazi domination. To no Europeans could those days have been darker than for Frenchmen abroad, not only contemplating the downfall of their country, but having to face the likely willingness of a new French regime in Vichy to cooperate with its Nazi victors. At such moments, what was most needed were valiant voices speaking words of defiance and hope. Jacques Maritain's would be just one such voice.

On the 13th of May 1940, the day the Germans broke through the Maginot line, the Prime Minister of Great Britain—appointed but three days before[7]—himself rose to speak for the first time to the House of Commons: "I have nothing to offer but blood, toil, tears, and sweat.... You ask what is our policy? I can say: It is to wage war.... You ask what is our aim? I can answer in one word: it is victory." Three weeks later, on June 4th, Chuchhill found himself able to report on the "miracle of Dunkirk": the successful evacuation of the British Expeditionary Force of 300,000, along with 30,000 men of the French army. He was unyielding: "we shall go on to the end, we shall fight in France, we shall fight on the seas ... we shall fight on the beaches, we shall fight on the landing grounds, we shall fight in the fields, we shall fight in the hills; we shall never surrender." Two weeks later, on June 18th—on the very day General Charles de Gaulle from London called on all Frenchmen to continue the fight against Hitler—Churchill's words were as memorable as those he had spoken on the 13th: "What General Weygand called the Battle of France is over; the Battle of Britain is about to begin. Upon this battle depends the survival of Christian civilization.... Let us therefore brace ourselves to our duties and so bear ourselves that, if the British Empire and its Commonwealth last for a thousand years, men will still say 'This was their finest hour.'"[8]

Across the Atlantic, Jacques Maritain had already been raising his own voice, with an identical message, tone, and goal. In the first essay of *Pour la justice*, and three weeks before Churchill was appointed,[9] he had spoken of the need to defeat Hitler (to a country, be it noted, still officially committed to neutrality). Whatever doubts may have paralyzed Frenchmen (and

7. Winston Churchill was appointed on May 10, 1940, as the German forces invaded the Low Countries.

8. For transcripts and audio versions of these speeches, and other of Churchill's great speeches at that time, see http://www.nationalchurchillmuseum.org.

9. Maritain, "Le Christianisme et la guerre," in *Pour la justice: Articles et discours (1940–1945)* (New York: Éditions De La Maison Française, 1945), 9–18. All translations of Maritain's writings in this essay are mine.

Englishmen) regarding how to respond to Hitler's actions against Czechoslovakia, his invasion of Poland had made the justice of their cause clear beyond doubt.[10] The present conflict was more than a national war; neither was it an ideological war; nor even rightly named a "holy war"; rather, it was nothing less than "a war of civilization."[11] Its aim was to establish a European federation of states, including Germany, thereby avoiding another return to war. Not only was it necessary to defeat the cynical and ruthless Machiavellianism of Hitler, but it was also necessary to reject its timid, "bourgeois," variety; in its place, an ideal of true political justice would have to guide the will to battle, a will informed equally by a love that was stronger than death and whose aim was to seek a true and lasting peace for all.[12] What was demanded was a commitment to a renewed vision of Christian civilization for our time.

In the black days of early June—while, as his diary entries of the time more than attest, he himself was trying to fight off the blackness of despair[13]—Maritain seemed to be everywhere. On June 8, to American professors of French, he again declared that for which France fought: again, nothing less than for Western Civilization and a renewed commitment of democratic states to the ideals of political justice, the equal dignity of all persons, fraternal friendship, and a freedom based on self-discipline and the gift of oneself.[14] The stark choice facing all was the possibility of a new temporal Christianity or an "enslaving pagan Empire a thousand times worse than the Empire of Nero."[15] While ironizing that he "admired" priests and pacifists sufficiently "detached" from temporal affairs to insist that Christianity was not of this sinful world, he commented that "young Frenchmen are dying by the thousands so that, in tomorrow's world, these same priests and paci-

10. Ibid., 12.

11. Ibid., 13–14. Earlier, at the outbreak of the war, Maritain had rejected false characterizations of the war, but had concluded not that it was a war of "civilization," but that it was a "just war." See "La Guerre-Juste," the second essay (of four) in *De la Justice politique: Notes sur la presente guerre* (Paris: Plon, 1940).

12. Ibid., 17–18.

13. June 13: "The news is atrocious.... Save for a miracle, France is defeated." June 14: "Paris is taken. How can one still live and engage in the ordinary acts of life?" June 20: "Frightful days of the crucifixion of France. One weeps, one hits one's head, one understands nothing." June 21: "I had never thought that I would be ashamed of France.... For the moment, I despair." See Mougel, "Les années de New York, 1940–1945," 10–12. Maritain's despair and shame came chiefly from France's voluntary capitulation, not its defeat.

14. Maritain, *Pour la justice,* "Ce que la France défend," 19–23, 19–20.

15. Ibid., 22.

fists are not thrown into concentration camps or exposed to the temptation to sell their soul to vanquishers little interested in the kingdom of heaven or of peace and virtue."[16] He called upon Americans not to abandon their own dream of a renewed world of goodness and fraternity, of people working together simply and generously. Four days later, he reminded them of the greatness of the French culture presently at risk: of the contemporary capital of painting in Paris—of Cezanne, Rousseau, Braque, Picasso, Matisse, and Rouault; of Baudelaire and Proust; of Debussy and Satie; of Gide, Mauriac, Bernanos, and Julien Green; of its open arms to others who came to France from other countries—of a Chagall, a Stravinsky, or a Nabokov.[17] He ended this talk as he had his previous speech, by recalling Joan of Arc, the true living icon of France's indomitable spirit.

Finally, in an essay published in *Commonweal* on June 21st, but already penned in late May (even before de Gaulle was readying his call to Frenchmen and Churchill was to ask Englishmen to rise to their finest hour), Maritain raised his own voice of defiance and hope.[18] He pulled no punches: "Western civilization is paying a terrible price for its mistakes. The enemy arising against the West is not called civilization: it is called Crime and Slavery."[19] Against this enemy, his only *absolute* hope is in God alone; but his *temporal* hope resided in the *people*, especially the suffering people of his country.[20] He admits this hope could be dashed: "it is precisely one of the abominations of the hellish sadism of the totalitarian dictatorships to force every man to ask himself whether the people, too, do not run the danger of being utterly perverted."[21] Against such an enemy, the half-measures

16. Ibid.

17. Ibid., "L'Esprit de la culture française," 24–26, 24–25.

18. On May 31, in his *Carnet Noir*, he writes of finishing his revision of an article to appear in *Commonweal* that is no doubt to be correctly identified as this one; its timely appearance came three weeks later.

19. Ibid., "Ten Months Later," 27–34, 28.

20. Ibid.

21. Ibid. Indeed, as the example of Germany showed, a people's moral sense could be perverted. Even when "left to themselves" under democratic rule, it can seriously err (as the contemporary example of abortion makes plain, as did the earlier instance of American slavery). Maritain's "faith in the people" here seems to be too unqualified, perhaps a remnant of his youthful "romanticism." To "exist *with*" the people seems importantly different than having a "faith *in*" the people. (For a more sober list of the errors to which "the people" are prey, save under the guide of "the wise," as instructed by God, see Aquinas, *Summa Theologiae* I–II, q. 100, a. 11.) On the other hand, when he wrote, it was important to support the French people against tyranny. And, when he speaks of his faith being "in the people," he means in relation to their not giving in to false Vichy propaganda or Nazi ideology, and not that they could not fall into other serious errors.

of men guided by "Cartesian reason" could not and did not prove effective: "Not human reason, imprisoned in its little systems and its illusions, but human reason fortified by divine energies—faith armed with all the powers of man—will triumph over hell on earth."[22] This war is "the supreme test of Christianity … with regard to the temporal life of which it should also be the leaven."[23] He admits that Hitler could succeed: "It is possible that everything which we love and which we have reason to love should be lost without remedy and that for a time, which can last for a long time, the world should be handed over to slave merchants and to those who do violence to souls." He knows that, supposing such a horror, "we must always bless God, asking only that Job's comforters spare us their consolations."[24] Nevertheless, recalling yet again the ardent flame of Joan of Arc, he absolutely rejects this future: "I say once more today what I said ten months ago. Whatever abominations we must perhaps yet see, at the end Hitler will not triumph. It is possible that Hitler should triumph—Hitler will not triumph. It is possible that Europe should perish—Europe will not perish. It is possible that liberty should be overwhelmed—liberty will live."[25]

Dark times try men souls. They also show their true worth. Maritain's words of hope fought against the blackness of men's despair. Their radiance shone forth in his day; it reaches even to our own.

III. His Work

I wish now to call our attention to three of his principal concerns in the years that lay ahead: with his American hosts, his fellow Frenchmen, and the Jewish victims of Hitler's "final solution."

We are accustomed to thinking of Maritain as at home in America, knowing that he not only spent his war years there, but also returned to Princeton for a twelve year stay as Emeritus Professor. We can perhaps forget his limited contact with it before he came to the New World in early 1940. After a lecture series at Toronto, he had visited the University of Chicago for the first time in 1933, where he met and became friends with men such as Robert Hutchins and Mortimer Adler. He returned there to lecture

22. Ibid., 30. (I have corrected the translation, removing "the" twice before "human reason.")

23. Ibid., 31.

24. Ibid., 32.

25. Ibid., 34.

the following year, where he met John Nef, who became a close friend. That year he also was able to meet people in New York, Dorothy Day among them, and visit The Catholic University of America. In 1936, he briefly passed through New York on his way to Toronto and again went to Chicago to give a lecture (on "Socialist Humanism and Integral Humanism").[26] In 1938, he again returned to Chicago and first visited Notre Dame, where he presided at a symposium.[27] Later that year, being again in Toronto, he briefly passed through New York, where Thomas Merton first encountered him. Certainly Maritain was a famous man, and many American intellectuals (non-Catholic as well as Catholic) were eager to hear him speak. Yet over a seven year period (1933–1939), to make only five brief trips to America, and for lectures only, is hardly enough to feel "at home" in another country.[28] With the exception of Chicago, where he occasionally visited for several weeks at a time, he mainly visited America passing through to, or on side trips from, the University of Toronto,[29] where he gave courses. Nor had the Catholic university community been effusive in its support, never offering him (for example) even a semester's visit as a visiting lecturer (much less an appointment). His unwillingness to support Franco in Spain had made him a person many in the Catholic hierarchy were not yet ready to welcome with open arms. (When leading the symposium at Notre Dame in 1938, he and Raïssa had ended up being housed in the student infirmary!)[30]

Thus he arrives in Manhattan in March of 1940 feeling very much "uprooted"[31] from his home and removed from his friends in France (a situation that its fall made only more acute for him). He, Raïssa, and Vera will

26. See Barré, *Les Mendiants*, 429, quoting from Mougel's "Les années de New York."

27. See his "Integral Humanism and the Crisis of Modern Times," first published by *The Review of Politics*, I (January, 1939): 1–17, and then later as chapter I of *Scholasticism and Politics*, translation edited by Mortimer J. Adler (New York: The Macmillan Company, 1940).

28. We should not think of Maritain in these years as visiting America "regularly." He gave lectures at the University of Chicago, but the positivism of its philosophy department, and general university politics, prevented Hutchins from finding a place for him (as he had for Mortimer J. Adler in its Law School). Maritain did not visit America in 1935, 1937, or 1939. He was only briefly in Notre Dame and Washington, and he was in New York City going to and from France. Also, his then-poor English hampered his public lectures.

29. Not too long after the founding in 1929 (by Étienne Gilson and others) of the Pontifical Institute of Medieval Studies at the University of Toronto, Maritain was regularly invited to give courses there.

30. For details on his American trips, see Julie Kernan's *Our Friend*, chapter VI: "A Thomist in America," 84–101 and Barré, *Les Mendiants*, 428–29.

31. This is the word he uses to describe their state when prefacing *Raïssa's Journal* for this period: see 286.

continue to live out of a suitcase for the next three months.[32] When they begin to settle into their new apartment, Raïssa will write in her journal that she has "the feeling of starting all over again."[33] Isolated due to her limited English, she agreed to the inspired therapy of writing her memoirs.[34] Jacques had experienced a similar dislocation when he had gone to Toronto to give a course in 1936, leaving her behind. He had then written to Yves R. Simon and Charles Journet that he felt like an "exile."[35] Now, in the dark days of May 1940, he writes Simon in a similar vein: "I have passed an atrocious week among the colleges of Virginia, amongst Americans who seem to me as strange as the inhabitants of the moon, with their commentaries on events [in France] that are tearing our own hearts apart."[36] In the depth of his own anguish at the fall of France, he will send a telegram to President Roosevelt on June 15th asking him to "assure the triumph of democracy over barbarism."[37] Marooned in a foreign land, he was well aware, as was

32. The Maritains and Vera moved into *the* Manhattan apartment near Washington Square (30 Fifth Avenue) that was to be their "home in New York City" for four years in September, 1940: see Kernan, *Our Friend,* 134. Her date is confirmed by a note (no. 9) that Jacques makes on Raïssa's journal entry for September 14th, 1940, that it was *then* that they moved into this apartment: see *Raïssa's Journal,* 294. However, Jacques confuses us in this note by saying that, "up until then," they had been "living in a hotel." In fact, they moved from a hotel to *an* apartment at 30 Fifth Avenue on June 13th—having rented it on June 3rd—as his *Carnet Noir* makes clear. Barré (*Les Mendiants,* 475) approximates the time and place as July. Maritain himself, in his June 18th correspondence with Simon, speaks of "subletting an apartment" at this time for three months (*Correspondance* I, 415) and the address on that letter is 30 Fifth Avenue. In effect, they moved from a hotel to 30 Fifth Avenue on June 13th and moved *upstairs* on September 14th. It was not until *then* that they established their "New York home," which must be what Jacques was recalling in his note. They were able to "settle" in this apartment—while still being able to give notice after six months—because that summer Jacques was asked to teach at universities such as Columbia and Princeton. An initial idea of teaching at Fordham fell through. (Ironically, he never was to hold a position at *any* American *Catholic* university.) Until the matter of his teaching posts for 1940–1941 was settled, in the late summer, they must have continued to feel they had an "itinerant" and uncertain life, as though they were still "living in a hotel."

33. Raïssa Maritain, *Raïssa's Journal,* 294.

34. According to Julie Kernan (*Our Friend,* 123), it was Étienne Gilson who had first urged Raïssa to write her memoires, when she was in Toronto (presumably in early 1940). She began writing them that summer.

35. Barré, *Les Mendiants,* 428.

36. *Correspondance I,* 411. The date is May 19th, the day they listened in anguish to the radio news with Fathers Ducatillon and Couturier in Julie Kernan's New York apartment: see *Our Friend,* 11.

37. See John Hellman's "World War II and the Anti-Democratic Impulse in Catholicism," in *From Twilight to Dawn: The Cultural Vision of Jacques Maritain,* edited by Peter A. Redpath (Notre Dame, Indiana: American Maritain Association, 1990), 96. Mougel gives the text of the telegram in his "Les années de New York (1940–1945), 11, note 11: "Mr. President recalling the gracious

Simon,[38] that the fate of France and of Europe rested on the military might of the United States.[39]

Maritain's telegram to Roosevelt did not come "out of the blue." Not only was he an officially delegated representative of the French government, but he also had met Roosevelt personally. Before leaving New York in 1938, he had been invited to tea at the White House, and his name even appears on Roosevelt's calendar for that day as his principal guest.[40] The time was brief, from 5:05 to 6:00 PM, and, as he wrote John Nef on his return trip to France, he only had a moment for the briefest of conversations with the President (on the Spanish Civil War), but he spoke of their meeting as a "charming" one.[41] Back in France less than two weeks, he must have been very heartened to read Roosevelt's State of the Nation address for 1939, delivered on January 4th. It is worth quoting at length:

> Storms from abroad directly challenge three institutions indispensable to Americans, now as always. The first is religion. It is the source of the other two—democracy and international good faith.

---

reception I had from you eighteen months ago I dare [(?)] to express my anguish in this present moment for democracy of France and England stop I fear that if a public expression against nazism is not made by the U.S. of A. at once to support the will of the French people France will be influenced into making a separate peace inspite [sic] of the avowed conviction of the Premier Reyaud stop I implore you to act in order that the great Democracy of America assures the triumph of Democracy over Barbarism stop In entire appreciation of your understanding sympathy I am with profound esteem yours J.M." (I have put a question mark after Mougel's translation of "dare" ["j'ose"] because the word in the *Carnet Noir* text apparently is unclear. The text given here, which confirms Mougel's French translation, is taken directly from the *Carnet Noir*.)

38. "... the Nazis will not win the war. The war will be won by the USA. For me, this is just about certain." Yves R. Simon to Jacques Maritain in a letter of June 12, 1940: see *Correspondance I*, 412.

39. Indeed, this has already been implied by Churchill at the end of his June 4th speech to the House of Commons: "Even if, which I do not for a moment believe, this Island or a large part of it were subjugated and starving, then our Empire beyond the seas, armed and guarded by the British Fleet, would carry on the struggle, until, in God's good time, the New World, with all its power and might, steps forth to the rescue and the liberation of the old." The ending contained an implied plea to the United States to enter the fray.

40. For FDR calendar, see www.fdrlibrary.marist.edu/daybyday/daylog/december-8th-1938/. It appears that a good friend of the president, Mde Eustis (a cousin of Charles Du Bos), arranged for this meeting: see his unpublished letters to Raïssa from this time (letter of December 6th) in the Archives Maritain, transmitted by René Mougel, in the Bibliothèque Nationale et Universitaire de Strassbourg. (My thanks again to Florian Michel for helping to clarify this point for me by reference to these letters.)

41. Barré, *Les Mendiants*, 462, quoting a letter of December 23rd to John Nef in the Kolbsheim archives. (According to Barré, he had arrived that very day at Meudon.) In truth, he had hoped for more from this meeting and was disappointed in his expectations: see his letter of December 9th from the same source as noted in footnote no. 40.

> Religion, by teaching man his relationship to God, gives the individual a sense of his own dignity and teaches him to respect himself by respecting his neighbor.
>
> Democracy, the practice of self-government, is a covenant among free men to respect the rights and liberties of his fellows.
>
> International good faith, a sister of democracy, springs from the will of civilized nations of men to respect the rights and liberties of other nations of men.
>
> In a modern civilization, all three—religion, democracy, and international good faith—complement and support each other.[42]

In this speech, Maritain must immediately have recognized a kindred spirit. Indeed, he had already been made aware of this by Roosevelt's Thanksgiving Proclamation of the previous November:

> We, like all mankind since the earliest origin of mankind, turn to God in time of trouble and in time of happiness.... In the time of our fortune, it is fitting that we offer prayers for unfortunate people in other lands who are in dire distress in this, our Thanksgiving time.[43]

The reference to the Jewish victims of Kristallnacht of but ten days previous seemed evident. Roosevelt had withdrawn the American ambassador from Berlin in protest. The reference to the "freedom of religion" in his State of the Nation address also looked back to that black night.

Maritain was quick to signal his own accord with Roosevelt. Only one month after his address, he delivered his own at the Marigny theatre, the conference later published as *The Twilight of Civilization*. In it, he explicitly links Roosevelt's Thanksgiving Address to the plight of the Jews, his prayers for the "unfortunate people in others lands," referencing *their* "dire distress."[44] And he goes on to note FDR's State of the Nation address and its importance, endorsing these words of Walter Lippmann: "'The message ... registers a change of ideas which is absolutely fundamental.... The message marks the reconciliation which is now in progress, after more than a century of destructive conflict, between patriotic freedom, democracy and

42. FDR's State of the Nation address (January 4, 1939): see www.presidency.ucsb.edu/w/?pid=15684.

43. FDR's Thanksgiving Proclamation (November 19, 1938); see www.presidency.ucsb.edu/?pid=15575.

44. Maritain, *Le crépuscule de la civilisation* (Paris: Éditions Les Nouvlles Lettres, 1939); English: *The Twilight of Civilization*, translation by Lionel Landy (New York: Sheed and Ward, 1943), 47. It was given on February 8, 1940; it reworks an earlier text of January 23, 1937: see Jacques et Raissa Maritain, *Oeuvres Complete*, vol. 7: 1939–1943 (Paris/Fribourg, Switzerland: Éditons St. Paul/Universitaires, 1988), 1355.

religion. . . . [T]hat the President . . . should recognize religion as the *source* of democracy and of international good faith is not a mere matter of words; it is a fundamental re-orientation in the liberal democratic outlook upon life.'"[45] Nor will Roosevelt be alone in making this kind of connection. His Vice-President, William A. Wallace, will famously go even further, affirming that "democracy is the only true political expression of Christianity."[46] All of this could not but be "music to Maritain's ears."

Roosevelt will continue to support the line Maritain so desperately had urged of him, both in his Christmas "fireside chat" of 1940, in which he declared that America "must be the great arsenal of democracy,"[47] and in his great State of the Nation address of 1941—in which he proclaimed the "Four Freedoms" (freedom of speech and expression, freedom to worship, freedom from want, and freedom from fear) as the great democratic "charter," to be guaranteed "anywhere in the world" (as he repeated again and again)[48]—until he finally brings America into the war against Japan and Hitler.[49] Maritain found in Roosevelt a leader he could not only admire, but also love. In his telegram to *Commonweal* at his death, we cannot miss his true feelings:

> Our country has lost a peerless friend: the world has lost a statesman of genius for whom it had pressing need. And it is likewise the President's greatness of humanity, the light which dwelt within him, which the French people, like the American, so deeply regrets. Two words say all that can be said: *he loved*. . . . Allow me to add a personal word; I have been deeply stricken by the blow which has come to our

45. Ibid., 55–56, quoting Walter Lippman's column in *The New York Herald Tribune* of January 7, 1939.

46. William A. Wallace, in a speech to the Free Work Association of May 8, 1942, quoted in John C. Culver and John Hyde's *American Dreamer: The Life and Times of Henry A. Wallace* (New York: Norton, 2001), 276, as referenced in www.wikipedia.org/wiki/Henry_A._Wallace.

47. For the fireside chat of December 29, 1940, see www.millercenter.org/president/speeches/speech-3319. The Lend-Lease bill that effected this aim was signed into law twelve weeks later (March 11, 1941).

48. For this address of January 6, 1941, see www.americanrhetoric.com/speeches/frdthefourfreedoms.htm.

49. Maritain might even have seen Roosevelt endorsing a balance between truth and love that he had urged first to Jean Cocteau—"one must have a hard mind and a meek heart" (see *Art and Faith* [New York: Philosophical Library, 1948], originally published in 1926, 114—and then repeated as his motto for ecumenical dialogue in *The Peasant of the Garonne* [New York: Holt, Rinehart and Winston, 1968], 80: "*We must have a tough mind and a tender* .") Here is Roosevelt in his last-mentioned address: "As a nation we may take pride in the fact that we are soft-hearted; but we cannot afford to be soft-headed."

country, and with all my heart I am one with my friends throughout the United States.[50]

In truth, Maritain discovered in America the home of his own political views. He began to work these out, and publish them, in *Du régime temporel et de la liberté*, before he ever came to America.[51] His effort was to craft a "political center" for *Catholic* countries—for France, for Latin America, for Portugal, Spain, and Italy—for all of those Latin countries in which the established Catholic faith of 1500 years standing had led to a deep cooperation with the state, one that was then violently opposed by modern political movements for freedom. His point to all of these lands was that there was an alternative between a fascist or quasi-fascist order and a "Masonic-style"[52] democracy that was anti-clerical and hostile to faith.

What Maritain was urging, in his "*evangelical* Catholic" stance—as opposed to a "*political* Catholic" stance[53]—was nothing less than a return to the pre-Theodosian order, when the Catholic faith was not tied to the State, as its "established religion," over against which minorities might be persecuted. He was advocating the end to a state of affairs that had begun with

50. Maritain, "Telegram to the Directors," *Commonweal* 42, no. 2 (27 April, 1945): 45–46.

51. Maritain, *Du régime temporel et de la liberté* (Paris: Desclée de Brouwer, 1933) ["Questiones disputées" 11]. The second essay, "Religion et Culture II," was published in *Nova et Vetera* in January 1933, before Maritain ever came to America, and contains the "first draft" of his political views. The first essay, "Une philosophie de la liberté" (also published in *Nova et Vetera* in 1933) symbolizes the transition of Maritain's view from the speculative to the practical realm: it begins with a metaphysical analysis of freedom reminiscent of his first work on it, in *La Philosophie Bergsonienne: Études Critiques* (i.e. Part Two, Chapter VI), and then goes on to speak of political liberty, in its third and final section. In fact, Maritain's attention began turning to practical matters by the beginning of the 30s: on this, see Barré, *Les Mendiants*, 395–419. His positions already appear in outline in "Religion et Culture," *Nova et Vetera* 5 (July–September, 1930): 229–64, which appeared as the second chapter—"La Religion Catholique et la Culture"—of *Religion et Culture* (Paris: Desclée de Brouwer, 1930); English: *Religion and Culture: Essays in Order I*, Introduction by Christopher Dawson, translation by J. F. Scanlan (London: Sheed and Ward, 1931), chapter 2, 13–36.

52. It is of course true that many American presidents (including the Roosevelts) were Masons. However, Masonry functioned very differently in Protestant countries that had already broken with the authority of the Catholic Church: it was not there regarded as essentially opposed to Christian faith. By contrast, in Catholic countries, Masons were almost certain to be implacably opposed to any "Catholic order," even to the point of persecuting the Catholic Church and its faithful (as occurred in Mexico in the 1930s).

53. For but one example of this contrast—in which the views of Lisbon's Catholic Patriarch are often placed against those of Spanish nationalists—see p. 399 of the *Commonweal* interview referenced in my note 2 above. For excerpts from the Patriarch's discourse of November 18, 1938, see *Twilight*, 48–49.

the forced conversion of Donatists in the late-fourth century. He was advocating for the civil right to religious freedom that Vatican II would come to endorse. Now, American democracy had been religiously pluralistic from its inception; it had not needed to establish itself by violently breaking with an established Christian faith or church. What he discovered was that a democracy such as he was urging—one that was religiously pluralistic yet open to the sacred and to the Christian faith—had in truth been "alive and well" in America.[54] This was one of the principal reasons that drew him to the country and made him desirous of continuing in it. Before accepting de Gaulle's plea to be Ambassador to the Vatican, he was already hoping to work out a way of splitting his post-war time between France and America.[55] His 1948 Princeton appointment came as an answer to a strong desire that he had begun to feel in his war years.

America had welcomed him and nourished him. He was not one to take that for granted. He returned any favor in abundance, as is evidenced by the works he produced during his four years of war-time in America, giving their English titles when translated: *France, My Country, Through the Disaster*; *Confession of Faith*; *The Living Thoughts of St. Paul*; *Ransoming the Time*; *The Rights of Man and Natural Law*; *Saint Thomas and the Problem of Evil*; *Christianity and Democracy*; *Education at the Crossroads*; *Sort de l'Homme*; *Bergsonian Philosophy and Thomism* (the Second Part); *Principes d'une politique humaniste*; *À travers la Victoire*; *Messages*, and our *Pour la justice*. Remarkable! The bibliographical references for 1940–1945 occupy sixty-eight pages in the final volume of his *Oeuvres Complètes*, roughly double the space of almost all other five year stretches.[56] This was surely the busiest, and one of the most productive, periods of his life.

Although he revisited the thought of his old master, recently deceased, and the metaphysical problem of evil that preoccupied him all his life, the center of his war-time concern lay in crafting the outlines of, and in educating for, a Christian humanism that could guide the West out of the

54. As Maritain often notes, the antecedent to American democracy is more Locke than Rousseau: see *Twilight*, 58, for but one example. The democracy that Maritain favored really had its roots in English law and government. It is but one of the reasons Maritain insists on the need for British-French post-war unity.

55. On this, see Barré, *Les Mendiants*, 508 and 512.

56. See Jacques and Raïssa Maritain, *Oeuvres Complètes*, vol. 17 (Paris/Fribourg [Swiss]: Saint-Paul Éditions Religieuses/Academic Press Fribourg, 2007). The closest 5-year period is 1934–1939 (65 pages).

devastation of the war. Many of his works were the direct result of lectures given at American universities, such as Columbia, Princeton, and Yale (the latter's Terry Lectures leading to his *Education at the Crossroads*). Maritain believed America could vigorously support the pluralist yet theocentric democracy he hoped would guide the future. He was already having an impact on young Americans similar to the one he had previously had on young Frenchmen: many were asking him to be their godfather.[57] After his stint as Ambassador to the Vatican, he would return to America for another dozen years, intent upon nourishing Thomism in the United States.

While his engagement with America would continue to increase, his immediate concern in June 1940 was with his French friends and fellow intellectuals endangered by France's fall. He used his status as an appointed "ambassador of French culture" to do what he could for them. Relying strongly on the advice of Yves R. Simon,[58] and with the invaluable help of Alvin Johnson—director of New York's New School of Social Research—he sought to get American visas for, among others, Abbé Oesterreicher, Baldwin Schwarz, Dietrich von Hildebrand, Gustave Cohen, Jean Wahl, Vladimir Jankélévitch, Arthur Lourié, Georges Gurvitch, Paul Vignaux, Hélène Iswolski, Marc Chagall, and Ossip Zadkine, and, at great length and through many channels, for his friend Alfredo Mendizibal, then a refugee in France.[59] He also intervened on behalf of Raymond Aron's wife, then in Morocco, on behalf of Clara Malraux, and of Léon Blum.[60] Maritain was in a position to act to help others and he did. No doubt his frequent interventions to obtain visas helped save many lives.[61]

While involved in helping to get Frenchmen to America and help them obtain work here, the other focus of his attention throughout 1940 was

57. Amongst these, Kernan mentions John and Emily Coleman and Dorothy Rothchild (see *Our Friend*, 133).

58. For his letter to Simon of July 9, 1940, asking him for this help, see *Correspondance*, 426.

59. See the thorough work of Michel Fourcade on this subject, "Jacques Maritain et l'Europe en exil (1940–1945)," *Cahiers Jacques Maritain*, 28 (June, 1994): 5–38, especially 11–12.

60. Ibid., 13–14.

61. Aristide R. Zolberg gives a moving account of the fate of the historian Marc Bloch during this same period. Unable to obtain an American visa for his extended family, he refused the offer of a visa and a teaching job in America for himself. He managed to avoid initial persecution due to his prestige, background, and being twice a soldier in the French army, but the German occupation of Vichy led him to join the underground, and he was executed by the Nazis 10 days after D-Day. (See Aristide R. Zolberg, with the assistance of Agnès Callamard, "The Ecole Libre at the New School, 1941–1946," *Social Research 65, no. 4* [Winter, 1998]: 921–51, especially 924–28.) Maritain helped people avoid that fate.

on all those in occupied France under the Vichy regime. As he indicates in its preface,[62] he wrote *À travers le Désastre* both for the American people—to help them understand the causes of the disastrous collapse of the French forces—but also and perhaps even more for conquered Frenchmen in his beloved country. He wrote to show his entire solidarity with them and his confidence in their undying spirit, which he sought to support. He committed himself to an objective, non-partisan account. His judgment was often quite severe, yet even-handed; he refused to vilify anyone or to "take sides." This extended even to de Gaulle. From the first, he admired de Gaulle's call to arms;[63] yet, like most Frenchmen in America,[64] he kept a cautious distance from one who was something of an "unknown quantity," who lacked a popular mandate, and whose natural "hauteur" made his "democratic credentials" perhaps suspect. (Barré rightly characterizes Maritain's initial response to de Gaulle as similar to Roosevelt's "clear-eyed temporizing.")[65] Later, through their correspondence, he grew closer to him, but he resisted becoming a member of his "team," ever guarding his own philosophical independence.[66]

Maritain not only was "loyal" to Roosevelt in maintaining an early re-

62. See *À travers le Désastre* in *Oeuvres Complétes*, vol. 7, 335–425; *Avant-Propos*: 343–44.

63. "The leader [of French soldiers who continue to fight for a Free France] said *"no"* to the enemy from the first day: an act such as that cannot be effaced ... De Gaulle has lifted up the honor of France." *Pour la justice*, "Il faut parfois juger," 184–85.

64. Yves R. Simon was one of the few Frenchmen who, from the beginning, was ready to give his full support to de Gaulle. He faults Maritain for not being willing to give him an unreserved support. (See his critical comments on *À travers le Désastre*, in *Jacques Maritain-Yves Simon Correspondance, Tome II: Les années américaines [1941–1961]*, edited and annotated by Florian Michel with the collaboration of René Mougel and Anthony O. Simon, Introduction by Michel Fourcade [Paris: Éditions CDL, 2012], 30–41: letter of February 11, 1941.) Simon, whose instincts were those of a "man of action," realized that times of war force one to land more squarely "on one side." Maritain—ever guided by spiritual instincts that made him wary of temporal "parties" (as they did Raïssa)—was inclined to hold back, looking for a "higher position," but one that Simon felt was not then practical. In this respect, there is a certain similarity between Maritain's unwillingness to give de Gaulle his full support and his unwillingness to give his support to either party in the Spanish Civil War (despite the two situations obviously being deeply dissimilar in other respects!).

65. Barré, *Les Mendiants*, 485: "lucid attentisme."

66. For the later history of his relation with de Gaulle, see Barré, *Les Mendiants*, 488–94 and 498–501. De Gaulle displayed a remarkable patience in trying to "win over" Maritain. He had at least some measure of satisfaction in persuading him to accept the ambassadorship to the Vatican. Yet he had hoped for a deeper connection and, had Maritain accepted his offer, no doubt his post-war experience—and, in all probability his influence in France—would have been different. America was to be the beneficiary of his independence.

serve or distance from de Gaulle; he even went so far as not openly to protest the pragmatic appointment of Admiral Darlan.[67] This was surely a bitter pill to swallow for anyone who was as outspokenly opposed to the officials of Vichy as was Maritain. One can see this in his reaction to an open letter that Antoine St. Exupéry addressed to his fellow Frenchmen just at that moment, when any pretense of Vichy independence came to an end.[68] He had pleaded that all Frenchmen should now unite in the common cause against Germany. While sharing this sentiment, the main point Maritain wished to make in criticizing his appeal was that a Frenchman had to *begin* by saying "No!" to the political *leaders* of Vichy and "no" to the ignominious armistice they had accepted. Even were some leaders to have a "political conversion" to the Allied cause, "honor and the common good forbid that they assume any authority whatsoever in the conduct, or in the reconstruction, of the country."[69] Increasingly appalled at the actions of the Vichy government, by the end of 1942 Maritain was in no mood to "forgive and forget." France's future required firmly rejecting the politics of Vichy.

À travers le Désastre was a good example of Maritain's ability to combine his tender heart—that reached out in complete empathy with his fellow Frenchmen—with his tough-minded objectivity. It made the book important for those in occupied Europe, as the famous Polish poet, Czeslaw Milosz explained, in the preface to his translation:

67. Maritain himself uses this term: "loyalty towards its [America's] President ... [is one of] the strict obligations of devotion to the common cause" *Pour la justice*, "If faut parfois juger," 184. I do not mean to suggest that he "followed Roosevelt's line" (rather, say, than Churchill's) in relation to de Gaulle; in fact, he had his own independent reasons for maintaining his reserve. However, it seems likely that Maritain was glad to find himself in accord with Roosevelt.

68. Admiral Darlan was appointed to be head of the French forces in North Africa on November 14, 1942, and confirmed on November 20th. (He was assassinated a month later, on December 24th.) St. Exupéry wrote his open letter to The *New York Times* on November 29, 1940. Maritain responded on December 19, 1940. Curiously, Maritain implies St. Exupéry wrote his open letter *before* Darlan's appointment: see *Pour la justice,* "Il faut parfois juger," 177. In objecting to St. Exupéry, Maritain was able to object to the appointment of Darlan without having directly to take issue with Roosevelt.

69. Ibid., 179–80. Perhaps Maritain might have felt Darlan was less a "political" than a "military" leader; nor was he then involved in the "reconstruction of the country." Yet the elevation of a former Vichy official to a position of authority over Free French forces likely provoked Maritain to exclaim "no" to this becoming a "precedent" for other prominent men of Vichy. (Indeed, it is hard not to regard the *strength* of his "no" addressed to St. Exupéry as motivated mainly by his desire to make plain his "no" to *Vichy politicians* and not by any objection to *St. Exupéry* himself.) He had earlier written to Simon (on December 4th) that "the Darlan affair is terrible for France"; see *Jacques Maritain, Yves Simon: Correspondance, Tome 2,* 114. The assassination of Darlan removed his concern.

> When a thinker as eminent as Maritain takes up his pen, one hopes to find from him certain explanations; and it is just these explanations that he, in large part, offers us here.... Little by little, our spirit is freed from unfounded horrible generalizations and passes to ideas much more precise and well organized. It is not true that the defeats or failures that led to the fall of France are vices consubstantial with democracy: that is the first axiom that Maritain establishes. Nor is it any more true that these defeats came from the decadence of the French nation: that is the second axiom.... Thus, the importance for us of Maritain's work resides not only in that it places the mechanisms of the French disaster in the light of day; it resides equally in reflections of a certain rational order it offers on the current state of the world. In truth, one of the most difficult things today is to put forward a lucid, yet pitiless, condemnation of the faults and vices of one's own country, without for that leading one to put in doubt its [true] values and qualities. With Maritain, his frank recognition of the faults of, as well as his profound faith in, the French people arouses our profound admiration.[70]

Milosz was not alone in his admiration. Everyone wanted to know what Maritain thought. The Éditions de la Maison Française promptly brought out a German translation. 1941 also saw a Portuguese translation in Brazil and a Spanish one in Chile. Most importantly, his work was clandestinely smuggled into France and later printed there.[71] It there strongly served, again in Milosz's words, "as a means of fighting against despair" and as a help in resisting tyranny. He continued to make his voice heard in France throughout the war. (Indeed, the first of his radio-broadcasts to France, transmitted by the BBC, was entitled "À travers le désastre.") Over the course of the war, he would transmit some fifty messages to France, mostly through the Voice of America.[72]

It may well be fair to say that no other philosopher in the period from 1935 to 1945 had a greater political impact than Jacques Maritain—a worldwide impact that would culminate in his important contribution to the 1948 UNESCO Mexican conference that produced the United Nations' *Univer-*

70. See Barré, *Les Mendiants,* 483–84; my translation (from the French).

71. For the various translations, see *Oeuvres Complètes,* Volume XVII, 183–84. It also was translated into Italian towards the end of the war (1945). For a moving account of its immediate and important influence in Occupied France, see Michel Fourcade's detailed and illumining article "Jacques Maritain, inspirateur de la Résistance," *Cahiers Jacques Maritain,* no. 32 (June, 1996): 14–57.

72. See *Messages (1941–1944)* in *Oeuvres Complètes,* Volume VIII (Paris/Fribourg [Swiss]: Éditions Saint Paul/Éditions Universitaires, 1989), 377–508. The original edition (New York: Éditions de la Maison Française, 1945) is presently out of print and not easy to find.

sal Declaration of Human Rights.[73] One's importance is well measured by how seriously one is taken by one's political enemies. It is hard to think of anyone whom the Nazis would have more liked to capture. (Dietrich von Hildebrand is one of the few others who might come to mind.) There were many philosophers and Thomists in occupied France. Although the Gestapo left them alone, its first "order of business" in conquered Paris was to try to hunt down Maritain. His voice mattered.

Perforce, Maritain's main connection with his fellow Frenchmen was in America. One of the most remarkable feats of Jacques, Raïssa, and Vera during the war was to make their apartment in Manhattan into a "second Meudon": a warm place of meetings and of friends, a home where Europeans of diverse backgrounds, experience, and creeds were welcomed and felt supported in their temporal and spiritual struggles. Here is the witness of Elisabeth de Mirabel:

> His home was open to all, to friends and to friends of friends. There I found Chagall, Focillon, Sigrid Unset and a number of intellectuals of Jewish origin.... With his wife Raïssa and his sister-in-law Vera, Jacques Maritain made a home for refugees of the spirit, those who preferred exile to the prostitution of thought. In his home, all passion was calmed. One entered into his living room as into a sanctuary. Maritain impressed me profoundly.[74]

Here is another witness, the Bavarian essayist and psychologist Karl Stern:

> I thought that, were I to find in the Church a single man who would have a response to offer to a good number of my questions, it would be him.... I briefly told him my history, and, from the beginning, he seemed to be profoundly interested in it. We spoke of Reformed Judaism and Orthodox Judaism, of Hassidism, of the "Grand Inquisitor" of Dostoevesky, and of the problem of the iniquity of the visible Church.... He expressed himself with a particular imprecision, proceeding by light touches more than by affirmations. And yet all that he said gave an impression of substance and clarity.... We were despoiled of the accidental features of our national and social origins.... In moments of great intensity, the historical time disappeared. I could just as easily have found myself in the catacombs, a disoriented and babbling catechumen at the side of an apostle.[75]

73. For his influence on this document, see René Mougel's "Jacques Maritain et la Déclaration universelle des droits de l'homme, 1948" *Cahiers Jacques Maritain*, no. 61 (December, 2010): 65–77.

74. Barré, *Les Mendiants*, 476; Barré is quoting from her *La Liberté souffre violence* (Paris: Plon, 1983).

75. Ibid., 177–78; Barré is quoting from his *Le Buisson ardent* (Paris: Le Seuil, 1953). For

The Maritains had a genius for friendship. Their goodness and their welcome touched many.

It thus is hardly surprising that, when French intellectuals, again working with Alvin Johnson and the New School, chose to found a French university in exile, they should turn to Maritain as one of their leaders. He was a Vice President of L'École Libre de Hautes Études, founded at the beginning of 1942, and then a year later succeeded its first President—the well-known art historian Henri Focillon—as it second President. Maritain, along with the medievalist Gustave Cohen and others, was involved in this university project from its beginnings. He saw in it not only the possibility of Belgian-French co-operation, but also one between Catholics and secularists, thus creating that practical union between men of diverse theoretical commitments that he believed essential for the "open democracy" of the future.[76] The school had a remarkable group of scholars: the Belgian Byzantinist Henri Gregoire and statesman Paul van Zeeland; the jurist Raoul Aglion; the sociologist Georges Gurvitch; the mathematician Jacques Hadamard; the structural linguist Roman Jakobsen, and the anthropologist Claude Levi-Strauss, whose own structuralism he influenced at that time; the historian of science Alexander Koyré; the scholar of constitutional and international law Boris Mirkine-Guetzévitch; and the physicist Jean Perrin. Nevertheless, of this most illustrious faculty, Raoul Aglion tells us that "far and away [Maritain's] course ... was the one most followed. It was many times necessary to give him a larger amphitheater, and his courses were given in the most spacious room of the establishment."[77] Students were crammed together, sitting "at the foot of chairs or on the steps of the amphitheater, as young Frenchmen 'had previously at the courses of Henri Bergson at the Collège de France.'"[78] It is hard to think of higher praise.

Founded only after America had entered the war, it was no surprise that most of its professors returned to France and Belgium at the war's end. Maritain himself (along with a number of others) would resign, in the Spring of 1944, in order, as he wrote Allen Tate, to protect his "freedom of

another testimony of the warm atmosphere of their gatherings, this time featuring Chagall, see Kernan's *Our Friend*, 132.

76. See Zolberg's "The École Libre," 929–30.

77. Barré, *Les Mendiants*, 494–95; Barré is quoting from Aglion's *De Gaulle et Roosevelt* (Paris: Plon, 1984).

78. Ibid., 494.

mind."[79] Yet he was able to use his position as President of an institution of growing renown to speak of matters close to his heart and to pay tribute to many. A good example of the latter was his address on the second anniversary of the founding of the school, which provided him the occasion to thank the British, in the person of Lord Halifax, for their heroic stand early in the war:

> For me, your Excellence, it is a profoundly moving privilege to have the occasion to express before you the admiration and the gratitude of all those who fight for civilization and for liberty ... to Great Britain and to the English people. I do not have need to recall the feelings which filled our hearts when, at the moment when all seemed lost, the heroism of your people and the inflexible resolution of your Prime Minister saved all. We will never forget that unique moment when the destinies of the world were suspended on the force of soul of the English people. Delivered from that nightmare, nations will [ever] remember what they owe to the prodigious effort of this great people.[80]

Here, as is so often the case in his war writings, Maritain's nobility of soul is unmistakable.

That nobility was perhaps most in evidence in his outspoken defense of those whose lives were most at risk: the Jewish people. There is no reason to rehearse Maritain's well-known and constant defense of them, and his absolute condemnation of the anti-Semitism that had become a cancer in the side of Western civilization.[81] I have already referred to his stand. (Nor, by the way, was he one to deny that "the religious-minded anti-Jewish prej-

79. John Dunaway, *Exiles and Fugitives: The Letters of Jacques and Raïssa Maritain, Allen Tate, and Caroline Gordon* (Baton Rouge, Louisiana: Louisiana State University Press, 1992), 20. There was a division in the school at that time, with men such as Claude Levi-Strauss accepting that it should come to be associated with the interests of de Gaulle and men such as Maritain, Gregoire, Koyré, and Guetzévitch, desiring that it maintain its former independence. See Zolberg, "The 'École Libre,'" 943–44.

80. Maritain, *Pour la justice*, "Second Anniversaire de L'École Libre des Hautes Études," 316–17.

81. For a summary of Maritain's writings on the Jewish people, see Charles P. O'Donnell's list of 17 works, "A Select Bibliography on Jacques Maritain's Writings on Jews, Christians, and Anti-Semitism," in *Jacques Maritain and the Jews*, edited by Robert Royal (Notre Dame, Indiana: American Maritain Association, 1994), 273–75. The first is from 1921 "Á propos de la Question Juive"; the last is a review from 1953. In his preface to Henry Bars *La Politique Selon Jacques Maritain* (Paris: Éditions Ouvrières, 1961), Maritain says he regrets expressions in his earlier work: "If I were to reedit my essay on "Impossible Anti-Semitism," I would rework certain of my formulas and refine them. When an entire people has been put on the cross, and six million of your own have been abominably massacred, one cannot use too much reverence or a language that is too considerate when touching on the questions with which it deals" (8).

udice and fanaticism of old was the shameful spot in Christian history."[82]) However, Maritain—as virtually all others—at first regarded Hitler's fanaticism as somewhat unreal. As late as his *Confession of Faith,* in 1941, he spoke of "the *dream* of exterminating certain groups,"[83] using words similar to those in his 1938 address on "Les juifs parmi les nations": "there are, in the Europe of today, those who want extermination and death, and first of all the extermination of the Jews ... the crazed hope of a general massacre of the race of Moses and Jesus. This massacre remains a *dream.*"[84] By 1942, there were growing signs that this dream might become a reality. Only once that year did Maritain raise his voice in a message broadcast to France, and it was just to condemn in absolute terms the shame of Vichy's newly promulgated anti-Jewish laws. Let us listen to his impassioned voice:

> A new shame has been inflicted on our country: the atrocious measures taken against the Jews, not only in the occupied region, but in the so-called free zone. Twenty thousand foreign Jews have been arrested by the Germans in the occupied zone. In the non-occupied zone thirteen thousand are being hunted by the police.... It is not only the Jews, it is France as well who is being struck and wounded by the abject results of the politics of collaboration. To betray her traditional laws of political hospitality, to accept for herself and for her own laws the bestial ignominy of Nazi racism, to betray foreign Jews received by her since 1935 as into a humane and faithful country, to betray even those who fought for her and in her army in the course of the present war: never in history has an equal infamy been imposed on France. It is not only for the injury given to human dignity and to human rights in the person of the persecuted Jews; it is for the soul of France that anguish grips us all, we who remember the saints of France and the days when honor meant something to the leaders of our country.... My Jewish friends, my brothers, permit a Christian to speak not only of the compassion but the sacred respect that your suffering inspires in him. In the abyss of suffering into which you are plunged, you bear witness, by your inexpressible agony, to the greatness of Israel, to the people who were given promises without repentance, to the olive tree onto which the Christian nations have been grafted. And it is for those nations, too, that you mysteriously suffer, and for that France, herself also tortured by these same butchers, delivered and betrayed by the same men who are your persecutors.[85]

82. Ibid., "Anti-Semitism as a Problem for the Jew," 158 (originally published in *Commonweal,* September 25, 1942).

83. Maritain, "The Confession of Faith" in *The Social and Political Philosophy of Jacques Maritain: Selected Readings,* edited by Joseph W. Evan and Leo R. Ward (New York: Charles Scribner's Sons, 1955), 337.

84. Quoted in Barré, *Les Mendiants,* 452.

85. Maritain, "La Persécution Raciste en France," *Messages, Oeuvres Complètes* VIII, 400–02.

It was to prevent words such as these that the Gestapo hunted him.[86] We can see why.

Unfortunately, by the time Maritain's voice was raised, the butchery had been underway for a year. Directly following Operation Barbarossa, and in the wake of the advancing German army, the *Einsatzgruppen* had begun their bloody work, as Churchill himself had noted, in a BBC address of 1941: "As his armies advance, whole districts are being exterminated. Scores of thousands, literally scores of thousands of executions in cold blood are being perpetrated by the German police troops upon the Russian patriots who defend their native soil."[87] In November, he again spoke on the BBC: "None have suffered more cruelly than the Jew the unspeakable evils wrought in the bodies and souls of men by Hitler and his vile regime."[88] The situation was worse, far worse, than even Churchill had proclaimed. The *Einsatzgruppen* had begun by instigating pogroms that hunted down thousands of Jews. Odessan and Kievan Jews were slaughtered by the tens of thousands.[89] Over 33,000 Jews were summarily shot that September at Babi Yar. The "Rumbla" operation against the Jews of Riga had killed some 25,000. Almost all of Latvia's Jewish population was wiped out, with Himmler estimating that some 134,000 Jews had been killed in the Baltic

The date was September 8, 1942. Here are Churchill's own words at this time: "... the most bestial, the most squalid and the most senseless of all their offences, namely, the mass deportation of Jews from France, with the pitiful horrors attendant upon the calculated and final scattering of families. This tragedy fills me with astonishment as well as with indignation, and it illustrates as nothing else can the utter degradation of the Nazi nature and theme, and degradation of all who lend themselves to its unnatural and perverted passions." (See www.bbc.co.uk/history/worldnews/genocide/Churchill_holocaust_01.shtml.) A year earlier, as the murder of the Jews (unbeknownst to him) was underway, Maritain had already spoken out in Reinhold Niebuhr's *Christianity and Crisis* (October 6, 1941): see *Pour la justice*, "On Anti-Semitism," 48–54.

86. Regarding this address of Maritain, Aristide R. Zolberg makes this poignant remark: "I was especially moved to learn of Maritain's broadcast, as the notion of Jews as 'Christ's own people'—was invoked shortly after the liberation of Brussels (September 1944) by Father Goossens, principal of the Institut Notre-Dame, to explain to the assembled student body why the boy they had known as—'Henri Van den Berghe'—could now resume his original name, Aristide Zolberg"; see, "The École Libre," 949 n. 10.

87. Churchill, in a BBC address of August 24, 1941 reporting on his recent meeting with Roosevelt. See www.jewishvirtuallibrary.org/jsource/ww2/churchill/082441.html.

88. See the same internet reference of note 85 above.

89. For an account of the brutal workings of the Einsatzgruppen, see Richard Rhodes, *Masters of Death: The SS-Einsatgruppen and the Invention of the Holocaust* (New York: Knopf, 2002). I am grateful to my colleague Elliot Neaman for referring me to this book and to others on the Holocaust noted in this essay.

States alone and over a quarter million all told by the year's end.[90] The executioners were savage and thorough, and few escaped to bear word of their atrocities, but by the end of 1941, over five hundred thousand people had been murdered in cold-blood.[91] This was only the beginning.

At the Wannsee conference of January 1942, the systematic murder by gassing was agreed upon. The first victims were the Jews of Poland. Even here, word was slow to reach the West. In an inside page, the *New York Times* of May 18th reported 100,000 Jews killed in the Baltic States, a similar number in Poland, and twice that in "Western Russia" (i.e., the Ukraine). On June 19th, the British *Jewish Chronicle* reported that some 85,000 Polish Jews had been killed. By July, *The London Daily Telegraph* even reported as many as a million Jews were being killed.[92] Finally, in August, Gerhart Rieger, the secretary of the World Jewish Congress in Switzerland, confirmed that some 700,000 Polish Jews had been systematically wiped out and that Hitler intended to exterminate all the Jews under his control. The report was initially met with incredulity, but Jan Karski was able to smuggle evidence from Poland to London by November putting matters beyond doubt.[93] Thus, in November of 1942, Hayim Greenberg, the editor of the *The Jewish Frontier*, was able to publish a report detailing the many thousands of Jews that had already been murdered.

Summaries such as this mislead one to think that a "—'hue and cry'" was

90. See Richard J. Evans, *The Third Reich at War* (New York: Penguin, 2009), especially part 3: 'The Final Solution' for a very recent summation of the killing. See also www.wikipedia.org/wiki/einsatzgruppen, www.jewishvirtuallibrary.org/source/holo.html, and www.theguardian.com/media/greenslade for but three of many internet sites on all these matters. (Ukrainians and Romanians were particularly complicitous in these mass murders, the latter killing some 280,000 to 380,000 Jews within a year's time: see Ibid., 233.)

91. This is the figure calculated by Evans: see Ibid., 239.

92. For these references, among others, see www.historyplace.com/worldwar2/holocaust/timeline.html. (It is worth remembering that, of the 5.7 million Soviet prisoners of war, some 3,300,000 died in the murderous conditions of transport and makeshift camps the Germans set up. Of course, many other Soviet officials were shot outright: see Evans's *The Third Reich at War*, "Operation Barbarossa," especially pages 175–86.)

93. See E. Thomas Wood and Stanisław M. Jankowski, *Karski: How One Man Tried to Stop the Holocaust* (Lubbock, Texas: Texas Tech University Press and Gihon River Press, 1994), especially 99–140. See also www.wikipedia.org/wiki/Jan_Karski. On December 19, 1942, the British Foreign Secretary, Anthony Eden, read a Joint Declaration by Members of the United Nations in the House of Commons condemning Germans for "carrying into effect Hitler's oft-repeated intention to exterminate the Jewish people of Europe": see www.wikipedia.org/wiki/Joint_Declaration_by_Members_of_the_United_Nations. By early 1943, some 1,700,000 Jews had been gassed in Belzec, Sobibor, and Treblinka alone: see *The Third Reich at War*, 294. Auschwicz-Birkenau consumed 1,500,000. Perhaps over 3,000,000 had been killed by 1943.

being made over what—from the issue of *The Jewish Frontier* on—was to be known as "the Holocaust." This was hardly the case.[94] Throughout 1942, only sporadic reports had surfaced, and these were often disbelieved. The American government, for example, did little to make an issue of it. The general silence and inertia before such appalling news—a numbness and general inaction that continued throughout most of the war—in fact remains a matter of shame. Surely, had more spoken up, more lives could have been saved. Evil lives off of the inaction of good men.[95]

Jacques Maritain was not to be counted amongst those who were inactive. He became the second President of L'École Libre de Hautes Études in January of 1943, just a little over a month following the November publication of *The Jewish Frontier*. In his first speech to the faculty, he spoke out against racism and detailed before all the murderous slaughter that was falling upon the Jewish people:

> Of the 250,000 Jews chased from Bessarabia towards the southern part of the Ukraine occupied by Rumania, about 190,000 have been shot, burned alive, or tortured to death during transport. At Odessa, 25,000 Jews have been massacred by the Rumanian troops in October of 1941.... In Kiev, according to information received from the Soviet government, 52,000 men, women and children—of whom a large portion (40,000) were Jews—have been massacred.... At Pinsk, 8,000 Jews have been machine-gunned, at Brest Litovsk, 6,000, at Marioupol the entire Jewish population: massacred in groups of 500 before trenches into which their cadavers were pushed. In a town near Smolensk, 7,000 Jews were led into the country, forced to dig their own graves and shot. Many of them were buried alive. At Riga, in Latvia, more than 20,000 Jews have been massacred by the Germans. At Jassy, in Moldavia, 10,000 Jews have been put to death, in a pogrom of three days, mercilessly machine-gunned or, by far the greater number, closed in sealed trains where they could receive neither food nor water. The Rumanian authorities left them for eleven days, until no sign of life was perceptible. When they opened them, on the 10th of August, all these unfortunates had died of asphyxiation or the torments of hunger. In Bukovina [Romania], 29,000 Jews have been killed by German armies and by Rumanians in Cernivtsi or in the surrounding neighbor-

94. For press coverage of the Holocaust during the war, see the essays edited by Robert Moses Shapiro in *Why Didn't The Press Shout? American and International Journalism During the Holocaust* (Jersey City, New Jersey: Yeshiva University Press, 2003). For the response of American Jewry to the Holocaust, see Henry L. Feingold's careful analyses in *Bearing Witness: How America and Its Jews Responded to the Holocaust* (Syracuse, New York: Syracuse University Press, 1995).

95. For a number of essays (especially Henry L. Feingold's) that assess this issue in relation to persons and groups, see *FDR and the Holocaust*, edited by Verne W. Newton (New York, St. Martin's Press, 1996).

hoods.... The government of Czechoslovakia has just made it known that 77,000 Jews have been killed in concentration camps of the protectorate.... If France has not lost its soul [by cooperating with this murderous campaign], it is due to her people and to those Christians who have cried out their indignation before this iniquity and who have done everything and risked everything to aid and defend—by shielding in their hearths or hiding in their mountains and forests—the victims of these infamous measures.[96]

Maritain was not silent. He made the iniquitous horror known, in all its detail: first before his fellow professors and then before at least the Catholic world, through the publication of the same article in *Commonweal* later that spring.[97] At just this time, Maritain was to comment: "At sixty it is suitable to begin one's self-examination; one thing at least I don't regret in my life—having always taken a stand against the antisemitic plague."[98] Would that more had done as he had!

IV. Conclusion

This, then, is the man who is at the center of our concern in our work here. Certainly, he sets us all a very high standard indeed! Here is someone who gave unstintingly of himself to help save lives, to push back despair and give hope, to encourage people to resist tyranny and fight for their true spirit. Here is a man in a foreign land, one deeply shaped by its Protestant past, who embraced the right to religious freedom and the freedom of conscience indelibly etched into the soul of any American. A man in a land proud of its democratic traditions, who embraced pluralism not just as the "inevitable way of the future," but as something good and right that flowed out of the principles of his own Catholic faith. Here is a man who defended the hunted and the powerless, who sought to protect those he could and who called others to do the same, fighting against the anti-Semitism that had indeed been a blight upon past Christian history. Here is a man who embraced inter-religious dialogue and who, without for one instant ceasing to be himself and a man of deep and committed Catholic faith, nevertheless was not just "talking words," but meant it when he spoke of his

96. Maritain, *Pour la justice,* "Le droit raciste et la vrai signification du racisme," 198–218, 207–10.

97. Maritain, "Racist law and the true meaning of Racism," *Commonweal* 38 (June 4, 1943): 181–88.

98. Maritain, *Pour la justice,* "A Mis Amis de New York," 195–96.

Jewish "brothers," so many of whom (like Marc and Bella Chagall) were his dear and true friends.[99] When we look at Jacques Maritain in these dark war years, we find nothing not to like and everything that is cause for admiration and emulation. Those who study and who seek to be instructed by such a noble man are truly fortunate. The Greeks spoke of right action as "kalos," and this can be rightly translated not only as "noble" but as "beautiful." His actions were beautiful, as was his soul's radiance that shone forth in them.

99. The Maritains were to lose a number of Jewish friends (many who were converts) to the Holocaust: the Jacobs—Babet (a godchild of Raïssa's), her mother, and younger brother Manuel—Jean and Suzanne Marx, and the poet-artist Max Jacob, among others; see Kernan, *Our Friend*, 128.

RICHARD SCHENK, OP

Maritain and the Possibilities for Cooperation in a Still Divided World

I. Introduction

THE THEME OF THE American Maritain Association's 2015 conference—"Maritain Engagé: Thomism Confronts the Global Challenge"—implies questions both of *what* and of *how*: what is the global challenge today, and what can we learn from Maritain and his use of Thomas Aquinas about how we should face this challenge? How are we to use and not to use Maritain's works to confront his issues as they have developed since his time? How does Maritain's message affect his medium, and how is Maritain's method already a good part of what he most wanted to say? The context for our dual question is defined by a particular *genius loci et temporis*: the beginnings of the United Nations in San Francisco some 70 years ago, between the foreseeable end of World War II and the Universal Declaration of Human Rights in 1948; and the 50th anniversary of the final year of the Second Vatican Council in 1965. This essay will focus on the global challenge of religious conflict and the suggested path toward the important right to religious freedom found first in Maritain's contributions to the work of UNESCO in 1947 and 1948 and then in his indirect involvement with the Council, particularly in the four *memoranda* answering questions for Paul VI in the final year of that synod.

II. Maritain and UNESCO

By the time that the Second Session of the General Conference of UNESCO met at the Palacio de Bellas Artes in Mexico City on November 6th, 1947, the first two drafts of a Universal Declaration of Human Rights, commissioned the previous year by the Economic and Social Council of the United Nations, had been completed by John Peters Humphrey and René Samuel Cassin and had been circulated widely by the United Nations Commission on Human Rights for general critique and commentary. Johannes Morsink sees here the first two of seven drafting stages prior to the adoption of the declaration in Paris on the 10th of December 1948.[1] Humphrey's initial list of forty-eight rights was received and reduced by Cassin first to forty-four, and would eventually be pared down to thirty rights in the final text.

Maritain was not directly involved with this process of drafting the Declaration,[2] but consultation on and debate about this UN project had widened progressively. The shadows of the impending Cold War and the continuing struggle for decolonization were revealing an increasing diversity of standpoints, and the discussions seemed headed towards a confrontational impasse. Prominent among the many invited respondents to initial drafts of the Declaration was UNESCO, whose reactions were sought, and Maritain's most immediate influence on the final form and initial acceptance of the Declaration stems from his involvement with UNESCO.[3] The UN project was chosen as the major focus of a Second Session of the General Conference of UNESCO, organized by the seven members of the "UNESCO Committee on the philosophical principles/theoretical bases of Human Rights."[4] An early planning conference for this subcommittee's work for UNESCO had been organized in Paris, June 26 to July 2, 1947, by the chair, Edward H. Carr, and the members of the committee. The commission expected that the examination of the diverse bases for acknowledging rights

1. Johannes Morsink, *The Universal Declaration of Human Rights: Origins, Drafting and Intent* (Philadelphia: University of Pennsylvavia Press, 1999), 4–12.

2. Cf. Rene Mougel, "J. Maritain et la Déclaration universelle des droits de l'homme de 1948," *Cahiers Jacques Maritain* 37 (1998): 13–15.

3. Ibid.

4. *Human Rights: Comments and interpretations. A Symposium of the UNESCO. With an Introduction by Jacques Maritain*, edited by UNESCO (Paris: July 25, 1948): Appendix II 15. http://unesdoc.unesco.org/images/0015/001550/155042eb.pdf

could anticipate and eleviate severe disagreements. In preparation for the meeting in Mexico, the commission circulated a set of six questions and a sample of the diverse written responses from among the one hundred and fifty persons and organizations contacted, including one by Maritain on the "Philosophical Examination of Human Rights," which Maritain had sent from Rome in June 1947.[5] Maritain's and several other solicited written responses were first published in the UN *Weekly Bulletin* during the second half of 1947, prior to the General Conference in November.[6] The organizing commission had also offered along with some of its own initial conclusions from the submitted answers two possible, complementary lists of rights, one with fifteen more "fundamental" rights,[7] the other with twenty-five "special" ones.[8] Selections from the preparatory material would be sent again after the conference in Mexico to the United Nations in the summer of 1948, but now, at the request of Julian Huxley and the commission,[9] prefaced by nine pages written by Maritain in July and August of 1948, summarizing the theses of his own talk at the Mexican conference.[10] This documentation was consulted by Cassin as he prepared the final drafts of the Declaration. The conference had hosted thirty-seven delegations of varying size, and with the invited and advance written responses, the materials under discussion by UNESCO had become unwieldly in terms both of sheer quantity and of philosophically and politically motivated disagreements about the theoretical bases of human rights.

Already in 1942, Maritain had completed at Princeton his work on *The Rights of Man and Natural Law.*[11] Developing René Mougel's remarks on the impact of this work in the two Americas, where it quickly found English, Spanish, and Portuguese translations,[12] Benedikt Ritzler and Herbert Hartl interpret twenty-two of the twenty-six rights listed there by Maritain in 1942

5. Jacques Maritain, "Philosophical Examination of Human Rights," in *Human Rights,* 59–64, esp. 67–71.

6. Cf. Catherine M. A. McCauliff, "Cognition and Consensus in the Natural Law Tradition and in Neuroscience: Jacques Maritain and the Universal Declaration of Human Rights," *Villanova Law Review* 54, no. 3 (2009): 435–78, here 462 n. 117.

7. UNESCO, Appendix II, 11–15, beginning with "The right to live."

8. UNESCO, Appendix I, 7–8, beginning with "Freedom of conscience or worship (a) for individuals (b) for organized religious groups."

9. Cf. Mougel, "J. Maritain et la Déclaration universelle," 15.

10. UNESCO, pages I–IX, dated on the final page, "New York, July–August 1948."

11. Jacques Maritain, *The Rights of Man and Natural Law,* translated by Doris C. Anson (New York: Charles Scribner's Sons, 1943).

12. Mougel, "J. Maritain et la Déclaration universelle," 13–15.

as recurring in some form among the thirty rights of the final UN Declaration of 1948.[13] It is far easier to localize the contribution Maritain made by his three communications to UNESCO towards the general acceptance and understanding of the developing UN Declaration than to guage the influence of his writings from the 1930s and 1940s, together with their early reception in Europe and the two Americas, on those initial drafts.[14] Still France's ambassador to the Vatican at the time of the conference in Mexico, and having already submitted his paper, Maritain was chosen, Jean-Luc Barré tells us, "at the last moment ... to replace Léon Blum who was sick, and it was his duty, as head of the French delegation, to give the opening speech."[15] As head of a heterogenous French delegation of four, Maritain delivered an influential address at the opening meeting of the Second Session of the General Conference of UNESCO in Mexico City on November 6th, 1947. Quite different from the initial written response that Maritain had submitted already in June for the conference, that November address would be published as "La Voie de la Paix" in Mexico that very November[16] and subsequently reproduced in whole or in part well over ten times in the original or in translation.[17] The text translated into English in *The Range of Reason*, "The Possibilities for Co-operation in a Divided World," follows the November talk closely, revising the title and the numbering. Some three months later, Maritain's talk

13. Cf. Benedikt Ritzler, "Maritain, Jacques," in *Thomistenlexikon*, edited by David Berger and Jörgen Vijgen (Bonn: Nova et Vetera, 2006): 426–36, here 429–30. Ritzler builds here on his 1999 dissertation, *Freiheit in der Umarmung des ewig Liebenden. Die historische Entwicklung des Personverständnisses bei Jacques Maritain* (Bern: Lang 2000); and Herbert Hartl, *Christliche Weisheit und neues Mensch-Sein. Leben und Werk des Kleinen Bruders Heinz R. Schmitz. Auf den Spuren Charles de Foucaulds und Jacques Maritains* (Würzburg: Echter 2013).

14. Cf. Paul Gordon Lauren, *The Evolution of International Human Rights: Visions Seen*, second edition (Philadelphia: University of Pennsylvavia Press, 2003), 148, where Lauren writes that "the publication of a book by Jacques Maritain entitled *Les Droits de l'homme et la loi naturelle* (1942) stimulated still further discussion about the prospects for some kind of bill of rights." For Morsink's caution about a direct influence of Maritain on the actual composition of the text, see the presently unpublished doctoral dissertation by Carrie Rose Stibora, *Jacques Maritain and Alasdair MacIntyre on Human Rights* (Washington, D.C.: The Catholic University of America Press, 2013): 5 n. 9; http://aladinrc.wrlc.org/bitstream/handle/1961/15223/Stibora_cua_0043A_10442display.pdf?sequence=1

15. Jean-Luc Barré, *Jacques and Raïssa Maritain. Beggars for Heaven*, translated by Bernard Doering (South Bend, Indiana: Notre Dame University Press, 2005), 393. Barré refers to Roger Seydoux, "Jacques Maritain à Mexico," in *Cahiers Jacques Maritain* 10 (October 1984).

16. Mexico (D.F.: Librairie Française, 1947); now in Jacques and Raïssa Maritain, *Oeuvres complètes* IX (Fribourg: Éditions universitaires/Paris, Éditions St. Paul, 1992), 143–64.

17. Jacques and Raïssa Maritain, *Oeuvres complètes* XVII (Fribourg: Éditions universitaires/Paris, Éditions St. Paul, 2007): 254–56: 47 L 3–47 L 3–11.

would be highlighted on the front page of the very first issue of the *UNESCO Courier*.[18] It was given more prominence in this inaugural issue than the address by Julian Huxley, the founding general director of UNESCO. It was likely Huxley himself who arranged it so.[19] René Mougel and Jean-Luc Barré suggest that Maritain's arguments had convinced Huxley to relax his insistance on a materialistic rationale for rights as the only path to neutrality. Barré claims that Maritain's insight had liberated the conference from the growing fear that they would sink into the isolation of the separate language-games that Maritain calls "Babelism." Barré and Mougel follow Seydoux' account: "Captivated, the thirty-seven delegates of the nations represented listened to him in silence."[20] At the very least, Maritain's address suggested a bold change of topic for the conference: not the debate about the best rationale for the theoretical bases of human rights, but an acknowledgement of the fact and extent of the genuine but merely practical consensus among those with theoretically incompatible justifications for it. The affirmative answer that Maritain offers to the question he poses in the second half of his talk, "Can intellectually divided men co-operate in practical matters?" is rooted in a theoretical justification quite his own that, consistently enough, he does not propose for discussion in this talk. It had been the topic of his written suggestion before being tapped to assume Blum's wider role. Instead, he offers here not foundations, but three necessary but not yet sufficient conditions for even practical agreement on the issue of rights, conditions that, if not fulfilled, will corrode even genuine practical consensus on the need for and the compass of a declaration of rights. He groups these conditions together as "Three Problems."[21]

The first condition is the liberation from what he calls "Machiavellianism and Realpolitik," which would admit, demand, or deny human rights only as deemed opportune for what seems to be of practical advantage for the party staking its claim.[22] Maritain's rejection of all notions that human rights are first constructed and extinguished by social contract or state agreement is only hinted at here, so as not to endanger the consensus. What it is that transcends merely pragmatic advantage is left open for the

18. Paris, February 1948, continuing on p. 8.

19. Cf. UNESCO, *Human Rights*, where Huxley's own response comes only on pages 302–308.

20. Jean-Luc Barré, *Jacques and Raïssa Maritain*, 393.

21. Jacques Maritain, "The Possibilities for Co-operation in a Divided World," chap. 13 in *The Range of Reason* (New York: Charles Scribner's Sons, 1952), 172–84, here especially 174–79.

22. Ibid., 176.

moment, but Maritain will enunciate his answer elsewhere, as he had in his written submission for the conference, arguing in his talk that this moment of transcendence beyond an all-engulfing pragmatism and functionalism can be forceful even while remaining implicit. The explication of Machiavellianism as the temptation to assess human rights as a mere matter of pragmatic expediency is also the theme of one of the seven chapters that he adds along with the UNESCO address to revise earlier versions of *The Range of Reason*.[23]

The second condition described here for accepting and maintaining a practical consensus on rights even without agreement on their theoretical foundations is arguably the most important and illuminating of the three: the memory of suffering, especially of the sufferings of others and the sufferings for which one is at least to some degree personally or collectively responsible. Like the first condition, this feature, too, will play a role in Maritain's later thematization of the rights issue at the Council. His suggestions to at least two popes to thematize more sharply the past failings committed in the name of the Church never received the degree of acknowledgement he had hoped for.[24] Maritain would return to this theme up to and including his final monograph, *On the Church of Christ*,[25] although a papal answer to match his request would wait arguably until the "purification of memory" called for in connection with the marking of the third millenium.[26] This condition is not restricted to nor even yet directly applied in this address to ecclesial existence or to a future declaration of religious liberty by a Church cognizant of her own failings in granting the religious freedom of non-Christians. Maritain acknowledges, however, that the practical consensus on rights in the late 1940s was possible because of the memory of the suffering resulting from great recent war crimes, and he

23. Maritain, "The End of Machiavellianism," chap. 11 in *The Range of Reason*, 134–64.

24. Cf. Barré, *Jacques and Raïssa Maritain*, 391; and the references to the testimony of Journet in Herbert Hartl, *Christliche Weisheit und neues Mensch-Sein*, 6 n. 9.

25. Jacques Maritain, *On the Church of Christ: The Person of the Church and Her Personnel*, translated by Joseph Owens (Notre Dame, Indiana: The University of Notre Dame Press, 1973). The distinction, used here by the translator for the subtitle, and taken by Maritain from Charles Journet, stood chiefly in the service of a greater frankness regarding the failings of Christians. It is the topic of all the final chapters, 11–14.

26. On the relative novelty of this theme during the pontificate of John Paul II, see International Theological Commission, *Texts and Documents, 1986–2007*, edited by Michael Sharkey and Thomas Weinandy (San Francisco: Ignatius Press, 2009), 187–228. The ITC dealt with the theme in the year 2000 at the suggestion of Joseph Ratzinger.

foresaw the challenge that would arise for the community of nations when the gradual loss of shared memory would lay bare the lack of common principles for acknowledging human rights. In particular, Maritain argues here for the acknowledgement of "the collective moral transgression" of the German nation.[27] His concern about other political crimes of the century is more palpable in his treatment of the third and final problem.

This third problem or condition explicates the implied bond between the first two.[28] The eclipse of moral conscience by instrumental reason, described as the first problem, and the loss of the memory of the violent consequences of that decline, discussed as the second problem, are implied by the third "problem of the human value and human use of science and technology."[29] The urgency for a still unrealized reconciliation of science and ethics in wisdom recalls the wider history of suffering that had resulted from the unchecked primacy of instrumental reason: "It is not enough to draw the attention of the peoples to the world-destroying catastrophes which the discoveries of modern (atomic) physics may well lead to, if another armed conflict should occur. Fear is not enough to make men wise."[30] The need for an international organization for educational, scientific, and cultural concerns could not be doubted; though such organizations, like universities, would be judged not least by their wisdom on the ethical dimension of the sciences. The implications for the urgency of the humanities and interdisciplinary discourse at the university level had already been a topic in his war-time Yale lectures, *Education at the Crossroads*,[31] a topic to which he will return in his first and especially in the final section of his fourth memoranda in 1965. At Yale he could still claim, with no apparent irony, that "the practical aspect of this question is of no difficulty for denominational colleges."[32] In that final memorandum for Paul VI in 1965 he will show a greater concern about studies even at such institutions.[33] Following Newman, Maritain sees every uni-

27. Maritain, *The Range of Reason*, 176.

28. Ibid., 177–79.

29. Ibid., 178.

30. Ibid.

31. Jacques Maritain, *Education at the Crossroads* (New Haven: Yale University Press, 1960), 75. This task of dialogue across the disciplines cannot be replaced by courses in any one field alone: "Nor can experience, which is an incommunicable fruit of suffering and memory, and through which the shaping of man is achieved, be taught by any school or any courses. There are courses in philosophy, but no courses in wisdom." Ibid., 23.

32. Ibid., 75.

33. Jacques and Raïssa Maritain, "III. Les Études," in *Oeuvres complètes XXVI* (Fribourg: Éditions universitaires/Paris, Éditions St. Paul, 1999): 1124–30.

versity as "a place of *teaching* universal *knowledge*."[34] The task of interdisciplinary, sapiential dialogue not just at universities lies in any case not merely in the critique of reason, but in its defense. The critique of merely intrumental reason is itself in the service of the advancement of a more genuine, more encompassing reason. The recognition of human rights by the forces of education, science, and culture is presupposed by every genuine form of education, science, and culture that could contribute to human flourishing.

> Today we have to defend science against those who, after asking of it more than it could give, now accuse it, just as unreasonably, of being bankrupt. And, on the other hand, we see men of science engaged in a serious internal examination, in which is questioned the relationship between their conscience as men and the possible use of their work as scientists. We even see them in danger of being treated by states as mere industrial ore made particularly valuable by its output in terms of discoveries. Thus it is the very dignity of science and of the scientist which is at stake.[35]

Maritain argues at the UNESCO conference for a sense of the newly recognized "need of a powerful renewal of the disciplines of wisdom and of a reintegration of ethical, metaphysical, and religious truths into its culture" as a third condition for the acknowledgement of human rights even among those with irreconcilable views of their ulimate foundations.[36]

None of these three necessary conditions is as yet sufficient to explain the simple fact that Maritain will underscore in the remaining section of his talk: that at this particular point in history, and under the three conditions mentioned, there is in 1947 a widespread consensus about a finite set of human rights. It is his direct but unexpected thesis that, although the conference was designed as a search for common theoretical foundations of the recognition of rights, and as important and interesting a topic as that might be, the more important conclusion would be to realize that a practical consensus already exists—or still exists—and has its own plausibility, perhaps not directly—but all the more strikingly—precisely because of that plurality. To introduce a conference by arguing that its topic and the very title of its organizing committee were ill-conceived would not normally be a recipe for success; but here Maritain's remarks were greeted as rescue from a

34. *Education at the Crossroads*, 76, quoting the conclusion of the first and programmatic sentence of John Henry Newman, *The Idea of a University* (South Bend, Indiana: Notre Dame University Press, 2009), xxxvii.

35. Maritain, *The Range of Reason*, 178–79.

36. Ibid., 179.

seeming impasse. Staying with his (and he tells us, not just his) image of Babelism, he sees UNESCO's task as providing methods for translating between non-identical languages for a common understanding of a peace attained in the justice defined by an accepted set of human rights. He returns to the comments he had cited at the beginning of his talk from Léon Blum at the preparatory conference in San Francisco 1944 and at the founding of the organization in London, in 1945. The goal of UNESCO is practical: the pursuit of peace by the development and communication of education, science, and culture. Maritain also cites with approval Blum's successful invitation to UNESCO to locate its future headquarters in Paris. In thoughts congenial to Maritain's own writings from the early forties (*Pour la justice*), and cited at the beginning of Maritain's address in Mexico, the three-time former Prime Minister of France saw in his country a characteristic tendency towards "universality," insofar as "the sciences, general culture, literature, the arts, and technology in so far as it borders on art have always developed side by side and in reciprocal connection."[37] It should be possible, Maritain adds, especially in France to reconcile the particular and the universal, but he does not recall here what he had maintained in his initial submission the previous summer that the adequate foundation for human rights should be sought elsewhere than in what was most often associated with French developments in the late-eighteenth century.

The comparison of Maritain's November address with his original written submission some four months earlier, in as much as it is represented by the version in the 1948 UNESCO publication,[38] reveals a facet from which he quietly abstracted but which was also just as quietly presupposed in the spoken address in Mexico and in his introduction to this edition of selected preparatory statements. Only the first of seven sections of the original written response addresses the topic of the distinction between the current possibility of consensus on a list of rights and the current impossibility of consensus on the principles and philosophical justification for just such a declaration.[39] Maritain claims for himself as a philosopher the right to be interested especially in the latter, even if he admits that he will be formulating

37. Ibid.

38. The biographical references at the beginning of the article on page 59 do not correspond to 1947 but only to the summer of 1948 (July 25th, 1948 is the date noted here), after Maritain's resignation as ambassaor and prior to the clarity that Maritain's position at Princeton was to be a general appointment outside the philosophy faculty.

39. UNESCO 59, Nr 2. unesdoc.unesco.org/images/0015/001550/155042eb.pdf

quite particular theoretical reasons for living with and working towards the common practical consensus. He begins his written response by rejecting "the view that the 18th Century's concept of Human Rights was an extension to the individual of the idea of the Divine Right of Kings or of the indefeasible rights which God granted to the Church":[40] a nearly exact quotation from and open contradiction of the "Memorandum and Questionnaire Circulated by UNESCO on the Theoretical Bases of the Rights of Man."[41] Maritain's alternative was a foundation of rights in "natural law," which he says was articulated together with the law of nations by reflecting on ancient and medieval traditions. Natural law is understood at other times by Maritain as the even more generic category for all theories of inalienable rights that do not result from governmental decision, contract, or positive law. Catherine M. A. McCauliff draws attention to the ideas that Maritain will state best some four years later (1951) in an article, "On Knowledge through Connaturality,"[42] which provides a natural law justification not just of human rights themselves, but also of the possibility of the United Nations consensus about them.[43] Maritain saw in the consensus about rights in the late forties an eminent example of the dynamics of connaturality. Just as Maritain's sometimes clumsy doctrine of the distinction between person and individual, which he had gleaned from Garrigou-Lagrange and then applied to the critique of totalitarianisms, autocratic or populist,[44] so, too, is Maritain's

40. Ibid.

41. UNESCO Appendix I, page 1, where the original has "imprescriptible" for Maritain's "indefeasible."

42. Jacques Maritain, "On Knowledge through Connaturality," *Review of Metaphysics* 4, no. 4 (1951): 473–81; now as chap. 3 of *The Range of Reason*, 22–29, as well as chap. 1 of *Maritain, Natural Law: Reflections on Theory and Practice*, edited by William Sweet (South Bend, Indiana: St. Augustine's Press, 2001), 13–24.

43. McCauliff, "Cognition and Consensus." McCauliff also underscores the abiding affinity of Maritain to key insights of Bergson, which became more evident after the 1932 publication of *The Two Sources of Morality and Religion*, translated by R. Ashley Audra, Cloudsley Brereton and W. Horsfall Carter (Notre Dame, Indiana: University of Notre Dame Press, 1977). That Bergon's thought remained present in Maritain's reading of Thomas's epistemology even prior to 1932, see also Benedikt Ritzler, *Freiheit in der Umarmung des ewig Liebenden. Die historische Entwicklung des Personverständnisses bei Jacques Maritain* (Bern: Lang 2000), 51–96.

44. Cf. Richard Schenk, OP, "Jacques Maritain and Vatican II: Resources for the Future? Approaching the Fiftieth Anniversary of the Council," in *The Vocation of the Catholic Philosopher: From Maritain to John Paul II*, edited by John P. Hittinger (Washington, D.C.: The American Maritain Association, 2010; distributed by The Catholic University of America Press), 3–29, here 23–25. The critique of totalitarianism plays nearly as central a role in Maritain's works from the 1930s on as in Hannah Arendt's writings. Much of what is said on other topics is meant first and foremost to elaborate this critique.

generic doctrine of natural law first and foremost the denial that the rights of human beings result only from state recognition of them; it is a challenge to the totalitarianisms of the right and the left. But here in preparation for the 1947 conference Maritain is also keen to distinguish among the many conceptions of natural law. "The concept of natural law has been so much abused, so much pulled about, distorted or hypertrophied that it is hardly surprising if, in our age, many minds declare themselves weary of the whole idea."[45] Maritain distinguishes between natural law itself, as a principle, and "doctrines of natural law." He does not cite John Henry Newman in this reply, but Maritain's distinction here between principle and doctrine parallels Newman's second note of genuine development.[46] Natural law calls for formulation and application, but it is itself unwritten ("which is interior to the creature and precedes any explicit expression"), a task which is the subject of slow and painful evolution, subject as well to "the immense influence of economic and social conditions," and therefore never "exhaustive and final."[47] Here is the core of Maritain's particular account of how there can be consensus about rights without a consensus about their origins: doctrines about the principles are secondary to the convictions that they articulate.

Flawed theoretical doctrines can, but need not, eclipse the practical strength of the natural law making itself felt by means of those doctrines. This is also not to deny that the natural law can be a force in articulating or correcting concrete positions in the political, legal, and ethical world. For example, Maritain's most biting remarks are directed here towards excesses of capitalism. The newer doubts in socialist systems about the unbridled application of capitalism are a justified impetus to the reflection of conscience upon the natural law, although it is "an irony stained with blood" that the "revolutionary proletariate" adopted "atheistic ideology" from "the most 'bourgoise' representatives of the bourgeoisie, who after calling on the God of the Deists that they might base their own demands on the natural law, rejected that God and the God of the Christians alike when they were come to power and sought to free the all-embracing exercise of proprietary rights from the shakles of the natural law and to close their ears to the cry of the poor."[48] The extremes of left and right consider "it ... today permissible to

45. Cf. UNESCO, 61, Nr. 5.
46. "Essay on the Development," chap. 5, sec. II, 178–85.
47. UNESCO, 60, Nr. 3.
48. Ibid., Nr. 5.

violate any right of any man, if this be necessary for the purpose at hand."[49] An interpretation of natural law along the historical, social, and narrative lines suggested here by Maritain could be an additional argument in favor of Carrie Rose Stibora's recent thesis about the "unexpected links" in the lives and concerns of Maritain and Alasdair MacIntyre as they regard the issues around human rights discourse.[50]

III. Maritain and Vatican II

The influence of Maritain's thought on the Second Vatican Council is no less difficult to pinpoint than his contribution to the UN Declaration. In both cases, his most significant contributions seem to stem from works published prior to the process of drafting those documents and then again during the early phases of their reception. Having returned to France after Raïssa's death in 1960 with the intention of a less public role in the debates of the day, and despite Paul VI's unfulfilled and—given the critique of Maritain prior to 1966 especially from the "Right"[51]—unfulfillable wish to see him as a formal advisor (or observer) at the Council, Maritain was not involved in the Council's labors of composition.[52] Maritain's writings, especially on practical and political concerns since his 1936 publication of *Integral Humanism,* had been widely received and also critically debated in France, Italy, and on the two American continents. The sense of the end not

49. Ibid.

50. Stibora, *Jacques Maritain and Alasdair MacIntyre on Human Rights,* 301. Stibora's analysis of Macintyre's discussion of rights is intentionally provisional, but she argues that the reduced level of MacIntyre's criticism of a Catholic embrace of the rights discourse, while not signaling MacIntyre's positive acceptance of this discourse, does reflect his growing appreciation of the Maritain's Thomistic answers to contemporary challenges. See ibid., 301–310.

51. Yves Congar, *My Journal of the Council* (Collegeville, Minnesota: Liturgical Press, 2012), recorded repeated rumors of attempts to have Maritain's writings condemned by the Council: see the entries on 17 XI 1960, 23 I 1961, 10 VI 1963. On the difficulties Montini encountered for being too closely associated with *Integral Humanism,* see 7–9 II 1965, 2 V 1965 and 30 IX 1966. As marginal as such efforts were, they show that Maritain's loudest critics at the Council were to be found among the opponents of declaring religious freedom a right. They included, not suprisingly, given the source of the thesis/hypothesis distinction, proponents of an article by Antonio Messineo in *Civiltà Cattolica;* see Peter Hebbeltwaite, *Paul VI: The First Modern Pope* (Glasgow: Harper Collins/Fount, 1993), 287.

52. Maritain is therefore not mentioned in the otherwise helpful commentary by Roman A. Siebenrock, "Theologischer Kommentar zur Erklärung über die religiose Freiheit *Dignitatis humanae,*" in *Herders Theologischer Kommentar zum Zweiten Vatikanischen Konzil,* vol. 4, edited by Peter Hünermann and Bernd Jochen Hilberath (Freiburg i. Br. 2005), 125–218.

just of the medieval but even of the Constantinian era, and the previously unsuspected chances provided by this ending for a new beginning, together with a capacity drawn from the self-understanding of the person and of Christian faith to embrace and defend democracy, the search for alternatives both to excessive capitalism and totalitarian collectivism, the need for a more positive appreciation and defense of Judaism *post Christum*, the importance of the laity not just to the temporal but to the spiritual life of the Church, and most notably support for the Declaration of Human Rights, in particular for the inalienable right to religious liberty: these were all topics towards which Maritain had contributed much already prior to 1960.[53] "Many of the bishops were able to accept this perspective because they knew the *Humanisme intégrale* of Jacques Maritain."[54] For the purposes of these reflections, I will focus on what arguably was Maritain's most significant input during the Council on the most significant issue with which he was involved: the question of religious liberty, thematized especially in the second of four memoranda that he submitted to Paul VI in March of 1965.

The question of religious liberty was among the topics slated for discussion from the beginning of the Council,[55] but the state of the question took several surprising turns in 1964 even prior to the third session of the Council.[56] The need noted by Cardinal Bea and Bishop De Smedt just prior to the Council to move beyond what had been what Bea could refer to as "the traditional teaching" since the mid-19th century,[57] had by then gathered sufficient support, that the defenders of the so-called "Roman position," who initially had hoped for a conciliar censure of Maritain's writings

53. Congar noted that Cardinal Wright defended the draft of the Declaration by appealing in the plenum to Maritain's thought; see *My Journal*, 28 IX, 1964.

54. Giuseppe Alberigo, "Chapter VII: The Conclusion of the Council and the Initial Reception," in *History of Vatican II*, vol. 5, edited by Giuseppe Alberigo and Joseph A. Komonchak (Maryknoll/Leuven: Orbis/Peeters, 2006): 541–71, here 546 n. 8.

55. Cf. Pietro Pavan, Professor at the Lateran University in Rome and advisor to John XXIII on *Pacem in Terris* and to the Council, especially on the Declaration, for an early account of the genesis of the "Declaratio de Libertate Religiosa," in *Lexikon für Theologie und Kirche*, vol. 13: *Das Zweite Vatikanische Konzil* (Freiburg i. Br., Herder 1967/1986): 703–48, and in *Commentary on the Documents of Vatican II*, vol. 4, translated and edited by Herbert Vorgrimler et al., (London, Burns and Oates/New York, Herder and Herder, 1967–69). Pavan identified six different schemata submitted to the Council.

56. Cf. Pavan, "Declaratio," 705; and Siebenrock, "Theologischer Kommentar," 153–61.

57. Cf. Giovanni Miccoli's contribution to vol. 4 of Alberigo and Komonchak, here cited from Miccoli's, "II. Zwei Schwierige Problemfelder: Die Religionsfreiheit und das Verhältnis zu den Juden," in *Geschichte des Zweiten Vatikanischen Konzils (1959–1965)*, edited by Giuseppe Aberigo and Günther Wassilowsky (Mainz, Günewald/Leuven, Peeters, 2006), 115.

on this topic,[58] now saw as their best remaining chance the withdrawal of the theme from the Council's agenda.[59] Not only was the matter considered by the majority to be important enough to be treated in a declaration of its own (and no longer merely as a sub-section of the decree on ecumenism), but—despite the widespread concerns for the homogeneous development of Catholic doctrine—as an issue significant enough to warrant an open shift of doctrine, whereby the proportions and *loci* of continuity and discontinuity still remain today a matter of debate.[60] The position developed in 1863 in the year before *Quanta cura,* but at the behest of Pius IX, by Carlo Maria Curzi, SJ, and the other contributors to the semi-official periodical *La Civiltà Cattolica,* distinuished between the substantial "thesis" of a rejection in principle of religious freedom, to be practiced in lands with Catholic majorities, and the very contingent "hypothesis" of a merely practical demand for religious toleration, for lands where Catholics were in the minority and for as long as they would be.[61] Maritain had expressed his dissatisfaction with the thesis/hypothesis distinction already in 1949 in chapter 6 of *Man and the State.*[62] Although the logical construction of thesis/hypothesis might be "quite respectable" and in principle capable of being "used in a valid manner," especially as regards the toleration of morally deficient private practices, and notwithstanding its violation of the rules of ordinary language or its not having, as he believes, "very deep traditional roots," and its thus being "often incorrectly construed," Maritain sees its application to the question of human rights as an outright self-contradiction, in that it makes out of a matter of principle—the human right to religious freedom—a matter of occasional expediency. One recalls Maritain's earlier critique of Machiavellian expediency: the practice of admitting, denying, or demanding rights only for the pragmatic advantage of those staking a claim.

58. Cf. Congar, *My Journal,* 35–37. In another common, if not altogether united, cause with Congar, Maritain was also considered by the same circles as suspect for stressing the spiritual task of the laity.

59. Cf. Miccoli, "II. Zwei Schwierige Problemfelder," 115 for Cardinal Ottaviani's forceful opposition already in the spring of 1964.

60. John T. Noonan Jr., *A Church That Can and Cannot Change: The Development of Catholic Moral Teaching* (South Bend, Indiana: University of Notre Dame Press, 2005), especially 145–53.

61. Cf. Martin Rhonheimer, *Christentum und säkularer Staat. Geschichte—Gegenwart—Zukunft.* Mit einem Vorwort von Ernst-Wolfgang Böckenförde (Freiburg et al., Herder, 2012), 149–63.

62. *Man and the State,* 154ff. In an initial "Acknowledgement" prefacing that work, Maritain thanked Journet, who "was good enough to pay special attention to Chapter VI." Ibid., iii.

The support for the Conciliar declaration came above all from the Americas, where Maritain's works were well-known prior to the Council. Already in 1963, John Courtney Murray could refer to the question of religious liberty as the "American" problem at the Council.[63] Not merely a source for these convictions, Maritain had also been a learner during his two sojourns in the USA. In *Man and the State* he had returned several times to his positive assessment of Murray's 1949 address to the Catholic Theological Society of America.[64] Murray will refer to a divergence at the Council even among the majority supporters of the Declaration between characteristically French and American instincts,[65] the former being of a more limited, historical, political, or juridical bent, for which Murray himself showed particular sympathy, but both supporting sides convinced that the state could hardly be a competent judge of "true religion."[66] Joseph Ratzinger will complain soon after the third session that "the American model came perhaps too clearly through these supposedly timeless natural-law doctrines,"[67] reflecting what conventional images of natural law had been presupposing, especially prior to Maritain and Murray's influence on the issue of religious liberty. The text proposals which would occupy the last two sessions of the Council were largely the work of Murray, and the opening words and title of the final declaration clearly show more than

63. John Courtney Murray, "On Religious Liberty," *America* 109 (November 1963): 704–706. The brief but influential description of the *status quaestionis* would be published during the Council in French, German, Spanish, and Italian: see John Courtney Murray, *Religious Liberty: Catholic Struggles with Pluralism*, edited by J. Leon Hooper (Louisville, Kentucky: Westminster John Knox Press 1993), 256.

64. Cf. first in *Man and the State*, 157 n. 11.

65. Cf. Hermínio Rico, *John Paul II and the Legacy of "Dignitatis Humanae"* (Washington, D.C.: Georgetown University Press, 2002), 41–51.

66. For a detailed account of the often surprising constellations of national and individual supporters, as well as the indifferent (often at odds with the typical clichés about the Council), see Gilles Routhier, "II. Finishing the Work Begun: The Trying Experience of the Fourth Period," in Alberigo and Komonchak, *History of Vatican II*, 49–184, especially 49–122. Murray's absence due to illness during the final session led to a stronger theological emphasis.

67. Ratzinger, *Theological Highlights*, 155. For a measure of Ratzinger's development on the validity of natural law discourse, see the address by Pope Benedict XVI to the German Parliament on September 22, 2011: "The Listening Heart. Reflections on the Foundations of Law" and the theme of "human ecology": http://w2.vatican.va/content/benedict-xvi/en/speeches/2011/september/documents/hf_ben-xvi_spe_20110922_reichstag-berlin.html. For his predecessor's dual use of natural law and, usually far more pronounced, strictly theological arguments in favor of the dignity of the person and religious freedom, see Hermínio Rico, *John Paul II and the Legacy of "Dignitatis Humanae,"* 105, for Wotyla's general position in the Conciliar debates around *Dignitatis Humanae*.

a political and juridical logic: "A sense of the dignity of the human person has been impressing itself more and more deeply on the consciousness of contemporary man, and the demand is increasingly made that men should act on their own judgment, enjoying and making use of a responsible freedom, not driven by coercion but motivated by a sense of duty." After the second major draft, the *Declaratio prior,* was rejected on September 23, a new, less dogmatic schema, composed largely by Murray, was presented in the final days of the third session, on November 11, 1964. Given the continuing dissatisfaction, not just among the determined minority, but even among supporters of the majority,[68] Paul VI followed the lead of the Council of Presidents (under Cardinal Eugenio Tisserant) and postponed the final vote until the beginning of the fourth and final session, as he assured would happen, in order to allow time for discussion and for the improvements of the text that had been suggested in the plenaries. The lack of clarity, however, about the Pope's ultimate intentions and the future of the declaration added to new controversies around the Council's stance toward ecumenism, collegiality, Mariology, and the conciliar process itself, and led many to call this week of 15–21 November 1964 the Council's "Black Week": that "salutary embarrassment" "that no one would want … to ever happen again."[69] In the end, even the supporters of the Declaration would come to admit that the additional consultation in 1965 proved advantageous to the intrinsic quality of the text and to the depth, if not so much the quantity, of its acceptance by the Council.[70] In late 1964 and for most of 1965, however, the future of the declaration seemed anything but certain.

It was in this extremely polarized situation in late December that Maritain received in Toulouse two "envoys," Jean Guitton and Monsignor Pasquale Macchi, who brought questions from Paul VI regarding certain topics of the coming fourth session of the Council and its reception, on which he would gladly hear Maritain's views.[71] After a bout with bronchitis,[72] Maritain formulated his answers in March 1965 in four memoran-

68. Cf. Luis Antonio G. Tagle, "VI. Die 'Schwarze Woche' des Konzils (14–21 November 1964)," in *Geschichte des Zweiten Vatikanischen Konzils* (1959–1965), edited by Giuseppe Alberigo and Günther Wassilowsky, vol. 4 (Mainz, Günewald/Leuven, Peeters, 2006), 461.

69. Cf. the brief reports immediately after each session by Joseph Ratzinger, *Theological Highlights of Vatican II* (1966; repr., Mahwah, New Jersey: Paulist Press, 2009), 160 and 193.

70. Cf. Tagle, "VI. Die 'Schwarze Woche' des Konzils," 471–73.

71. Cf. Maritain's note to "Sur la vérité," in *Oeuvres complètes* XVI , 1085.

72. Maritain tells of this illness in his cover letter to Msgr. Macchi; see Piero Viotto, *Paolo VI–Jacques Maritain: Un'amicizia intellettuale* (Rome: Edizioni Studium, 2014), 209–37, 209–11

da sent via Macchi, who assured him that he had forwarded them to the pope. Montini had long been Maritain's avid reader, translator, defender, and (especially during Maritain's ambassadorship in Rome 1945–48) regular conversation partner.[73] He had referred to Maritain as his teacher and to himself as a disciple.[74] It is not surprising, then, that Paul sought the philosopher's advice on these very public issues (together with one smaller but more delicate issue discussed during Maritain's suboptimal visit to Rome in September: the ceremonies to conclude the Council). It is unknown what influence the responses had on Paul's thoughts or actions in 1965. Paul certainly did not always heed Maritain's advice, e.g. concerning the need for *Nostra Aetate* not only to deplore but also to condemn ("damnat") antisemitism,[75] to exercise a more robust self-critique of ecclesiastical failings, or to issue an encyclical on truth. They differed in their conceptions of the implications of natural law.[76] And yet the further written observations that Maritain would offer Pope Paul in November of 1965,[77] the Pope's consultation with Maritain about, and his choice of him for, a symbolic role in the concluding ceremonies of the Council, the allusions by Paul VI on the previous day to the credit due the Council for its effort "to recognize our own new type of humanism," a private meeting of the two on December 10, two days after the ceremonies to conclude the Council, as well as the incorporation of Maritain's thoughts and formulations in Paul's *Credo of the People of God*,[78] along with the two references to Maritain in

---

Congar will learn of the papal request for Maritain's views and of the sickness that delayed them first through Dominican channels, then from Journet, and finally from Maritain himself on the occasion of his second visit to Rome in 1965. Cf. Congar, *My Journals*, for 1 II 1965, 7 X 1965, and 7 XII 1965.

73. Cf. Philippe Chenaux, *Paul VI et Maritain: Les rapports du "Montinianisme" et du "Maritainisme"* (Brescia, Istituto Paolo VI/Rome: Edizioni Studium, 1994); and Barré, *Jacques and Raïssa* Maritain, 389–97, 419–29.

74. Cf. Catherine M. A. McCauliff, "Jacques Maritain's Embrace of Religious Pluralism and the Declaration on Religious Freedom," *Seton Hall Law Review* 41, no. 2 (2011): 593–624.

75. On Maritain's disappointments with two popes on this matter, see Barré, *Jacques and Raïssa* Maritain, 425. On the complexities of Maritain's own positions, see the diverse voices in *Jacques Maritain and the Jews*, edited by Robert Royal (American Maritain Association, 1994; distributed by Notre Dame University Press).

76. Cf. Bernard Doering, "Jacques Maritain and Charles Journet on Human Sexuality," *Theological Studies* 62 (2001): 597–606.

77. The reflection on the importance of non-violence in the political order, "*Amour* et *Pouvoir*," touches again several times on religious freedom, but its focus is broader: *Oeuvres complètes* XVI, 1131–1135.

78. Maritain's text, passed on to the Pope by Journet, is appropriated to a larger degree than Maritain had anticipated.

Populorum Progressio,[79] show that these conversations would continue after the conclusion of the Council, and despite remarkable differences, would share a common type of stance toward the projects of a "renovatio accommodata" of Christian thought and practice, and the need for a "creative fidelity" with regard to the innovative future of traditions.

Of the four memoranda, the first two deal most directly with the matters under discussion here. The first memorandum, "On Truth," is the only text of the four not to refer to previously published material.[80] Maritain would present it with minor modifications as a lecture later that month for the Little Brothers in Toulouse. It was published subsequently in this slightly revised form in *Approches sans entraves*.[81] It is a defense of the reality of absolute, divine truth, but also a clarification of some very non-absolute features of our human participation in it. Maritain claims "that *a doctrine essentially grounded in truth is possible* only if one recognizes at the same time the pluralism of philosophic doctrines" and that "truth is not the work of one person." Diversity is a necessary, but not yet the sufficient, condition of truth; and this very insufficiency is what makes genuine dialogue possible. With its necessary pluralism, truth demands as "an integral part of fraternal dialogue" an "element of suffering and of heartbreak" over the error of partners in conversation.[82] The search for truth has this motivation in genuine mercy, which allows us to consider the suffering of the other also as our own, yet truth motivated by mercy cannot be reduced to or replaced by technocratic and pragmatic indifference or populistic expediency.[83] Maritain recalls again the Newman-like distinction between principles and doctrines to underscore the necessary development of doctrinal truth, the inevitable and genuinely desirable rise of distinctively new, true doctrines in each and every epoch living from older, shared, and abidingly true principles.[84] Two of the five sections apply these features of a necessarily organic and interpersonal truth to study of "The Role of the Common Doctor" and "The Popes and the Common Doctor," stressing the need for the development of Thomism

79. Notes 17 and 44 of the encyclical refer to J. Maritain, "Les conditions spirituelles du progrès et de la paix," in an anthology entitled *Rencontre des cultures à l'UNESCO sous le signe du Concile Oecuménique Vatican II* (Paris: Mame, 1966), 66, and to *Integral Humanism*.

80. "Sur la vérité," in *Oeuvres complètes* XVI, 1085.

81. Now in "Approches sans entraves," *Oeuvres complètes* XIII, 514 sqq, translated in *Untrammeled Approaches*, 49–62.

82. Ibid., 53.

83. Ibid., 52.

84. Ibid., 53.

and therefore the need for an open conversation between Thomas and other thinkers, suggesting some features of how Maritain would see Thomism facing the global challenges of the times. "Authentic Thomism (I do not like this word *Thomism*) ... is not an end point. Nor is it the doctrine of any single man."[85] The necessity of development will be also a central point in the message addressed in the name of the Council to thinkers and academicians during the closing ceremonies of the Council on December 8, 1965, which Maritain not only received symbolically but might well have had a hand in composing. A sentence borrowed from St. Augustine formed the heart of the message and underlines the necessity of development: "Let us seek with the desire to find, and find with the desire to seek still more."[86]

Given the importance of the debates about the development of ecclesial and especially papal teaching on human rights, in general, and on the right to religious liberty, in particular, this first memorandum provides a kind of methodological introduction to the second memorandum: "Religious Liberty."[87] Maritain begins these six pages by recalling that he had stated the issues better and at greater length in the sixth chapter of *Man and the State*, and he included a copy of the work with his reply.[88] That is the chapter on "Church and State" containing Maritain's critique of the 100-year old application of the thesis/hypostasis distinction to the problem of religious liberty. In accord with the lectures of 1949, Maritain encouraged Paul VI in the memorandum to support the Declaration on Religious Liberty as a human right, and not as a calulated concession for situations in which the

85. Ibid., 55. For somewhat parallel thoughts on Thomistic learning, yet without direct reference to Maritain, see Richard Schenk, "*Communicatio imperfecta*: The Dominican Order and Thomism in the Service of the Church's Intellectual Life and Universal Mission," *Nova et Vetera*, English Edition, 12, no. 4 (2014): 1063–1090.

86. *Acta Apostolicae Sedis* (LVIII 1966): 10–11. See Augustine, *De Trinitate* IX 1: "Sic ergo quaeramus tamquam inventuri; et sic inveniamus, tamquam quaesituri." The text of the message, translated into English by Richard Lemp and John P. Hittinger in *Reassessing the Liberal State: Reading Maritain's* "Man and the State", translated and edited by Timothy Fuller and John P. Hittinger (American Maritain Association, 2010; distributed by The Catholic University of America Press), continues: "Do not forget that, if thinking is something great, it is first a duty. Woe to him who voluntarily closes his eyes to the light. Thinking is also a responsibility, so woe to those who darken the spirit by the thousand tricks which degrade it, make it proud, deceive and deform it" (245). For an impassioned critique of these closing messages and Maritain's influence on them, see Peter Hünermann, "The Final Weeks of the Council," in Alberigo and Komonchak, *History of Vatican II*, vol. 5 (Maryknoll/Leuven, Orbis/Peeters, 2006), 481–83.

87. "La liberté religieuse," first published by Philippe Chenaux, 111–14, now in *Oeuvres complètes* XVI: 1086–91.

88. Ibid., 1087 n. 1.

Church happens to be in the minority. In both writings, Maritain stresses the right to freedom from coercion to a religion and the right of believers to the formation and self-definition of a religion. Freedom of religion is "freedom from" and a "freedom for." Even without citing the United States Bill of Rights for freedom both from state establishment and from state prohibition of religion, Maritain seeks to identify the advantages to the Church of being liberated from State interference, even ostensibly in her favor, while identifying areas where cooperation between Church and State could and should be sought. The presence of the societal force of religious convictions and insights not mandated or suppressed by the state is necessary for the flourishing of the state itself. With his notion of the free cooperation of church and state in an overarching body-politic, Maritain anticipates a much cited remark by a later German Supreme Court Justice: "A free and secular state lives by presuppositions that it cannot itself guarantee."[89] Freedom of religion implies both the freedom from coercion and the freedom for self-definition, as the final drafts of the Declaration would assert.[90] The development of secular history and of the Christian conscience both confirm the Conciliar declaration that the legitimate limits that a state can impose upon a religion to protect the rights of its citizens should not be extended into a pretense for the state control or repression of religion. Maritain sees the end of the sacral state in itself not as a corruption, but as a development of Christian principles. Maritain reminds Paul VI, whose constant support for the Declaration would help to overcome attempts in 1965 to remove it from the Conciliar agenda, of his own arguments for the dual human right of liberty from and for religion. Charles Journet joined Maritain in encouraging the Council and the Pope to support the Declaration for these very reasons.[91]

89. "Der freiheitliche, säkularisierte Staat lebt von Voraussetzungen, die er selbst nicht garantieren kann." Ernst-Wolfgang Böckenförde, *Staat, Gesellschaft, Freiheit: Studien zur Staatstheorie und zum Verfassungsrecht* (Frankfurt am Main: Suhrkamp, 1976), 60.

90. Cf. Richard Schenk, "Voices of the Conscience," in *Villanova Law Review*, 54, no. 4 (2009): 593–607.

91. Cf. *Journet—Maritain: Correspondance*, vol. VI (1965–1973), edited by Georges Cottier, Fondation du Cardinal Journet, Michel Cagin, et al. (Saint-Augustin, 2008), especially 906–909; and Piero Viotto, *Paolo VI—Jacques Maritain. Un'amicizia intellettuale* (Rome: Edizioni Studium, 2014), 209–237.

IV. *Maritain engagé* and Thomism Facing Global Challenges

The significant historical work on the Council occasioned by its forthieth anniversary has continued over the last ten years with a growing—although not yet unanimous—sense that the tensions between moments of discontinuity and continuity at the Council were not merely *de facto* struggles, albeit with battlelines that changed from issue to issue (as is clear with the American episcopate, notably Cardinal Spellman, on the issue of religious liberty, or with efforts by German theologians, notably Karl Rahner, in the spring of 1965 to prevent the pastoral constitution, *Gaudium et spes*).[92] These real tensions at the Council which found expression in the agreed upon texts remain important ideal and normative coordinates for the synthetic work of theology and philosophy today. Along the lines of Maritain's own logic, the continued development of Conciliar doctrines is necessary, but a genuine development of the Council's doctrines and spirit cannot ignore the terms of the often elusive synthesis established as a task for the future by the texts themselves. The wounds of the conciliar spirit have yet to heal without scars, and there is no lack of those clamoring for a return to the mimetic rivalry of political strife in the Church between left and right.[93]

92. The attempts by the German theologians of the Council, represented above all by the talks of Karl Rahner and Oswald von Nell-Breuning on August 31, 1965 at a meeting of the German Episcopal Conference in Fulda, sought to reduce the status of Schema 13, the draft of *Gaudium et spes,* to a message of the Council or to entrust it to a post-Conciliar commission. The German episcopate seemed poised to accept the recommendation, but in the following weeks before the final session of the Council was persuaded by the French episcopate that this would harm the Council as a whole. Cf. Giovanni Turbanti, *Un Concilio per il Mondo Moderno. La redazione della costituzione pastorale "Gaudium et spes" del Vaticano II* (Il Mulino, 2000), 615–26; and Hans-Joachim Sander, "Theologischer Kommentar zur Pastoralkonstitution über die Kirche in der Welt von heute *Gaudium et spes*," in Hünermann and Hilberath, vol. IV, 581–886, esp. 650–63. Although the edition of Karl Rahner's thirteen-page critique of *Gaudium et spes*, "Anmerkungen zum Schema DE ECCLESIA IN MUNDO HUIUS TEMPORIS (in der Fassung vom 28.5.1965)," remains a *desideratum* of Conciliar research even after the recent volumes 21, 1–2 of Rahner's *Sämtliche Werke* (*Das Zweite Vatikanum* [Freiburg i. Br., Herder, 2013]), Sander and especially Turbanti have provided helpful excerpts. The author wishes to thank the Karl Rahner Archiv in Munich for its kind assistance in consulting two copies of Rahner's remarks. The systematic attention to this minority voice in the genesis of *Gaudium et spes* could help today's readers to recognize in the accepted text moments of the "theologia crucis" and hamartiology that Rahner feared might be overlooked by the initial reception.

93. For arguments for privileging a program of discontinuity over a hermeneutics of reform, see the accomplished commentator, Roman A. Siebenrock, "Siehe, ich mache alles neu!" "Hermeneutik der Wandlung." Von der rechten Weise, das Zweite Vatikanische Konzil zu realisieren,

There are those who wish first to view the Council under a hermeneutic of rupture and then to approve it or dismiss it (even if by "augmenting" it by a soon to be engineered and "uncompromising" Vatican III) on the basis of that simplistic abstraction. The rejection of the compromise that characterized the Council and its reception is a common feature of today's extreme ecclesiologies of the right and the left. In fact, the very alternative between distincontinuity and continuity is, as Maritain suggests, too facile, since these features are not only compatible but necessary for one another. If it had been read from a "hermeneutic of reform," like that to which Benedict XVI called the Church in the first year of his pontificate, a hermeneutic of retrieval for understanding what the Council actually agreed upon in the difficult negotiations for its final texts, with all the *nova et vetera* of a scribe turned disciple, the unity-in-tension of a *renovatio accommodata,* then Maritain's *Peasant of the Garrone* might not have been received simplistically as a renunciation of the Council, but as a celebration of that "true new fire," to which the greater number of chapters had been dedicated and which Maritain fanned against those who would extinguish at least half of it, allowing to shine only the statements of discontinuity and stylish accommodation (the sheep of Panurge) or only the statements of evident continuity (the Manichean ruminators of the covenant).[94] Maritain's description of the true new fire of the Council continues a theme that had been begun by John XXIII in his initial conception of the Council, briefly but with an already nuanced programmatic.[95] The false conclusion drawn at times today

in *Zweites Vatikanisches Konzil. Programmatik—Rezeption—Vision,* edited by Christoph Böttigheimer (Freiburg i. Br. i.a.: Herder, 2014), 101–39.

94. Cf. Schenk, "Jacques Maritain and Vatican II."

95. Recalling his own prayer of 1959, John repeated his hopes for the Council in its official announcement on Christmas Day, 1961, "Humani salutis," nr. 23: "Renova aetate hac nostra per novam veluti Pentecosten mirabilia tua, atque Ecclesiae Sanctae concede, ut cum Maria, Matre Iesu, unanimiter et instanter in oratione perseverans, itemque a Beato Petro ducta, divini Salvatoris regnum amplificet, regnum veritatis et iustitiae, regnum amoris et pacis. Amen." (http://w2.vatican.va/content/john-xxiii/la/apost_constitutions/1961/documents/hf_j-xxiii_apc 19611225_humanae salutis.html), and in his allocution at the conclusion of the Council's first session on December 8 of the following year: "Tunc procul dubio exoptata illucescet nova Pentecoste, quae Ecclesiam spiritualibus viribus uberius ditabit eiusque maternum afflatum salutaremque vim per omnes humanae navitatis provincias latius propagabit. Tunc Regnum Christi in terris novo amplificabitur incremento. Tunc denique altius ac suavius in orbe laetus resonabit humanae Redemptionis nuntius, quo confirmantur suprema Omnipotentis Dei iura, fraternae caritatis vincula inter homines, pax, quae his in terris promissa est hominibus bonae voluntatis" (http://w2.vatican.va/content/john-xxiii/la/speeches/1962/documents/hf j-xxiii_spe_19621208_closing i period .hrml)

from the true premise that the Council was looking for a new Pentecost needs to resist Marcionistic interpretations of Pentecost by recalling that the gift of the Spirit was given even on the Church's first feast of its own Pentecost in continuity and discontinuity with the First Covenant feast of the decalogue. To expect the kind of "new" Pentecost that would dismiss the previously known structures of the Church implies rather a kind of Joachite misconception even about the quality of the abiding "novum" of that first Christian transformation of Pentecost.

Maritain's sense that the practical consensus on human rights in the late 1940s was fragile has proven all too true, both within consumerist societies and in the conflict of civilizations. Joining the older rivalries of national and international power blocs, there is a quickly spreading "contagion of rivalries" (Girard) on the part of subnational organizations, including religiously colored ones, with the propensity towards, and the technological means of, massive violence. That would make a discourse on the theoretical bases of human rights even more difficult than in the years following the Second World War. The three conditions for cooperation in a still divided political and economic world need to be defended and healed: the liberation from Machiavellian self-interest in the process of defining rights, the memory of the sufferings of others, and the sapiential task of humanizing science and technology. Consumerist nations can hardly demand these conditions from less advantaged regions without holding themselves to the same standards at home and abroad, a kind of imperative: to move beyond merely positive law to the recognition of inalienable rights, to grow more sensitive to the unequal distribution of advantage, and to become more suspicious of the darker sides of the manipulation of natural and human ecologies. There is a need for consumerist societies to look again closely at the original list of declared rights and to ask, self-critically, if they themselves are honoring the rights they see violated elsewhere, including the rights of their minorities to religious identity. Religiously enhanced rationalities, including what many proponents of Maritain's thought and in keeping with it have chosen to call "Christian philosophy," need to show for their part their own unique potential and their uncommon resources for securing and furthering the common good and for joining genuine self-interest to something like altruism in the service of a flourishing whole.

To read Thomas Aquinas with a keener eye on his principles (such as the freedom necessary for the beginnings of Christian faith) than on his many explicated doctrines (such as the possible coercion of those who have lost that faith) is to follow Maritain's Thomistic methodology, and one should read Maritain himself in the same Maritainian way—and with the same aims. Maritain returned to this theme of the first memorandum: his goal in seeking an alternative to functionalist, totalitarian, or forgetful, a-historical domination was to secure a place of consensus for the dignity of persons by searching out strategies for cooperation in a still divided Church, academy, society and among un-united nations. He was convinced that an uncoerced sense of spiritual realities and of the personal God who calls free persons to answer was needed in order to continue to perceive and protect human dignity.

A little more than one year after Jacques and Raïssa Maritain, during a summer afternoon walk in Paris' Jardin de Plantes in the year 1901, had determined to end their lives in a year's time if they could discover no meaning in them, another young twenty-something, the poet Rainer Maria Rilke, wrote (1902 or 1903) from those same gardens what would become one of the German language's classic poems, "The Panther: In the *Jardin des Plantes*, Paris," about a panther pacing around and around in a cage of the zoological section of the gardens. The once magnificent wild cat has lost its ability to see outside the cage. It is clear to the poet that this is the result of violence, not nature. This incapacity for the transcendence needed to have a world means that, in such captivity, even its occasional glimpses of fleeting events mean nothing.

His sight has so tired from the bars he's passed
That it retains nothing more.
It seems as if there were a thousand bars
and behind the thousand bars no world.

The quiet gait of steps, both soft and strong,
trace the smallest circle as he turns
like a dance of power around a center
in which a great will stands bound and drugged.

At times the veil frees the eyes
for a moment. Some image enters them,
passes through the tense silence of the limbs
to his heart, where it ceases to be.[96]

96. Translated from Rainer Maria Rilke, *Die Gedichte* (1986; repr. Frankfurt: Insel, 2004), 451.

In teaching us to look beyond the cage of secular and even ecclesiastical functionalism, Maritain taught us to engage the world by sharing both in its *gaudium et spes* and in its *luctus et angor*. He taught us to retrieve principles in order to gain a new vision of humanity that would not cease to exist when it reached the heart. A true godson of Leon Bloy, he taught us to listen especially to the sufferings of others in order to engage the truth of our common nature.

FLORIAN MICHEL

Jacques Maritain Engagé in Social Questions

The Early Years between Revolution and Democratic Socialism[1]

TO BERNARD DOERING AND CLIO

I. Introduction

WHAT WERE MARITAIN'S politcal positions before his entrance into the Catholic Church (1906) and before his first connection with the Order of Saint Dominic? Those who know that the political conscience of Maritain did not originate at the time of "Action Française," already know that the young Maritain was at one and the same time a socialist, an anarchist, a revolutionary, a Dreyfusard, a feminist, a republican at times, a libertarian sometimes, a Péguyist in his own way, and a Proudhonian on occasion. Indecisions, provocations, and paradoxes are all characteristics of an adolescent intelligence. When he was eighteen, Maritain declared forcefully to Charles Péguy, who had just published an article very critical of Jean Jaurès: "I have already told you that I loved Jaurès."[2]

1. I would like to warmly thank Bernard Doering, who translated the text; and Michael D. Torre, who gave precious suggestions.

2. Letter of Maritain to Péguy, 1901, *Amitiés Charles Péguy*, no. 177 (May 1972): 13. On the relations between Péguy and Jaurès, see the article by Geraldi Leroy, "Péguy-Jaurès: bref essai de synthèse," *Cahiers Jaurès* no. 192 (April–June 2009): 51–65. Jean Jaurès was one of the great leaders of French social-democracy. He was assassinated in the summer of 1914.

What is the meaning of Maritain's attachment to this socialist leader? Can ramifications of this attachment be discerned throughout his writings?

In 1944, while she was in the United States, Raïssa Maritain wrote that as a young man Jacques was a "democrat," and in confirmation of this recalled the attitude of the Dominican Father Clérissac, who became their spiritual guide in 1908. He "was pitiless in his mockery of the democratic tendencies and the socialist ideas that remained dear to Jacques' heart, seeing in them only the remains of the old man that had to be stripped away."[3] In this way Raïssa intended to underline, excessively without a doubt, the continuity between the Jaurésian Maritain and the Maritain of *Christianity and Democracy* (1942). In 1951, Henri Massis used this very same citation from Father Clérissac to draw an opposite conclusion and to better defend the thesis of Charles Maurras concerning the "Maritainian ruptures" in the days of Action Française: "the royalist Maritain" turned coat to put himself in the pay of the "Christian-democrats."[4]

In 1954, Maritain himself affirmed his attachment to Jean Jaurès during his adolescence: "When I was 13 or 14 years old I became a socialist. Articles by Jaurès and Gerault-Richard set me on fire."[5] One year before he died, Maritain again wrote: "I was an ardent socialist from the first years of my adolescence, and I had for Jaurès not only enthusiastic admiration, but also those sentiments of gratitude and affection that a grand and generous figure arouses among many of his unknown disciples."[6] In her memoirs, Raïssa herself tells how she studied philosophy under the Marxist theorist Charles Rappoport, "a collaborator of Jaurès."[7] Are the socialist roots of the Maritain couple a reconstruction of memory? Can a true measure be taken of the traces of this early Maritain engagement, in face of the fact that the figure of Jean Jaurès is scarcely present at all in the political writings of his

3. Raïssa Maritain, *Les Grandes Amitiés*, 1944, *Oeuvres complètes* [OC], vol. XIV, 957.

4. Henri Massis, *Maurras et notre temps* (Paris: La Palatine, 1951), 155. On these questions, see for example Charles Maurras, *Le bienheureux Pie X, sauveur de la France* (Paris: Plon, 1953), 217: "Born a Huguenot, grandson of the disarmament advocate and the tearful complainer Jules Favre, Maritain passed through three stages," which Maurras then tries to characterize.

5. Jacques Maritain, *Carnet de Notes*, 1964, *OC.*, vol. XII, 135.

6. Jacques Maritain, preface to the Peguy-Maritain correspondence, *OC.*, vol. XII, 1255.

7. Raïssa Maritain, *OC.*, vol. XIV, 657. Raïssa described him in this way: "He was a very good man, completely unselfish. He was perfectly convinced of the truth of Marxism and believed in the coming of an era of liberty and universal happiness." Charles Rappoport was a convinced socialist, at first Jaurésian, then Guesdist, then founder of the PCF before denouncing the crimes of Stalin at the beginning of the 1930s. See *Une vie révolutionnaire, 1883–1940* (Paris: Éditions de la Maison des Sciences de l'Homme, 1991).

maturity—whether in *Integral Humanism* in 1936, or in *Man and the State* in 1951?

II. False Tracks

Contemporary historical writings concerning the years of Maritain's youth, when they are not simply overlooked, are quite uneven. The milieu of his origin is often evoked, marked by an attachment to the Republic, and by both liberal and bourgeois values, whose titular figure was Jules Favre, Jacques' grandfather, a member of the 1870 government of national defense, whose secretary was Paul Maritain, Jacques' father.[8] Also very important were Jacques' close friends, Charles Péguy and Ernest Psichari, the grandson of Renan. This approach by way of his milieu is useful to portray Maritain's early years, but, unless one believes in sociological determinism, in no way furnishes us a clear definition of his political position. This would mistakenly presume an identity of views between an adolescent and his family.

Several authors maintain that Maritain's political position had its origin within the bounds of Action Française. The "first serious Maritain" must have been a Maurassian. This antimodernist Maritain is supposed to have been a "member" of Action Française and to have been deeply committed to the theses of this nationalist movement. For this "first Maritain," the pontifical condemnation in 1926 is supposed to have been less a "liberation" than a "complete break." The partisans of this thesis found themselves on diverse political horizons. The denizens of French Christian democracy who submitted willingly to the patronage of Maurice Blondel, and who had always been opposed to Maurras, did not look favorably on what appeared to them as a simple act of obedience on the part of Maritain to the pontifical condemnation. On the other hand, those who followed Action Française in its "*non possumus*," multiplied their criticisms of the one who from then on was portrayed as the intellectual spokesman for the papacy and as a traitor.

Maritain, the erstwhile "fellow-traveler of Action Française," certainly must not be overlooked. On this question there is the text of a letter to Massis in 1914, which shows his hostility to the democratic model, or rather what he then called "démocratisme," never defined *stricto sensu*, and referring rather vaguely to a form of corruption of democracy by the Free-

8. See especially Jules Favre, *Mélanges politiques, judiciaires et littéraires*, edited by Arthur Rousseau (Paris: 1882).

mason anticlericalism characteristic, according to him, of this period of the Third Republic[9]:

> A catalogue of the causes of this evil would be very valuable. From my point of view, it is not only naturalism, democratism, scientism, etc., but essentially the mediocrity of Catholics ... who want to be in conformity with the century and who have been punished by a weakening of intelligence itself. The ... more I think of it, the more I am persuaded that we must all have a political doctrine; this doctrine can be nothing other than anti-revolutionary, anti-republican, anti-constitutional, and therefore monarchical.[10]

It must be added however that this Maritain, undeniably anti-democratic on the eve of the First World War, remained an "irregular," never fully aligned with the positions of Maurras. The archives furnish evidence of a disagreement on the part of Maritain, in the very act of his adherence to the movement, concerning points that are in no way minor with regard to Maurras' doctrine. Maritain never swore the monarchist and anti-Semitic oath of Action Française; the Jewishness of Raïssa was naturally incompatible with the anti-Semitism of Maurras. Maritain, however, would later regret his "unpardonable irresponsibility" caused by a "docility without experience."[11] This point should be commented on at length in order not to simplify in any way so complex a dossier.[12] However, this "docility," admitted and recognized, is not synonymous with blindness. In a number of extracts from his writings and correspondence, there is evidence that Maritain put a pointed distance between his own and certain details of Maurras' politics. In his short book of 1926 entitled *Une Opinion sur Charles Maurras*, Maritain accepts Maurras' criticism of democracy as understood by Rousseau, but he qualifies as inadmissible Maurras' criticism of "political democracy as understood by Aristotle and Saint Thomas, or for example the ancient Swiss democracy."[13] In a letter to Massis, dated October 1, 1925, Maritain wrote again: "I read in the *Revue catholique des idées et des faits* a message of Maurras to latinity which

9. On this point, see also Raïssa Maritain, *We Have Been Friends Together*: "Official democracy had allied its cause to that of all the antireligious myths"; "the parliamentary procedures of the Third Republic seemed to support the criticisms of Action Française."

10. Letter of Maritain to Massis, April 3, 1914, Maritain Archives at "Bibliothèque Nationale et Universitaire de Strasbourg" [BNUS].

11. Remarks of Jacques Maritain quoted by Raïssa Maritain, *OC*, vol. XIV, 975.

12. Guillaume Bourgeade, "Jacques Maritain et la *Revue universelle*," *Cahiers Jacques Maritain* [*CJM*], no. 46 (June 2003) : 2–30.

13. Jacques Maritain, *Une Opinion sur Charles Maurras*, 1926, *OC*, vol. III, 753–754.

seems hardly satisfactory to me. Latinity, I have no idea what this is, any more than what organity is, or germanity, and other racist fictions." In a letter to Dom Delatte, Abbot of Solesmes, at Easter 1920, Maritain presented the new *Revue universelle* "as an extension of Action Française—abstraction having been made of immediate political realizations and of Orléanism." The new review would be a non-political enlargement of Action Française.

Without a doubt, this wishful thinking was evidence of a kind of utopianism. Maritain, to borrow an expression of Guillaume Bourgeade, was the victim of a "trafficking in dupes," because he "believed he was Christianizing the movement, whereas in reality he was winning Catholics over to Maurras."[14] The thesis of Maritain as the ideologue of Action Française certainly comes across better if Maritain's political interests as a young man are discredited. This rigorous Thomist, developing arguments *closely related* to those of Action Française, *should* be taken into account more seriously to better understand his later evolution as a philosopher.

It is true that the young Maritain is at times difficult to grasp. Maritain the adolescent took aim at the bourgeois society of his time, but with an ironic distance that did not keep him from entering into the system;[15] he passed the *concours général*, the baccalaureate, and the *agrégation* in philosophy. From time to time he adopted the platitudes of the "revolutionary dance-halls,"[16] as is revealed in a letter to Ernest Psichari of November 29, 1900, in which Maritain laments the fact that his aunt has committed "the great sin, the irreparable sacrilege" of becoming a property owner. This young "libertarian" Maritain—he used this expression in several letters to Psichari—became engaged in 1902 at 20 years of age, then got married at 22, and in this way rejected one of the essential demands of "free love," made by the anarchists of the generation before his own, the generation of Ravachol and Émile Henry—marriage being for them a typical "bourgeois" institution. Although an admirer of the anarchists, Maritain criticized them in private.[17] Maritain, "a traitor to his class," as he called himself, would ap-

14. Bourgeade, "Jacques Maritain et la *Revue universelle*," 29.

15. Letter of Jacques Maritain to Émile Clermont, July 31, 1900, BNUS: "You pay me great compliments about the *Concours général*. This is really nothing worth bothering about. This is essentially a bourgeois institution, where bourgeois competition appears with even more ugliness, which is surely the basest form of the struggle for life."

16. Jacques Maritain, *Carnet de Notes*, *OC*, vol. XII, 136.

17. Letter of Maritain to Émile Clermont, July 31, 1900, BNUS: "In general, though I admire them, I do not approve of the anarchists, and their method seems to me defective."

pear to be a young bourgeois, who would not assume responsibility for the contradictions between his social affiliations and his political aspirations.[18] Viewed from a distance, there is a very real temptation not to take seriously the political affirmations of Maritain as a young man. From a purely historical point of view, however, this would be a mistake, since it cuts the story off from its beginning and does not recognize what, in Maritain's own words, he *escaped* from in the first place.

III. An Historiographic Turning Point

Another historiographic vein, represented by several quite recent publications,[19] develops *a contrario* a position that follows the conclusions of an article by Lucien Mercier published in the *Cahiers Jacques Maritain* in 1986.[20] Following this article, which is a veritable watershed, these authors write that the early Maritain is a Dreyfusard, a republican, a socialist—which is not new—and that this commitment is very significant, which is new. Maritain himself suggested that the keys to the positions of his maturity be sought in his young years: "the vow to serve 'the proletariat and humanity,' all the while making use of very unexpected forms for its realization, and by subordinating all to the service of God above all else, has never been revoked."[21] However, to assume and admit the political continuity of Maritain is nevertheless problematic.

Lucien Mercier, uninvolved in the historiographic debates of French Catholicism, is a specialist in popular universities, where for a time Maritain was a militant activist. They were, writes this historian, "on the front line of the republican combat . . . if not the goad of the social revolution."[22] Mercier also published an important contribution on the networks of Lycées students around Jean Jaurès. He once again described the socialist commitment of Maritain, who met Jaurès on several occasions in the salon of the Psichari family.[23]

18. Maritain, *O.C.*, vol. XII, 136.

19. Philippe Chenaux, "Humanisme intégral" (*1936*) *de Jacques Maritain* (Paris: Cerf, 2006); Nora Possenti, *Les trois Maritain* (Paris: Parole et Silence, 2006); Sylvain Guéna, "Maritain et la Révolution," *CJM* no 61 (December 2010): 34–64.

20. Lucien Mercier, "Jacques Maritain avant Jacques Maritain: un engagement dans le siècle," *CJM*, no. 13 (June 1986): 7–26.

21. Jacques Maritain, *OC*, vol. XII, 136.

22. Lucien Mercier, *Les Universités populaires: 1899–1914. Éducation populaire et mouvement ouvrier au début du siècle* (Paris : Les Éditions ouvrières, 1986).

23. Lucien Mercier, "Les réseaux lycéens," in *Jaurès et les Intellectuels*, edited by Madeleine Rébérioux and Gilles Candar (Paris: Éditions de l'Atelier, 1994), 169–79.

The contribution of the writings of Mercier is considerable. The author analyses the essential elements of Maritain's correspondence with Ernest Psichari (1883–1914), whom he met at the Lycée Henri IV in 1898. On the basis of these documents, the author shows that for a certain time Maritain frequented the socialist school of Lucien Herr, on the slopes of la Montagne Sainte-Geneviève. The biography of Psichari makes the tableau more complex by mentioning the different popular universities that Maritain and Psichari were led to frequent: first, the one on rue Fourneaux, which the two friends left because it was too "bourgeois," then the one on rue Mouffetard and the one in the Faubourg Saint-Antoine, which was more working-class.[24] At that time Maritain was militating for Jean Jaurès against Jules Guesde. We learn also that in 1900 Maritain was a member of the "Democratic Union for Social Education," whose name is scarcely equivocal.[25] It is easy to find the status of this union in the socialist press of that time.[26] The Democratic Union was created by the students and professors of the Sorbonne in 1896. The manifesto of the Union clearly indicates the objectives it pursued:

> The Democratic Union was founded to work toward the education of French democracy. France now has the fundamental institutions of a democratic regime, universal suffrage and universal primary education: it does not yet have the political and social practices of a democracy.... The masses of the nation, kept apart from public life, have not acquired the habits of discussion and association necessary for a free people. We are behind our neighbors the Swiss.

Considerable prejudice is necessary to end up doubting the evidence: in 1900, "French socialism," as it was called to distinguish it from the "German socialism" of Marx, was democratic in its heart. In addition, Maritain's socialism has a shade of avant-garde feminism, as revealed in these lines of Psichari: "It is impossible to be a socialist with that ignoble concept of woman, for socialism, from a rational point of view, is justified by this fact, that it is the struggle for a conscious and equal humanity, in which there will be neither men-machines, nor men enslaved, nor women-objects, but persons, nothing but persons."[27] On this point, there is also the letter to Psichari of October 4, 1900: "Tell Chantavoine [their professor of French literature],

24. Frédérique Neau-Dufour, *Ernest Psichari. L'ordre et l'errance* (Paris : Le Cerf, 2001), 94–95.

25. Mercier, Les Universités populaires: 1899–1914, 17.

26. Albert Livet, "Le mouvement socialiste au Quartier latin," *La Revue socialiste* (October 1897) : 560–93. The manifesto and the status of the "Union démocratique" are published on 578–80.

27. Mercier, Les Universités populaires: 1899–1914, 23.

if you are lucky enough to meet him, that I am abandoning the Lycées, the Ecole Normale and the professorship. Tell him that I want to be a militant, libertarian socialist and write a thesis on Marx in Latin and on feminism in French."

IV. Complementary Elements of This Analysis

Lucien Mercier based his analysis on the correspondence of Maritain with Psichari. Does other archival evidence confirm his conclusions? Few substantial documents permit us to reconstitute with precision the political positions of the young Maritain, which are—it must be admitted—rarely developed and often paradoxical. As a consequence of the Dreyfus Affair, which he followed passionately, the question of politics is very present in Maritain's adolescent years, not only because of his familial environment and, more broadly, his sociological environment, but also in his first writings and in his correspondence.

The first page, now made public, of his philosophy notebook when he was still a student at the Lycée Henri IV (1899), establishes a few horizons of sensitivity—Dreyfusism, anticlericalism, Proudhonism, revolutionary socialism, feminism.[28] Here is a brief anthology: "Long live the social"; "Death to the Bourgeois"; "Proletarians of every land, unite"; "Christianism is the greatest calamity that has fallen upon the world"; "Hang the last of the kings with the bowels of the last of the priests"; "Neither God, nor Master"; "Equal pay for equal work"; "Blessed are those who hunger and thirst for justice"; "the 19th century has proclaimed the rights of man; the 20th century should proclaim those of the woman and the child," etc. However, it is a delicate matter to deduce from all this any formal conclusions about the young Maritain, whose political sources, from Diderot to Marx, passing through Proudhon and Blanqui, are so very eclectic. What is the value, *stricto sensu,* of all these disjointed slogans scribbled on the cover of a student's notebook?

Maritain's first public positions were concerned with Russia. First there is the manifesto in favor of Russian students, published in the *Cahiers de la Quinzaine,* in April 1901. Under the leadership of Louis Lapique of the faculty of Science at the University of Paris, a committee of students set out to circulate a tract "without distinction of political opinion" to gather

28. See Frédérique Ripoll, *Les grandes amitiés de Jacques et Raïssa Maritain,* Éditions du Carmel (1995), 15; 2e éd., (2009), 19.

signatures in defense of the Russian students "in the name of university liberties"; hundreds of students in Kiev, following on the "school disorders," had been condemned to military service. Maritain and Péguy were among the first signatories and were active members on the committee. At the *Cahiers*, Péguy sheltered the administrative support committee; Maritain collected signatures, among which was that of his future spouse, Raïssa.[29] From 1903 to 1905, Maritain acted as secretary of *La Tribune russe*,[30] a semi-monthly bulletin of the revolutionary socialist movement in Russia, toward which a large part of the French republican forces converged.[31] Here Maritain published an article against the overly prudent attitude of Tolstoi during the 1905 revolution.[32]

Among the publications of Maritain's young years, mention must be made of his six contributions to the review *Jean-Pierre*, the review destined for the children of the working class, under the direction of Jeanne Maritain, Jacques' older sister.[33] The life span of this review, presented as an extension of the *Cahiers de la Quinzaine*, was brief (1901–1904). The articles that Maritain published there between 1902 and 1904 and which have been reprinted in the *Oeuvres completes*,[34] are more interesting for their sociability than for what their content reveals. Maritain explains in one of them that little boys must not play with lead soldiers; in another he describes a scientific expedition to the North Pole; in the final issue, in May 1904, Maritain presented the labor union stakes in the "workingman's glassware factory of Albi," a Jaurésian center *par excellence.*

Besides his letters to Psichari, a few other items of his correspondence emerge to give an idea of the young Maritain between 17 and 22 years of age. Shortly after having received the second place prize in the *Concours général* for philosophy in 1900, Maritain wrote to one of his fellow students:

29. "Pour les étudiants russes. Appel aux étudiants français," *Cahiers de la Quinzaine*, tenth cahier of the second series (1901) : 5–25.

30. On this point, see the heading of the letter to Angèle Baton, postmark of September 21, 1903 (BNUS): "La Tribune Russe. Bulletin bimensuel. 50 rue Lhomond, Paris. Secrétaire. J. Maritain." This review was published between 1904–1905 and 1909–1910.

31. On this question, and more generally for a detailed reevaluation of the revolution of 1905, see the contribution of Wladimir Berelowitch, "La révolution de 1905 dans l'opinion républicaine française," *Cahiers du monde russe* 48 (2007): 379–92.

32. Jacques Maritain, "Tolstoï et le Matin," *La Tribune russe*, March 1905, *OC*, vol. XVI, 574–681.

33. Lucien Mercier, "Enfance et socialisme. *Jean-Pierre* et *Les Petits Bonhommes*, deux journaux des années 1900," *Le Mouvement social* (October–December 1984): 29–59.

34. Jacques Maritain, *OC*, vol. XVI, 611–58.

My only consolation is to read some Vigny and some Baudelaire ... and to be active in socialism and feminism, that is, in humanism. I am ashamed to tell you this now that everybody and his brother is a little apostle of a more or less scientific or Christianizing socialism. I am thinking seriously of becoming a Bonapartist so as not to be confused with the protecting members and founders of working class soup kitchens and the honorable zealots of the people's universities. By the way, Jeanne [Maritain] has told me that you hold it against me for hanging around a few U.P.s [Universités Populaires]. But I'm a Dreyfusard, damn it, and I want to criticize only what I know. But, can't you see, friend, that nothing, not even pride, will lead me to take off my revolutionary cap.[35]

Published in Maritain's *Carnet de Notes,* a letter of 1898 to Angèle Baton, the cook in the Favre family, already took on the form of a defense of the people and of the Revolution: "I will be a socialist and live for the Revolution.... All that I will be able to think or to know, I will consecrate to the proletariat and to humanity: I will use all of it to prepare the revolution, to work, however little it might be, toward the happiness and the education of humanity."[36] Two other letters of 1899 were published in the *Cahiers Jacques Maritain* in 1994. In the first of these letters, August 28, 1899, Maritain recounts the meeting between Psichari and Jaurès: at Rennes, on the occasion of the Dreyfus trial, the two men exchanged verses of Latin poetry. There is a sense of the adolescent's measureless admiration for the great politician: "As for Jaurès, what a marvelous brain, in the midst of all his occupations and preoccupations, to still maintain all his literary knowledge and all his erudition.... You would do me a great favor by copying for me a sentence from the preface of the sublime Jaurès, the one where we find: 'Enter, here is the city of men.'" From the second of these letters, September 6, 1899, the same admiration for this socialist leader is evident: "What a luminous and admirable spirit is this Jaurès! How well he *understands* things, how he takes everything into account, and how, without neglecting any of the elements of life, he arrives at the truth by his sincerity." Here Maritain seems in love with Jaurès' prose, underlining the suppleness of his sentences: "Jaurès is a poet, and an inspired one, a leader of men. But enough of these elucubrations and divagations and verbocinations on the greatest man of our century." The conclusion of this letter is precious, since it enables us to tie together at one time Maritain's anti-bourgeois sen-

35. Jacques Maritain to Émile Clermont, July 31, 1900, BNUS.
36. Jacques Maritain, *Carnet de Notes,* 1965, *OC,* vol. XII, 136–37.

timents, his anticlericalism, his socialism, and at the same time a kind of understanding, almost nostalgic, of religion:

> O the vile bourgeoisie, sanctimonious, squared away with God, with its hypocritical formulas, having lost even the grandeur of religious faith and Christian enthusiasm. It's possible for them to be religious without believing in God. I say, I affirm, I proclaim that there is no religion more profound, more sincere, more feeling, and greater than atheism. Let us distinguish between belief in a religion and religious understanding of the universe, what I mean is respect before the mystery of things and of life, the mystical experience of listening to the song of beings and of nature, and that faith which alone inspires sacrifice and devotion.[37]

The correspondence with Angèle and François Baton at the Maritain Archives has not been published in its entirety. In any case, the three documents already made public permit us not only to conclude a love for the proletariat and the revolution, but also to understand the precise significance of this attachment to Jaurès. Throughout this correspondence, one is led to realize how sensitive Maritain's political conscience actually was. In 1901, he called off engagements already made in order to be able to attend a colloquy in which Jaurès was to appear (letter of May13, 1901). In a following letter he comments on the socialist congress at Lyon, the difficulties of the French socialist union, the varied movements and tendencies, the question of party unity.[38] Sometimes Maritain dreams of an "interior revolution," "the only true one."[39] In another undated letter—probably in the summer of 1899 since Maritain writes in it about "the criminal and venomous manifesto of the French Worker Party," which, following Mille-

37. Letters of Jacques Maritain to Angèle and François Baton, "Jacques Maritain à 17 ans," *CJM*, no. 28 (1994) : 44–45.

38. Letter of Jacques Maritain to Angèle Baton, May 29, 1901, BNUS: "And the congress at Lyon? And our sacred unity? I am delighted with everything that happened there.... Guesde and Millerand disgust me, one as much as the other. Millerand is too guesdist, and Guesde is too millerandist. The true revolutionary situation is well beyond these parliamentary slogans, in the workers' revolutionary movement, which alone will bring about, by its autonomous Federations, the unity of the proletariat, collectivist as well as libertarian." The letter concludes with these words: "Goodbye, my dear Yeule [his name for Angèle], I embrace you with all my heart, thanking you once again. For Baton [Angèle's husband], all my expressions of *revolutionary and anti-governmental* friendship."

39. Letter of Maritain to Angèle Baton, undated [doubtless in August 1903], BNUS: "How desirable it would be for the Revolution, about which all the newspapers are constantly talking, to cross over a bit into their lives and into their sincerity. The interior revolution is the only true one, and alone will be able to give some meaning to economic development. But Marxism itself has already been abandoned, and we are rotting under the socialism of the State."

rand's entrance into the government, set about to weaken the unity of the socialist movement—Maritain goes on to write: "The attitude of Jaurès was the only one to take. I have always admired Jaurès, and I love him more and more. I even have a mind to write him a letter to tell him all about my friendship for him. You should do so as well. I detest Guesde and Vaillant. And Zévaès too." On July 26, 1900, Maritain wrote again to Baton: "I have plunged into reading newspapers and also *Histoire socialiste,* which I have been lucky enough to find. Jaurès is decidedly the greatest of our contemporaries. But how sad are these quarrels that divide French socialism." In a note to François Baton on April 15, 1904, after the setbacks of *La Petite République,* Maritain announced the imminent appearance of Jaurès' *L'Humanité* and commented: "This will be the moment to organize our propaganda."

The most developed document is a letter of March 13, 1901, to Péguy,[40] whose political characterization was hardly monochromatic. He had just published a critique of Jaurès in an article entitled "Casse-Cou" (daredevil).[41] Péguy, half-way between socialism and anarchism, was at times closer to social democracy than is generally admitted. The *Cahiers de la Quinzaine* were financed by Alexandre Millerand,[42] a socialist and a minister in the government of Waldeck-Rousseau, to whom the *Cahiers de la Quinzaine* would render strongly supportive homage, since—and it is worth insisting on this point—Maritain published in the *Cahiers,* in 1904, the "political testament" of Waldeck-Rousseau, consisting of a group of articles and unedited notes on his work in the Parliament.[43]

This is how Raïssa Maritain described the opposition between Péguy and Jaurès: "Péguy had a falling out with Lucien Herr, and a little later with Jaurès, whom he reproached for having forgotten the struggle for pure Justice that had brought them together during the Dreyfus Affair, and losing

40. See Feuillets mensuels de l'Amitiés Péguy, no. 176.

41. C. Péguy, "Casse Cou," *Cahiers de la Quinzaine,* 7th cahier, 2nd series, 1901.

42. See the Péguy-Millerand correspondance, *Feuillets mensuels de l'Amitiés Péguy,* nos. 178 and 179.

43. See the *Cahiers de la Quinzaine,* 5th cahier of the 6th series, November 22, 1904. Charles Péguy, in the preface (x–xi), rendered homage to Jacques Maritain for his work as editor of the manuscripts: "Our collaborator M. Jacques Maritain has proof-read all the manuscripts and recopied them for the printers much better than I could have done myself; we submitted a few particularly difficult texts to M. René Waldeck-Rousseau; M. René Waldeck-Rousseau was pleased to tell me that M. Maritain's copy was like a photograph of the text."

his way in the pettiness of political opportunism."[44] Against Péguy, Maritain took up the defense of Jaurès:

My dear Péguy,

I just read the 7th cahier of the 2nd series; since you are telling Jaurès what he ought to do, permit me to offer a few observations, which are rather requests for supplementary explications rather than definitive impressions. Let me tell you right away that you have hurt me by criticizing Jaurès with a suspicious bitterness that just does not fit in this case. I certainly approve of your making criticisms that you consider just, and by them showing that in socialism there is no place for slogans, for high priests, or for faithful on their knees, and that one can be truly faithful while being neither Guesdist, nor Jaurèsian, nor in between the two, but only beyond them. But we love Jaurès; and certain forms seem too hard, too cutting, applied to him.... You know very well that "at the present it will not be necessary to be materialist and atheist." It will not be necessary that I, that Baudouin, that Deloire, that Péguy, that we all be materialist and atheist with citizen Vaillant." I do not think that Jaurès has ever had the intention of forcing your thought; you are so afraid that your freedom may be trampled upon, that you attribute to others malevolent designs, tyrannical calculations, and that finally you keep them from expressing their own particular thought. Jaurès certainly has the right to call himself a materialist and an atheist along with Vaillant, and to tie his political conceptions to metaphysical conceptions. Besides, if Jaurès is a monist, he is not a materialist. Has he not said in one of his most beautiful speeches: "As far as I am concerned, I have no prejudice of offense or disdain toward the great religious aspirations.... I believe, gentlemen, that a few mechanistic explications do not exhaust the meaning of the universe and that the network of algebraic formulas and abstract theorems which we cast over the world lets reality pass through, just as the meshes of a net let the river pass through" (*Action socialiste*, 277–278)? ...

Revolutionary and libertarian socialism does not dispense one from the bourgeois politeness nor from the respect that is properly owed to a man of the intellectual and moral value, of the devotedness and goodness of Jaurès. I know very well, because I have been reading the *Cahiers* from the very beginning, that you too love Jaurès, and that the bitterness of your reproaches comes perhaps from that fact....

For me, socialism is not a body of doctrine set apart. It is much more a state of mind, which like a general tint, colors all the thoughts and all the sentiments of the socialist, of anyone who "lives in the state of socialist grace," and gives them their specific character, their particular quality....

Socialism is not a simple economic doctrine. It is a general philosophy of life, it

44. Raïssa Maritain, *Les grandes amitiés*, *OC*, vol. XIV, 677; see also Géraldi Leroy, "Péguy-Jaurès: bref essai de synthèse," 2009.

is a *spirit.* It is the synthesis . . . of all of life's activities, and in turn it imprints its own spirit on each particular order of vital activity. Look at Paris from Montmartre. All the monuments and all the houses are disposed in an order and with determined relationships. Look at Paris from Buttes-Chaumont: it is still Paris that you are seeing, but there things are in another order and with different relationships.[45]

Jacques Maritain, too, is not to be viewed solely from "Montmartre," from the flight of stairs that Raïssa Maritain described in her memoirs and which led them to Léon Bloy and to baptism. He must also be viewed from Buttes-Chaumont, the high ground of socialism during the "commune" in 1870. It is always Maritain who will be in one's sights, but "things" there will be "in another order and with different relationships."

V. Conclusion

In conclusion, it may not be entirely useless to underline, after many authors,[46] the strong democratic coefficient that existed at the very center of the French socialism of those days. The aim of revolutionary socialism must not be set against the Republic, but against what was bourgeois in that Republic; that is, not against social democracy as a concrete regime. Alexandre Millerand, a close friend of Péguy, must be read again on this subject. He described "the irresistible movement that has advanced French democracy" and responded in the famous speech of Saint-Mandé (1896) to those who reproached him for wanting to overthrow the Republic: "As Republicans before all else, we do not nourish the mad thought of appealing to the illusory prestige of a royal pretender or to the sabre of a dictator to help our doctrines triumph. We address universal suffrage alone; here it is our ambition to bring economic freedom."[47] Jaurès wanted "to connect socialism to the Republic, to complete political democracy by means of social democracy."[48] He considered "universal suffrage" as "revolutionary

45. Letter of Maritain to Péguy, March 13 1901, *Feullets mensuels de l'Amitié Péguy,* no. 176.

46. See especially Jacques Droz, *Le socialisme démocratique 1864–1960,* edited by Armand Colin (Libraire Armand Colin, 1966); André-Jean Tudesq, *La démocratie en France depuis 1915,* (Paris : Presses Universitaires de France, 1971) . See the article by Romain Ducolombier, "Socialisme et démocratie: une affinité élective," *Cahiers Jaurès,* no. 191 (January–March 2009) : 69–104.

47. A. Millerand, the speech of Saint-Mandé, May 30 1896, *Amitiés Charles Péguy* (August 25, 1972): 11.

48. Jean Jaurès, *Le socialisme et le radicalisme en 1885,* cited by André-Jean Tudesq in *La démocratie en France depuis 1915,* 148.

legality,"[49] and he permits no equivocation to continue: "French socialism will be passionately republican; we would never separate economic questions from political questions, social justice from freedom, socialism from the Republic," even if his speeches double their virulent criticism of the Republic of the social and political elite.[50]

Maritain, who was a Jaurésien at the time of his baptism in 1906, never completely abandoned the idea of revolution. Traces can be found even in the middle of the 1960s, because Maritain still presented himself, despite his age, as a revolutionary.[51] At the same time as he wanted to "withdraw from politics,"[52] Maritain continued to insist on his "left-leaning temperament" from the time of the famous *Lettre sur l'indépendance* of 1935 until the *Paysan de la Garonne* thirty years later. Among the socialist friendships of his Lycée years—Robert Debré, Maurice Reclus, Jean-Paul Coulon, Jean Dietz—not a single one remained, with the exception of Jean Marx.[53] Apropos the latter, Maritain insists in his *Carnet de Notes* that his former network of relations was completely reorganized because of his conversion to Catholicism.[54]

From 1907 on, in private, Maritain criticized socialism in very harsh terms: a letter to Elie Roubanovitch, his old friend from the *Tribune russe* and one of the leaders of the SR (socialistes révolutionnaires) in Paris, points out that Maritain came to a new understanding of socialism and put a good distance between it and himself.[55] In *Integral Humanism*, Maritain

49. André-Jean Tudesq, *La démocratie en France depuis 1915*, 150: "Jean Jaurès is a socialist because he is a democrat, and because he is a democrat, his socialism, reformist as it is, brings about a progressive transformation of society."

50. Jean Jaurès, *Œuvres* (Paris : Rieder, 1931) : 160–161.

51. Jacques Maritain, *Le Paysan de la Garonne*, 1966, *OC.*, vol. XII, 698.

52. *Personal Notebook*, July 22, 1907, BNUS. He wrote this after his meeting with E. Roubanovitch.

53. Concerning Jean Marx (1884–1972), eminent member of the French diplomatic corps, see "Jacques Maritain pendant la drôle de guerre. Notes et Documents," *CJM*, no. 59 (December 2009): 4–57.

54. See Jacques Maritain, *Carnet de notes*, 1965, *OC*, vol. XII, 191, dated April 26 1909: "Jean and Suzanne, among all the friends from before our baptism, are almost the only ones who come to see us."

55. Letter of Jacques Maritain to Elie Roubanovitch, December 4 1907, BNUS: "Socialism has seen the horror of modern poverty, and glimpsed the responsibility of the bourgeoisie. But it draws its life from the same root as bourgeois society does, to the point that the history of the 19th century is from one point of view the history of the contamination of the people by the bourgeoisie. The socialists have the same essential principles as the bourgeoisie: to do without God, to establish on earth the power of man without the help of the Almighty, to seek its well-being and security above all else, to hate and flee poverty, to love and desire property to the extent of wishing it be universal, to work fiercely against the Church and detest all spiritual

denounces what seem to him its intrinsic vices: "Socialism has its origin in a conception of man, of work and of society that is stricken with errors and deficiencies, for which only new syntheses can offer a remedy."[56] Later on, Maritain would come to regret "the manicheism" of socialism.[57] At the same time, however, Maritain recognizes his debt to it.

This acknowledgment was undoubtedly, in his first gesture, a desire to redo his "criticism of anthropocentric humanism and socialism,"[58] which Maritain intended to go beyond, without, however, rejecting their reasons:

> We also believe that what we call integral humanism is capable of saving and of promoting, in a fundamentally different synthesis, all the truths affirmed and presented by socialist humanism, by uniting them in a vital and organic way to many other truths. This is why the very name of integral humanism seems to us particularly appropriate here.... However serious have been its errors and illusions, socialism has been, up to the present century, a protestation of the human conscience and of its most generous instincts against the evils that cried to heaven.... Socialism has loved the poor. It cannot be criticized efficaciously except by remaining indebted to it. The deceptions that it has already caused to men is only the more bitter because of this.[59]

In *Integral Humanism*, Maritain did not silence his invariable antibourgeois vein, since his project was to succeed only through the "liquidation of the bourgeois man."[60] In June 1936—a fact that has never been emphasized—Maritain, a realist, was thrilled that the Popular Front had not rekindled the religious quarrel, and conscious of the fragility of the "good dispositions" of the new government, advised that the ecclesiastical authorities advise Catholics to support the Popular Front: this was an "occasion that had to be seized."[61]

---

authority, to think of nothing but one's body and one's own 'skin,' as M. Hervé says, and to insist that neither God nor nation nor anything else in the world is equal in value to that skin; to calculate what one gives according to the pleasure to be gained.... I have already spoken of doctrinal socialism: it is based on the prejudice of the omniscience and the omnipotence of man carried to their maximum, and pretends to put man in the place of God. If it rightfully recognizes the struggle of the classes, it does not understand that this is an historical phenomenon, partial and often superficial, a tendency and not a law, introduced into the world along with the bourgeoisie, and that it is not, and never will be, the sole driving force in history."

56. Jacques Maritain. *Humanisme intégral*, 1936, *OC*, vol. VI, 393–94.

57. Jacques Maritain, *Carnet de notes*, 1965, *OC*, vol. XII, 153.

58. Jacques Maritain, *Questions de conscience*, 1938, *OC*, vol. VI, 748.

59. Maritain, *Humanisme intégral*, *OC*, vol. VI, 393–94.

60. Ibid., 398.

61. Jacques Maritain, June 1936, *OC*, vol. XVI, 923: "Catholics actually have an opportunity,

In radio broadcasts to France in 1944, Maritain called for closer collaboration between socialists and Christians: "What is in question here, and what has proved possible, is to work together, despite doctrinal oppositions, toward a temporal, political, and social objective, which each one conceives in his own fashion but which contain enough similarities, in the realm of practical realizations, that each may contribute to the common effort."[62] In 1945, Maritain chanced to meet Léon Blum in Naples, Italy where a friendly affection was born between the two men.[63] They met again in 1947 when Maritain attended the UNESCO Congress in Mexico.[64] In 1945, Blum sent him *A l'échelle humaine* with this dedication: "To Jacques Maritain, in memory of the informal broadcast talks which we waited for each week with such impatience, and whose memory brings us such a tender satisfaction."[65] At Blum's return to power in 1946, from the French Embassy to the Holy See, Maritain sent him a letter of congratulations: "Mister President and dear friend, let me tell you with what great emotion I learned that you are accepting the responsibilities of power. After so many and such trials as you have endured, it is a beautiful thing that the country have recourse in this way once again to your moral authority and turn again toward you."[66] In the last half of the 1950s, along with Eleanor Roosevelt, André Gide, Léon Jouhaux, Edouard Herriot, and Roger Martin du Gard, Maritain found himself, despite his objections, honorary president of the Society of the Friends of Léon Blum.[67] In June 1954, in a letter to Cletta Mayer, general secretary to the Friends of Léon Blum, Maritain asked that his name be removed from this list of presidents:

---

which it is important to seize upon without losing an instant, to have their rights recognized, by generously and loyally doing their part in this social effort carried out by the nation. Whatever may come of the Blum experiment, they will have a strong position if a sufficient number of them support this experiment in all the measures of utility and social justice that it proposes."

62. Jacques Maritain, "Socialistes et chrétiens," 1944, *OC*, 499.

63. On this point see Maritain's letter to Journet, June 24, 1945, *Correspondance Maritain-Journet*, vol. III, 323. In March 1944 or 1945, Blum commented very favorably on a speech by Maritain in which the latter criticized an American project of an "Atlantic federation": "Maritain wonders if this 'ideological basis' is broad enough to include the federative organization (to which, he emphasizes once again, the spirit of the French Resistance aspires). Maritain doubts this. I do too evidently.... A federation of free peoples would be at least in the beginning a federation of the conquerors." Léon Blum, *Oeuvres complètes, 1940–1945*, vol. 5 (Paris: Albin Michel, 1955), 508–509.

64. Maritain's letter to Journet, October 23, 1947, *Correspondance*, vol. III, 589–90.

65. Maritain Archives, BNUS.

66. Maritain's letter to Blum, January 1, 1947, BNUS.

67. Bulletin of the Society of the Friends of Léon Blum, under the heading of Léon Blum, Oeuvres complètes, 1940–1954, vol. 5, Albin Michel, 1955.

"The fact that I have been listed, as I see in Bulletin no. 1, among the honorary presidents, entails for me a serious difficulty of conscience: in fact, whether from a philosophical or a religious point of view, my positions are too different from those of our friend for me to be able, without the risk of serious misunderstandings, to appear to be in agreement with his positions. If it were a question of giving witness to the person of Léon Blum, the situation would be very different. But it is a question of ideas, and here the responsibilities of the intelligence are involved."[68] This fact is full of meaning, first of all for the French socialists who one day would have to weigh the reception—or not—of Maritainism, and for Maritain, torn between his friendships and the demands of intellectual independence.

Maritain's democratic ideal would undergo profound transformations. Its visibility and the use of a democratic terminology, from that time on based on Thomist philosophy, would continue to grow ceaselessly after the beginning of the Second World War: "It is the philosophy of St. Thomas that became the first authentic democratic philosophy,"[69] even though Thomism has certainly not been the matrix of Maritainian democracy. Even if Maritain did not subscribe to the formulations of "liberal democracy," since this was never his political horizon, Maritainian democracy would be recharged by his American experience,[70] which for him reconciled the Christian tradition, the Thomist tradition, and New Deal social-democratic aspirations,[71] so freed from Rousseauian myths and anticlerical elements,

68. Letter of Maritain to Madame Cletta Mayer, June 3, 1945, MA, BNUS. Maritain throughout the letter underlines his "feelings of affection": "In my heart I am in the number of his friends."

69. Jacques Maritain, *Principes d'une politique humaniste,* 1944, *OC.,* vol. VIII, 210. For a commentary on this statement, see Ruedi Imbach, "Démocratie ou monarchie? La discussion sur le meilleur régime politique chez quelques interprètes français de Thomas d'Aquin (1893–1928),", *Saint Thomas au XXe siècle, Actes du colloque du centenaire de la Revue Thomiste,* edited by Serge-Thomas Bonino (Paris : Saint Paul, 1994), 335–50. We mention only the author's conclusion: "The recall of a few thomist passages justifies our affirmation that it is undeniable that there are powerful democratic elements in the thought of Thomas Aquinas. In this sense, Father Schwalm and J. Maritain express a real and authentic aspect of the thought of Thomas Aquinas. However these elements are not developed by Thomas Aquinas who expresses them on the level of general principles."

70. Florian Michel, "L'expérience de la démocratie américaine chez Jacques Maritain," *Penser la mondialisation avec Jacques Maritain,* edited by Jean-Dominique Durand et René Mougel, coll. "Chrétiens et Sociétés," RESEA, LARHRA (Lyon, 2013), 99–114.

71. On this point see the contribution of Maurizio Vaudagna, "The New Deal and European Social Democracy in comparative perspective. The trend toward convergence," in Jean Heffer, *Pourquoi n'y a-t-il pas de socialisme aux Etats-Unis?* (Paris : EHESS, 1988), 237–52.

that he became not the "philosopher of Christian-democracy," as the well-known expression would have it, but the Christian philosopher of democracy.[72]

Maritain, the convert, was also a smuggler perhaps on the level of politics. First he was a Jaurésian socialist, with all that the term implied, then a Catholic close to the monarchists, with certain nuances spread about to explain his proximity to Action Française, and finally a Thomist democrat, friend both of the revolution and of authority.[73] His Thomist democracy, simultaneously close to, yet distinct from, "Christian Democracy," renewed it after the political failures of the period between the two wars by a graft brought from "elsewhere," to use the term of Émile Poulat, a graft that came from Maritain's experience of democratic socialism, among other sources.[74] The unity of man, always involved in a dynamic and hence dangerous search for 'the best regime,' will have to be sought both in the mystique of the poor and in the thirst for liberty. Philosophers and even political scientists can have a certain propensity to "essentialize," politics included, often lacking the complexity and the paradoxical singularity of such a trajectory.

72. Jean-Dominique Durand, *L'Europe et la Démocratie chrétienne* (Bruxelles: Complexe, 1995), 126–27.

73. Jacques Maritain, *Principes d'une politique humaniste,* 1944, *OC,* vol. VIII, 211–12. Maritain's democracy does not suppress authority, that is to say, "the force at hand and with the help of which the other can be obliged to listen and to obey."

74. Émile Poulat, "Maritain revisité. Sur les traces françaises de Jacques Maritain," *Maritain en Europe* (Paris: Beauchesne, 1996), 209 (my translation): "It has been too much forgotten, or even conceived with great difficulty: Jacques and Raïssa Maritain are people from elsewhere, and this cannot be erased, especially when there is question of strong personalities. There has always been a profound misunderstanding—insurmountable?—between them and Catholic milieus."

JOHN MARSON DUNAWAY

Maritain's Role in the American Civil Rights Movement

I. Introduction

THE WORK OF JACQUES AND RAÏSSA Maritain had a very significant impact in the United States. An area of this impact little-studied is the role it played in the American Civil Rights Movement of the mid-twentieth century. Even as early as in *Pour la justice,* written during his World War II exile in the US, Maritain speaks often of the national callings of France and the United States: "America and France [are] both called to an enfranchising mission in the world ... fusing historic and racial diversities [and] opening a vaster field to Humanity and the rights of the Human Person" (78–79). He further states that democratic political philosophy "claims the right of suffrage for every adult of whatever race or social condition" (250). Such declarations demonstrate Maritain's position and are typical of the kind of Thomistic foundation that led Americans, Catholic and non-Catholic alike, to feel conscience-bound to activism for racial justice.

The racial reconciliation efforts of John Howard Griffin, and particularly his landmark classic book, *Black Like Me* (1961), were a conscious and direct living-out of the social philosophy he discovered in Jacques's books, particularly *Scholasticism and Politics.*[1] Throughout the rest of his life after the *Black Like Me* experiment, Griffin drew heavily on not only his godparents' writings but their loyal friendship as well. Saul Alinsky's tireless radical community-organizing work may not have been the direct fruit of his very

1. Jacques Maritain, *Scholasticism and Politics,* translated by Mortimer Adler (New York: Macmillan, 1940).

close relationship to Maritain, but the two otherwise apparently opposite personalities certainly shared many commitments, and the French Thomist's faithful friendship and admiration certainly had to inspire the American provocateur. Moreover, the acknowledged leader of the civil rights movement, the Rev. Dr. Martin Luther King Jr., was not only a disciple of Ghandi but also a careful reader of Maritain. It must certainly have been a natural outgrowth of lived experience as the husband of a Russian émigrée Jewess, particularly during the growth of anti-Semitic sentiment in France and the threat of German Nazism in the late 1930s, that Jacques's writings took up the issue of racial injustice. In their early years, he and his wife had both drunk deeply of the prophetic social philosophies of Charles Péguy and Léon Bloy, whose championing of the cause of the poor is echoed in King's work in the 1950s and '60s.

This essay will explore the role that the Maritains' ideas and commitments concerning racial justice played in the civil rights movement, focusing particularly on John Howard Griffin and Saul Alinsky, with briefer remarks about Martin Luther King Jr. and Thomas Merton.

I. John Howard Griffin

As a teenager, John Howard Griffin applied for and won a scholarship to finish his high-school studies in France, since the classical formation that he desired was not available to him in his native Texas. It was during his studies in France in the late 1930s that he first became aware of his own racism. Ironically enough, it was during those same years that Jacques and Raïssa were being widely attacked for their defense of the Jews. They became so wearied of the anti-Semitic form of French racism that their subsequent exile in the United States during the war years, though a painful deprivation in most ways, must have been at least in that one regard a relief.

Griffin started his French schooling at the Lycée Descartes in Tours in 1935, later studying medicine at the Université de Poitiers, as well as musicology and psychiatry. At the outbreak of World War II, he joined the Resistance, specifically Défense Passive, and helped smuggle Jews out of Tours by ambulance. He returned to the US in 1941 and enlisted in the Army Air Corps, serving in the Pacific theater. A severe war injury caused him to endure blindness for a full decade, starting in 1947. He converted to Catholicism in 1951. Of his conversion he writes: "Then and later, religious faith influenced my developing consciousness. The study of music, of the chants, led me to a fascination with monastic systems, and my association with Jacques Maritain and Father Gerald Vann coaxed me out of the agnosticism I had drifted into and led me eventually into the Catholic Church."[2] In a letter to Maritain he called Jacques and Raïssa the "two people who have (after St. Thomas) been the greatest formative influence since [my] adolescence."

When his eyesight was restored in 1957, it was a totally unexpected miracle of grace for Griffin and his family. One is hard pressed to imagine the wonder of seeing for the first time the woman to whom one has been married for four years. Griffin's decade of blindness had already introduced him to the experience of discrimination, and he had been involved in the fight to desegregate the Mansfield, Texas, schools in 1956. In 1959, however, he made the first step toward what would become one of the boldest, most courageous experiments in the history of American race relations. He wrote to *Sepia* magazine, proposing to darken his skin and travel as a black man across the heart of the segregated South and publish a series of articles chronicling the experience, the title of which was originally to be *Journey into Shame.*

For those who have not read the resulting account, renamed *Black Like Me,* Griffin spent over six weeks hitch-hiking and riding buses through the heart of the segregated South, from New Orleans to Atlanta, in the fall of 1959. He not only suffered first-hand the discrimination, abuse, and even potential danger to his life that were common for blacks in those Jim Crow days, but the experience also made him confront the depth of his own unconscious racism. On seeing himself in the mirror for the first time after having used a sunlamp and undergone a dermatologist's darkening treatments using Oxsolarem, Griffen found his "transformation" "total and shocking."[3] He was staring with fear and hatred at a black man who did not resemble himself. "I had tampered with the mystery of existence and I had lost the sense of my own being. This is what devastated me. The Griffin that was had become invisible."[4] In *Man in the Mirror,* Robert Bonazzi writes of Griffin that "[h]is despair was not merely a matter of the transformation,

2. Robert Bonazzi, *The Man in the Mirror: The Story of John Howard Griffin and Black Like Me* (Maryknoll, New York: Orbis, 1997), 17.

3. John Howard Griffin, *Black Like Me* (New York: New American Library, 2010), 10.

4. Ibid., 11.

but a sense of utter hopelessness that he 'had come all this way, had myself transformed chemically into a black man, *because* of my profound convictions about racism, only to find that my own prejudices, at the emotional level, were hopelessly ingrained in me.'"[5]

Griffin's book, which is still in print today over a half-century later, exerted a profound influence on public opinion during the early civil rights struggle. It amounted to a revelation for many whites who had not taken seriously the claims of racial discrimination in the South, and it gave Griffin a platform in the years following its publication for lecturing and serving on community groups that were trying to negotiate peaceful settlements of racial issues. In those groups, he always found himself called upon to serve what he termed "one ridiculous but necessary function.... In city after city we had these meetings to communicate, and in each one my function was to say those things that black men knew much better than I could hope to know, but could not communicate as yet for the simple reason that white men could not tolerate hearing them from a black man's mouth."[6]

Griffin stated in a 1976 letter to me that *Black Like Me* "was in reality the 'living out' of Jacques's ideas on racism." He saw his 1959 experiment as enacting the notion of redemptive suffering that was so dear to Maritain. Bonazzi quotes a letter from Griffin to Jacques and Raïssa: "How to say thank-you to two people who have (after St. Thomas) been the greatest formative influence since one's adolescence?"[7] He also quotes Griffin's private *Journal*, in which not long after Maritain's death he was recalling a conversation with his mentor: "He had told Maritain that he had been 'obedient to you insofar as my actions have consistently been the incarnation of your thought,' which Griffin believed to be the work of the Holy Spirit in Maritain." Griffin then explained to Maritain that thus attempting to live out the Thomist philosopher's philosophy "permitted me to function in a way that helped me overcome my cowardice."[8]

In a 1961 letter to Griffin, one that he no doubt cherished, Maritain had written: "I want to tell you of my profound admiration for what you have done and my joy that you have accomplished an action so great, which is a magnificent expression of love, and which will have a sure and beneficial

5. Bonazzi, *The Man in the Mirror*, 47.
6. Griffin, *Black Like Me*, 177.
7. Bonazzi, *The Man in the Mirror*, 140.
8. Ibid., 162.

effect on souls."[9] Bonazzi also provides one final testimony to Maritain's influence that I will quote from *Man in the Mirror*:

> In an interview with Thomas P. McDonnell, published in the January 1963 issue of *Ramparts*, Griffin revealed that his experiment had been carried out "without Maritain's knowledge but at his inspiration and at Aquinas's (after reading St. Thomas on justice and Maritain on racism)." In particular, he had been struck by Maritain's statement "that all that can save us is a return of authentic charity and metaphysics, and that some must be prepared to be martyrs for the love of humanity."[10]

Though Maritain certainly had exerted a profound influence generally on Griffin's spiritual life, the *Black Like Me* journey specifically was inspired by *Scholasticism and Politics*, where he read this challenge to Christians to be prepared for martyrdom.

II. Saul Alinsky

The case of Saul Alinsky is considerably different from that of Griffin. Best known perhaps for his ground-breaking work in community organizing and social activism, Alinsky was a secular Jew and repeatedly reminded Maritain of his theological skepticism. He was also known for his irreverence, on occasion coming up with rather crude ideas for shaking up the status quo. Nicholas von Hoffman tells of two particularly uncouth stunts that he threatened to pull off, one at a Rochester Philharmonic concert and another at Chicago's O'Hare airport. In both instances he planned for protesters, rather than chanting or sitting in, to engage in bodily functions that would have been egregiously unpleasant to the public. Neither of these had to be actually carried out, as the simple threat of them got the desired results.[11] Some of today's political junkies may not be aware that Alinsky was the founder of the Industrial Areas Foundation, the community organizers who inspired President Barack Obama's early activism, and that Secretary Hilary Clinton was an avid admirer of Alinsky in college. Indeed, Bernard Doering has given us a valuable glimpse of Alinsky's relationship with Jacques Maritain in his admirable editing of their correspondence.[12]

9. Ibid., 185.

10. Ibid., 185–86.

11. Nicholas von Hoffman, *Radical: A Portrait of Saul Alinsky* (Philadelphia: Nation Books, 2010), 83–84.

12. *The Philosopher and the Provocateur*, edited by Bernard Doering (Notre Dame, Indiana: University of Notre Dame Press, 1994).

Doering points out in his preface that it was Maritain who repeatedly urged Alinsky to finish writing and publish his first book, *Reveille for Radicals,* which has served as a primer for radical socialist activism ever since.[13] Alinsky states clearly that "I began to write this book at your (Maritain's) personal request."[14] Doering also quotes Rev. Charles Curran, who he says is correct in observing that "Maritain probably learned more about the practical functioning of real democracy than Alinsky did from Maritain."[15] Yet it is obvious that the radical provocateur was also subject to a measure of hero-worship in the relationship:

> This aggressively fearless and unflappable social organizer [writes Doering] seems strangely ill at ease in asking 'one great favor' of Maritain which he must put in writing because he is too embarrassed to ask him face to face. He explains his embarrassment by his aversion to sentimentality, idols or hero worshipers. "But what I am trying to say is that a picture of you with some personal statement on it would be one of my most cherished possessions. There I have said it." This certainly does not betoken irreverence.[16]

Another instance of what high regard Alinsky had for Maritain is found in the letter he wrote to thank the philosopher for the above-mentioned photograph:

> The picture is wonderful—it is you. I can't tell you how deeply appreciative I am of your inscription. It is only natural that many of my actions of the future will be dictated by my conscience plus that inner voice that will say, "Would Jacques Maritain think this is right."[17]

WWJMD ... a secular Jewish activist's version of the What Would Jesus Do Movement!

For his own part, Maritain expresses near boundless admiration for Alinsky's work and his writing. In a review of *Reveille for Radicals* for the *New York Post,* he writes that "this book will be epoch-making." While conceding that Alinsky does not share his faith, and that "his religious philosophy seems to me rather inconsistent," he states that "I would wish that many Christians may exhibit, in their approach to social matters, as deep an understanding of the moral implication of our basic temporal problems,

13. Saul Alinsky, *Reveille for Radicals* (New York: Random House, 1946).

14. Doering, *The Philosopher and the Provocateur,* 9.

15. Quoted in ibid., xxvii.

16. Ibid., xxxi.

17. Ibid., 5.

as bold a courage in fighting for the dignity of the people, and as ardent a thirst for justice and freedom as Alinsky does."[18] In perhaps his last letter to Alinsky (at least the last one published in Doering's book), Maritain calls him "the greatest man of action in our modern age."[19]

Nevertheless, considering all the religious and temperamental contrasts between these two men, we should not be surprised to see Maritain express some reservations. Doering admits that "though Maritain seems never to have been dissatisfied with what Alinsky did, he did on occasion express his fear that what Alinsky said about means and ends might be subject to misinterpretation."[20] And Maritain does go to some lengths in his letters to point out to Alinsky the dangers of his pursuit of power. Here let me quote at some length a letter Maritain wrote from Kolbsheim in 1964:

> In the temporal realm (civilization) it is normal to aim primarily at power in the ordinary sense (implying coercion, pressure), but such power will inevitably become corrupted if the only incorruptible power, the power of love, is not quickening the whole business. (Your own case, my dearest Saul.... All your fighting effort as an organizer is quickened *in reality* by *love for the human being, and for God,* though you refuse to admit it, by a kind of inner *pudeur*.)[21]

In this passage, while reminding Alinsky of a conversation he had with a cemetery guard in which he admitted that he did what he did for love of the people, Maritain still feels the need to remind Alinsky of that love in warning him about the dangers of seizing power in political action. Indeed, Alinsky uses rather harsh language in his books to talk about the need to wrest power from the establishment. "*The Prince*," he says, "was written by Machiavelli for the Haves on how to hold power. *Rules for Radicals* is written for the Have-Nots on how to take it away."[22] Alinsky's approach to social activism is indeed Machiavellian through and through, even if it is nobly motivated by love for the people. Let us not forget that Machiavelli himself was inspired to write his classic by a desire to help end the chaotic political instability of Florence in his lifetime.

In his 1971 letter from Kolbsheim, responding to *Rules for Radicals*, Maritain questions some of the statements from Alinsky's new book, in

18. Quoted in ibid., 18–20.
19. Ibid., 110.
20. Ibid., xxv.
21. Ibid., 106.
22. Saul Alinsky, *Rules for Radicals: A Practical Primer for Realistic Radicals* (New York: Random House, 1971), 3. This was Alinsky's sequel to *Reveille for Radicals*.

particular this one: "In war the end justifies almost any means." Maritain goes on to ask Alinsky: "Torture? Indiscriminate bombing? Annihilation of cities? (OK for Hitler and like?)"[23]

In *Reveille for Radicals,* Alinsky defines a radical as someone who identifies with people, who genuinely likes them and has confidence in their capacity to work for justice. "In the final analysis," he writes, "the answer to all of the issues facing us will be found in the masses of the people themselves, and *nowhere else*."[24] This description is strikingly similar to the way Maritain repeatedly expresses his own love of the people and his confidence that the way to meet the challenge to freedom posed by the totalitarianism of the war years lies in the strength of the people, whether in France or in the US. But it is one thing to express love for and confidence in the basic wisdom of the people; it is an altogether different matter to advocate the raw use of power in social action out of the rationale of the ends justifying the means.

In 1964, Alinsky sent Maritain a copy of Charles E. Silberman's *Crisis in Black and White.*[25] Jacques's lengthy letter in response reveals some of the subtleties of their relationship. While Maritain does praise the book, he does so in spite of its inadequacies, specifically, its "disregard of moral power and the power of love." He goes on to say that "there will be no solution to the racial crisis in the US if people like you and Silberman and people like Martin Luther King do not meet together and recognize the essential unity of their effort, and the essential complementarity of their methods and inspirations, different as they may be and appear."[26] Maritain here is clearly implying that Alinsky's sociopolitical methods share the same inadequacies as Silberman's. He undoubtedly would have wished that his American activist friend's social action program could be softened somewhat by the passive resistance philosophy of King, which he pointedly describes in this letter as "inspired by Gandhi and the Gospels."[27]

III. Martin Luther King Jr. and Thomas Merton

Among the papers of Martin Luther King Jr. at the King Center there is an outline of Maritain's thought that he wrote during his seminary stud-

23. Doering, *The Philosopher and the Provocateur,* 111.
24. Saul Alinsky, *Reveille for Radicals* (1946; repr. New York: Vintage, 1969), 40.
25. Charles E. Silberman, *Crisis in Black and White* (New York: Random House, 1964).
26. Doering, *The Philosopher and the Provocateur,* 106.
27. Ibid.

ies at Crozer in 1951.[28] The bibliography for the document lists five titles: *Christianity and Democracy, Freedom in the Modern World, Scholasticism and Politics, The Angelic Doctor,* and *True Humanism*. Michael G. Long believes that King embraced Maritain's notion that the sovereignty of the state was only a derivative sovereignty, not an absolute sovereignty, since the state derives its authority from God. He says King's views on communism owed a significant debt to Maritain, who as we know did not eschew the economic program of communism but rejected its rigid philosophical reliance on atheism.[29] The King document also affirms essential agreement with Maritain's general views on democracy as the most desirable political system and specifically a statement from *Christianity and Democracy*: "The democratic impulse burst forth in history as a temporal manifestation of the inspiration of the gospel."[30]

Michael Long notes also that King, like Maritain, recognized that Western democracies still had a long way to go before reaching their potential. "If democracy has its virtues," writes King, "it also has its concomitant vices, and its vices are found in the fact that it has failed to remain true to its virtues."[31] He quotes Maritain again: "The tragedy of modern democracies is that they have not yet succeeded in realizing democracy."[32] Long concludes that Martin Luther King's reflections on the state had mostly been formed by the preaching with which he grew up and his previous studies at Morehouse. Thus, rather than Maritain serving as a formative influence, he believes that "King found a soul mate in Maritain."[33]

My exploration of this topic would be sorely lacking without a few thoughts on the civil rights advocacy of Thomas Merton. The author of *The Seven Storey Mountain* was, after all, among Maritain's closest American friends, along with Griffin and Alinsky. Naturally, the vows of a Trappist monk would not have allowed Merton to engage directly in social activ-

28. Martin Luther King Jr., "Jacques Maritain," *Papers*, 1:438.

29. Some of this thinking was undoubtedly filtered through King's Morehouse professor Samuel Williams, another student of Maritain's writings.

30. Michael G. Long, *Against Us, But For Us: Martin Luther King, Jr. and the State* (Macon, Georgia: Mercer University Press, 2002), 44–45.

31. King, "Jacques Maritain," *Papers*, 1:438.

32. Maritain, Christianity and Democracy, 17.

33. Long, *Against Us, But For Us*, 46. I venture to speculate that if King had been a Catholic rather than a Baptist, Maritain might have initiated a relationship with him, though the difference in their ages and Maritain's retirement to Toulouse in the early 1960s would have made the likelihood of that rather remote.

ism or demonstrations, but his strong antiracist testimony was consistently voiced publicly in his writings. George Kilcourse draws a striking parallel between Merton's "Letters to a White Liberal" and King's "Letter from a Birmingham Jail." Merton writes epistles from the claustration of a cell himself, albeit self-imposed. King too had willingly made himself available for incarceration as a redemptive act in the Birmingham campaign, and both letter-writers explicitly cite a third partner and model in their situations—namely, Saint Paul, writing from his own imprisonment.

"Letters to a White Liberal" is part one of a three-part series of essays that Merton published in 1964 in *Seeds of Destruction*.[34] These three open letters, addressed to a putative white liberal, are hard-hitting indictments of American Christians who have hypocritically espoused liberty and justice while refusing the same to people of color.

> It would not be easy for a Christian to mutilate another man, string him up on a tree and shoot him full of holes if he believed that what he did to that man was done to Christ. On the contrary, he must somehow imagine that he is doing this to the devil—to prevent the devil doing it to him. But in thinking such thoughts, a Christian has spiritually apostatized from Christianity and has implicitly rejected that basic respect for the rights of the person on which a truly Christian and free society depends. From then on anything such a man may say about "Christianity" or "freedom" has lost all claim to rational significance.[35]

One can easily imagine such a passage flowing from the pen of Jacques Maritain.

Merton demonstrates in this book that he understands the American civil rights struggle as much more than a sociopolitical issue. For him, as for Maritain, it is most deeply a spiritual issue. He understands that Martin Luther King's movement is grounded in Christian principles and that King "has clearly spelled out the struggle for freedom not as a struggle for the Negro alone, but also for the white man."[36] Even more deeply, he perceives that blacks do not aspire to integrate themselves into white America. He notes that white liberals in the 1960s assume "that, since the white man is superior, the Negro wants to become a white man."[37] This assumption is still far too prevalent among whites today, much like our unawareness or denial

34. Thomas Merton, *Seeds of Destruction* (New York: Farrar, Straus and Giroux, 1964).
35. Ibid., 17.
36. Ibid., 43.
37. Ibid., 58

of the reality of white privilege. "A genuinely Catholic attitude in matters of race," writes Merton, "is one which concretely accepts and fully recognizes the fact that different races and cultures are *correlative. They mutually complete one another.* The white man needs the Negro, and needs to know that he needs him."[38]

Finally, Merton tells white America that they have some very important lessons to learn from black America. He suggests that African Americans have been observing their white counterparts for centuries and that they actually know a great deal about the white man "and, in fact, understand him in some ways better than he understands himself."[39] His advice for whites is still valid for white America today. The message or lesson that African Americans have been offering us is one we whites need to listen to. We can find it in Moses and the Prophets, Martin Luther King, James Baldwin, and a host of others. Merton concludes, "Read them, and see for yourself what they are saying."[40] I myself only started on this road a few years ago. "And," as Frost once wrote, "that has made all the difference."

38. Ibid., 61.
39. Ibid., 58–59.
40. Ibid., 70.

GREGORY M. REICHBERG

Jacques Maritain, Spain, and Holy War[1]

I. Introduction

It will soon be eighty years since the onset of the Spanish Civil War in July 1936. Outside of Spain and apart from historians of the period, the conflict is now largely forgotten. Yet this civil war, in which about 500,000 died and about the same number were displaced, certainly merits our attention today. This was the last major conflict in which Catholics were actively engaged on religious grounds. The sort of violence that we currently associate with Islamic militancy was then regularly perpetrated by self-styled defenders of our Catholic faith. These included not only the leaders of the July insurrection, but also well-established members of the Church hierarchy, who actively promoted the idea that the Nationalist rebels were waging a "holy war."

One of the most authoritative books on the Spanish Civil War and the repression that followed, Paul Preston's *The Spanish Holocaust*,[2] includes a chapter, "Theorists of Extermination," which traces out the lineage of ecclesiastical ideologues (*inter alia* Juan Tusquets Terrats, Pablo Leon Murciego, and Aniceto de Castro Albarrán), who justified the rebellion by an appeal to Catholic moral doctrine. Indeed, the last-named did not shrink

1. This paper was first presented at a colloquium on "Maritain et la théologie" (Toulouse, 17–18 May, 2014). A French version subsequently appeared in the *Revue thomiste* 115, no. 2 (2016): 215–33.

2. Paul Preston, *The Spanish Holocaust: Inquisition and Extermination in Twentieth-Century Spain* (New York: Norton, 2012).

from publishing a book on this subject with the title *Guerra santa* (1938).[3] Should one think that these were "merely" regional excesses that enjoyed little or no support from the wider Church, one could have pause for thought in reading these lines from (the newly elected) Pope Pius XII's radio message to the Spanish nation ("Con immenso gozo") on April 16, 1939:

> With an immense joy we address you, our very dear sons of Catholic Spain, to express our paternal congratulations for the gift of peace and victory by which God has deigned to crown the Christian heroism of your faith and charity.... We acknowledge also our duty of gratitude toward all those who sacrificed themselves heroically on the field of battle for the defense of God's inalienable rights and of religion.[4]

While Pope Pius refrained from using the term "holy war," it remains true however that the rationale he so fervently applauded—*defending on the battlefield the rights of God and religion*—was one of the chief religious justifications for war that had been advanced by St. Bernard and other medieval proponents of the crusades.

It was into these turgid waters that Jacques Maritain cast his own reflection on the events in Spain with an essay, published in July 1937, with the title "De la guerre sainte."[5] The thrust of essay was to deny—emphatically—the Nationalist pretention that it was waging a *guerra santa.* The essay was addressed mainly to a French Catholic—and in some measure British—readership, in order to encourage a stance of neutrality vis-à-vis the conflict. Chairman of the *Comité français pour la paix civile et religieuse en Espagne* (French Committee for Civil and Religious Peace in Spain), Maritain's political objective was to persuade France and Britain to adopt energetic measures, short of armed intervention, to compel the two sides, Re-

3. Aniceto de Castro Albarrán, *Guerra santa: el sentido católico del Movimiento National Española* (Borgos: Editorial Española,, 1938).

4. My translation of the French text as reproduced in *Les Enseignements Pontificaux: La Paix Internationale*, ed. Moines de Solesmes, vol. 1, *La guerre moderne* (Tournai: Desclée and Cie, 1956), 203–204.

5. *La Nouvelle Revue Française* 49, no. 286 (July 1937): 21–37. This essay subsequently formed part of Maritain's preface—"Considerations françaises sur les choses d'Espagne"—to the French edition of Alfred Mendizabel's book *Aux origines d'une tragédie: La politique espagnole de 1923 à 1936*, which appeared in September 1937. In what follows I cite from the edition of the preface which is reproduced in *Oeuvres complètes Jacques et Raïssa Maritain*, vol. VI, pp. 1215–1255 (unless indicated otherwise, all translations are my own). For background on Maritain's engagements vis-à-vis Spain, one can usefully consult Jean-Miguel Garrigues, OP, "Espagne 1934–1937: J. Maritain face à un Catholicism de croisade," *Cahiers Jacques Maritain* 63 (2011): 34–55.

publican and Nationalist, to reach a negotiated settlement of their conflict. There is much in Maritain's engagement that could provide guidance to us in the present.

II. Maritain's Critique of Nationalist Appeals to "Holy War"

Writing in defense of Maritain, who had come under vociferous attack by French and British (and, of course, Spanish) Catholics for his stance of "neutrality," François Mauriac, a fellow member of the Comité, wrote that as an "homme de droit" (a man of the right) he had originally lent a sympathetic ear to Nationalist claims that they were defending the religious patrimony of the country against the aggression of foreign-led communists. Yet the excessive means employed by Franco and his military eventually led Mauriac to dampen his original support for this seemingly Catholic cause. He adds, tellingly, that "What determined our attitude was the Spanish generals' claim that "they were leading a holy war, a crusade, that they were soldiers of Christ."[6]

In considering Nationalist appeals to "holy war," Maritain defines it as a war raised to the level of the sacred, and consecrated by God."[7] Thus understood, holy war serves as a functional equivalent of the more traditional term "crusade."[8] He adds that on the medieval conception, a holy war was directed *ad extra*, namely "against foreigners who threatened temporal communities [that were deemed] sacred ("communautés temporelles sacrales") and in this sense it could not be waged between fellow Christians and citizens."[9] This restriction of the medieval crusade to warfare against infidels seems intended, on Maritain's part, to undercut the Nationalist claim that it was qualifying its own war-effort as "holy" in the traditional meaning of the term. However, in this respect, Maritain's conceptualization seems

6. François Mauriac, *Le Figaro*, 30 June 1938; reproduced as an annex in OC IV, pp. 1188–1190.

7. "[U]ne guerre élevée elle-même à l'ordre du sacré, et consacrée par Dieu" ("Considerations," in OC VI, pp. 1237–38)

8. Along these lines Alphonse Dupront (*Le mythe de croisade*, vol. III, pp. 1384–85) writes that "la croisade est guerre sainte," "[c]elle-ci est en effet l'état de la croisade en acte." In his very last reflection on this theme, in a section of *De l'Eglise du Christ* entitled "Les exactions des croisés et l'idée de la guerre sainte," Maritain took some distance from his earlier conflation of the crusades and Christian holy war: "L'idée pure de la croisade a été envahie et souillée dès le depart par l'idée impure de la guerre sainte" (OC, vol XIII, p. 260).

9. "Considerations," OC VI, p. 1239.

overly narrow. The idea of "crusade" as it was applied in medieval Latin Christianity could signify both (a) Church-sanctioned warfare against "external" infidels who had invaded Spain and the Holy Land, as well as (b) warfare against heretics, schismatics, and other such "internal" enemies of the Church.[10] Maritain's much later treatment of this theme in *De l'Eglise du Christ* evinces a broader perspective, for here he acknowledges that "holy war" in the middle ages also encompassed conflicts fought within Christendom, for instance as "in France against the Albigensians."[11]

As will become apparent in what follows, we should be aware that there is no commonly received definition of "holy war." This is unsurprising, as although the term is frequently used in the Christian context to describe the medieval crusades and analogous phenomena, it did not come into usage until well after the middle ages. We would look in vain for "bellum sacrum" in Thomas Aquinas or other medieval authors. The term is in large measure the product of modern medievalist historiography, with authors framing definitions that best suit their theoretical needs. Finally, as concerns Maritain, although his aim was to critique the usage that Nationalist ideologues made of the term, he does not engage in an exegesis of their texts to see whether his definition of the term in any way corresponded to theirs. In fact, the definition given above by Maritain cannot be found in the article he cites by the Dominican Ignacio Menendez-Reigada,[12] who, without trying to define exactly why Franco's war was in his eyes holy, suggests that this was so by reason of its primary objective: defense of the Catholic religion in Spain and ultimately throughout the entire world.[13] The *sanctity* of this militant activity—the central element in Maritain's

10. For a good treatment of these two forms of crusade, see Norman Housley, "Crusades against Christians: Their Origins and Early Development, c. 1000–1216," reproduced in *The Crusades: The Essential Readings*, edited by T. F. Madden (Oxford: Blackwell, 2002), 69–98.

11. OC, vol. XIII, p. 262.

12. Ignacio G. Menéndez-Reigada, OP, "La guerra nacional española ante la Moral y el Derecho," *La Ciencia Tomista* (1937): fasc. 1–2, pp. 40–57; cited in "Considerations," OC VI, p. 1238, n. 18.

13. After defining holy war in general terms as any military engagement that has for motive some religious factor ("todos aqûellos que tenían por móvil y determinante algún asunto religioso"), and which can be directed against both external and internal enemies ("la obligación de defender su propia religión, que es la católica, por medio de las armas… contra cualesquier enemigos exteriores o interiores"), Menendez-Reigada goes on to explain that the "Spanish national war" was especially holy because it was directed against individuals who wholly denied the existence of all religion (in contrast to the Moors and Protestants who at least were believers in God): "En la actual Guerra nacional se discute la existencia misma de toda religion, natural o positiva." "La guerra nacional española", 48–9.

definition—was not expressly drawn out by Menendez-Reigada. Maritain seems not to have been mistaken, however, when he identified the issue of sanctity as essential to the Nationalist mindset. A recent historian has described the spiritual atmosphere of the period as follows:

Boys abandoned their Catholic youth groups for the militias; girls forsook philanthropy for voluntary war work. In general, they took up their duties with enthusiasm, convinced that they were part of God's purpose. A new society was being forged by the war: even at the front, young soldiers were exhorted to conduct themselves as 'armed apostles'.... These new crusaders were to be 'the most valiant, the most obedient,' worthy heirs to the mantle of St. James the Moorslayer....

Those who fell were not simply heroes, they were martyrs. Their names became litanies, the stuff of pious legend.... [And] out of suffering came redemption. Spain would be purified by the blood of its martyrs who were, in the words of one young nun, the "living stones" of the new monument the Heart of Jesus was building in Spain....

Franco's crusaders saw a competing and antithetical vision of society: the anti-Spain that had to be extirpated if the true Spain were to flourish.... [When] Franco marched victorious into Madrid in April 1939.... Spanish Catholics attended mass rosaries rather than mass rallies, celebrating their *caudillo's* triumph with Te Deums in every church in the land. The ancient hymn of Thanksgiving rang out again when Franco was anointed, at the hands of the cardinal primate, in a ceremony of consecration which combined the medieval liturgy of the kings of Castile with devotion to the Christ of Lepanto, at whose feet Franco's sword was laid. Centuries of Christian history apparently culminated in the *caudillo*, whose reign would ensure the preservation of the Spanish Church.[14]

Returning now to Maritain, alongside his proper definition of "holy war," he also recognized that the term is sometimes used in a wider sense to designate a war waged on behalf of values that those fighting hold high. On this usage, and taking into account the "laicized transposition of the ancient idea of Crusade" into the "myth of Revolution,"[15] it would make perfectly good sense to say that "the red militiamen likewise wage their own holy war."[16] More generally, anyone who wages a war he believes to be just "can also say he wages a holy war."[17] However, it was not "holy war" under

14. Mary Vincent, "Spain," in *Political Catholicism in Europe 1918–1965*, edited by T. Buchanan and M. Conway (Oxford: Clarendon Press, 1996), 119–20.

15. "[T]ransposition laïcisée de l'antique idée de Croisade" en "myth de la Révolution," "Considerations," OC VI, p. 1249.

16. Ibid., 1250.

17. Ibid., 1241.

this very wide signification that occupied Maritain in the Spanish context. His aim was rather to assess in what measure there could be any validity in maintaining, as did the theological ideologues cited above, that the Nationalist military offensive against the Spanish Republic had a religious character which merited for it the honorific title "holy war."[18] Maritain wished to examine, in other words, whether engagement in this violent struggle (purportedly to uphold Catholic Christianity in Spain) might rightly be described as an activity that emanates from sanctifying grace, on a par with the medieval crusading ideal, as promoted for instance by St. Bernard.

Paradoxical as it might appear to us today, from the perspective of medieval crusading theology, war-making "for Christ" was viewed as an expression of divine faith and charity. Crusaders fallen in battle were likened to martyrs. Thus, in a famous canon from Gratian's *Decretum* we read that those who "combat with all [their] strength the enemies of the holy faith" will "obtain a celestial reward."[19] In the words of one historian of canon law, such a war was "not only just, but justifying; that is a war that confers positive spiritual merit on those who fight in it."[20] On Maritain's reading, the theological apologists of Franco wished to make similar claims about their co-religionists participation in the war against the Second Republic.

In taking up this question, Maritain implicitly assumes that the supernatural acts which flow directly from the theological virtues must have their own natural rectitude.[21] This rectitude serves as the *sina qua non* support for these acts of the theological virtues. Almsgiving (*eleemosyna*), for instance, is traditionally listed as one of the acts of *caritas*. St. Thomas takes care, however, to point that out money wrongfully gained, say, from theft or fraud, cannot be donated *ex caritatem*.[22] Working along a similar line of reasoning, Maritain suggests that acts manifestly unjust could never, *objectively considered*, serve as the support for a holy war, namely a war fought for a divine end under the motion of sanctifying grace. Another way of put-

18. These names are not mentioned by Maritain, who refers instead to the article (cited above) by Menendez-Reigada, who had maintained a similar line of argumentation.

19. *Decretum*, bk. II, causa 23, q. 8, canon 9.

20. James A. Brundage, "Holy War and the Medieval Lawyers," article reproduced in his volume *The Crusades, Holy War and Canon Law* (Farnham, Surrey: Ashgate, 1991), 116.

21. An exception would be an act directly commanded by God, as when Abraham was commanded to sacrifice Jacob. However, Maritain does not suppose that any of the Spanish apologists sought to justify the civil war as holy on grounds that the rebels had benefited from a special revelation from God. Hence this line of justification can here be set aside.

22. See ST II-II, q. 32, a. 7.

ting this point would be to say that a war can be holy only under condition that it should also be just, both with respect to its cause and its execution.[23]

Maritain discusses the justice of the nationalist war-effort on the two levels of *ius ad bellum* and *ius in bello* (as we would say today). Regarding the first—the very ground or rationale for resorting to armed force—he expresses some doubt that the military insurrection of July 17, 1936 could meet the standard set by Catholic moral teaching: those who employ violence against an illegitimate ruler must beforehand assure themselves that the foreseeable damage to life and property will not outweigh the harms he had originally caused. While Maritain hesitates to express a firm conclusion (in keeping with his stance of neutrality), he suggests nonetheless that the perpetrators of the rebellion callously failed to meet this condition of *ad bellum* proportionality. Moreover, the related just war requirement that force may licitly be resorted to only when no other alternative course of action is available ("necessity" or "last resort"), likewise seemed to have been violated by Franco and his associates. Indeed, Maritain insinuates that they had put into practice the "pagan principle of preventive war"[24] and in so doing exceeded the bounds that might be justifiable on the Catholic understanding of legitimate defense.[25]

Maritain's most severe comments on the injustice of the Nationalists' war-effort are framed by reference to the *ius in bello*, namely the moral (and legal) conditions to be observed in prosecuting a war. On this score, he expresses little doubt. The forces led by Franco willfully violated the most elemental norms of war. Arial bombing of civilian population centers, direct attacks on fleeing civilians, summary executions and the like in Maritain's words "are crimes and will always be crimes, for which no ideology can provide an excuse."[26] The fact that the opposing side also perpetrated

23. Whereas some authors place just war and holy war into two wholly separate categories, as for instance Roland Bainton, *Christian Attitudes toward War and Peace* (Nashville, Tennessee: Abingdon Press, 1960), others view holy war as a special mode of just war. Brundage writes in "Holy War and the Medieval Lawyers" that "the canonists recognized holy war as a specific variety of just war; one that, like the others, had its own proper legal characteristics and limitations. The holy war was the most favored variety of war known to canon law, for it allowed the widest latitude of action to its participants." Cf. Leroy Walters, "The Just War and the Crusade: Antitheses or Analogies?," *The Monist* 57, no. 4 (1973): 584–94.

24. "Considerations," OC VI, 1229.

25. In this respect I think Maritain's assessment was correct; see the chapter "Preventive War" in my *Thomas Aquinas on War and Peace* (New York: Cambridge University Press, 2017), 201–222. On the Nationalist strategy of preventive attack, see Preston, *The Spanish Holocaust*, 46, 114–15.

26. Jacques Maritain, "La guerre et le bombardement des villes" (1938), OC VI, 1169–71, on

atrocities, including the massacre of priests and religious, can in no way justify the reciprocal violation of basic moral norms. In arguing this, Maritain makes clear that he is not endorsing pacifism ("We do not condemn the use of force as such"[27]); in fact, in earlier writings,[28] he had already affirmed the traditional doctrine of just war. This would some two years later become the title of one of his articles.[29] He does not deny that resort to force for purposes of defense can be permissible and sometimes even obligatory. He does however condemn the enterprise of total war, namely a war conducted without norms or limits. And despite all the lip service paid to the holiness of his war, if truth be told Franco showed little or no interest in the related doctrine of just war, which after all was a prominent teaching among his compatriot Spanish Scholastics. To the contrary, Maritain emphasizes how the leaders of the military uprising espoused a form of Machiavellianism, namely the doctrine that in the political sphere, and especially in war, whatever conduces to success, no matter how evil, may politically and militarily be considered good. This separation of morality into two entirely different spheres—public and private—and the supposition that evil may deliberately be done so good will emerge is how "the devil makes his way" in the world.[30] "This would be to betray Christ, the good of human beings, and the truth of politics, to say *thus it must be* in the face of this denial of ethics and the Gospel."[31]

Maritain's critique of the Nationalists' invocation of holy war is at its most trenchant when he accuses them of having committed sacrilege. What could be more distant, indeed opposed to, the holy than the desecration

---

p. 1170. Beforehand Maritain had commented that "[l]es conditions de la guerre moderne ont ruiné toutes les constructions du droit positif en matière de guerre. Il reste le droit naturel, et les lois non écrites qu'Antigone invoquait" (ibid.). It can be noted however that Article 25 of the Hague Regulations respecting the Laws and Customs of War on Land (the Annex to Convention II Respecting the Laws and Customs of War on Land, signed in the Hague on July 29, 1899), stated that "[t]he attack or bombardment of towns, villages, habitations or buildings which are not defended, is prohibited." Spain was a signatory to this treaty, as were Germany and Italy.

27. "Considerations," OC VI, p. 1242.

28. *Du régime temporel et la liberté*, "Moyens de guerre spirituels et charnels," OC, V, 1982, 465–83; and *Humanisme intégrale*, OC VI, p. 565.

29. "La guerre juste," *Temps Present*, no. 96 (29 Sept 1939): 1 and 3; reproduced in OC, vol. VII, pp. 295–300. See Gregory M. Reichberg, "Jacques Maritain—Christian Theorist of Non-violence and Just War," *Journal of Military Ethics*, forthcoming 2017. Machiavelli's attempt at justifying evil for the promotion of the good was later treated by Maritain at greater length in his essay "La fin du machiavélisme," OC VIII, pp. 307–355.

30. "Considerations," OC VI, p. 1235.

31. Ibid.

of what God holds dear? Directing to them the self-same accusation that they had flung at the Republications, he explains that whereas the latter had insulted "God in what is physically consecrated to him"[32] (killing clergy, burning Churches, ridiculing the exposed cadavers of priests and nuns, profaning the Holy Sacrament and images of Jesus and his saints, etc.),[33] the Francoists had committed "sacrilege in a more spiritual but no less grave sense, by insulting God in what he had made his own through his love"[34]:

> massacring the poor in the name of religion,—even were they 'Marxists'. . . ; covering Muslim soldiers with images of the Sacred Heart [of Jesus] so as to sanctify the killing of persons descended from Christians (*fils de chrétiens*); claiming to have enrolled God into the passions of a fight wherein the adversary was regarded as unworthy of all respect and compassion. . . ; executing by firing squad (*fusiller*) hundreds of men while celebrating the feast of the Assumption, and on top of everything to annihilate by aerial bombing . . . an entire city, as at Guernica, with its churches and tabernacles, while machine gunning all those who attempted to flee.[35]

The historical record would alas provide numerous other additions to Maritain's list,[36] yet his point is crystal clear: to have committed such atrocities, not simply in the heat of battle and under the sway of emotion, but out of a concerted strategy, is wholly incompatible with anything even remotely connected with the Catholic conception of the holy.[37]

Maritain does not rest his case against appeals to holy war with this

32. Ibid., 1244.

33. See Mary Vincent, "'The keys of the kingdom': religious violence in the Spanish civil war, July–August 1936," in *The Splintering of Spain: Cultural History and the Spanish Civil War, 1936–1939*, edited by Chris Ealham and Michael Richards (Cambridge: Cambridge University Press, 2005), 68–89.

34. Ibid., 1244.

35. Ibid., 1245.

36. Outrages against women would certainly merit inclusion; see Preston, *The Spanish Holocaust*, xix.

37. Some (but by no means all) historians of the crusades would argue the contrary, namely that a divinely sanctioned frenzy of violence was part and parcel of the crusading élan. Dupront sums this up well: "La logique interne de la guerre sainte, autant que les passions déchaînées des troupes croisées, expliquent, pour une bonne part, l'intensité de massacre, et meme la frénesie de pillage qui marque la liberation de Jérusalem. . . . Il n'est point probleme de l'humanité: le massacre devient le signe de la victorire, et donc du service de Dieu. . . . Mais comme la mort en soldat de Dieu entraîne la gloire du martyre, la lutte les signes sanglantes et déstructeurs de la lutte sont autant de causes de l'acceptation, par le Dieu présent de l'oeuvre violent de foi. Sainteté donc de cette guerre, d'être le pacte sanglant, à tous et à chacun manifeste, que le sacrifice est accepté." *Le mythe de crusade*, vol. III, pp. 1392–1393. A similar comment is made by Bainton, who places excess in the very definition of holy war: "The crusading idea requires that the cause be holy . . . , that the war be fought under God and with his help, that the crusaders shall be godly

analysis of the contradiction between high-minded rhetoric and actual practice. He takes the analysis a good deal further when he proceeds to question whether the very idea of holy war can have any valid applicability for Christians within the modern age. At this stage his argumentation is explicitly doctrinal. He alerts us that this is a question "that engages fundamental issues in the philosophy of culture as well as theology, and is of extreme importance for all of modern civilization."[38] This question has lost none of its actuality in our own day, although its center of gravity has shifted from a consideration of war in the context of Christian culture to the parallel developments within Islam.

III. Maritain on Christian Holy War

In examining the status of holy war in relation to Christian thought and practice, Maritain builds his argument on two key points.

First, he assumes that waging war is an inherently profane activity, in other words that "by its essence war is part and parcel of those things that belong to Caesar, and par excellence pertains to the temporal [sphere]."[39] Unlike, say, the conferral of the sacraments or the preaching of divine truth, the employment of military might on the battlefield does not pertain to the Church as such. Even when carried out for purportedly divine ends or at the instigation of spiritual authorities, it is still, with respect to its concrete implementation, a matter for temporal communities and their rulers. It is for this reason that Maritain raises the question of holy war by reference to Christian civilization (*le chrétienté*), and by the same token he avoids framing it in terms of the exigencies proper to the Christian religion (*le christianisme*). Writing about three years after Maritain's intervention on the Spanish civil war, abbé Charles Journet captured the spirit of his friend's distinction in the following lines from *L'Eglise du Verbe incarnée*:

> To be responsible for a just war, for just bloodshed, was no sin for a temporal power; it was ethically good and so could be made meritorious by charity; but it would have been a sin for the Church, who has to conquer by being ready to shed her own blood, like Christ, not by spilling the blood of others. What is allowable for

and their enemies ungodly, and that *the war shall be prosecuted unsparingly.*" *Christian Attitudes toward War and Peace*, 148; italics mine.

38. "Considerations," OC VI, p. 1238.

39. Ibid., p. 1239.

the kingdoms of this world, whose ends and means are temporal, would certainly be illicit for the Kingdom of God, whose end and means are spiritual. The Crusade might very suitably be a war waged by *Christendom* against Islam. It could not be a war of *Christianity* against Islam: Christianity never takes up arms.[40]

If we transpose Journet's assertion from the context of the medieval crusades to the civil war in Spain, taken in isolation it would not have seemed alien to those Nationalists who promoted the idea of holy war. They viewed their war as a struggle in defense of Spanish Christendom, which for them amounted to a very struggle for Spain, for, in their eyes, the Catholic faith was essential to the very identity of *España*.[41] In the measure that the war was fought against unbelievers who were purportedly seeking to replace Christianity in Spain with a secular ("atheistic") humanism, it was but an extension (in their eyes) of the medieval Christian crusade to wrest the Iberian peninsula from its Muslim occupiers.[42] Similarly, to the extent that

40. Charles Journet, *L'Église du Verbe Incarné,* vol. 1 [1941], *La hiérarchie apostolique,* in *Oeuvres complètes,* vol. 1 (Fribourg [Switzerland]: Éditions Saint Augustin, 1998), 668–69. English translation (slightly modified) by A. H. C. Downes, *The Church of the Word Incarnate,* vol. 1, *The Apostolic Hierarchy* (New York: Sheed and Ward, 1955), 328.

41. "E alma española es naturalmente critiana, totalmente cristiana, universalmente cristiana." Menendez-Reigada, "La Guerra nacional española ante la Moral y el Derecho," 41. The author uses this assertion of the Christian identity of Spain to argue that Franco's civil insurrection was not only licit and even obligatory, but that, in addition, it was the most holy war ever documented in history: "guerra más santa registrada en la historia." Ibid., 46. To this claim Maritain responded that: "Il est permis de douter que la Providence n'ait d'autre moyen de sauver ces bases primordiales de la vie humain que le triomphe militaire des nationalists espagnoles et de leurs allies." "Considerations," OC, vol. VI, p. 1238, note 18. He further observes that even if Menendez-Reigada's claim were true, it still would prove only that Franco's war was just, not that it was holy. Ibid.

42. Responding to a telegram (1 April 1939) from Pope Pius XII, congratulating him for the victory of Catholic Spain ("Nous Nous réjouissons avec Votre Excellence de la victoire tant désirée de l'Espagne catholique"; reproduced in *Les Enseignements Pontificaux : La Paix Internationale,* 203), Franco spoke of his country's "croisade héroïque contre les enemies de la religion, de la patrie et de la civilization chrétienne" (cited in *Correspondance Journet-Maritain,* vol. II, p. 828, note 139). Preston explains how in the racist ideology then prevalent among ideologues of the Spanish right, it was believed that leftist Jews had enslaved the Spanish working class, so that the latter, as manifested by their darker skin, were thought to be "imbued with Jewish and Muslim treachery and barbarism." *The Spanish Holocaust,* 43. Thus, Antonio Primo de Rivera associated the Spanish left with the Moors; in his eyes, all of Spanish history was "an endless struggle between Goths and Berbers," the former identified with monarchical, aristocratic, religious, and military values, and the latter with the rural proletariat. See ibid., 48. In this vein, the Second Republic was denounced as a "new Berber invasion" against European and Catholic Spain. See ibid. Gils Robles, for his part, frequently justified violence against the left as a "reconquest," and in this manner he "linked enmity toward the left in the 1930s to the central epic of Spanish nationalism, the battle to liberate Spain from Islam between 722 and 1492." Ibid.

these "unbelievers" were baptized Catholics who had become "apostates," Franco's war also had the character of an internal crusade. Indeed, once victorious, Franco conducted a post-war repression that in significant respects was styled after the medieval inquisition.

Without too much trouble, one could show that mainstream Catholic theologians, from the twelfth to the seventeenth centuries, likewise supported the idea that Christian rulers and their subjects should wage war in defense of God and religion. St. Thomas himself gave voice to this understanding when he wrote that

> Christ's faithful often go to war (*bellum movent*) against unbelievers, not indeed for the purpose of forcing them to believe ... but to prevent them from hindering the faith of Christ. [Moreover] unbelievers who at one time had accepted the faith, and professed it, such as heretics and apostates ... should be submitted even to bodily compulsion (*corporaliter compellendi*), that they may fulfill what they have promised and hold what they at one time received.[43]

Let us turn now to the second key point in Maritain's analysis of holy war in relation to Christian thought and practice. After affirming how in the medieval period wars of this kind had legitimately been waged by Christians on behalf of Christendom, he then denies that a war of this kind can have any legitimacy under the conditions of modern Christendom. His analysis (which was later applied with considerably more detail by Journet)[44] rides on the contrast between two forms of Christendom,[45] sacral and profane. Acknowledging that Christianity has always upheld a distinction between the temporal order of the earthly city, on the one hand, and the spiritual order of the Church and the kingdom of God, on the other, Maritain showed how the relationship between these two orders must not be represented as fixed and unchanging throughout history. Thus, in the Christian middle ages, the unity of the temporal order was conceived of as dependent upon a shared faith. On this sacral conception of Christendom, goods associated with the human being's temporal existence were deemed valuable in light of the assistance that they provided for the achievement

43. ST II-II, q. 10, a. 8.

44. *L'Eglise du Verbe incarnée*, in Journet, OC, vol. I, pp. 618–674 (Downes trans., pp. 304–330).

45. Maritain speaks alternatively of sacral and profane *civilizations* (OC VI, 1239). His suggestion is that the contrast between the sacral and profane phases of Christendom may have parallels within other cultural-political settings, Islamic and Jewish, for example. See his *On the Philosophy of History* (New York: Charles Schribner's Sons, 1957), 111–15 (OC X, pp. 705–709).

of spiritual ends. From such a standpoint, religious pluralism would be viewed as an inherent evil; and religious minorities, while tolerated, would never be accepted into the temporal community as full-fledged citizens.

By contrast, under the historical conditions of modernity, Maritain maintained that a new model of the relationship between the spiritual and the temporal (and by extension between Church and state) would have to be elaborated. This model could not be premised on a pure and simple separation of the two orders. Rightly understood, the two should be conceptualized as in vital interaction with each other. However, within a "profane" instantiation of Christendom, shared theological faith would no longer provide the primary bond of unity between citizens, nor would the temporal order be valued chiefly for its instrumentality vis-à-vis our spiritual end. Fundamental Christian truths would still be reflected in the temporal order, but they would function more as sources of inspiration for the promotion of human dignity than as constitutive elements of civic unity.

Having distinguished these two forms of Christendom, sacred and profane, at some length in his *Humanisme intégral* (delivered in 1934 as lectures at the University of Santander), three years later Maritain summed up the implications for the doctrine of holy war:

> In a form of civilization like ours ... where the temporal is more perfectly differentiated from the spiritual [than was the case during the medieval period] and henceforth enjoys considerable autonomy, [the temporal order] no longer exercises a purely instrumental role vis-à-vis the sacred. In these civilizations of profane type, the notion of holy war loses all meaning. Just or unjust, a war against a foreign power or fellow citizens necessarily remains what it is by its essence, namely something profane and secular, not sacred.... And if sacred values are somehow implicated in the struggle—defended by some or contested by others—this does not in itself render sacred this profane complex of elements. Instead, with respect to the objective movement of history, the sacred values are themselves secularized by this profane complex, and are drawn into its temporal finalities. War does not thereby become holy; rather it risks blaspheming that which is holy.[46]

Maritain's argumentation is straightforward: while it previously enjoyed some legitimacy, the idea of holy war is now entirely outmoded (*périmée*). On his account, the Hapsburg-Polish victory over the Ottomans at the gates of Vienna (1683) was the very last historical manifestation of the medieval holy

46. "La guerre n'en deviant pas sainte: elle risque de faire blasphémer ce qui est saint." "Considerations," pp. 1239–41.

war.[47] Appealing to holy war now, within the confines of post-Enlightenment modernity, is not only to err; even worse, it inflames religious strife, and in the eyes of unbelievers brings Christianity itself into discredit.

Maritain does not deny that Christians can henceforth take part in just wars, nor in doing so must they leave their Christian faith and charity behind. In his earlier *Du Regime temporal et de la liberté* (1933) he emphasized how the theological virtues could purify battlefield courage, so that in standing firm against grave injustice, force, which has been "soiled and dishonored" in the modern world, would recover its "natural dignity."[48] Nevertheless, when violence is thus applied in view of a just cause and with due restraint, and while it can (and indeed must) be regulated by charity, the essentially natural character of the act does not disappear.[49] Rephrased in the language of St. Thomas, Maritain is saying that while a just war can indeed be "commanded" by charity (when for instance it is ordained to the protection of the innocent), it would be improper to say that it is "elicited" by this same virtue—as though waging just war were a direct manifestation of *caritas*,[50] on a par with its acts of beneficence, joy, or mercy.[51] Engagement in a just war may be compatible with the life of grace, but it is not itself an activity of grace.[52]

47. Ibid., p. 1240, n. 19.

48. OC V, p. 481. See the chapter "Battlefield Courage" in *Thomas Aquinas on War and Peace*, 82–109.

49. Maritain follows Yves Simon in terming "violence" any usage of force that is not implemented as an instrument of positive law. In this sense, a just war would represent an instantiation of violence. "Violence," on this understanding, can be good or bad, just or unjust (and hence it should not be defined simply as "an unjust usage of force"); see OC VI, p. 565, n. 16.

50. For an analysis of medieval views that appear to posit crusading as a direct manifestation of charity, see Jonathan Riley-Smith, "Crusading as an Act of Love," reproduced in *The Crusades: The Essential Readings*, edited by T. F. Madden (Oxford: Blackwell, 2002), 31–50.

51. For the distinction between acts elicited and commanded by charity, see ST II-II, q. 23, aa. 7–8. Significantly, when St. Thomas wishes to cite an activity which is defined by reference to a *natural* human good, one nonetheless that (because it represents a *verum bonum*) can be further ordained to a supernatural *divine* end (in this case it will be ordained but not elicited by charity), he mentions the activity ("conservatio civitatis") by which people preserve their city from harm (a. 7); cf. *De caritate*, a. 2, c.

52. Judging from St. Thomas's brief comment on the military-religious orders (ST II-II, q. 188, a. 3), he seems to have thought the contrary, namely that military activity can be directly elicited by *caritas*. This can happen when religious who are engaged in the "active life" (*opera vita activa*, i.e., charitable action behalf of the neighbor—*ad dilectionem actum proximi*, q. 188, a. 2) employ force for the protection of the innocent. Such activity, he adds, may pertain to the way of perfection (*potest ad perfectionem pertinere*): "Potest autem officium militare ordinari ad subventionem proximorum; non solum quantum ad privatas personas, sed etiam quantum ad

It is possible to wage just war while preserving our integrity as Christians (*en chrétiens*), but henceforth, under the conditions of the profane Christendom which is ours, we can never do so precisely by virtue of our identity as Christians (*en tant que chrétiens*).[53] During the Second World War, Maritain remained faithful to this teaching. Opposition to National Socialism—which he identified as an essentially anti-Christian movement—did in his eyes count as a just war.[54] Still, when Christians were engaged in this "war of civilization,"[55] as was his friend the Carmelite Admiral Thierry d'Argenlieu, and when these same Christians were thereby willing to risk their lives,[56] even then their struggle could not rightly be termed "holy."[57] Since, on this understanding, Christian princes can no longer have "any just title for war beyond that which natural reason dictates" (to borrow a formulation from Suarez),[58] for the same reason their warfare, no matter how just it may be, should henceforth never be waged under the banner "Christian."

While recognizing how, over the course of the last three centuries, the trajectory of history has decisively moved beyond the sacral civilization

totius reipublicae" (q. 188, a. 3, c. and ad 1). In formulating this last clause, St. Thomas evinces a sacral conception of the *res publica,* since in the same passage he also says that the religious who undertake activity of this sort do not do so in view of some worldly object, but for the defense of divine worship and the public well-being ("non quidem propter aliquid mundanum, sed propter defensionem divini cultus et publicae salutis," q. 188, a. 3, c.).

53. Maritain does not explicitly draw out this implication himself, but it is in line with the logic of his distinction between agir *en tant que chrétien* et agir *en chrétien*. See *Humanisme integral,* in OC, VI, p. 620.

54. As Maritain wrote in 1940, "si jamais une guerre a été juste, c'est bien celle dans laquelle nous entrions tout en la détestant." "Le christianisme et la guerre," OC VII, p. 518.

55. "Maritain, "Le christianisme et la guerre," 520.

56. See Gérard Bardy, *Les moines-soldats du Générale* (Paris: Plon, 2012).

57. In this connection it is worth citing these lines from "La guerre juste" (1939): "[C]ette guerre contre l'Allegmagne … ne s'agit pas … d'une guerre idéologique.… Il ne s'agit pas non plus d'une guerre sainte.… Il s'agit d'une guerre juste. Combattant Pour La Justice, souffrant et mourant pour qu'une barbarie bestiale ne règne pas sur la face de la terre, ils savent, ceux du moins que la foi éclaire, qu'ils peuvent compter sure le secours de Dieu. Ils ne dissent pas: notre cause est divine, notre cause est la cause de Dieu, nous sommes les soldats de Dieu. Ils disent: notre cause est humaine, elle est celle de cette communauté humaine voulue par Dieu dans l'ordre de la nature et qui s'appelle notre patrie.… Et parce que notre cause est juste, Dieu aura pitié de nos soldats et de notre people." OC, vol. VII, p. 296. And even when recognizing that this war "apparaît comme baignée des reflets des lutes surnaturelles, et comme située déjà en decà du *Sieuil de l'Apocalypse* …, [qu'elle] est dans la relation la plus étroite avec le bien sacré des âmes," [encore] "[i]l ne s'agit pas … du'une guerre sainte. Il s'agit d'une guerre juste." Ibid.

58. In his *Disputatio de bello,* section 5, Suarez responds negatively to the question "Utrum principes christiani habeant aliquem justum titulum belli praeter eum, quem ratio naturalis dictat" (p. 746).

of the middle ages, Maritain nonetheless acknowledges that by virtue of an anachronistic ideation (*idéation anachronique*)[59] our habits of thought and speech can often lag far behind. The words of Pope Pius XII, cited at the outset, give testimony to this phenomenon of linguistic regression.[60] The Pope seems later to have grasped the problem, for (to my knowledge) he never subsequently asserted that upholding the "rights of God and religion" could justify the resort to armed force.[61] Nor, for that matter, have his successors. Doctrinally, within Catholic Christianity, holy war is a page that has now definitively turned.[62] By his courageous intervention in the Spanish crisis, Maritain did much to undermine the legitimacy of holy war within our tradition.[63] For this he merits our gratitude today.

59. OC VI, p. 1240, n. 19.

60. In correspondence with Maritain (letter dated April 12, 1939), we find Journet alluding to Pope Pius's words of congratulation to Franco (see above n. 42), with the discrete comment that "[i]l faut laisser au pape le temps de faire ses experiences" (vol. 2, p. 826). Yves Simon was characteristically more emphatic: "Je ne peux éviter d'être affligé de cette dernière manifestation.... Mais quelle épreuve pour tant de consciences! ... Dans vingt ans, ces garcons-là [enfants basques refugiés en Angleterre] seront des incendiaires d'églises. Très Saint-Père, y avez-vous pensé?" *Correspondance Maritain-Simon*, vol. I, letter n. 337, dated April 19, 1939, p. 365.

61. Pope Pius XII subsequently altered the formula to "the rights of God and of man." See his address on 7 October 1947 to members of the US Congress, apropos the anniversary of the battle of Lepanto; reproduced in Moines de Solesmes, *Les Enseignements Pontificaux* , vol. 1, *La guerre moderne*, 457.

62. Appeal is occasionally still made to some version of holy war. In this connection, see the recent testimony of As'ad Shaftari, a former intelligence officer in a Lebanese Christian militia, who admits (and now deeply regrets) having tortured and killed Palestinians, to defend "what I thought was Christianity in Lebanon." Cited by Robert Worth, "A lonely apology rises from war's ashes," *New York Times*, April 17, section A, 2010. Fortunately, such a view is now wholly rejected within mainstream Church teaching.

63. Maritain traces the "official" repudiation of holy war to the pontificate of John XXIII and the Second Vatican Council, but without citing specific texts: "Une omission plus grave encore concerne l'idée de la guerre sainte. Il a fallu attendre Jean XXIII et l'enseignement general de Vatican II pour qu'elle se trouve *ipso facto* frappée d'interdit, et chassée enfin des obscurs sous-sols où gisent dans l'âme les fantömes du passé. Jusque-là je ne vois pas que le haut personnel de l'Église ait rien fait pour empêcher la conscience chrétienne d'être contaminée par l'idée de la guerre sainte, idée impure qui a empoisonnée des siècles d'histoire, et qui est en elle-même un sanglante injure à l'Évangile." *De l'Eglise du Christ,* OC, XIII, p. 259. In this passage he seems to be defining holy war as a divinely sanctioned frenzy of violence, along the lines of Dupront and Bainton (cited above, n. 35).

II

EDUCATION AND CULTURE

NOEL ADAMS

Market Pressures, Outcomes Assessment, and Catholic Higher Education

At the Crossroads—Again

I.

In his 1943 work entitled *Education at the Crossroads,* Jacques Maritain outlines his vision for higher education while at the same time expressing concerns about the direction colleges and universities could be pushed if the wrong forces were to gain undue influence. His vision for higher education called for a system in which there occurs an awakening of the mind and soul of the student leading to inner freedom, as opposed to a system in which students are trained mechanistically and narrowly so as to produce specialized workers who lack a unified, coherent worldview. Whereas Maritain expresses optimism that his vision would win out, it turns out that the very sorts of improper influences he anticipated are indeed responsible for dictating a departure from his vision for higher education.

Among these influences are three interrelated yet distinct forces: market pressures, the outcomes assessment movement, and a gradual victory of anthropocentric humanism over Christian humanism. The political and social conditions that made possible the rise of these forces include the educational implications of the G.I. Bill of 1944 and the 1971 Supreme Court case *Tilton v Richardson.* The Church recognized the rising influence of secular forces and their implications in several directives contained in *Gaudium et Spes,* published at the end of the Second Vatican Council in 1965, and *Ex Corde Ecclesiae,* published in 1990. Whereas one might reasonably hope and think that the leaders of Catholic universities and colleges would actively resist the forces that would make Catholic institutions of higher education virtually indistinguishable from their secular counterparts, unfortunately, such active resistance is not taking place, and Maritain's vision for higher education is hardly recognizable in practice at many, if not most, Catholic universities and colleges. Although there is little evidence that Maritain's vision for higher education is shared by those who hold positions of leadership in Catholic institutions of higher education, nevertheless those of us who teach, research, and serve at Catholic universities and colleges are obligated to live out the principles that Maritain envisioned, regardless of the risks entailed by doing so.

II.

Maritain maintains in *Education at the Crossroads*[1] that education is an ethical art[2] whose prime goal is "the conquest of internal and spiritual freedom to be achieved by the individual person."[3] He sees education as a human awakening of the mind and spirit[4] in which the principles of morality play an essential role.[5] Other crucial components of this awakening include the cultivation of "inner resources and creativity," precisely because "what matters most in the life of reason is intellectual insight or intuition."[6] Instead of serving as professional schools (in which students are trained for a specific job) or institutes of specialization (in which students are given a concentrated training in a very narrow field), higher education should provide human beings with "the foundations of real wisdom, and with a universal and articulate comprehension of human achievements in science and culture."[7] Maritain's vision of education is a spiritual transformation of the human person in which both faith and reason play essential roles in the search for truth.[8] He concludes his book by acknowledging that a competing secular conception of education based on pragmatism and scientific-materialism stands in direct opposition to his vision.[9] Maritain maintains that the rise

1. Jacques Maritain, *Education at the Crossroads* (New Haven: Yale University Press, 1943).
2. Ibid., 2.
3. Ibid., 11.
4. Ibid., 9.
5. Ibid., 26, 27.
6. Ibid., 43.
7. Ibid., 48.
8. Ibid., 115.
9. Ibid., 113–118.

of pragmatism would lead to the extinction of the spiritual dimension of the human being, and that it would result in morality playing a purely instrumental role. He anticipates that the rise of scientific-materialism would lead to an educational model that emphasizes the cultivation of memorization skills, in which the chief aim would be to churn out specialists who are able to do impressive work in a narrow area, but who would lack a unified worldview. Notwithstanding, Maritain expresses great confidence that education would not go in such a direction. He is confident—even in the extremely dismal point of World War II in 1943—that the immense value of a humanities-based education would continue to be seen as valuable on account of what it produces and cultivates in students. He was confident that a humanities-based education, which cultivates the whole person, including not only the intellectual, but also the moral and spiritual dimensions of the person, would be recognized as the best kind of education, since it cultivates in human beings what is most valuable, and what needs most to be expressed in life. Maritain takes it for granted that a proper university education should prepare a young person to be well informed and versatile, someone who is prepared not simply to enter the labor force, but who is also civically concerned and active, and whose moral and spiritual conscience is integrated into all aspects of life, both private and public.

Only a year after the publication of *Education at the Crossroads*, the passage of The Servicemen's Readjustment Act of 1944, better known as the "G.I. Bill," sparked a number of substantial developments in higher education in the United States. Over the next few decades following World War II, the number of college students exploded, and institutions of higher education grew as never before. In order to help colleges and universities expand in order to meet the staggering numbers of students seeking higher education, the US government offered federal funds for the purpose of building new classrooms, research facilities, student housing, along with the need to hire new faculty members who were needed to teach and serve the ever growing student body. Catholic institutions of higher education faced a number of legal challenges before accessing such funding, however.[10] In par-

10. For a thorough analysis and excellent presentation of the details of this history, see Alice Gallin's book, *Negotiating Identity: Catholic Higher Education Since 1960* (Notre Dame, Indiana: University of Notre Dame Press, 2000). For other monographs that examine the way in which Catholic institutions of higher education were transformed by economic, social, and legal developments, see the following: Andrew M. Greeley, *From Backwater to Mainstream: A Profile of Catholic Higher Education* (Hightstown, New Jersey: McGraw-Hill, 1969); Alice Gallin, *American*

ticular, they had to prove that they would not use federal funds for sectarian[11] purposes.[12] The Supreme Court decided, in the 1971 *Tilton v Richardson* case, that so long as Catholic institutions of higher education could prove that they were not "pervasively sectarian," and that their "predominant higher education mission is to provide their students with a secular education," that they were qualified to receive federal funds.[13] Whereas this Supreme Court decision did not spell out what a secular education consisted in, the legal worry was that Catholic institutions of higher education would have a significant religious and spiritual influence on their students, thus violating the Establishment Clause of the US Constitution. Thus in order to compete for the millions of dollars from the government, Catholic universities needed to demonstrate that their educational mission was indeed primarily to provide a secular education in which the religious and spiritual influence on students was minimal.

III.

Given the influence and contents of documents such as *Gaudium et Spes*,[14] a "Pastoral Constitution on The Church in the Modern World," published on December 7, 1965, at the end of Vatican II and just over five years before the *Tilton v Richardson* case, there was very good reason to believe that the Church's religious teachings would indeed be lived out with renewed vigor in Catholic universities and colleges. This is especially so, given that the Church conceived of Catholic universities and colleges as a natural extension of the Church's work. The document was a kind of profession to the world of how the Church saw itself as relevant in the modern world, and how it would engage the world. As such, it is worth clarifying what the

---

Catholic Higher Education: Essential Documents, 1967–1990 (Notre Dame, Indiana: University of Notre Dame Press, 1992); *The Challenge and Promise of a Catholic University*, edited by Theodore M. Hesburgh (Chicago: University of Chicago Distribution Center, 1994); Alice Gallin, *Independence and a New Partnership in Catholic Higher Education* (Notre Dame, Indiana: University of Notre Dame Press, 1996).

11.

12. Gallin, Negotiating Identity, 37, 38.

13. Ibid.

14. The English text of *Gaudium et Spes* was published as a *Pastoral Constitution on the Church in the Modern World* (Washington, D.C.: National Catholic Welfare Conference, 1965). See also http://www.vatican.va/archive/hist_councils/ii_vatican_council/documents/vat-ii_const_19651207_gaudium-et-spes_en.html. References to this document will indicate the corresponding paragraph number from the text, i.e., *Gaudium et Spes*, 2.

Council declared.

The stated purpose of *Gaudium et Spes* is to explain clearly to the entire world "how [the Council] conceived of the presence and activity of the Church in the world today."[15] The stated goal of the Church is "to carry forward the work of Christ under the lead of the befriending Spirit."[16] The Church recognizes that the human race is undergoing a "cultural and social transformation" that is having "repercussions on man's religious life."[17] For instance, the rise of science and technology is recognized for its powerful impact on the cultural sphere.[18] A new, dynamic, evolutionary conception of reality is recognized as having replaced an old, static conception, thus giving rise to new problems and questions that call for new analysis and synthesis.[19] Not surprisingly, these "new conditions have [had] their impact on religion."[20] In particular the Council points out that a

> growing number of people are abandoning religion in practice. Unlike former days, the denial of God or of religion or the abandonment of them, are no longer unusual and individual occurrences. For today it is not rare for such things to be presented as requirements of scientific progress or of a certain new humanism. In numerous places these views are voiced not only in the teachings of philosophers, but on every side they influence literature, the arts, the interpretation of the humanities and of history and civil laws themselves. As a consequence, many people are shaken.[21]

Echoing the way in which Maritain anticipated and discussed such matters in his *Education at the Crossroads,* the Council observes the way in which technological advances affect us:

> Within the individual person there develops rather frequently an imbalance between an intellect which is modern in practical matters and a theoretical system of thought which can neither master the sum total of its ideas, nor arrange them adequately into a synthesis. Likewise an imbalance arises between a concern for practicality and efficiency, and the demands of moral conscience; also very often between the conditions of collective existence and the requisites of personal thought

15. *Gaudium et Spes,* 2.
16. Ibid., 3.
17. Ibid., 4.
18. Ibid., 5.
19. Ibid.
20. Ibid., 7.
21. Ibid.

and even of contemplation. At length there develops an imbalance between specialized human activity and a comprehensive view of reality.[22]

Gaudium et Spes addresses also the problem of atheism, especially the kind that purports to be based in the "power which modern technical progress generates in man."[23] The remedy for atheism "is to be sought in a proper presentation of the Church's teaching as well as in the integral life of the Church and her members."[24] "While rejecting atheism, root and branch, the Church sincerely professes that all men, believers and unbelievers alike, ought to work for the rightful betterment of this world in which all alike live; such an ideal cannot be realized, however, apart from sincere and prudent dialogue. Hence the Church ... courteously invites atheists to examine the Gospel of Christ with an open mind."[25]

The Council insists that the truths of revelation, which human beings can access only by faith, must be sought after because they are a critical component to the solution of humanity's most pressing social problems: "Christian revelation contributes greatly to the promotion of [the] communion between persons, and at the same time leads us to a deeper understanding of the laws of social life which the Creator has written into man's moral and spiritual nature."[26] Whereas technological advances contribute to human progress, they cannot, by themselves, actually bring it about.[27] Notwithstanding, the Council recognizes that there are many people who "fear that a closer bond between human activity and religion will work against the independence of men, of societies, or of the sciences."[28]

The contentious matter of how human affairs and human reason are autonomous from divine influence took center stage in the 1960s,[29] and they remain so to this day.[30] "The Land O'Lakes Statement"[31] in particular illus-

22. Ibid., 8.

23. Ibid., 20.

24. Ibid., 21.

25. Ibid., 22. It is worth noting how much has changed in the intervening years. With the rise of the so-called "new atheism," as found in antagonistic thinkers such as Sam Harris, Richard Dawkins, Daniel Dennett, and Christopher Hitchens, it is clear that it is no longer possible to issue to atheists an honest invitation to discuss such matters in an open, serious manner.

26. Ibid., 23.

27. Ibid., 35.

28. Ibid., 36.

29. See, for example, Philip Gleason, *Contending With Modernity: Catholic Higher Education in the Twentieth Century* (New York: Oxford University Press, 1995), especially 308–317.

30. See, for example, Garcia, *Academic Freedom*.

31. The contents of this brief yet profoundly important document can be found in Gallin, *American Catholic Higher Education*, 7–12.

trates the way in which contemporary concerns regarding academic freedom were first raised within Catholic intellectual and academic circles. The Council, recognizing that these sorts of issues were about to take center stage, addresses matters of academic freedom head on, and for that reason there are some passages from *Gaudium et Spes* worth quoting at length. These passages illustrate that the Church was recommending and investing in an approach to life that was perfectly in keeping with the views put forth by Maritain just over two decades earlier. In light of these passages, it is also not surprising at all that the about the Supreme Court would go on to express concern, in *Tilton v Richardson,* the degree to which Church's religious teachings would play an essential part on the campuses of Catholic universities.

The relevant passages from *Gaudium et Spes* read as follows:

If by the autonomy of earthly affairs we mean that created things and societies themselves enjoy their own laws and values which must be gradually deciphered, put to use, and regulated by men, then it is entirely right to demand that autonomy. Such is not merely required by modern man, but harmonizes also with the will of the Creator. For by the very circumstance of their having been created, all things are endowed with their own stability, truth, goodness, proper laws and order. Man must respect these as he isolates them by the appropriate methods of the individual sciences or arts. Therefore if methodical investigation within every branch of learning is carried out in a genuinely scientific manner and in accord with moral norms, it never truly conflicts with faith, for earthly matters and the concerns of faith derive from the same God. Indeed whoever labors to penetrate the secrets of reality with a humble and steady mind, even though he is unaware of the fact, is nevertheless being led by the hand of God, who holds all things in existence, and gives them their identity. Consequently, we cannot but deplore certain habits of mind, which are sometimes found too among Christians, which do not sufficiently attend to the rightful independence of science and which, from the arguments and controversies they spark, lead many minds to conclude that faith and science are mutually opposed.[32]

But if the expression, the independence of temporal affairs, is taken to mean that created things do not depend on God, and that man can use them without any reference to their Creator, anyone who acknowledges God will see how false such a meaning is. For without the Creator the creature would disappear. For their part, however, all believers of whatever religion always hear His revealing voice in the discourse of creatures. When God is forgotten, however, the creature itself grows unintelligible."[33]

32. *Gaudium et Spes,* 36.

33. Ibid.

Clearly, the Council here echoes the very concerns first voiced by Maritain two decades earlier. His worries in *Education at the Crossroads* that technological advances would lead to a disintegration of a unified world view, and his concerns in *Pour la justice* that an impoverished and incomplete anthropocentric humanism would displace a Christian humanism,[34] are elaborated on at length in *Gaudium et Spes* as the very concerns that the Church insists need to be addressed in the modern world. What better place to address such concerns than on the campuses of Catholic universities?

IV.

Notwithstanding the legal battles waged in the 1960s and 70s regarding the influence of religion in higher education, it cannot be denied that, until very recently, in both theory and practice, higher education has long been conceived of as having intellectual, moral, and spiritual components. As late as 1983—four decades after the publication of Maritain's *Education at the Crossroads*—the US Department of Education's report entitled "A Nation at Risk,"[35] mentions no less than four times that the purpose of higher education is to develop the intellectual, *and* moral, *and* spiritual powers of students. Without a doubt, Maritain would find that encouraging. Just over two decades later, however, the Department of Education's Spellings Report[36] of 2006 entitled "A Test of Leadership: Charting the Future of U.S. Higher Education" contains not a single sentence in which higher education is mentioned as to have anything *at all* to do with matters moral or spiritual. In fact, in the Spellings Report matters moral and spiritual are *entirely* absent in the discussion of the purpose of higher education. Instead, the worth of higher education is linked—well over a dozen times—primarily to economic security or economic prosperity. Much had changed in just over two decades in the United States. Indeed, the Spellings Report conceives of higher education in terms that have, unfortunately, become all too familiar. That is, higher education is seen as but a part of the engine for economic prosperity in a knowledge driven marketplace. Institutions

34. Jacques Maritain, *Pour la justice* (New York: Editions de la Maison Francaise, 1943), 139–41. For an excellent discussion of the distinction between the anthropocentric and Christian conceptions of humanism and its implications for democracy, see James V. Schall's book *Jacques Maritain: The Philosopher in Society* (Lanham, Maryland: Rowman and Littlefield, 1998), 99–119.

35. See http://www2.ed.gov/pubs/NatAtRisk/.

36. See https://www2.ed.gov/about/bdscomm/list/hiedfuture/reports/pre-pub-report.pdf.

of higher learning are addressed in the Spellings Report as if their primary role is to deliver job training; as if the academy's product is none other than specialists who are in high demand in a globally competitive, diverse, quickly changing, technologically advanced, short-sighed and increasingly impatient marketplace.[37]

In other words, the very sorts of worries identified by Maritain in *Education at the Crossroads* as educationally corruptive have today become an integral part of the values, standards, and background assumptions of higher education. Among scholars who reflect upon the nature, purpose, and function of higher education, there is deep and wide ranging concern that it is on the wrong path. Even those who are either opposed to or unconcerned with issues regarding the relation between the divine and the academic express worry that the higher education is being transformed fundamentally for the worse.[38] In other words, educational theorists who

37. More recently, in a 2011 study entitled "Strength through Global Leadership and Engagement: U.S. Higher Education in the 21st Century" (Report of the Blue Ribbon Panel on Global Engagement, Washington D.C.), the American Council on Education maintains that "[t]oday, colleges and universities are asked to prepare citizens not for a single career but for a life of unpredictable velocity and volatility. Simultaneously, they are asked to produce graduates who are capable of communication across borders and citizens who are invested with the capacity to navigate a transparent, permeable world."

38. There is a rapidly expanding body of literature that discusses these concerns along the lines of what is often referred to as the insidious nature of neo-liberalism or globalization that departs from a model of public funding of higher education in which the aim is to serve the greater or larger good of all society, to a model of private funding in which the aim is to serve primarily the interests of narrower (private) parties within society. See, for example, the following works: *Learning Under Neoliberalism: Ethnographies of Governance in Higher Education*, edited by Susan Brin Hyatt, Boone W. Shear, and Susan Wright (New York: Berghahn Books, 2015); *Neoliberalizing Educational Reform: America's Quest for Profitable Market-Colonies and the Undoing of the Public Good*, edited by Keith M. Sturges (Rotterdam: Sense Publishers, 2015); Dieter Lenzen, *University of the World: A Case for a World University System* (New York: Springer, 2015); *Advancing Knowledge in Higher Education: Universities in Turbulent Times*, edited by Tanya Fitzgerald (Hershey, Pennsylvania: Information Science Reference, an Imprint of IGI Global, 2014); Henry A. Giroux, *Neoliberalism's War on Higher Education* (Chicago: Haymarket Books, 2014); *Equal Scrutiny: Privatization and Accountability in Digital Education*, edited by Patricia Burch and Annalee G. Good (Cambridge, Massachusetts: Harvard Education Press, 2014); Jeffrey R. Di Leo, *Corporate Humanities in Higher Education: Moving Beyond the Neoliberal Academy* (New York: Palgrave Macmillan, 2013); *International Perspectives on Higher Education: Challenging Values and Practice*, edited by Trevor Kerry (London: Continuum International Publishing Group, 2012); *Universities and the Public Square: Knowledge Creation and State Building in the Era of Globalization*, edited by Brian Pusser, Ken Kempner, Simon Marginson, and Imanol Ordorika (New York: Routledge, 2012); *Globalization, Education, and Social Justice*, edited by Joseph Zajda (New York: Springer, 2010); *Global Neoliberalism and Education and its Consequences*, edited by Dave Hill and Ravi Kumar (New York: Routledge, 2009); Carlos Alberto Torres, *Education and Neoliberal*

are non-Christian, agnostic, or atheistic share many of the concerns facing educational theorists in Catholic higher educational circles.

In recent years market forces have pressed hard on Catholic colleges and universities to comply with what Maritain calls the pragmatic, scientific-materialistic model of education. What led to this model of education in the US is, I suggest, fairly straightforward. There have been specific developments in higher education that have directly contributed to the depreciation of all things spiritual and moral. These developments are the rise of the outcomes assessment movement, coupled closely with the growing influence of accreditation agencies that create and transform the standards for institutions of higher education in keeping with market-based criteria. In addition, there has been a cultural change in which discourse about God, spirituality, and moral values has come to be seen as no longer properly belonging to the public realm in which rational discourse holds sway, but rather as belonging primarily, if not exclusively, to the private realm in which reason plays no essential role.

In order for institutions of higher education to confer degrees upon their students, they must meet the standards of the authoritative accreditation agencies[39] that grant universities and colleges their legal, official accreditation credentials. In conjunction with what drives these accreditation standards are the market trends that shape and inform the perception of what is most valuable in higher education. The accrediting agencies have had a profound affect on the structural framework within which colleges and universities function. Accreditation agencies dictate the direction that universities are to take in order to continue to be officially sanctioned schools with legitimate degree programs; in addition, they strongly influence the way in which the values are ordered in the universities over which they hold the power of accreditation.[40] In so far as the values of the market-

Globalization (New York: Routledge, 2009); *Structure and Agency in the Neoliberal University*, edited by Joyce E. Canaan and Wesley Shumar (New York: Routledge, 2008); *Learning to Seek: Globalization, Governance, and the Futures of Higher Education*, edited by Walter Truett Anderson, Jim Dator, and Majid Tehranian (New Brunswick, USA: Transaction Publishers, 2007).

39. The following accreditation agencies cover most of the universities and colleges in the United States: the Accrediting Commission for Community and Junior Colleges Western Association of Schools and Colleges; the Higher Learning Commission; the Middle States Commission on Higher Education; the New England Association of Schools and Colleges Commission on Institutions of Higher Education; the Southern Association of Colleges and Schools Commission on Colleges; the WASC Senior College and University Commission.

40. See, for example, the procedure that is followed by the Higher Learning Commission

place have slowly but surely entered into the academic sphere as the default measuring stick of what constitutes academic success, economic and quantitative measures of academic success have slowly but surely become the measures that universities use to determine their own progress. A primary challenge confronting Catholic universities today is that of salvaging their distinctive Catholic, non-secular identities while undergoing the scrutiny and examination of the accreditation associations which use standards, methodologies, and values that become more and more secular with each passing year. As it now stands, distinctly Catholic religious practices, methodologies, and values must be reducible to something objectively quantifiable, and must be translated into non-religious terms, in order to be properly assessed in accordance with the relevant criteria. Only to the extent that matters spiritual and moral can be measured in accordance with empirically quantifiable and objectively verifiable standards can they be assessed. Given that the standards against which institutions of higher education are to be measured have less and less to do with matters moral and spiritual, and more and more to do with graduation rates and job-placement, it is easy to see how Catholic universities and colleges are having a hard time showing that their moral and spiritual identities are even relevant. Indeed, in keeping with *Tilton v Richardson,* Catholic universities and colleges must prove that they are succeeding in their primary mission of providing their students a *secular* education. Given that a secular education values moral and spiritual matters less and less each year, institutions of higher education that tout such things as essential to their identity would seem to be fighting a very steep uphill climb. As such, only to the degree that Catholic universities and colleges can demonstrate that their moral and spiritual educational mission can be translated consistently and without remainder into a secular model can they be seen to be measuring up properly.

In order to prove that they are indeed measuring up properly, Catholic universities and colleges must do what is required of any other institution of higher education that wants to remain accredited: they must clearly identify and articulate the school's primary goals and aspirations; and on account of *Tilton v Richardson,* these goals and aspirations must be secular. In actual practice, these goals and aspirations receive additional clarification in terms of learning objectives and outcomes. Schools must then pro-

when it determines whether a university will be granted accreditation: http://www.ncahlc.org/HLC-Institutions/how-institutions-are-accredited.html.

vide clear, quantifiable, empirical data that serves as evidence that the stated objectives and outcomes are indeed being met. The task of measuring and verifying whether these goals are being met is called *outcomes assessment*.[41] Outcomes assessment takes place at a wide range of levels, including the classroom level of a specific course taught by a specific professor, the level of a specific academic program/department, and at the level at which the university, in a comprehensive matter, accounts for the way in which its various colleges are unified.[42] Over the past fifteen years or so, the outcomes assessment movement has become more and more important. Leading or aspiring universities have several assessment leaders who often answer directly or indirectly to a provost or dean. In addition, strategic plans are crafted by university administrators in conjunction with specific outcomes or goals that aim to line up with the critical reports written by the accreditation agencies after they have conducted their campus visits.

All of these academic outcomes are measured in accordance with criteria that are defined, with each passing year, more and more in accordance with the values and methods adopted by those who dictate the direction of higher education. Given the Spellings Report, the default criteria and methodologies used today for assessing the worth of higher education presupposes a thoroughgoing secular set of norms, with an increasing emphasis on short-term economic success in the job market.[43] As a result of this

41. See, for example, Alexander W. Astin and Anthony Lising Antonio, *Assessment for Excellence: The Philosophy and Practice of Assessment and Evaluation in Higher Education*, second edition (Lanham, Maryland: Rowman and Littlefield, 2012); see also Mary E. Huba and Jann E. Freed, *Learning-Centered Assessment on College Campuses* (Needham Heights, Massachusetts: Allyn and Bacon, 2000).

42. The outcomes assessment movement in a very short time period has dramatically impacted Catholic Jesuit universities. For example, as recently as 2003 Marquette University required its students in the College of Arts and Sciences to take four philosophy classes and four theology courses in order to have an integrated, comprehensive outlook on how knowledge is unified in accordance with the Catholic intellectual tradition. Today, just twelve years later, students in the College of Arts and Sciences must take only two philosophy and two theology courses, and the total number of credits needed for graduation has been dropped from 128 to 120. All along the way, Dr. Richard Holz, dean of Marquette University's College of Arts and Sciences, who pushed hard for these changes (over the strenuous objections of the departments of philosophy and theology) cited the need to become more like other universities on the basis of the way in which other universities had responded to market conditions identified by the outcomes assessment movement.

43. President Obama has recently called for an objective ratings system that measures the effectiveness of institutions of higher education for matters such as job placement. See, for example, http://www.whitehouse.gov/issues/education/higher-education.

increasing emphasis on standards and criteria that become increasingly secular and market based with each passing year, the challenges confronting Catholic colleges and universities are growing at an unparalleled rate of concentration. Only if these challenges are properly framed and understood in clear detail can there be any hope of successfully confronting them. Only then can administrators reasonably formulate strategic plans that maintain and foster the Catholic character of Catholic colleges and universities. Only then can they continue to direct new expressions of a vibrant Christian spirituality and faith in curriculum choices, research projects, and officially sponsored activities. It would be helpful to such administrators if there were an authoritative document that gave some directives in this area. Thankfully, there is.

V.

Twenty-five years ago, just before the dawn of the outcomes assessment movement, the Church issued an apostolic constitution regarding the very nature of Catholic universities entitled *Ex Corde Ecclesiae* on August 15, 1990.[44] In so far as the purpose of this document is to explain the way in which Catholic universities are the very heart of the Catholic Church, it is this very document that the leaders of Catholic institutions of higher education can and should draw inspiration from in order to carry out their mission of keeping Catholic universities distinctive from their secular counterparts. In this document, Pope John Paul II addresses a number of issues near and dear to Jacques Maritain's heart. For instance, at a Catholic university it must never be forgotten that "knowledge is meant to serve the human person," and that it is

> essential that we be convinced of the priority of the ethical over the technical, of the primacy of the person over things, of the superiority of the spirit over matter. The cause of the human person will only be served if knowledge is joined to conscience. Men and women of science will truly aid humanity only if they preserve the sense of the transcendence of the human person over the world and of God over the human person.[45]

44. Gallin, *American Catholic Higher Education*, 413–37. References to this document will indicate the corresponding paragraph number from the text, i.e., *Ex Corde Ecclesiae*. no. 4., 4.

45. *Ex Corde Ecclesiae*: no. 18.

Pope John Paul II sees Catholic universities as playing an essential role in the Church's active work of evangelization, or of "spreading the authentic message of Christ."[46] Such work, since it utilizes the power of the Gospel, will sometimes be at odds with "humanity's criteria of judgment, determining values, points of interest, lines of thought, sources of inspiration and models of life which are in contrast with the Word of God and the plan of salvation."[47] In other words, the teachings and truths discovered by faith can be at odds with the criteria taken to be authoritative by society, by accreditation agencies, and by certain academic members within the university.

The fact that Catholic universities recognize the Christian faith as a legitimate source in the search for truth, especially in the search for the unity of all truths, makes Catholic universities distinctive:

> While each discipline is taught systematically and according to its own methods, *interdisciplinary studies,* assisted by a careful and thorough study of philosophy and theology, enable students to acquire an organic vision of reality and to develop a continuing desire for intellectual progress. In the communication of knowledge, emphasis is then placed on how *human reason in its reflection* opens to increasingly broader questions, and how the complete answer to them can only come from above through faith.[48]

Thus it follows that Catholic universities are indeed qualitatively different from their secular counterparts,[49] and thus it would be a fundamentally flawed procedure to apply purely secular standards or criteria in order to measure the outcomes or objectives of Catholic universities. However, as outlined previously in this essay, such is the very predicament that Catholic universities face today in the United States.[50]

A cursory glance at the mission statements of Catholic universities gives hope that Maritain's vision of a Catholic educational model is alive

46. Ibid., no. 49.

47. Ibid., no. 48.

48. Ibid., no. 20.

49. See, for example, Alastair MacIntyre, *God, Philosophy, Universities* (Lanham, Maryland: Rowman and Littlefield, 2009).

50. Jesuit colleges and universities have recognized the importance of developing a framework for assessing the core Catholic values essential to a Catholic, Jesuit educational model. These matters are address in the document entitled, "Some Characteristics of Jesuit Colleges and Universities: A Self-Evaluation Instrument," a publication of the Association of Jesuit Colleges and Universities. See https://www.ajcunet.edu/Assets/Publications/File/Characteristics% 20 FINAL%20Dec%2020122.pdf.

and well. Most of these mission statements say something about the importance of faith in the search for truth, and about the integration of the student's intellectual *and* spiritual *and* moral life. So long as those in positions of leadership at Catholic universities take seriously the principles and directives in *Ex Corde Ecclesiae* and earnestly attempt to employ them, there is reason to hope that Catholic universities will continue to do much more than offer merely a secular education that is based on the values of pragmatism and scientific-materialism. However, most Catholic universities, hoping to remain competitive, or in an attempt to raise their profile in publications such as *U.S. News and World Report* have hired and promoted to leadership positions persons who prefer the pragmatic, scientific-materialistic model of higher education that Maritain opposed so ardently. Well-informed, polished advocates of what Maritain called *anthropocentric humanism* (divorced from its original *Christian* roots) have learned how to use the rhetoric of the Catholic intellectual tradition in order to advance the pragmatic, scientific-materialistic model that Maritain so ardently opposed. This rhetoric is used to give parents and donors the impression that the values of a Catholic university are consistently and regularly being lived out in the classroom and in the research projects carried out on campus when in reality they are not.

To an extent, it is not so surprising that things have come to this point. That is, it might be expected that agnostics and atheists who embrace a non-Christian, anthropocentric humanism that is rooted in a pragmatic, materialistic, scientific world-view would eventually become the majority in Catholic universities—contrary to what *Ex Corde Ecclesiae* dictates should never be allowed to happen.[51] After all, the market conditions are such that not only in recent years but also in years to come, the vast majority of academics will earn their PhDs from non-Catholic institutions. Indeed, most academics are not Catholic in the first place; an increasing number identify as having no religious identity at all (i.e., as "nones")[52]; and a growing number are outright hostile to religion. Thus, most of the best qualified academics—so long as by "best qualified" one means "measuring up to the highest secular standards set by the individual disciplines within the academy"—applying for jobs at Catholic universities are either unaware of or uninter-

51. *Ex Corde Ecclesiae*, Part II, Article 4, paragraph 4.

52. See, for example, the PEW Research Center's study at http://www.pewforum.org/2012/10/09/ nones-on-the-rise/.

ested in or hostile to the essential, distinctive role that faith plays in Catholic universities. This market reality is, I suggest, the most challenging factor of all for the future of Catholic higher education. Even if a Catholic university tries to use the mission statement of the school as a criterion to measure the worth of prospective candidates, which is sometimes referred to as "hiring for mission," the current market conditions make it hard to see how this will be rewarded.[53] After all, if a college or university hires faculty and staff who are deeply concerned with non-secular goals and outcomes, the market will see this sort of school as one that is not focused on the proper goals of higher education; and as a result, the school will be punished, not rewarded, by the market.

We live in an age when research projects and research grants count more and more for raising the profile of universities. Increasingly, the research dollars available have nothing to do with spiritual or moral matters relating to the Christian faith. The kinds of research projects being conducted today that attract the greatest research dollars, along with the scholars conducting those studies, are most likely to be seen as having nothing whatsoever to do with the Catholic faith or Catholic spirituality. The market simply does not recognize or value the Catholic faith as a legitimate source in the search for truth, nor does it recognize the value of spirituality as conceived of and promoted by the Catholic intellectual tradition.

VI.

Of course, markets can and do change. As Pope Francis recently indicated in *Evangelii Gaudium*,[54] it is our responsibility to oppose and resist a market-based system that is based on exclusion and inequality,[55] that sees human beings as no more than consumers,[56] and that sees the interests of

53. "Hiring for mission" is when Catholic universities and colleges take seriously their own mission statements so as to hire accordingly. The idea is that only if they do so will they be able to form a community of scholars and administrators who take seriously issues of faith and spirituality so as to actively weave them as seamlessly as possible into the overall academic mission of the school.

54. *Evangelii Gaudium: On the Proclamation of the Gospel in Today's World*, an apostolic exhortation, published December 4, 2013. See http://w2.vatican.va/content/francesco/en/apost_exhortations/documents/papa-francesco_ esortazione-ap_20131124_evangelii-gaudium.html.

55. *Evangelii Gaudium*: no. 53.

56. Ibid., no. 55.

a deified market as the only relevant rule.[57] What explains our current market conditions, according to the pontiff, is exactly what has been the focus of this essay. Namely, it is

> a rejection of ethics and a rejection of God. Ethics has come to be viewed with a certain scornful derision. It is seen as counterproductive, too human, because it makes money and power relative. It is felt to be a threat, since it condemns the manipulation and debasement of the person. In effect, ethics leads to a God who calls for a committed response which is outside the categories of the marketplace. When these latter are absolutized, God can only be seen as uncontrollable, unmanageable, even dangerous, since he calls human beings to their full realization and to freedom from all forms of enslavement.[58]

Such a papal exhortation is challenging for leaders at Catholic universities to follow, since it is much more likely to be punished than rewarded by the market. And, given the direction that the leaders in Catholic higher education continue to take, it appears that they are taking their directives from the market rather than the authority to which the pontiff appeals. Most administrators and leaders in Catholic higher education seem intent on following market-based directives—directives that, if followed, will lead to the complete disintegration of the Catholic model of the higher educational tradition that Jacques Maritain championed. True, it is very hard to see how one can oppose the current trends of the marketplace and still remain competitive within the marketplace; but to not oppose those market trends is intolerable.

When the leaders and administrators at Catholic institutions of higher education act in such a way that seems to indicate that they either are ignorant of or refuse to follow Pope Francis's most recent directives, which, as I see it, are but extensions of the directives contained in *Ex Corde Ecclesiae*, *Gaudium et Spes*, along with Maritain's vision in *Education at the Crossroads*, what ought to be done? I must confess that I do not have a grand or systematic solution to the difficult state of affairs facing those of us who currently work on the front lines of the Catholic academy. Perhaps among the most straightforward things that can be done is to conduct one's teaching, research, and service in such a way that the proper measure of our tasks is not measured by the market's criteria. Of course, this approach will be seen as

57. Ibid., no. 56.
58. Ibid., no. 57.

ridiculous from the point of view of the market, and, as a result, might not line up well with the school's strategic plan or even the goals of one's own department, whether short- or long-term. Indeed, this approach might be seen to be obstructionist or rebellious to the plans that our universities, colleges, and departments have set for themselves. Accordingly, one could very well be punished, or at least not rewarded, in an economic and professional sense, by administrators. After all, as is consistent with what was argued above, pay raises and promotions are determined within the academy according to the way in which the market measures one's worth. In this way, one's academic commitments will be rewarded or punished according to the relevant criteria of the market. So it would not be surprising if those who commit themselves to the vision of higher education described by Maritain, the Second Vatican Council, and Popes John Paul II and Francis, will be harshly treated or punished accordingly. That, however, will not deter those of us in academe if we truly believe that we are living our lives in accordance with the proper principles and the proper criteria. Plus, given that we are protected by the principles of academic freedom—at least as they currently stand—we can retain our positions of influence without fear of retribution, even in current conditions. Of course, taking this sort of path is especially risky for those who do not yet have tenure. And we should not be surprised when in the not too distant future the attempt will be made to eliminate tenure itself from the academy on account of the fact that it is not consistent with the principles of the market—for surely it is not, since tenure protects us from the conditions of the market.

We must abide by principles that conceive of higher education's goal to be the spiritual and moral development of human beings for the sake of their own awakening and freedom—not for merely, let alone primarily, economic advantage or utility. We must gather and foster a community of individuals who share this vision of higher education,[59] and work towards

59. Among the things that I find most promising in Jacques Maritain's conception of higher education is that it is universal and is committed to a vision of Christianity that is truly universal (i.e., catholic). It does not push toward a Catholicism that leans simply to the right or to the left or that does not want to engage with those who belong to another creed or way of life. In particular, what I have in mind is the vision of the relationship between learning and Christianity that he puts forth in *The Peasant of the Garonne: An Old Layman Questions Himself about the Present Time*, translated by Michael Cuddihy and Elizabeth Hughes (New York: Holt, Rinehart and Winston, 1968), as well as in *Pour la justice*. As I understand Maritain, the kind of learning that Catholic institutions of higher education are to offer should take place in a community in which all are welcome, regardless of one's orientation or identity, whether political, social,

the implementation and expansion of that vision and of that community. Of course, this vision, along with those of us who live in accordance with it, will be seen as absurd or ridiculous from the vantage point of the marketplace. However, as the apostles of the early Church first learned so very long ago, it will hardly be the first time such a judgment has been made regarding the Christian approach to life.[60]

---

sexual, or religious. In this sense of being open to all, the hopes of the Catholic Church are lived out in accordance with Maritain's vision.

60. See, for example, the book of The Acts of the Apostles.

WALTER SCHULTZ

The Two Universal Principles of Education

Intuition and Love

A bruised reed he will not break,
and a smoldering wick he will not snuff out.
In faithfulness he will bring forth justice;
he will not falter or be discouraged
till he establishes justice on earth.
In his teaching the islands will put their hope.
Isaiah 42: 3–4 (NIV)

I. Introduction

PEDAGOGY, AS THE DISCIPLINE concerned with teaching how to teach, is about discerning proper method in the teaching profession. Here it will be argued that there are two universal principles which must be adhered to in the classroom or lecture hall. These principles, intuition and love, are universal because they direct us to what is and what it is to be human; and it is Jacques Maritain who identifies these universal principles as primordial and the primary concern of education. As he writes in *Education at the Crossroads*:

For man and human life there is indeed nothing greater than intuition and love. Not every love is right, nor every intuition well directed or conceptualized, yet if either intuition or love exists in any hidden corner, life and the flame of life are there, and a bit of heaven in a promise. Yet neither intuition nor love is a matter of training and learning, they are gift and freedom. In spite of all that, education should be primarily concerned with them.[1]

Adhering to the two universal and primordial principles of education means that the teaching profession involves more than method and teaching itself. This is so because intuition and love designate the immediate, pre-conceptual apprehension of reality and the human person. Intuition is fully liberated in "the free adhesion of the mind to the objective reality to be seen."[2] However, intuition initially springs forth from a preconscious level: "The germ of insight starts within a preconscious intellectual cloud, arising from experience, imagination, and a kind of spiritual feeling, but it is from the outset a tending toward an object to be grasped."[3] Because they are foundational, intuition and love are prior to any instruction, training, or imparting of knowledge.

In addition to his focus on intuition and love, thereby placing the provenance of education beyond the institutional setting and standard curriculum, it is eminently clear that, for Maritain, all modes of education foster the achievement of our humanity, which of necessity involves personal fulfillment within a social setting. Maritain is adamant when he states that, "education must remove the rift between the social claim and the individual claim within man himself."[4] Furthermore, he insists that, "the education of tomorrow must provide the common man with the means for his personal fulfillment, not only with regard to his labor but also with regard to his social and political activities in the civil commonwealth, and to the activities of his leisure hours."[5] For Maritain, education contains pedagogy and every way of functioning as a human being. Quite simply, education establishes our humanity. This becomes evident in the opening page of *Education at the Crossroads*, where disparaging the failure of modernity to acknowledge our common human nature, Maritain forthrightly states that "the chief task of education is above all to shape man, or to guide the evolving dynamism through which man forms himself as a man. That is why I might have taken

1. Jacques Maritain, *Education at the Crossroads* (New Haven, Connecticut: Yale University Press, 1960), 23, hereafter referred to as *Education*.

2. Ibid., 44.

3. Ibid.

4. Ibid., 89.

5. Ibid., 90.

for my title *The Education of Man*."[6] Such a broad, all-encompassing view of the centrality of education for our humanity demands the marriage of individual and society, as it demands the marriage of theory and practice. Wherever education occurs, whether in the classroom or elsewhere, a very practical ambience is generated, with implications for economic development, social justice, democratic procedure, and environmental integrity.

According to Maritain, in order to establish our humanity, the educator must avoid nurturing the romantic lure of anarchic, self-indulgent individualism, while at the same time refusing to succumb to the seemingly secure mechanism of totalitarian control. Returning to the fundamental orientation to reality and the human person through intuition and love denies the hegemony of the rudderless will. Abandoning reality and the human person, such a will is left to its own selfish resources and is rendered vulnerable to the willful ideologues who peddle overly ambitious or presumptuous complexities in place of simple albeit often partial truths; reality and the human person can be known conceptually, but never encapsulated by any theory. The will of the student, which is naturally inclined toward reality and the human person, must be nurtured and guided toward conceptual clarity; too often even proper instruction and correction are delivered by way of imposition and coercion. It is the will of the individual student which must desire truth and attain clarification through the intellect.

Vittorio Possenti, a founding member of *L'Istituto Internazionale Jacques Maritain*, depicts the significance of intuition and love (as well as the significance of their absence) on the theoretical and practical levels. Maritain has unequivocally stated that "there is no knowledge without intuitivity."[7] Given the various modes of intuition discussed by Maritain, Possenti focuses beyond sense perception on the basic intellectual perception or intuition of the being of things through their intentional existence in the mind, ultimately focusing on the essentially analogous value of being attained in metaphysics. He informs us that such intuition "alludes to a noetic apperception of reality in which the intellect celebrates its marriage with the being of things and actualizes itself in contact with the nucleus of intelligibility and the mystery contained in being."[8] Furthermore, through the perennial

6. Ibid., 1.

7. Jacques Maritain, *Untrammeled Approaches* (Notre Dame, Indiana: University of Notre Dame Press, 1997), 326.

8. Vittorio Possenti, *Nihilism and Metaphysics: The Third Voyage*, translated by Daniel B. Gal-

philosophy of Aquinas identified as the pivotal advance over Greek speculation within the philosophy of being (*Seinphilosophie*), Possenti offers a frontal attack on those who would deny the intentional merger of the intellect with the reality of things through intellectual intuition and conceptualization, eschewing the consequent apprehension of being in metaphysics.[9] He argues that the forgetfulness of being, or the eclipse of reality and the human person evident in the nihilism of a thinker like Friedrich Nietzsche, explains the practical consequences of a will detached from reality, however much attired in a conceptual wardrobe when we come to the work of thinkers like Giovanni Gentile in Italy and Martin Heidegger in Germany. Although the evaluation of choice is formidably complex, one must not discount Gentile's bold allegiance to Fascism nor minimize Heidegger's infatuation with Nazism; and one must not forget that Gentile was the Minister of Education for the government of Benito Mussolini nor forget the contribution of Heidegger to National Socialist aspirations in education while Rector of Freiburg University under Adolf Hitler. In addition to the basic intuitive apprehension of reality, Possenti asserts that the philosophy of being must include a philosophy of love (*eros* and *agape*), observing "that the theme of love seems largely absent from the pages of Nietzsche, Gentile, and Heidegger. A philosophy of love is lacking because there seems to be a deficient consideration of the subject, the person."[10] Given the practical implications of Possenti's observations, it is imperative that educators in all disciplines and at every level nurture the originary orientation to reality and the human person in students.

The structure of this essay revolves around three assumptions based on

---

lagher (Albany, New York: State University of New York Press, 2014), 18. For a synopsis of the various modes of intuition discussed by Maritain with sources see John G. Trapani Jr., "The Air We Breathe: The Reality of Our Knowledge and Our Knowledge of Reality," in *Jacques Maritain and the Many Ways of Knowing* (Washington D.C.: American Maritain Association, 2002; distributed by The Catholic University of America Press), 186.

9. Although not to be developed within the context of this paper, Posenti contends that the great advocates of *Seinphilosophie* in the twentieth century failed to directly confront the challenge of nihilism; he even proposes a new determination of speculative nihilism which "reopens the way to a rediscovery of the philosophy of being as an expression of *onto-sophia*, radically demarcating itself from onto-phobia on a metaphysical level, and, on a gnoseological level, from *logos*-phobia or myso logia." Ibid., 313. I am grateful to Vitttorio Possenti for communicating to me the primary significance of his aim to foster an idea of nihilism coherent with *Seinphilosophie*, and profoundly differing from the nihilism of Nietzsche and Heidegger.

10. Possenti, *Nihilism*, 228.

experience as a professional educator: first, that Maritain provides the proper approach to reality within the teaching profession as he does for every human endeavor; second, that he is correct when he maintains that the will and freedom of the individual human person constitute the primary agency in the process of education; and third, that his approach to education as establishing human activity as such, enables us as educators to significantly broaden our horizon, delineating varied yet cohesive factors at play through global education, which exemplifies the universality of intuition and love. Here the classroom and lecture hall merge with other venues for education within the global forum working toward establishing our humanity, avoiding the pitfalls of self-indulgent individualism and totalitarian control.

We must remember that Jacques Maritain was very much a public intellectual in his time, extending his reach far beyond the academy, in this sense standing on common ground with a thinker like Cornel West in the United States or John Haldane in Scotland. Furthermore, there are important lessons for educators in the encounters which took place at Meudon between the two great wars of the twentieth century, where Jacques, Raïssa, and Vera (the "Little Flock") entertained and counseled, always with the utmost respect, those who may be called "the lost souls" within the flamboyant French culture of what has been called "the Jazz Age" (the Maritains' encounter with Jean Cocteau, a popular artist in French literature and cinema, is a prime example). Such openness is also evident in Jacques and Raïssa's lifelong interest in the work of Charles Pierre Baudelaire, an interest shared by Bob Dylan, the American artist Jacques came to appreciate through Thomas Merton while visiting in Gethsemane, Kentucky.[11] Finally then, this paper will briefly address the continuing relevancy and attraction of Jacques Maritain's approach to reality and the human person, exhibited so strongly in his openness to the other.

II. Reality and Education

Philosophical realism offers a conceptual approach to reality, as thinkers from Aristotle through Aquinas down to thinkers like Étienne Gilson and Jacques Maritain have affirmed in our time. Gilson makes it quite clear that this conceptual approach to reality remains humble before it, and he

11. John H. Griffins and Yves R. Simon, *Jacques Maritain: Homage in Word and Pictures* (Albany, New York: Magi Books, 1974), 35–36.

argues that it is Descartes who crossed the line when he reified the concept. In his *Methodical Realism,* Gilson states:

The person who *reified* concepts was not St. Thomas but Descartes, and he could not avoid doing so once he raised concepts to the rank of Ideas. He turned abstractions from reality into models of reality, about which it is not enough to say that reality is supposed to conform to them but which are reality itself. On this point the difference between the two philosophies leaps to the eye as soon as one realizes that for Descartes every substance is fully known because reducible to the content of its idea, whereas for a scholastic every substance as such is unknown, because it is something other than the sum of the concepts we extract from it.[12]

It is Maritain who informs us that the Cartesian reification of concepts eventually allows reason to become no more than the justification or narrative enabling the will to trick reason into its service through the pragmatic advance of technology. As Maritain writes in *Three Reformers*:

The essence of rationalism consists in making the human reason and its ideological content the measure of what is: truly it is the extreme of madness, for the human reason has no content but what it has received from external objects. That inflation of reason is the sign and cause of a great weakness. Reason defenceless loses its hold on reality, and after a period of presumption it is reduced to abdication, falling then into the opposite evil, anti-intellectualism, voluntarism, pragmatism, etc.[13]

Furthermore, when considering the cultural significance of Cartesian dualism, Maritain identifies a profound moral shift. He informs us in *The Dream of Descartes* that there is a difference between the traditional ascetic morality, whereby we strive to perfect ourselves with the aid of reason and grace, and the promise of material satisfaction through technical progress proposed by rationalism, "an entirely different morality, anti-ascetic, exclusively technological."[14] On this note Maritain asks a key question and answers it: "What remains of man? A consumer crowned by science. This is the final gift, the twentieth century gift of the Cartesian reform."[15] Cut off from reality, the "consumer crowned by science" can function for a time as the self-serving

12. Étienne Gilson, *Methodical Realism,* translated by Philip Trower (Front Royal, Virginia: Christendom Press, 1990), 87.

13. Jacques Maritain, *Three Reformers: Luther, Descartes, Rousseau* (New York: Thomas Y. Crowell, 1970), 85.

14. Jacques Maritain, *The Dream of Descartes,* translated by Mabelle L. Andison (New York: F. Hubner and Co., 1944), 182.

15. Ibid., 182–83.

atomistic individual, but most likely will succumb to the Idea with a utopian promise, i.e. to the ideologue justifying the will to power.

The conceptual approach to reality remains humble and subservient to what is, whereas the modern reification of the idea places us in bondage to the often complex rationalization of the ideologue engaged in liberating the will for technological advance and self-aggrandizement. As Maritain never tires of telling us, from the Cartesian reform, through a liberal society of autonomous individuals, and finally coming to rest in a variety of totalitarian structures, the rudderless will, often mixed with many truths and noble aspirations, has captured our world and seeks to perpetuate itself through false education or manipulative indoctrination which diminishes or even eclipses the simple and basic apprehension of reality and the human person. This primordial apprehension is prior to philosophical conceptualization and it must be nurtured through education on every level and in every discipline.

Harnessing the will to truth is the primary goal of education according to Maritain. Presenting five fundamental natural dispositions to be nurtured through education in *Education at the Crossroads,* Maritain notes that "the love of truth … is the primary tendency of any intellectual nature."[16] Related to truth is the natural love of the good and justice, which he presents as the second fundamental disposition to be nurtured.[17] Maritain also proposes a third disposition, namely, "simplicity and openness with regard to existence."[18] Skipping over the fourth fundamental disposition, we note that such "openness" in any being endowed with intellect entails acknowledgment of and cooperation with the other, as Maritain indicates when he states that, "the fifth fundamental disposition is the sense of cooperation, which is as natural in us, and as thwarted too, as the tendency to social and political life."[19]

The fourth fundamental disposition mentioned above "the sense of a job well done, for next to the attitude toward existence there is nothing more basic in man's psychic life than the attitude toward work."[20] It is noteworthy that Maritain emphasizes the implication for morality in this fourth fundamental disposition: "I am convinced that when this [fourth] fundamental disposition, which is the first natural move toward self-discipline,

16. Maritain, *Education,* 36.
17. See Ibid., 36–37.
18. Ibid., 37.
19. Ibid., 38.
20. Ibid.

this probity in regard to work is marred, an essential basis of human morality is lacking."[21] Presumably, Maritain intends that "self-discipline" mature beyond what is necessary to secure technical mastery over geometric extension, since he promotes an ascetic morality against the "anti-ascetic" and "exclusively technological" morality of "the twentieth century gift of the Cartesian reform," enslaving the intellect to will. Attention to truth, being, the good, justice, and the other together, as the goals of natural fundamental dispositions to be nurtured in the student, establishes the foundation of a good will wedded to the intellect, directed toward reality and the human person. Primordial, and therefore pre-conceptual, these dispositions come to form the basic apprehension of reality and the person.

It is primarily the will, but not a rudderless will, which is to be liberated in the classroom and lecture hall. Harnessing the pre-conceptual will to desire knowledge of reality through intuition and appreciate the other as a human person through love is foundational. Maritain is adamant when stating the importance in education of allowing the will to attain its natural inclinations:

> The upbringing of the human being must lead both intelligence and will toward achievement, and the shaping of the will is throughout more important to man than the shaping of the intellect. Yet, whereas the educational system of schools and colleges succeeds as a rule in equipping man's intellect for knowledge, it seems to be missing its main achievement, the equipping of man's will.[22]

III. The Human Person and Education

How Maritain understands the relationship between human subjectivity and love shows us what is essential in both the spiritual and temporal development of the human being. The development of personality is intimately connected with love, which is the central tenet in Christianity. Love is not connected with qualities (as Pascal said), but with the substantial or truly existential dimension of the beloved.[23] Love is connected with that which is capable of giving itself and receiving another self. Moreover, "to bestow oneself, one must first exist; not, indeed, as a sound, which passes

21. Ibid.

22. Ibid., 22.

23. See Jacques Maritain, *The Person and the Common Good*, translated by John J. Fitzgerald (Notre Dame, Indiana: University of Notre Dame Press, 1966), 38–39.

through the air, or an idea, which crosses the mind, but as a thing, which subsists and exercises existence for itself."[24] Moreover, a loving being must be master of itself, or self-possessed: "Personality, therefore, signifies interiority to self."[25] Love implies the existence of a subject.

In *Existence and the Existent,* Maritain argues that

> [t]he subject or *suppositum,* or person has an essence, an essential structure. It is a substance equipped with properties, and which is acted upon and acts by the instrumentality of its potencies. The person is a substance whose substantial form is a spiritual soul; a substance which lives a life that is not merely biological and instinctive, but is also a life of intellect and will.[26]

Arguing against contemporary existentialists, whose approach he perceives as being merely concerned with phenomena, Maritain states:

> They [contemporary existentialists] do not see that, because his *spirit* makes man cross the threshold of independence properly so-called, and of self-inwardness, the subjectivity of the person demands as its most intimate privilege communications proper to love and intelligence. They do not see that, even before the existence of free choice, and in order to make free choice possible, the most deeply rooted need of the person is to communicate with *the other* by the union of the intelligence, and with *others* by the affective union. Their subjectivity is not a *self,* because it is wholly phenomenal.[27]

Besides the Bergsonian intuition of duration, in *A Preface to Metaphysics* Maritain also criticizes Heidegger's encounter with anguish and Gabriel Marcel's experience of fidelity. However, it should be noted that Maritain, always appreciative of initial insights that testify to the truth by way of attachment to reality, allows for existential experience as a preparation for the intellectual apprehension of being proper to metaphysics.[28]

Maritain contends that the conceptual perspective of Thomism allows him to plunge into the ontological depths of subjectivity:

> [I]n relation to its essential structures, the subject is in no wise betrayed when it is made object. The objectization which universalizes it and discerns in it intelligible

24. Ibid., 39–40.

25. Ibid., 41.

26. Jacques Maritain, *Existence and the Existent,* translated by Lewis Gaalantiere and Gerald B. Phelan (Westport, Connecticut: Greenwood Press, 1975), 81—hereafter referred to as *Existence.*

27. Ibid., 82.

28. See Jacques Maritain, *A Preface to Metaphysics: Seven Lectures on Being* (New York: The New American Library of World Literature, 1962), 48–64.

natures, makes it known by a knowledge destined doubtless to continue to deepen, but not one that is in any sense unjust. Such a knowledge does no violence to the truth of the subject, but renders that truth present to the mind.[29]

Furthermore, he states that

personality, metaphysically considered, being the substance of the spiritual soul communicated to the human composite, and enabling the later to possess its existence, to perfect itself and to give itself freely, bears witness in us to the generosity or expansivity of being which, in an incarnate spirit, proceeds from the spirit and which constitutes, in the secret springs of our ontological structure, a source of dynamic unity and unification from within.[30]

According to Maritain, the philosophical notion of the *suppositum*, which expresses the core of the subject or person, safeguards the authentic ontology of the subject. Maritain refuses to reduce the subject to a mere object, either by way of rational abstraction or by way of phenomenal reduction. He insists that philosophical speculation be just to the dynamic subject, who in fact exists only by way of interpersonal relationship, and argues that a proper philosophical anthropology can occur only through a form of intellectual existentialism.

Thomistic philosophical conceptualization is seen by Maritain as adequate precisely because it points beyond itself toward the existent, apprehended conceptually as well as at the foundational level of awareness and intersubjectivity, whereby reality is known through inclination by way of natural affinity with the reality known. Functioning at this foundational level we apprehend reality and the human person through various modes of intellectual and affective connaturality.[31]

In the context of this essay, it is significant that there is, according to Maritain

[a] knowledge by intellectual connaturality with reality as *conceptualisable* and rendered proportionate in act to the human intellect. It goes along with the devel-

29. Maritain, *Existence*, 80–81.

30. Ibid., 81–82.

31. See Jacques and Raïssa Maritain, *The Situation of Poetry: Four Essays on the Relations between Poetry, Mysticism, Magic, and Knowledge*, translated by Marshall Suther (New York, NY: Philosophical Library, 1955), 65–67—hereafter referred to as *Poetry*; and Jacques Maritain, *Redeeming the Time*, translated by Harry Loren Binesse (London: Geoffrey Bles, The Centenary Press, 1946), 225–233—hereafter referred to as *Time*. Also, for other enumerations of the three types of affective connaturality see Maritain, *Existence*, 78; and *The Range of Reason* (New York: Charles Scribner's Sons, 1952), 22–29.

opment of the *habitus* of the intelligence; and it is from this knowledge that comes the *intuition*—intellectual and expressible in a mental work—of the philosopher, the scientist, of him who knows by mode of knowledge.[32]

A type of intellectual connaturality accompanies conceptual knowledge in the development of philosophy and science. Another type of intellectual connaturality concerns the presence of self to self, and can engender a form of natural mystical experience.[33] Affective types of connaturality identified and explored by Maritain are poetic knowledge, mystical experience, and moral feeling.[34] Furthermore, at this foundational level, we are able to encounter and affirm authentic humanity in the individual human person. Maritain tells us that "knowledge through connaturality plays an immense part in human existence, especially in that knowing of the singular which comes about in everyday life and in our relationship of person to person."[35] It has been observed that attaining the inconceivable uniqueness and personhood of the other appears to be similar to both the receptive side of poetic knowledge and affective mystical experience.[36]

The key words in Maritain's appreciation of connaturality are "existence" and the "existent." Connaturality designates the non-conceptual apprehension of reality, not to be confused with that mode of knowledge through conceptualization and discursive thought exercised by the philosopher and scientist. Here Maritain is quite adamant:

If one confuses the planes and orders of things, if poetic knowledge or mystical experience or moral feeling claim to become philosophical knowledge, or if a philos-

32. Maritain, *Poetry*, 66.

33. See Maritain, *Time*, 225–255.

34. See Jacques Maritain, *Natural Law: Reflections on Theory and Practice*, edited by William Sweet (South Bend, Indiana: St. Augustine's Press, 2001), 13–24—hereafter referred to as *Natural Law*.

35. Ibid., 15–16.

36. Artistic connaturality engenders knowledge of the self and things other than the self, and if we concentrate on this non-conceptual awareness apart from the creative surge toward the production of a work of art, we have something similar to knowledge by intersubjective, affective connaturality. And revelation itself, through the super-analogy of faith, offers us the self's love for others as an image of God's love for us. In the love between father and son, husband and wife, shepherd and flock, we experience something like the supra-natural, affective connaturality which is the experience of love between God and self. See Joseph J. Sikora, SJ, *The Christian Intellect and the Mystery of Being: Reflections of a Maritain Thomist* (The Hague: Martinus Nijhoff, 1966), especially 56–90. For an explanation of the super-analogy of faith, see Jacques Maritain, *Distinguish to Unite or the Degrees of Knowledge*, translated from the fourth French edition under the supervision of Gerald B. Phelan (Notre Dame, Indiana: University of Notre Dame Press, 2011), 256–259, and 298–301.

> ophy which despairs of reason tries to capture those kinds of knowledge through connaturality, and to use them as an instrument—everyone loses his head, knowledge through inclination and metaphysics are simultaneously spoiled.[37]

Maritain considers himself to be in line with many of his contemporaries in their struggle for authenticity, retaining the intellectual apprehension of being from the ancient Thomistic edifice for balance and precision, juggling the non-conceptual and conceptual apprehension of reality and the human person within the arena of the perennial philosophy, always humble before existence and the existent.

For Maritain, then, it is on the connatural level that the vital principal in education, the will of the student naturally inclined toward reality and the human person, is affirmed:

> [I]t is with reference to this preconscious spiritual dynamism of human personality that keeping personal contact with the pupil is of such great import, not only as a better technique for making study more attractive and stimulating, but above all to give to that mysterious identity of the child's soul, which is unknown to himself, and which no techniques can reach, the comforting assurance of being in some way recognized by a human personal gaze, inexpressible either in concept or words.[38]

IV. The Global Context

Above all else, the educator must present a human face to the student. Here we detect affinity with the "face to face" encounter described by Emmanuel Levinas, and the "I-Thou" relationship championed by Martin Buber. It is no wonder that the American philosopher of education, Thomas Groome, acknowledges joint inspiration from the merger of Buber with Maritain. Groome tells of how in the 1970s the Sisters of Jesus and Mary, a French order teaching in Pakistan where many of the Catholic schools were nationalized and predominantly Muslim in faculty and enrollment, remained confident in retaining their Catholic Christian identity as educators by promoting the value of the person in a way which is exceptional in Pakistani society. Many Muslims preferred the schools run by the sisters to the government schools. These parochial schools were successful, Groome tells us, because they would

37. Maritain, *Natural Law*, 23–24.
38. Maritain, *Education*, 41.

promote the value of the person, emphasizing the equal dignity of boys and girls—exceptional in this society; they encourage a positive outlook on life and challenge the fatalism that pervades the surrounding culture; they build up a sense of school community and promote friendship across class and ethnic divides. They also encourage students to develop a personal spirituality, to commit to justice and peace, to respect those who are different. They have strong academic curricula that encourage critical thinking (the government schools favor route learning).[39]

Clearly Groome intends that such a nuanced personal approach taps something fundamental and universal, applicable to the aspirations of the Muslim and Catholic Christian alike. Something fundamental and universal is trans-curricular, as well, in the sense that aspirations beyond the technical confines of any given discipline are awakened. Again from within a Christian context, Maritain asserts

that there are of course no Christian mathematics or Christian astronomy or engineering; but if the teacher has Christian wisdom, and if his teaching overflows from a soul dedicated to contemplation, the *mode* or manner in which his teaching is given—in other words, the mode or manner in which his own soul and mind perform a living and illuminating action on the soul and mind of another human being—will convey to the student and awaken in him something *beyond* mathematics, astronomy, or engineering: first, a sense of the proper place of these disciplines in the universe of knowledge and human thought; second, an unspoken intimation of the immortal value of truth, and of those rational laws and harmony which are at play in things and whose primary roots are in the divine Intellect.[40]

Every educator, the professed Catholic Christian educator and otherwise, must adhere to the two universal, natural, and foundational principles of education: intuition and love. Such adherence entails a profound respect for the freedom of each unique pupil, while respecting the integrity of each discipline through developing reason and imparting the appropriate knowledge. Maritain asserts that in the temporal order

the main duty in the educational spheres of the school as well as of the state is not to shape the will and directly to develop moral virtues in the youth, but to enlighten and strengthen reason; so it is that an indirect influence is exerted on the will, by a sound equipment of knowledge and a sound development of the powers of thinking.[41]

39. Thomas Groome, *Educating for Life: A Spiritual Vision for Every Teacher and Parent* (Allen, Texas: Thomas Moore, 1998), 10; and 9–11 for context.

40. Jacques Maritain, "On Some Typical Aspects of Christian Education," in *The Christian Idea of Education,* edited by Edmund Fuller (New Haven, Connecticut: Yale University Press, 1957), 180.

41. Maritain, *Education,* 27.

Nevertheless, intelligible truths can only be accepted by the primordial truth which is the *suppositum*, the activating core of each person. Succinctly stated: "the prime goal of education is the conquest of internal and spiritual freedom to be achieved by the individual person, or in other words, his liberation through knowledge and wisdom, good will, and love."[42] Maritain concludes that "the principle agent in education, the primary dynamic factor or propelling force, is the internal vital principle in the one to be educated; the educator or teacher is only the secondary—though a genuinely effective—dynamic factor and a ministerial agent."[43]

Liberating the will of each for the truth of each is the primary aim of education, and this means overcoming egoism and the twin disasters of individualism and totalitarianism which egoism engenders—egoism being the expression of a rudderless will detached from reality and the human person. Nothing less than combating the disastrous practical consequences of the philosophy of will is at stake when Maritain writes:

> If it is true that the internal principal, that is to say nature—and grace too, for man is not a merely natural being—is what matters most in education, it follows that the entire art consists in inspiring, schooling and pruning, teaching and enlightening, so that in the intimacy of man's activities the weight of the egoistic tendencies diminishes, and the weight of the aspirations proper to personality and its spiritual generosity increases.[44]

A discussion occurring within the United Nations in the final decade of the twentieth century clarifies and directs Maritain's concerns regarding the significance of education for establishing our humanity within the global community. This enables us to expand the horizon wherein education occurs and indicate the practical implications of this broad view of education for economic development, the improvement of social relations, democratic procedure, and environmental integrity. Here we can delineate some further implications of Maritain's integral education for integral humanism, as called for and briefly developed in *Education at the Crossroads*.[45]

In 1992, the UN Security Council convened in a first-time meeting as heads of State or Government, requesting then Secretary-General Boutros Boutros-Ghali to prepare a report recommending future reforms. The request contains the following choice observation:

42. Ibid., 11.
43. Ibid., 31.
44. Ibid., 35.
45. See ibid., 88–118.

> The absence of war and military conflicts amongst States does not in itself ensure international peace and security. The non-military sources of instability in the economic, social, humanitarian and ecological fields have become threats to peace and security. The United Nations membership as a whole, working through the appropriate bodies, needs to give the highest priority to the solution of these matters.[46]

In his response, *An Agenda for Peace,* Boutros-Ghali indicated the need for international dialogue involving smaller, intermediate communities concerning economic and environmental issues, human rights and democratic procedure, acknowledging prevention of the *casus belli* and peace-building after conflict as the goal.[47] Although Boutros-Ghali necessarily focuses on United Nations initiatives, and regional, local structures in co-operation with the body of the United Nations, a far more pervasive public dialogue is essential. The work of radical thinkers like Michael Hardt and Antonio Negri is helpful, suggesting a dialogue of singularities within the global multitude.[48] It is significant that Hardt, Negri, and Maritain all take issue with the notion of state sovereignty, Maritain pointing out the weakness of the United Nations as a vehicle for sustaining global peace, since it works within the context of sovereign nations.[49]

New economic developments, social justice movements, democratic organizations, and environmental initiatives catalogued and analyzed by innovative economists, David C. Korten and Gar Alperovitz offer a viable foundation for promoting dialogue engaging small, integral communities on a global basis—seeking to address global economic sustainability, environmental integrity, and the fostering of human rights and democracy beyond the boundaries of state sovereignty.[50]

Maritain argues that the human person is the key to peace, and education

46. *Repertoire of the Practice of the Security Council,* chapter 8, 1992, 05-51675, 821

47. See Boutros Boutros-Ghali, *An Agenda for Peace: With the New Supplement and Related UN Documents* (New York: United Nations, 1995).

48. See the trilogy by Michael Hardt and Antonio Negri, *Empire* (Cambridge, Massachuesetts: Harvard University Press, 2000); *Multitude: War and Democracy in the Age of Empire* (New York: The Penguin Press, 2004); and *Commonwealth* (Cambridge, Massacheusetts: The Belknap Press of Harvard University Press, 2011).

49. See Jacques Maritain, *Man and the State,* (Chicago: The University of Chicago Press, 1966), 193–94.

50. See David C. Korten, *Agenda for a New Economy: From Phantom Wealth to Real Wealth,* A publication of the New Economy Working Group (San Francisco: Berrett-Koehler Publishers, 2010); and Gar Alperovitz, *America Beyond Capitalism: Reclaiming our Wealth, Our Liberty, and Our Democracy,* with a new forward by James Gustave Speth (Takoma Park, Maryland: Democracy Collaborative Press; Boston: Dollars and Sense, 2011).

is the process establishing our humanity. He tells us that there is a universal human nature, and that we tap into this nature when we develop as persons within the intimacy of small, caring communities. Maritain tells us that the opposite of the person is the autonomous, self-serving individual, who operates by identifying with the large self-serving structures; according to Maritain, such was the case with Nazi Germany and other totalitarian structures in the twentieth century.

Certainly it can be argued that this gathering together of self-serving individuals too often continues to be the case within the huge impersonal, international corporations and monetary establishments in the twenty-first century. For Maritain, what is required is that all the small, local communities work together against the sources of instability—something anticipated in the community organizing of Maritain's friend and fellow revolutionary, Saul Alinsky, the agnostic radical who acknowledged Maritain as his spiritual father while admitting that he remained a prodigal and wayward son, and who Maritain appreciated as "an anti-racist leader whose methods are as effective as they are unorthodox."[51] Rather than collapsing into anarchy, diverse communities working together become the harbinger of global democracy, wherein we can detect a foundational (albeit not always articulate) agreement based on our universal human nature and the dignity and rights of every person. The classroom and lecture hall merge into the global "teach-in," where intuition and love enable individual human beings to become the collective expression of our humanity. In organizations like the International Forum on Globalization (IFG) and meetings like the World Social Forum (WSF)—both of which have benefited from the inspiration and direction of the Catholic Christian activist Maude Barlow and her Council of Canadians—we see research and education emerging from a North-South dialogue addressing economic sustainability, environmental integrity, and issues related to human rights and social justice. We see the dissemination of information and ideas from a plethora of sources in the global dialogue and activity within various anti-austerity and pro-democracy movements exemplified in the global Occupy move-

51. Jacques Maritain, *The Peasant of the Garonne: An Old Layman Questions Himself about the Present Time*, translated by Michael Cuddihy and Elizabeth Hughes (New York: Holt, Rinehart and Winston, 1968), 23 n. 16; and see *Reflections on America* (New York: Charles Scribner's Sons, 1958), 164–66. See also Bernard E. Doering, "Jacques Maritain and His Two 'Authentic Revolutionaries,'" in *Thomistic Papers III*, edited by Leonard A. Kennedy, CSB (Notre Dame, Indiana. University of Notre Dame, 1987), 91–116, especially 102.

ment which began with Occupy Wall Street in 2011. We see this coming together, this cohesion of otherness, even in the ubiquitous Guy Fawkes mask, originally adopted by Anonymous, rapidly becoming a symbol of revolt for many diverse causes throughout the world. Here we detect movement toward what Maritain presents, in *Man and the State,* as the ideal fully political world society, freely formed, encompassing multifarious institutions and communities within the global body politic, avoiding the merely governmental solution of world Empire.[52] Engaged and on the street is where we should be as educators, acknowledging and nurturing intuition and love, while guiding this natural process through the mine fields of the ideologues, away from the anarchy of rudderless wills with its totalitarian flipside.

The simple truth explaining this coming together is the consistent nature of the human being inclined through intuition and love, the nurturing of which is the task of every educator. Perspectives may differ, but adherence to reality and the human person through intuition and love can lead us to our humanity. Maritain drew attention to this camaraderie of diversity, this coming together of people with different points of view, when he formulated the notion of a shared "practical secular faith," whereby a very diverse human choir attains harmony through similar practical principles and in the end the same human goals, because, Maritain tells us, "they similarly revere, perhaps for quite diverse reasons, truth and intelligence, human dignity, freedom, brotherly love, and the absolute value of moral good."[53] Such reverence can only emerge from the pre-conceptual apprehension of reality and the human person, so with acceptance, generosity, and care the conceptual clarity available to us will follow. Maritain forthrightly states that the task of preparing a world society "will obviously develop first of all as a deep and continuing task of education and enlightenment, discussion and study."[54]

Returning to the classroom and lecture hall, this pluralistic perspective in tune with a common human identity and goals is paramount. The spirit of Meudon permeates Maritain's approach to education and the establishment of our humanity. Between the two great wars of the twentieth century, the openness of the Meudon gatherings and private encounters extended far beyond the strictly academic community, into the worlds of the

52. See Maritain, *Man and the State,* 188–216.

53. Ibid., 111.

54. Ibid., 213.

most controversial artists and poets. At Meudon, the intuition and love detectable in the popular poetry, novels, and films of a figure as controversial as Jean Cocteau was welcome, although in the end Cocteau managed to elude Maritain's nurturing and guidance of that intuition and love.[55] As already noted in the introduction to this essay, Maritain knew that "not every love is right, nor every intuition well directed and conceptualized"; nevertheless, he adamantly maintained that "if either intuition or love exists in any hidden corner, life and the flame of life are there, and a bit of heaven in a promise." In a broken world, we must suffer derailments; but, as indicated in this essay through the words of Maritain, the hope for our future remains with "the principal agent in education, the primary dynamic factor or propelling force, the internal vital principal in the one to be educated."

In one of his stories, "Teddy," J. D. Salinger, a controversial American author who undoubtedly would have been welcome at Meudon, has a more than precocious twelve-year-old lament his parents' failure to appreciate the fundamental significance of the person in regard to his sister and himself. "They don't seem able to love us just the way we are," Teddy says to his sister in reference to their parents, "unless they can keep changing us a little bit. They love their reasons for loving us almost as much as they love us, and most of the time more. It's not so good that way."[56] Without the subjugation of methodical pedagogy, and even the rationale of sound doctrine, to the human good of the internal vital principle captivated by intuition and love, in education as in every human endeavour, it is love and the authentic appropriation of knowledge that is being denied.

55. See Jean-Luc Barré, *Jacques and Raïssa Maritain: Beggars for Heaven*, translated by Bernard E. Doering (Notre Dame, Indiana: University of Notre Dame Press, 2005), 180–226; and Stephen Schloesser, *Jazz Age Catholicism: Mystic Modernism in Postwar Paris, 1919–1933* (Toronto: University of Toronto Press, 2005), 173–203.

56. J. D. Salinger, "Teddy," in *Nine Stories* (Toronto: Little, Brown, 1986), 187.

STEPHEN CHAMBERLAIN

Interpreting the Times

The Philosopher's Understanding in Engaging the World

I. Introduction

IN HIS BRIEF ADDRESS, "A mes amis de New York," Jacques Maritain states, "the great question for us is if the doctrine and inspiration of Thomas Aquinas are able to take new forms and to disengage their cultural potentialities in a manner pure and free enough to be accepted by and to quicken the mental structures of the world."[1] Throughout his life's work, Maritain tirelessly attempted to do just this—to engage the world and confront the challenges of his day in light of the universal and necessary principles of St. Thomas Aquinas. Indeed, one might suggest that Maritain's value as an intellectual lay as much in the practical ways in which he actively engaged the world and his intellectual contemporaries as it does in the more theoretical and strictly philosophical ways in which he developed a "living Thomism" in such fields as metaphysics, epistemology, political philosophy, and the philosophy of art.

This essay will examine the structural underpinnings that make a philosopher's engagement with the world both possible and fruitful. That is, rather than consider the particular challenges of Maritain's own day or even those of today, we will undertake a meta-analysis of the philosopher in relation to the particulars of his time; or, to put it another way, we will consider

1. Jacques Maritain, "A mes amis de New York," in *Pour la justice: Articles et discours (1940–1945)* (New York: Editions de la maison francaise, 1945), 194.

the intentional structure and virtue of the philosopher insofar as he takes on the role of cultural critic. In doing this, we will attempt to show how an Aristotelian-Thomistic philosophical psychology undergirds and explains the specific virtue or disposition (*habitus*) of the philosopher insofar as he interprets the times against the backdrop of universal values, principles, and causes. Such an aim is particularly significant and challenging to the Thomist philosopher who holds to the possibility of adequately grasping common natures such that the acquisition of universal knowledge is the very aim and end of philosophical activity as such. Thus, unlike many of his anti-metaphysical contemporaries who have taken the various byways off the hermeneutic turn, and in doing so, have reduced all philosophical activity to cultural criticism, the Thomist philosopher, if he is to maintain the proper orders of knowing, must clarify the intentional differences between the philosopher *qua* philosopher and the philosopher *qua* cultural critic.

In undertaking this task, we will focus on two central notions. First, we will examine the intellectual virtue of *understanding* (*sunesis*) as discussed by Aristotle in book 6 of the *Nicomachean Ethics*. Unlike the other well-known intellectual virtues discussed in book 6 (namely, *phronêsis, epistēmē, and technē*), most scholars have tended to neglect the virtue of *sunesis*. In the *Nicomachean Ethics*—and elsewhere to my knowledge—Aristotle does not elaborate in much detail upon *sunesis* as a specific intellectual virtue. Nonetheless, his rather brief analysis does suggest how *sunesis* can be considered a hybrid virtue that integrates qualities of both practical wisdom (*phronêsis*) and speculative wisdom (*epistēmē*). These qualities, we will argue, are essential for the cultural critic insofar as he offers a truthful analysis of the movements or trends of his day. As one who exhibits understanding (*sunesis*), the cultural critic shares certain attributes of both the virtuous statesman or ethicist and the virtuous philosopher as speculative scientist.

After offering a sketch of the intentional structure of *sunesis*, we will then show how the notion of understanding as an intellectual virtue can be developed and deepened through a Thomistic account of the cogitative power or particular reason (*ratio particularis*), that faculty which the cultural critic must sharpen and perfect in correctly interpreting the times. For it is through the cogitative faculty that intuitive reason, in its instrumental use of the internal sense power, is able to perceive and in turn interpret the particulars of one's age, not merely "in-themselves," that is, as possessing common natures, which is the proper aim and end of the cognitive activity of the philosopher as such. Rather, the judgment attained in understanding takes place through a comparative process that considers the *relational-being* of particulars within a semiotic nexus—that is to say, within a complex world of interrelated signs. Particular reason, then, is a contextual reason which, while employing speculative wisdom concerning common natures, eternal values and universal principles, likewise relies upon the acute and sensitive perception of particulars (*aísthēsis*) within this semiotic nexus or complex world of signs. Such perception is essential, we will argue, to the success or virtue of the philosopher as cultural critic.

II. The Virtue of Understanding (*Sunesis*) According to Aristotle

In book 6 the *Nicomachean Ethics*, Aristotle makes his well-known distinctions between the different orders of reason and the corresponding intellectual virtues of knowledge, namely, practical wisdom (*phronêsis*), speculative wisdom (*epistēmē*) and productive wisdom (*technê*). What is less known, however, is Aristotle's identification of another specific virtue of knowledge, that is, *sunesis* or understanding. As mentioned above, although Aristotle does not discuss this specific intellectual virtue in much detail, it is a highly suggestive notion in terms of his recognition of an intentional order that incorporates aspects of both practical wisdom and speculative wisdom and yet remains distinct from each one.

First, understanding (*sunesis*) is similar to practical wisdom (*phronêsis*) insofar as both virtues are concerned with the same objects, namely, those goods of the practical realm. In chapter 10 of book 6, Aristotle states that "understanding (*sunesis*) is neither about things that are always and are unchangeable, nor about any and every one of the things that come into being, but about things which may become subjects of questioning and deliberation. Hence, it is about the same objects as practical wisdom" (1143a5-8).[2] In other words, understanding is directed neither at universal essences (like speculative wisdom) nor at objects to be produced (like technical wisdom); rather it is concerned with the particulars of the practical realm that involve "questioning and deliberation." Previously in bk. 6,

2. Unless otherwise indicated, all references from Aristotle's *Nicomachean Ethics* will be from *Ethica Nicomachea,* translated by W. D. Ross in *The Basic Works of Aristotle*, edited by Richard McKeon (New York: Random House, 1941).

Aristotle defined practical wisdom (*phronêsis*) as one's ability "to deliberate well about what is good and expedient for himself" and "what sorts of thing conduce to the good life in general" (1140a26-28). *Phronêsis*, then, is "a true and reasoned state of capacity to act with regard to the things that are good or bad for man" (1140b 5–6). Insofar as understanding shares the same concern for the particular objects of practical wisdom, it is also concerned with what is good both for oneself and the good life in general.

Aristotle goes on to say, however, that the intellectual virtues of understanding and practical wisdom remain distinct, for the end or conclusion of practical reasoning is the concrete choice and in turn action (what is to be done or not done), whereas the end or conclusion of understanding is merely the judgment or act of cognition. As Aristotle puts it, "understanding and practical wisdom are not the same. For practical wisdom issues commands, since its end is what ought to be done or not to be done; but understanding only judges" (1143a8-10). In this manner, then, understanding is more like speculative wisdom insofar as it seeks knowledge for its own sake, at least in the intentional order of concluding with an act of cognition or apprehension of truth. For this reason, Aristotle compares understanding to speculative wisdom (*epistēmē*) in that both are forms of learning.[3] Hence, understanding is similar to speculative wisdom in concluding with a judgment or an act of cognition rather than a concrete choice, while remaining dissimilar to speculative wisdom insofar as it is not directed at universal natures or essences, but instead at the particular objects or goods that involve deliberation regarding how humans being should live or the good life in general.[4]

Now one of the most significant features of Aristotle's ethical theory is his emphasis upon the role of perception (*aísthēsis*) in practical reasoning.

3. Or, in other words, understanding is similar to *learning*, which is the acquisition of speculative or scientific knowledge. Aristotle states, "Now understanding is neither the having nor the acquiring of practical wisdom; but as learning is called understanding when it means the exercise of the faculty of knowledge, so 'understanding' is applicable to the exercise of the faculty of opinion for the purpose of judging of what someone else says about matters with which practical wisdom is concerned—and of judging soundly; for 'well' and 'soundly' are the same thing. And from this has come the use of the name 'understanding' in virtue of which men are said to be of 'good understanding,' viz. from the application of the word to the grasping of scientific truth; for we often call such grasping understanding" (1143a11-19).

4. As Aristotle states, "Nor is practical wisdom concerned with universals only—it must also recognize the particulars; for it is practical, and practice is concerned with particulars" (1141b14-16).

Unlike many rationalist accounts, Aristotle insists that practical reason involves the whole person insofar as proper deliberation or correct reasoning synthesizes or "is in agreement with" appropriate appetition and emotional dispositions.[5] Hence, the discernment of what is good or bad for human beings and in turn the good life in general is the acquisition of truth that essentially includes an acute and sensitively attuned perception of particulars. This perception (*aísthēsis*), as the root word indicates, is aesthetic, which should be understood in the broad sense of the term. Moreover, as Aristotle indicates, this aesthetic perception is intuitive.[6] This aesthetic, intuitive perception, then, involves the whole person insofar as the senses, imagination, and emotions, along with reason, are all employed.[7] As Martha Nussbaum, who has written extensively on the roles of the imagination and emotions in Aristotle's account of perception and in turn practical reason, puts it: "Good perception is a full recognition or acknowledgement of the nature of the practical situation; the whole personality sees it for what it is."[8] To summarize the distinction, the practically wise person can be defined as the one who *chooses* and in turn *acts* according to the correspondence of right reason and a perception that incorporates the appropriate emotional response in particular circumstances, whereas the understanding person is the one who *judges* correctly regarding this practical, contextual realm. [9]

Because the cultivation of the intellectual virtue of understanding, like the virtue of practical wisdom, involves the proper emotional disposition and attunement toward particulars, Aristotle specifically highlights the role

5. "[W]hile of the part which is practical and intellectual the good state is truth in agreement with right desire" (1139a30-31).

6. "[N]ot only must the man of practical wisdom know particular facts, but understanding and judgment are also concerned with things to be done, and these are ultimates.... [T]he intuitive reason involved in practical reasoning grasps the last and variable fact, i.e., the minor premise. For these variable facts are the starting-points for the apprehension of the end, since the universals are reached from the particulars; of these therefore we must have perception, and this perception is intuitive reason" (1143a33-1143b6).

7. 1139a33-35.

8. Martha Nussbaum, "The Discernment of Perception: An Aristotelian Conception of Private and Public Rationality," in *Love's Knowledge: Essays on Philosophy and Literature* (Oxford: Oxford University Press, 1990), 79.

9. One might suggest that the understanding person may well lack the effective *will* and in turn *habitus* of the practically wise person in *acting* upon this judgment, which is why the virtue of *sunesis* must be distinguished from *phronêsis*. Again, as Aristotle says, "For practical wisdom issues commands, since its end is what ought to be done or not to be done; but understanding only judges" (1143a8-10).

of sympathy in the discernment of what is equitable or just (i.e., true) in the concrete contextual situation. Aristotle writes that "the equitable man is above all others a man of sympathetic judgment, and identifies equity with sympathetic judgment about certain facts. And sympathetic judgment is judgment which discriminates what is equitable and does so correctly; and correct judgment is that which judges what is true" (1143a22-24). This "correct judgment" that apprehends what is true according to the particulars (i.e., "facts") is, then, a sympathetic cognition or judgment that again involves the whole person in the recognition of what is just or equitable according to the specific circumstances. Such a sympathetic cognition, in order to judge what is true according to the circumstances, does not "abstract" from the particulars, as does speculative reason, but rather remains within the immanent context in order to apprehend the particulars as particulars and not merely according to their common natures. This capacity to perceive the particulars as particulars requires an acute imaginative and emotional sensitivity toward the subtle complexities of the situation; or, to put it another way, this sympathetic judgment requires the apprehension of the *relational being* of the particulars in the concrete situation. Hence, it is a kind of aesthetic perception in which particulars are apprehended not only according to their common natures, but as particulars in relation to one another and in turn in relation to the whole. This ability to judge what is just or true within a specific context, Nussbaum calls "concrete focusing" or "deliberative imagination."[10] As the terms suggest, such an ability, cultivated as a virtue, requires one to be presently alive to the particular nuances of the present situation while also being expansively open to the possibilities required to maximize the goods to be attained or the harms to be avoided. Moreover, such an acute, sensitive perception of the particulars within their contextual, semiotic interrelations likewise requires the application of universal principles that helps to inform and direct this perception.[11] We can see, then, that both universals and particulars are involved in the true sympathetic judgment of understanding.

10. See Nussbaum, "The Discernment of Perception," 77–82.

11. We might note here that Nussbaum, despite her otherwise helpful development and analysis of the notions of concrete focusing and deliberative imagination, does not place sufficient emphasis upon the role of universal principles in the apprehension of what is true or correct in the concrete situation. See Hillary Putnam, "Taking Rules Seriously: A Response to Martha Nussbaum," *New Literary History* 15 (1983): 193–200.

III. The Role of the Cogitative Power in the Virtue of Understanding

In this next section, we will discuss the role of Thomas's particular reason (*ratio particularis*), or more specifically, the cogitative power (*vis cogitativa*), as it pertains to the cultivation of understanding, which is the virtue of the philosopher as cultural critic. In his *Commentary on Aristotle's "Nicomachean Ethics"*, bk. 6, Thomas's main focus, as is Aristotle's, is upon the elaboration of the essence of practical wisdom (*phronêsis*). In his analysis of bk. 6, chap. 10, however, Aquinas clarifies those same distinctions made by Aristotle regarding the virtue of understanding (*sunesis*).

Thomas begins by pointing out that understanding is directed at the same objects of practical reason (i.e., "matters worthy of deliberation"), which as an intentional mode makes it distinct from both speculative reason (*epistēmē*) and technical reason (*technê*).[12] At the same time, understanding remains distinct from practical wisdom in that it concludes in a cognition or judgment (i.e., an act of understanding) rather than in a practical choice and in turn a concrete action. [13] In this respect, then, understanding is more like speculative reason insofar as it is a form of learning such that its aim or end, in its intentional structure, is knowledge for its own sake. [14] Moreover, Thomas also points out that unlike speculative reason, understanding requires an appropriate emotional involvement and response, namely, sympathy or clemency, if one is to judge equitably or justly according to the particulars of the concrete circumstances. [15] This requires that the objects of

12. "Since *synesis* is concerned with matters worthy of deliberation which prudence also considers, as was noted above (1164), it follows that *synesis* is concerned with the things treated by prudence" (L.9, 1237). Thomas Aquinas, *Commentary on the "Nicomachean Ethics"*, translated by C. I. Litzinger, OP (Chicago: Henry Regnery Company, 1964).

13. "However, practical reason does not stop here but proceeds further to do something. Hence there is required a third work, as it were final and perfecting, viz., to command that the thing be done. This properly belongs to prudence" (1239). "Consequently, he says that prudence is preceptive inasmuch as the work of the end is to determine what must be done. But *synesis* merely makes a judgment" (L.9, 1240).

14. "But just as learning, which is the use of knowledge, is called *syniene* in Greek, so also the practical evaluation used by someone to judge things about which prudence treats is called *syniene*. This can even be called judging well, by another, for *eu* in Greek means the same as "well." Hence the name *synesis*, in accord with which some are called *eusyneti* (as it were men of good judgment or of good sense), is derived from this word *syniene* which is used in connection with learning. Indeed we often call learning *syniene*" (L.9, 1241).

15. "The equitable man is especially (*syngnomonicum*) inclined to kindness, as it were tem-

cognition are apprehended as singulars or "particular ultimates" according to their relational being within the contextual and semiotic totality, and so are not grasped merely as objects "in themselves." In other words, although these objects may be considered according to their common natures, they are also evaluated as goods in relation to one another. As Thomas puts it, "equitable things ... in general can be compared to all human goods inasmuch as each of them has a reference to another—a thing pertaining to the nature of justice."[16] That is, only by apprehending such particulars in reference to one another can one judge what is equitable or just (i.e., true) according to the situation.

Now one of the distinctive features of Thomas's epistemology is that the intellect only apprehends singulars according to their universal natures and hence not as particular, which is to say, not in their individuality, strictly speaking. For this reason, the apprehension of the particular as particular always requires, for rational animals, the employment of the sense faculties in some respect.[17] Thus, while identifying understanding (*sunesis*) as an intellectual virtue, Thomas ascribes the power which apprehends the objects of understanding, namely singularities or ultimate particulars, to a sense faculty. This specific power of understanding is the internal sense faculty of particular reason (*ratio particularis*), which in human beings is called the cogitative power (*vis cogitativa*).[18]

Before examining the cogitative power, which is specific to human beings as rational animals, it is worth noting a more general aspect that applies to all animals who possess the generic internal sense power of estimation. In *Summa Theologiae*, q. 78, a. 4, Thomas identifies four internal sense powers, namely, common sense, imagination, memory, and instinct (i.e., the estimative

---

pering judgment with a certain clemency.... The virtue *syngnome* rightly judges what is equitable, and is correct when it judges what is true" (L.9, 1244).

16. L.9, 1246.

17. Actually this is true of "abstract" speculative apprehension as well, though in a different respect, as shall be discussed in further detail below.

18. In the *Commentary on Aristotle's "Nichomachean Ethics"*, Thomas states, "Because singulars are properly known by the senses, it is necessary that man should have experience of these singulars (which we say are principles and ultimates) not just by exterior but by interior sense as well.... [P]ractical wisdom belongs to the sensory power of judging called particular reason. Hence this sense is called understanding whose object is the sensible and singular" (L.9, 1249). Also, "We say that prudence, *synesis*, and gnome pertain to understanding [*intellectus*]. However, this is called particular reason, inasmuch as it concludes from one to another.... Therefore he said it (particular reason) deals with particular ultimates" (L.9, 1255).

power). The estimative power or instinct is common to all higher animals insofar as they are able to judge particular objects or goods (intentions) as not immediately pleasurable but rather as useful or fitting. The recognition of an immediate good as pleasurable (e.g., food) only requires within its unified operation the two distinct acts of sense cognition and appetition, and therefore the external senses and appetite are sufficient to explain the apprehension of an immediate good or evil that, as pleasurable or painful, is directly sought or avoided. However, the apprehension of a useful good (what Aquinas calls a "difficult good") requires a third distinct act that judges the object to be useful or harmful according to the animal knower's overall well-being. Thus, as the estimative power, instinct judges the practical value of the sense object according to its contribution or threat to the well-being of the animal knower and perhaps its community. In other words, instinct interprets and evaluates the practical object according to its overall utility or harmfulness.[19]

Aquinas goes on to distinguish this generic power of instinct that is proper to all higher animals in terms of its specific difference in rational animals. Higher non-rational animals perceive particular intentions according to a natural instinct that evaluates singular objects within their environment. [20] For non-rational animals this environment is, as Jacob von Uexkull terms it, an *Umwelt,* which is to say, a bio-semiotic nexus.[21] In contrast, one can say that the world of the human animal is a *Lebenswelt* in which singular objects are evaluated and interpreted not merely by natural instinct but through a comparative process appropriate to rational animals. Such evalu-

19. As Aquinas states, "an animal has to seek and shun things not only because they suit or do not suit its senses but also because they are in other ways fitting and useful or harmful. Thus a lamb, when it sees a wolf approach, flees, not because it does not like the color or shape, but because it is its natural enemy. And likewise a bird collects straw, not because it pleases its senses, but because it needs it for building a nest. So the animal has to perceive things which no external sense perceives. And there has to be a distinct source of this perception since the perception of sense forms comes from their impact on the senses but not the perception of the intentions in question here." *Summa Theologiae* I, q. 78, a. 4, translated by Timothy Suttor (Cambridge: Cambridge University Press, 2006), pp. 138–39.

20. As Klubertanz also puts it, "Because the estimative is the highest power of the animal, it follows that all purely sense cognition will *ultimately* be practical. In other words, the final limit, the highest type of purely animal knowledge is the apprehension of the individual in so far as the latter is the term of material action or passion." George P. Klubertanz, *The Discursive Power: Sources and Doctrine of the* Vis Cogitativa *According to St. Thomas Aquinas* (St. Louis, Missouri: The Modern Schoolman, 1952), 274–75.

21. For a Thomistic reading of Jacob von Uexkull's notion of *Umwelt,* see Josef Pieper, "The Philosophical Act," *Leisure: The Basis of Culture,* translated by Alexander Dru (San Francisco: Ignatius Press, 2009), 95–97.

ation involves particular reason (*ratio particularis*) or the cogitative power (*vis cogitativa*). As Thomas says, "what we call natural instinct in other animals in man we call cogitation, which comes upon intentions of this kind in question through a process of comparison. Which is why it is also called the particular reason ... for it compares individual intentions the way reasoning intellect compares universal intentions."[22] The cogitative power, then, although it is a sense faculty, is nonetheless infused by the intellect such that it evaluates particular objects in several ways: (a) according to their common natures, (b) as particular individuals in their particularities, and (c) as particulars in relation to other particulars within the context of the concrete situation. While the cogitative faculty is understood, strictly speaking, to be an internal sense faculty, it is ordered toward and directed by the intellect such that it compares ultimate particulars or individual intentions in a way that is distinct from non-rational animals. As Aquinas puts it:

> the cogitative faculty differs from natural instinct. *The former apprehends the individual thing as existing in a common nature, and this because it is united to intellect in one and the same subject.* Hence it is aware of a man as this *man*, and this tree as this *tree*; whereas instinct is not aware of an individual thing as in a common nature, but only in so far as this individual thing is the term or principle of some action or passion.[23]

In this way, particulars can be variously apprehended as good or valuable: (a) in themselves as individuals (e.g., *this* man as good), (b) according to their common nature (e.g., this *man* as good), and (c) as particular in relation to other particulars within the concrete situation (this man as good *in relation to* and so *qualified by* other *particular goods*).

Above we related how, in the Thomistic noetic order of knowing, the intellect by itself cannot know particulars as particulars, requiring instead the mediation of a lower sense power that acts as the instrumental means

22. "Consider now that so far as sense forms are concerned there is no difference between men and other animals; they are affected in the same way by external sense objects. But when it comes to the intentions just discussed there is a difference, for other animals perceive such intentions solely by natural instinct, whereas man perceives them by a process of comparison. And so what we call natural instinct in other animals in man we call cogitation, which comes upon intentions of this kind in question through a process of comparison. Which is why it is also called the particular reason ... for it compares individual intentions the way reasoning intellect compares universal intentions." ST I, q. 78, a. 4, pp. 140–41.

23. *Thomas Aquinas, Commentary on Aristotle's "De Anima"* II. *6, lt.*13; translated by Kenelm Foster, OP and Sylvester Humphries, OP (New Haven, Connecticut: Yale University Press, 1951), html edition by Joseph Kenny, OP; italics mine.

through which the mind knows the particular. In *De veritate* (10.5), Thomas discusses how the mind in relation to the particular operates in two directions. In the abstractive process of speculative reason, the mind moves from particulars to universals, that is from individuals to common natures. In the application of practical reason, the mind moves from universals to particulars insofar as it recognizes common natures in individuals and so chooses and acts accordingly. In this first movement, the mind attains knowledge of the universal nature of singulars through an abstractive process of theoretical thinking. In this abstractive process the mind moves from the particular to the general in order to know the singular as universal through the abstract concept that returns to the phantasm in making its judgment. [24] Practical reason, on the other hand, remains within the immanent world of particulars in order to decide upon a proper course of action in regard to the particulars, typically doing so in light of common natures and universal principles. What is significant here is the distinction between the two internal sense faculties that are employed in the two movements. The first movement relies primarily on the sense faculty of imagination in returning to the phantasm of the speculative judgment, while the second movement relies primarily on the cogitative faculty in evaluating particulars within the context of the specific circumstances. [25]

In *De Veritate*, Thomas is concerned with making some essential distinctions between theoretical reason and practical reason. Given the above anal-

24. In *De Veritate*, Aquinas makes this distinction in the following way: "Nevertheless, the mind has contact with singulars by reason of something else in so far as it has continuity with the sensitive powers which have particulars for their object. This conjunction comes about in two ways. First, the movement of the sensitive part terminates in the mind, as happens in the movement that goes from things to the soul. Thus, the mind knows singulars through a certain kind of reflection, as when the mind, in knowing its object, which is some universal nature, returns to knowledge of its own act, then to the species which is the principle of its act, and, finally, to the phantasm from which it has abstracted the species. In this way, it attains to some knowledge about singulars." Thomas Aquinas, *Truth*, q. 10, a. 5, c., translated by James V. McGlynn, SJ (Chicago: Henry Regnery Company, 1953), p. 23.

25. Aquinas states, "In the other way, this conjunction is found in the movement from the soul to things, which begins from the mind and moves forward to the sensitive part in the mind's control over the lower powers. Here, the mind has contact with singulars through the mediation of particular reason, a power of the sensitive part, which joins and divides individual intentional likenesses, which is also known as the cogitative power.... The mind's universal judgment about things to be done cannot be applied to a particular act except through the mediation of some intermediate power which perceives the singular. In this way, there is framed a kind of syllogism whose major premise is universal, the decision of the mind, and whose minor premise is singular, a perception of the particular reason. The conclusion is the choice of the singular work, as is clear in *The Soul*." Ibid.

ysis of understanding (*sunesis*), we are now in a position to identify a third operation or intentional structure that is both similar to and distinct from these other two movements. Similar to practical reason, understanding is not concerned primarily with the universal natures of theoretical reason (*epistēmē*); likewise, it is not concerned with the objects-to-be-produced of technical reason (*technê*). Rather, as we have seen, it is concerned with the same objects or particular goods of practical reason. However, unlike practical reason, understanding is more like speculative reason in that it terminates not in choice and concrete action, but in the judgment or act of understanding. It is therefore a kind of knowledge for its own sake, though this knowledge pertains not to universal natures as such, but to the immanent world of the concrete situation. If the concrete situation in question need not be reduced to a rather confined concrete situation, but instead may be expanded to the larger cultural milieu of the present age, then the act of understanding is likewise the aim and end of the cultural critic: the intentional structure of the critic's understanding is distinct from the term or end of the political or social *activist* on the one hand, and the political or social *scientist*, on the other.

IV. The Philosopher as Cultural Critic

We have argued that the virtue of the cultural critic (insofar as she accurately interprets the times in making true or correct judgments) is a species of the virtue of understanding (*sunesis*). Hence, what is required in discerning the "present age" is both an adequate grasp of universal natures, values, and principles, as well as an acute perception and, in turn, interpretation of particulars, one which considers particulars as particulars, and so within the context of their semiotic interrelations, which is to say, in terms of their *relational being*, rather than merely their entitative or essential being. Given these assumptions, we can then ask what additional attributes or qualities are required for the Thomist philosopher to fruitfully engage the world as cultural critic, in order that, as Maritain puts it, "the doctrine and inspiration of Thomas Aquinas are able to take new forms and to disengage their cultural potentialities in a manner pure and free enough to be accepted by and to quicken the mental structures of the world." [26]

As we have seen, speculative wisdom as science is concerned with com-

26. Jacques Maritain, "A mes amis de New York," 194.

monalities, whereas understanding, like practical wisdom, is concerned primarily with particulars. Moreover, this perception of particulars, as we have also seen, can be called *aesthetic* in the broad sense of the term. The aesthetic nature of the perception of particulars suggests four additional attributes or qualities that the philosopher must embody as cultural critic in cultivating and perfecting the virtue of understanding.

First, although the cultural critic, as a person of understanding, is concerned with particulars, she is not (like the person of practical wisdom) primarily concerned with choice and in turn concrete action, for understanding is again more like speculative wisdom insofar as the aim and end of the intentional activity is the judgment or act of understanding. Thus, although cultural criticism can and typically should lead to political and social activism, the intentional aim and end of the cognitive activity of cultural criticism, strictly speaking, is not choice and concrete action, but rather knowledge insofar as such criticism leads to broader and deeper awareness of the cultural condition or situation. Because this intentional orientation is distinct from the statesmen, activist, or even concerned citizen as such, who are again more directly aimed at choice and concrete action, the cultural critic enjoys greater latitude or freedom in her critical analysis. Although the cultural critic engages the world insofar as she considers the particulars as particulars, she maintains a certain critical or aesthetic distance, one that is analogous, perhaps, to that of the speculative thinker in his theoretical or contemplative orientation toward the world.

Second, the perception of particulars is aesthetic not only in the apprehension of sensible objects in reading the signs of the age, but also in the intuitive judgment concerning what is "fitting" or "appropriate." Like the person of practical wisdom, the person of understanding must weigh or measure various particular goods in their interrelations in order to judge what is fitting or best. What makes ethical judgment so difficult, of course, is often the clash of competing goods or values such that one must consider them in relation to one another and with an eye toward the unforeseeable end or whole of the good life (individually or collectively). To put it another way, the critic must interpret the parts in relation to the whole so as to discern the right balance, proportion, and integrity—properties that are, *mutatis mutandis,* essential qualities of the classical notion of beauty. This is not to suggest that ethical judgment or the understanding of the cultural critic is reducible to aesthetic judgment, in the narrow sense of aesthetic beauty, but it is to claim that both kinds of judgment involve a subtle intuitive and interpretative perceptiveness of the parts or particulars in relation to the whole. Indeed, the role of the cultural critic is often not to disclaim or disqualify some cultural value or principle, understood universally, but rather to show how in the concrete cultural situation, there is or can be an imbalance, disproportion, or lack of integrity as concerning those particulars in relation to and as directed toward the individual or common good as a whole. In this respect, we suggest that the cultural critic is similar to a certain kind of literary writer, particularly the novelist, who is able to read the signs of the age and in turn "sniff out" various trends, movements, or tendencies within a local, national, or global culture. Such trends or tendencies, expressed universally, might well have merit and legitimacy, and yet in the concrete context are disproportionate, imbalanced, or lack integrity. Thus, the cultural critic must possess an intuitive perceptiveness—as well as, perhaps, a degree of hermeneutic suspicion—in reading and in turn interpreting the particular signs of the present age.

Thirdly, as we saw above, in making equitable judgments concerning particulars, the person of understanding must integrate appropriate emotional dispositions, such as sympathy or clemency. Here too, then, is an additional attribute not necessarily required for adequate speculative analysis, in the strict sense, but one that is required for adequate cultural criticism. Like the novelist, who must display a degree of sympathy for her characters, even the wicked ones, the cultural critic, who deals not with possible particulars but actual ones, must likewise habituate a sympathetic attitude in order to make equitable judgments. As Thomas states, "the equitable man is especially (*syngnomonicum*) inclined to kindness, as it were tempering judgment with a certain clemency... The virtue *syngnome* rightly judges what is equitable, and is correct when it judges what is true."[27] Now we might note that the particulars analyzed by the cultural critic are not typically concrete individuals or events, though these may well be the "leaping-off points" for critical analysis. Rather the proper objects of such critiques tend to be the particular trends, movements, and tendencies of the present age. These objects are more abstract than the concrete particulars typically considered by practical reason, since the judgment of understanding concerns a more generalized, though nonetheless contingent, aspect of the cultural situation.

27. L.9, 1244.

At the same time, however, these objects, remaining immanent within the relational being of the contextual situation, are at a lower level of abstraction than the universal natures considered by speculative reason. Here too, then, we find a kind of intentional middle ground of understanding that operates between the concrete contingencies of practical reason and the universal necessities of speculative reason. In this sense, we might suggest that the proper objects of cultural criticism be termed "abstract particulars."

Finally, because the knowledge or understanding of the cultural critic is directed at these so-called abstract particulars, it is neither attained nor expressed through a purely logical, abstract demonstrative reason; rather, it is attained through an intuitive reason, that although at times employing demonstrative reason, is essentially reliant upon the cogitative faculty in perceiving and evaluating particulars as particulars—which is to say, it remains within the immanent realm or relational being of the contingent contextual situation. Although the evaluative analysis happens at a higher abstractive or generalized level, it remains within the relational being of the interrelated semiotic context. Thus, what is required in the discovery and in turn communication of such understanding is not a purely, logical, analytic demonstrative reason that employs abstract concepts and arguments. Rather, what is required is a rhetorical skill, one that is able to enlighten and disclose the abstract particulars of the present age. This it must do in a persuasive and not analytically demonstrative way, precisely because again the abstract particulars it considers are contingent rather than necessary.

It is interesting to consider Maritain himself in light of the four additional attributes that we are suggesting are required for the philosopher as cultural critic, namely: (1) the disposition of a certain aesthetic or contemplative distance from the objects of one's analysis; (2) an acute intuitive and aesthetic attunement or perceptiveness of particulars; (3) the habit of sympathy or clemency; and (4) a rhetorical skill that complements a sharp, analytic acumen. For it would seem that Maritain possessed such additional attributes, along with the more strictly speculative qualities that belong to the philosopher as such. We should not be surprised, then, that Maritain exhibited such understanding as he interpreted the issues of his own day.

III

THOMISTIC ANTHROPOLOGY

BRIAN KEMPLE

Jacques Maritain and *Ens ut Primum Cognitum*

I. Introduction

"ILLUD QUOD PRIMO CADIT in apprehensione, est ens, cuius intellectus includitur in omnibus quaecumque quis apprehendit"—"That which first falls into the apprehension is being, which is included by the intellect in all else that it apprehends."[1] What is this being which is first known? Is it, as many seem to assume, that which exists independently of cognitive awareness, often called *ens reale*? For St. Thomas himself, this was not a question needing any further discussion than the few brief passages he sporadically gave. For today's student of the Angelic Doctor, however, living in the increasingly complex and developing world of socially-determined structures, we must make a deeper investigation. The posited existence of social realities—which all admit practically, if not speculatively—requires us to examine the most fundamental principle of a Thomistic theory of knowledge, being as it is first known.

This question remains, as of yet, underexamined in no small part because the first half of the twentieth century saw Thomists preeminently concerned with overcoming the philosophy of idealism. To this end, St. Thomas' teaching that being is the first known was very often interpreted within realist philosophies to mean that *ens ut primum cognitum* is *ens reale*. This assumption carries a train of unfortunate consequences, especially a theory of knowledge incapable of dealing adequately with the suprasubjective

1. Thomas Aquinas, *Summa Theologiae* I II, q. 94, a. 2, c. My translation

elements of human experience, including socially-constructed realities. The ardor of these Thomists for overcoming idealism does not, however, diminish the great benefits to be found in their teachings on the development of human knowledge, and indeed, it is not a far step from their position to ours. With the goal of taking this step, we propose to make a substantial investigation of the teaching of Jacques Maritain, especially in his *Preface to Metaphysics* and *Degrees of Knowledge*. We will show his contributions to the Thomistic doctrines of abstraction, namely, the emphasis he places upon the positive aspect of this act; second, the process of concept formation and the nature of the object of the concept; and we will conclude, third, by briefly considering the root of Maritain's philosophy of being as it relates to his philosophy of knowledge, and will provide a suggestion as to how we can develop our understanding of this teaching of St. Thomas beyond what Maritain has given us.

II. Maritain on Abstraction

Whereas Étienne Gilson shied away from using language which distinguished "object" from the term "thing," there is likely no distinction more important to Maritain's Poinsot-influenced interpretation of St. Thomas' philosophy of knowledge. While Maritain was also strongly concerned with overcoming the idealist hurdle, he nevertheless saw that the knowledge had by human beings is not simply and directly an immediate perception of things as things, but rather that "object and objectivity are the very life and salvation of the intellect,"[2] "object" being said here in the original sense of the Latin *obiectum* as that which is present to a power (and most especially to a cognitive power).[3] While the distinctive mark of the human intellect is its ability to think about a thing *as a thing*—that is, according to the subjective constitution of its own being, as possessing its own reality, independent of relation to the knower—such thinking is impossible unless the thing is *first* and *continually* an object. To quote Maritain:

> [The] object is the term of the first operation of the intellect (simple perception, or "simple apprehension"); what is it therefore if not, under a given specific aspect

2. Jacques Maritain, *Court traite de l'existence et de l'existant* (Paris: Pantheon Books, 1964). References are to the English translation by Lewis Galantiere and Gerald B. Phelan, *Existence and the Existent* (Garden City, New York: Image Books, 1956), 23.

3. Cf. John Deely, *Purely Objective Reality* (Belgium: Mouton de Gruyter, 2009), 9–16.

determined and cut out by abstraction, the intelligible density of an existent subject, rendered transparent in act to the mind and identified with the mind's vital activity by and in the concept? Briefly, the object as present in the mind is the intelligible objectisation of a trans-objective subject.[4]

By abstraction, a subjective being, a being outside the mind, becomes intelligible. This occurs only so long as a thing is made into an object for the intellect. We ought to note, however, that in terms of the actual experience of a human animal, things are first known as objects and only as objects. We do not, prior to intellectual experience of them, discern that they are things apart from their relation to ourselves; in other words, we have no conception of the *being* of the thing, and consequently cannot understand the thing as thing, but rather have it grasped only as an object.[5] At the same time, things, even while understood as things, are always at the same time still understood in their "objectisation" (to use Maritain's term), that something, through the fact that it is an object, stands in the relation given it by the intellectual grasp: "we must distinguish between the thing as thing—as existing or able to exist for itself—and the thing as object—when it is set before the faculty of knowing and made present to it."[6]

This distinction between "thing as thing" and "thing as object" is not to say that the two are unrelated, or that it is a problem of how we move from the object to the thing. This problem, the difficulty modernity found insurmountable, occurs only if we take the object as a pure object[7]—as though to be an object is to be something mutually exclusive from being a thing. Rather, as Maritain says:

the *thing* is given with and by the object, and ... it is even absurd to wish to separate them.... We would say in Thomistic language that the *thing* is the "material object" of the sense and intellect, whereas what we are calling *object* in this context

4. Maritain, *Existence and the Existent*, 23.

5. Cf. John Deely, *Intentionality and Semiotics* (Scranton, Pennsylvania: Scranton University Press, 2007), 98–100.

6. Jacques Maritain, *Distinguish to Unite, or The Degrees of Knowledge*, translated under the supervision of Gerald B. Phelan (New York: Charles Scribner's Sons, 1959), 91.

7. "In general, moderns take *object* as pure object, cut off in itself from any *thing* in which it has existence, I mean an existence independent of my *cogito*, an existence posited in its own right before my act of thinking and independent of it: existence which is called, in that sense, extramental without the 'exteriority' having the slightest spatial meaning; it might as well be termed premental, i.e., preceding the knowledge we have of it, or even metalogical." Maritain, *The Degrees of Knowledge*, 91.

... is their "formal object": material object and formal object are grasped at a single stroke and indivisibly by the very same perceptions.[8]

The object is the *terminus* of a relation of knowing: when someone actually understands, intellectually, the human nature in some human individual, that specific intelligible *quid* alone forms the object of the act of understanding, not the whole "thing." The particular human being is not the formal object of the intellect's act of understanding; but because of the *intellectus agens'* connection to the particular reason, the *vis cogitativa* working in conjunction with the *vires memorativa et imaginativa*, there is a cognitive grasp of the whole thing, what Maritain above calls the "material object." Because the relationship between these various powers is too complex for this essay, we will focus upon the notion that the formal object is the *terminus* of the relation whereby we have intellectual knowledge. To be such a *terminus* necessitates that there be also a *fundamentum*, something in the intellect connected to something in the thing.[9] Thus we may ask: how is this *fundamentum* produced?

All students of St. Thomas are, of course, familiar with the doctrine of abstraction as producing the concept, the fundament which provenates[10] a

8. Ibid., 93.

9. This "being-a-*terminus*" and "being-a-*fundamentum*," as modifications of that which is the formal object in the thing and that which is the foundation of the relation in the intellect, i.e., the concept, are accidents of objectivity constituted by the existence of the relation itself. Cf. Deely, *Purely Objective Reality*, 36–37: "It is easy enough to see that for triangle A really to be similar to triangle B, both triangles must exist. If either A or B is destroyed, the relation between them is destroyed. Yet consider the subjective characteristic of B whereby it is 'similar' to A, namely, its triangular shape. This shape is part of the subjectivity of B: it needs neither A nor the shape of A in order to be what it is; it needs only the existence of B. When A exists, however, B's shape does something it does not do when A does not exist, to wit, it *terminates* a relation of similarity to A founded on A's shape, and it *founds* a relation of similarity to A founded on B's shape. *Thus, for the foundation and the terminus of a relation,* even when the relation is a categorical relation, and even though the foundation and the terminus alike have a subjective dimension or being which is independent of the being of the relation as intersubjective, *precisely as foundation and terminus, it is not the subjective being of the inherent accidents that is decisive but the being of the relation itself.* Otherwise the being of the triangular shape as from one side foundation and from the other side as terminus could not cease when the relation ceases. In short, the *being of terminus* of a relation and the *being of foundation* of a relation *are alike creatures of the relation itself* in its suprasubjective character, even when the relation itself is an intersubjective reality (a categorical relation) and as such dependent upon the inherent, subjective reality of *both* fundament and terminus as modifications of substance."

10. Cf. John Deely, *Semiotic Animal: A Postmodern Definition of "Human Being" Transcending Patriarchy and Feminism* (South Bend, Indiana: St. Augustine's Press, 2010), xiii: "Here too, perhaps, is the place to mention a neologism introduced into my analysis from the Latin

relation to the terminal object. A certain tension emerges in many expositions of this Thomistic doctrine, however—namely, that the very etymology of the word suggests primarily a process of extraction or removal of the intelligible form from the unintelligible material thing. Maritain attempted to minimize this negative aspect of intellectual abstraction while preserving some sense of the divestment of form from matter spoken of so frequently by St. Thomas.[11] Maritain's primary concern was to emphasize the "positive perception" of being, as we read here:

> The essence of the process of abstraction, the eidetic visualisation, is not to remove baser minerals in which the precious metal is embedded but to find the metal. The essence of metaphysical visualisation is not to remove first the individualising notes, then the sensible qualities and finally the quantity, it is that of which all this is but the indispensable condition, namely the positive perception, the intuition of being as such.[12]

In Maritain's description, abstraction consists not so much in a removal or disengagement from the inferior surrounds, but rather a discovery of something distinctive within. It is not that the form is in some way extracted or copied from the thing and placed in the intellect, but that the form is discovered in such a way that the mind returns back to the form's source. As he warns us, "it is a radical error to restrict the object of the intellect to

---

semiotic of John Poinsot, namely, the English verb-form *provenate*. This verb in English derives from the Latin infinitive 'provenire', to come or issue forth, appear, arise, be produced; its closest relative in existing English being the noun-form 'provenance' ('where something originated or was nurtured in its early existence'). Hence, as will appear, a relation *provenates* from its fundament only *contingently* in *ens reale* restrictively conceived, but *necessarily* when the fundament is a psychological state. Thus, as psychologic states cannot be without being 'of' or 'about' something other than themselves, so as qualities they belong to subjectivity as entangled inescapably with suprasubjectivity, but they do not depend upon a *subjectively existing terminus* in order to give rise to relations. In this case, the relation *provenates*—i.e., issues forth from or 'on the foundation of' the psychological quality—*necessarily* regardless of any subjectivity on the side of its terminus."

11. Maritain, *Sept leçons sur l'être et les premiers principes de la raison spéculative* (Paris: Chez Pierre Téqui, 1934). References are to the English version, *A Preface to Metaphysics: Seven Lectures on Being* (London: Sheed and Ward, 1945), 86–7: "You understand what is meant by the term abstraction. It must never be separated from the intuition which it effects. That is why in many cases I prefer the term *visualisation*. To abstract means to disengage, to draw out. There is always *something to be disengaged*, a metal from the ore in which it is contained. But we often insist too exclusively upon the negative aspect of the process, the aspect implied by the term abstraction, on the divestment it involves, and fail to see that this divestment is simply a condition. So the term is understood in a purely material fashion, and it becomes incomprehensible how it can designate the supreme degree of human knowledge."

12. Ibid., 87.

the object of the first operation of the mind.... It is merely a preparation for the second, which achieves knowledge."[13]

While we wholeheartedly agree with Maritain that the "essence of the process of abstraction ... is not to remove baser minerals ... but to find the metal," his account of abstraction nevertheless leaves something to be desired in terms of clarity, at the very least. We can make our dissatisfaction clearer by looking at the way in which Maritain emphasizes two aspects of abstraction: one, the three degrees of physics, mathematics, and metaphysics; and two, the distinction between *abstractio totalis* (or "extensive visualization") and *abstractio formalis* ("intensive visualization"), which consist, respectively, in the initial abstractive grasp whereby we realize some more general or universal concept from the individuals encountered in experience, and the incisive abstractive insight that grasps the essential differentiation of beings.[14]

Maritain describes extensive visualisation as being of an object that "is not explicitly the type or essence abstracted by and for itself," such that "the essence is there, but contained in the notion after a fashion wholly implicit or blind, as it were hinted, not such that thought can employ or handle it."[15] He does not explain what he means by saying that the essence is present, but "wholly implicit or blind." Presumably, however, he means that there is a lack of clear distinction, that the intellect has grasped some "thing," though the nature of the thing is not yet known beyond the vaguest outlines, as though it were a surface encountered by touch in the dark. As Maritain goes on, "Contact has been made with the intelligible order, the order of the universal in general; but nothing more."[16] Contrariwise, intensive visualisation penetrates to the "form or regulative type perfected, complete in its distinctive intelligibility."[17] In this case, not only does the visualisation perceive the outline of the understood thing, but also its distinctions and details; the object of intensive visualisation is clear and distinct. We have then not only found the precious metal amongst the lesser

13. Ibid., 20.

14. Maritain, *The Degrees of Knowledge*, 36. This twofold notion is taken from Cajetan and John Poinsot. Maritain's references are to Cajetan c.1493: *In de Ente et Essentia*, proem., q. 1, and Poinsot 1632: *Artis Logicae Secunda Pars*, vol. 1 in *Cursus Philosophicus Thomisticus*, edited by Reiser, q.2 7, a. 1, pp. 822, 829.

15. Maritain, *Preface to Metaphysics*, 75.

16. Ibid., 75–6.

17. Ibid., 76.

ore, but have succeeded in precisely distinguishing it from its surroundings.

In his *Preface to Metaphysics,* Maritain adds to the degrees of abstraction his own elaboration. On the one hand, he maintains the traditional sense of the degrees abstracted according to the *ratio formalis objecti ut res,* the "inspect" under which that thing appears to a knower and the division of sciences which follows from such distinctions. On the other hand, he speaks also of the "objective light," the *ratio formalis objecti ut objectum,* of "a certain characteristic immateriality in the medium of knowledge, the peculiar mode of visualising and defining it demanded by the object in question if we are to attain and penetrate it."[18] Maritain thus distinguishes between the object as belonging to a specific sort of thing, or being in a thing in a specific way, and the object precisely as "objectised" through some act of knowledge, through the way in which it is grasped. In the sense of the formal object as thing, *ratio formalis objecti ut res,* we are considering the formal object precisely as it belongs to a thing, and thus the objects are distinguished according to the existence proper to their subjective constitutions. In the sense of the formal object as object, *objecti ut objectum,* on the other hand, we are considering how objects themselves are distinguished precisely in their mode of being as object, and thus they are distinguished according to the manner of their reception and subsequent presence in the one knowing.

In this latter sense, Maritain speaks of four degrees of communicability, from absolute opacity to sheer transparence, in terms of what and in what manner something is communicated, and consequently understood through some objectisation. (The lowest degrees, which deal with matter and form, are omitted here for the sake of brevity, except to point out that even pure nothingness and prime matter, of themselves nothing, are capable of being cognized and therefore made objects.)[19] The third degree of

18. Ibid., 79.

19. The lowest and most opaque of these is the degree of pure nothingness—about which there is little to say, but about which we ought to note that, while it cannot be a formal object as thing, it is nevertheless known as an object—we can objectise even that which is not a thing. Second to pure nothingness is the object we call prime matter, totally unknowable in itself and not something which communicates itself to any other; indeed, there really is no "itself" of prime matter, for it exists only as the indefinite and wholly indeterminate realm of possibility for change. Prime matter does not exist on its own, but "it communicates with the form which actualises it. This is a reminder that transparence to the mind, communicability, is co-extensive with being." (Maritain, *Preface to Metaphysics,* 79.) In other words, prime matter—which is distinct from the matter actualized by the form—communicates with forms as being receptive of

communicability is that whereby a form is received, in a soul, by the virtue of a transitive action of one body upon another—namely, what occurs in the sensation of the external sense powers. Yet the form as known is received not in the order of the receiver's subjective constitution, but rather with an intentional existence. Thus, though a transitive action occurs, a kind of reception of some form by the one sensing, the form transitively impressed upon the organs, does not come to exist in those organs in the way it exists in the thing sensed: the roughness of sandpaper does not make the finger rough, but the form of roughness is received in sensation, existing intentionally and making known the roughness in the sandpaper. This intentionality of the form in the animal awareness is constituted only through a grasp of the accidents, and consists in a kind of corroboration of them so as to form a substitute identity, that sense knowledge is attained.[20] In other words, by collating the various sense perceptions had of a thing's sensible accidents—including the *sensibile per accidens* or what we might call "incidental sensibles"—an animal considers something outside of itself in a particular and determinate way through an intentional form.[21]

---

them. It does not contribute anything to them, but only receives; it is a one-way communication, and prime matter always stands, as it were, "outside" the existing, material thing actualized by some present form. This being of pure possibility is, however, still a being and not pure non-being, and is therefore an object which can be known by a mind. Subsequently, Maritain speaks of "the second degree of communicability, that of bodies in their material existence," which occurs when matter is no longer mere possibility, but by its conjunction with some form becomes *signate* matter, as Thomas would say. The occasion of signate matter becomes known to us by the observation of a change wrought upon those bodies in some way or another, which bodies, Maritain says, "can communicate only by the modifications which they receive from each other, each of which is bound up with a corresponding loss." (Maritain, *Preface to Metaphysics*, 80.) Such communication, between things which are strictly bodies, is nothing other than the communication of transitive action—i.e., the form received is communicated to the body of the receiver as something which contributes to, detracts from, or even constitutes the receiver's subjective constitution: "Between one being and another whose form is *entirely* absorbed in informing its matter, namely an inanimate being, no other communication is possible than transitive action"; "At the upper limit, two bodies communicate their natures to each other *by destroying* each other, to exist henceforward only virtually in a third of a different species. This is substantial generation." Maritain, *Preface to Metaphysics*, 80.

20. We might even say that, in Maritain's own terminology, sense cognition or perception is always and intrinsically *perinoetic*—that is, it essentially cannot get at the essence of anything. Cf. Maritain, *The Degrees of Knowledge*, 205.

21. For more on the role of incidental sensibles in the working of the interior sense powers, see Daniel De Haan, "Perception and the *Vis Cogitativa*: A Thomistic Analysis of Aspectual, Actional, and Affectional Percepts," in *American Catholic Philosophical Quarterly* 88, no. 3 (2014): 397–437, as well as Anthony Lisska, "A Look at Inner Sense in Aquinas: A Long-Neglected Faculty Psychology," *Proceedings of the American Catholic Philosophical Association* 80 (2007).

The fourth degree of communicability is that of intellectual knowledge. Maritain distinguishes this from the third degree in that the intentional existence of the form attained in sensation is the product only of "accidental transitive action," whereas the intentionality of the intellectual form is "in virtue of an object's being itself ... in virtue of what it is."[22] This is the communication of the very form itself, not by virtue of some proxy, but in its own proper mode.[23] At this point, the intentional existence of the form in the intellect is the same in terms of *what* it is as the substantial existence of the form in the order of subjective constitution. In this communication, Maritain sees a divergence from the material object of experience, in that "the individuating notes bound up with sensible knowledge, which is itself psychophysical, necessarily fall away."[24] The human intellect cannot know the sensible as the sensible itself is.[25]

It seems that there is something problematic in the schema of communicability Maritain has here outlined, especially with the notion that we are losing something in abstraction—that this is ultimately a problematic way of considering matter, and especially signate matter. It is easy to begin to treat such matter, combined with, determined, and actualized by a specific form, as though it is a positive thing in its own right. Because it is a principle in something actually existing, we can make the mistake of treating the matter as though a thing itself, a *res* with its own content apart from the form—as though the matter is responsible in a positive manner for the singularity of the individual material being.

We can raise the problem this way: when we "abstract" from matter, what is it we are really pulling away from? Of what is the form truly divested? If we conceive of the combination of matter and form as though one thing simply gives structure or even meaning to another, then we are doomed to be mistaken about the nature of abstraction. If, contrariwise,

22. Maritain, *Preface to Metaphysics*, 81.

23. Cf. Maritain, *The Degrees of Knowledge*, on perinoetic and dianoetic intellection as a similar kind of distinction.

24. Maritain, *Preface to Metaphysics*, 81.

25. Maritain is certainly in line with the teaching of St. Thomas. Cf. Thomas Aquinas, *Summa Contra Gentiles* I, chap. 65, no. 9: "Forma igitur rei sensibilis, cum sit per suam materialitatem individuata, suae singularitatis similitudinem perducere non potest in hoc quod sit omnino immaterialis, sed solum usque ad vires quae organis materialibus utuntur; ad intellectum autem perducitur per virtutem intellectus agentis, inquantum omnino a conditionibus materiae exuitur; et sic similitudo singularitatis formae sensibilis non potest pervenire usque ad intellectum humanum."

we see that signate matter is nothing other than a determinate set of potencies, then we can perceive that the form grasped is divested not of anything that the being itself actually is, but only what it might be; it is divested only of potency. Let it suffice here to say that much more needs to be said about the operation of the *intellectus agens*, in both its aspects as illuminating and abstracting, to fully grasp how intellection occurs.

In summary, what Maritain has to say concerning the various degrees of communicability whereby the objects of our understanding, understood as and distinguished from one another in their objectivity, contains a great insight. We can see, indeed, that the realm of that which can be grasped as object, wherein we can make formal distinctions of kind, exceeds that whereby we may grasp things as objects formally distinct from one another as things. Further, by distinguishing between the grasp of a formal object as belonging to a thing and of the formal object in its objectivity, we can more properly see the continuity in the objects of intellection—that all being is communicable, no matter the kind of thing in which the being is found, even if that "thing" is actually no-thing—nothing at all. To grasp further the value of these insights, however, we need now to turn our attention to Maritain's interpretation of concept formation.

III. Maritain on Concept Formation

Maritain summarizes his take on a Thomistic doctrine of knowledge by saying that "knowing appears to us to be an immanent and vital operation that essentially consists, not in making, but in being; to be or become a thing . . . in a way other than by an existence that actuates a subject."[26] This being or becoming of the other is accomplished in a union which does not constitute a *tertium quid* in the way that matter and form do, but rather in a union where the object becomes present through the *species* which is a "presentative" form. This germination of knowledge constitutes only the first half, the prerequisite to knowledge being accomplished: "intellectual knowledge is accomplished thanks to a mental word or concept, a presentative form uttered by the intellect within itself, and in that form the intellect intentionally becomes . . . the thing taken in one of its intelligible determinations."[27]

26. Maritain, *The Degrees of Knowledge*, 117–18.
27. Ibid., 118.

A major point Maritain is keen to make concerning the nature of the concept is a common one among Thomists of the twentieth century, namely, that the concept and that which is known are not each distinct *quods*. That is, each is not a distinct "that which," such that the concept stands as something in the mind which is the direct object of understanding, one *quod*, and that representationally directs the understanding to the thing outside the mind, another *quod*. Rather, the concept is a *quo*, a "that by which" or a means which operates to make known something other than itself, a formal sign.[28] To be a *quo*, according to Maritain, is to be a pure means, i.e., something which is not a terminal object, a *quod*, before it signifies something other. The *quo* is understood in one of two ways:

> in general, in the sense of a *pure means* (and then the concept is a *quo* just as the *species impressa* is), or in particular, in the sense of a means by which (as from a *principle*) the act of intellection is produced (and then the word only suits the *species impressa*, whereas the concept is *in quo*, a means in which, as in its *term*, the act of intellection is completed).[29]

Both the *species impressa* and the *species expressa* are *quo*, but not in precisely the same way. To be a pure means or a *quo* is not necessarily to be a formal sign, but could entail merely being the principle or incipient stage whereby a formal sign comes into being, as is the case with the *species impressae*, which are "part of the preconscious equipment of knowledge."[30]

28. "[The concept] is not known by 'appearing' as an object but by 'disappearing' in face of the object, for its very essence is to bear the mind to something other than itself. All that we have established up to this point enables us to understand that the *species expressae*, or the elaborated presentative forms which intervene in knowing, are formal signs, not instrumental signs. A remembrance, or presentative form retained in memory and used by the memory *hic et nunc* is not *that which* is known when we remember. It is the *means* by which we know. And what we know by that means is the past itself, the thing or event woven into the web of our past. The concept or mental word is not *that which* is known when our intellect is at work; it is the *means* whereby intellection takes place. And what we know by that means is the very nature or intelligible determination of an actually or possibly existing thing" (ibid., 121); "[P]resentative forms, concepts in particular, are pure means of knowing; shcolastics called them *objectum quo*, mental objects *by which* knowledge takes place. What is known through these immaterial *species*, they called *objectum quod*, the object *which* is known" (ibid., 120); "[W]hile existing in two different states (1° in the concept, in a state of abstraction and universality which allows it to be handled, divided, compared by the mind, and to enter into the concatenations of discourse; 2° in the thing, in a state of individuality and concreteness), nevertheless the *object* and the *thing* do not constitute two known terms, two *quod*'s, but only one. One and the same term of knowledge, one and the same *quod*, exists for itself as a thing, and is attained by the mind as object" (ibid.).

29. Maritain, *The Degrees of Knowledge*, 393 n. 2.

30. Ibid., 120 n. 3. The preceding comments of the footnote are worth considering as well:

Maritain sees, between the terms *quo* and *in quo*, a distinction whereby the former refers merely to being a pure means, and thus the *quo* is indifferent to the manner in which something is a means, while the *in quo* refers specifically to the term of the process whereby knowledge is attained. The concept, the "elaborated presentative form," is the term, the *species expressa*, the *in quo*.[31] This *in quo* is a "means in which"—in other words, the concept is that in which the object is known, and this term, *in quo*, signifies the simultaneity of "the concept signifying and the object signified" united in the act of understanding.[32]

Thus, while Maritain sees no problem in applying the term *quo* to that of the concept, as a generic term, he does note that a more precise signification can be given to the concept than what *quo* alone suggests. It is unfortunate that, having seen something of a distinction between the *species impressa* as an incipient *quo* and the *species expressa* as a terminal *in quo*, Maritain did not further investigate the nature of this distinction. For although true that the concept alone is a formal sign, it is not enough to merely speak with greater specificity of the *species expressa* as a means "in which," as opposed to the generic notion of a "pure means," a *quo*. Nor is it sufficient to distinguish the concept by *quo*, said either generically or specifically as *in quo*, and the object by *quod* as, respectively, the "means by which" or "in which" and "that which."[33] This does not fully explicate the distinction between the form im-

---

"Received presentative forms (*species impressae*) are not called formal signs by the scholastics because they are at the beginning, not at the end, of the act of knowing and, hence, are not themselves known (*in actu exercito*) by the same knowledge that grasps the object."

31. Ibid., 393: "The concept is not a pure means in the sense of a principle or fertilizing seed, like the presentative form which is received (*species impressa*); it is a pure means as *term* or fruit (*species expressa*, presentative form which is uttered). But since this produced term—term *quod* in respect to intellection as productive—is a pure means in respect to intellection as intellection, it does not arrest in itself the intellection which fulfills itself in it. By the fact that understanding is completed in it as in a *quo* which makes known, by that very fact is understanding achieved in the object as in the *quod* which is known. Whence we have the expression *in quo*, an expression which in no way destroys or diminishes the force of the word *quo* as applied to the concept, but only makes it more precise, and signifies that the act of understanding indivisibly includes, at once and by the same token, both the concept signifying and the object signified."

32. Ibid., 393.

33. Cf. Deely, *Intentionality and Semiotics*, 56–71. To quote just a part, on p. 71: "Whence to insist simply that the expression 'in quo' in no way 'destroys or diminishes the force of the word "quo"' is to miss a crucial point and to beg the question. For the *quo* as *species impressa* simply conveys iconically the otherness of its source, whereas the *in quo* normally and necessarily (by virtue of its function to engender *a perception* and not merely to duplicate *a sensation*) adds to that iconicity 'relations of reason' (*entia rationis*), whether only materially (as in the perception of brute animals rendering the cognized environment meaningful *for them*) or also formally (as

pressed upon the intellect, the inception of the concept, and the form expressed by the intellect when the concept is formed, the *verbum mentis* or *species expressa*.[34]

Maritain was well aware that the two were different, noting that the conceptual task is "highly complicated and slow moving," admitting "of a large measure of construction and artifice," running "the risk of error in proportion as it advances."[35] Maritain adds that the "word itself is not perfect within us at the first stroke; on the contrary, it is constantly taken up once more, elaborated step by step and matured in the course of discursive activity."[36] In other words, between the impression of the presentative form

---

in the intellection of rational animals rendering the perceived environment something able to be understood in terms of being, both *reale* and *rationis*). And it is as *terminus* of the relations *founded in* (provenating from) the *species expressae* that the object perceived exists, which includes but does not reduce to the relations of the environmental source which provenate from the *species impressae* as sensory stimulus."

34. Maritain, *The Degrees of Knowledge*, 389 n. 4: "[I]t seems that St. Thomas was much more concerned with the relation between the *extramental thing* and the presentative form [Maritain's term for the *species impressa*] thanks to which it is made object than with the relation between the presentative form and the *object* itself taken as such. That is why, as we will see later, it often happens that he deals with thte concept not by distinguishing between *mental concept* and *objective concept*, but rather by speaking of it, at one time, in the sense of mental concept (*intentio intellecta* could then be translated as "the mental aim") and, at another time, in the sense of objective concept (*intentio intellecta* could then be translated as "the object aimed at mentally"). This is to say, he speaks of the concept by thinking of the mental concept not precisely as *species* but from the point of view of the *object* it presents to the mind."

35. Maritain, *The Degrees of Knowledge*, 127: "[T]he conceptual task is highly complicated and slow moving.... [I]t proceeds from the indeterminate and generic to the determined.... [I]t admits of a large measure of construction and artifice.... [I]t makes us take very indirect or 'confused or partial or derivative or negative' views of things, and finally ... it runs the risk of error in proportion as it advances—not only from the fact of judgment and reasoning but from the fact of abstractive perception as well, because when our intellect is already busied with forms, the new concepts it engenders (whose formation no longer depends on the thing alone, but on objects already possessed and in virtue of which the new object is placed before the mind) can be formed awry."

36. Maritain, *The Degrees of Knowledge*, 125 n. 2: "Once the intellect is actuated into first act by the *species impressa*, it is a sufficient principle of its own operation. That is why Aristotle and St. Thomas call intellective action *actus perfecti*, the act of a thing that is already in act.... The actuating of the intellect, insofar as the object is not formed in the word, still remains imperfect on the side of its term, and that is why this *processus de actu in actum*, which is 'perfect' as regards its principle of intellection and as the *species impressa* has formed and actuated the intellect, at the same time constitutes a *fieri* for understanding wherein, in the very instant it takes place, it *perfects* the actuating of the intellect, as regards its term, by producing the word and forming the object in it. Moreover, the word itself is not perfect within us at the first stroke; on the contrary, it is constantly taken up once more, elaborated step by step and matured in the course of discursive activity."

or *species impressa* and the formation of the *verbum mentis* or concept proper, a *discursive* process unfolds—the intellect does not produce the word, the concept, as a static and inert product to be preserved, but gives birth to a living and dynamic reality, capable of constant and continual revision and deepening. The *species expressa* is an *elaborated* presentative form; this elaboration results in "the complex products fashioned by the intellect, for instance, definition and division (which have to do with the mind's first operation) and proposition (which has to do with the second)."[37]

Yet while he posits a discursive process of concept formation, clearly distinguishing the content of the *species expressa* from that of the *species impressa*, such that the mental composition of the concept makes it to be something properly "ours," Maritain, in his alacrity for overcoming the quagmire of modernist epistemology, posits an identity of the concept and the formal object inasmuch as it belongs to the subjective constitution of the extramental thing. As he says, "the concept is therefore [identical] with the object—not, certainly, as if it were *that which* is known: that is not what I mean; rather I mean precisely this: it is identical insofar as it is the inner sign and term *by which* the intellect becomes, in ultimate act, what it knows."[38] Even more strongly, he states that the *species expressa* is "the object's pure likeness ... because its entire specification comes from the object."[39]

While it is certainly true that there is a genuine sameness between the *species impressa* out of which any concept is formed and the formal object, as *terminus* of the act of understanding, yet, because the concept is formed discursively, there is still the possibility of a non-identification between the concept and the formal object *as it exists in the thing*. In other words, there may exist in the concept some specification which is *not from the thing*, as it exists according to its own subjective constitution. Note that we are not

37. Ibid., 395.

38. Ibid., 124.

39. Ibid., 127: "[T]he form that the intellect, once it has been placed in first act by the *species impressa*, engenders within itself, under the uninterrupted irradiation of the agent intellect, is truly, as we have said, the object's pure likeness, spiritually on fire, or rather the object itself now made spirit and *intentionally* present (not as object but as sign): because its entire specification comes from the object. The intellect that illumines and the intellect that knows are by themselves equally undetermined. Thus, the concept (in its intentional role) and object are indistinguishable, save that one makes known and the other is known, one is sign and the other is signified, one exists only in the mind and the other exists at the same time in the mind and in the thing."

simply referring to the false or pseudo-concepts which involve some falsity entailed in contradictory elements of a definition, of which Maritain was well aware, though the method of elaboration—composition or division—is the same in these "pseudo-concepts" as it is in the true concepts.[40]

It appears that such objective constitution is left out of Maritain's account from the fact that he takes "ens reale" to be "the direct object of the intellect," which is exhaustively divided into "something which exists or can exist for itself (a thing as thing)" and "something that exists or can exist for the mind—something attained by it and made present to it (thing as object)."[41] This limitation of the concept to be directly of only *ens reale*—a term not once used by St. Thomas himself—misses the very complexity of concept formation which Maritain insightfully acknowledges, the truth that the mental composition whereby we elaborate upon the presentative forms of knowledge is properly ours.

IV. Maritain on *Ens ut Primum Cognitum*

It is quite probable that Maritain did not see the consequences of the assumption that *ens ut primum cognitum* is the so-called *ens reale* of being existing outside of the mind in the order of subjective constitution; indeed, the question of *ens ut primum cognitum* ignores the aspect of its relation to *entia rationis,* hemmed-in as it is by the dichotomy between realism and idealism.[42] As he says, "what is the object first attained by the human intellect"? It is "being as enveloped or embodied in the sensible quiddity, being 'clothed' in the diverse natures apprehended by the senses, *ens concretum sensibili.*"[43] What Maritain evidently fails to realize here is the relevance

40. Ibid., 128: "Undoubtedly, they always present to the mind some aspect of the real—or some being of reason based on the real—when they are not pseudo-concepts giving the mind a complex of contradictory elements (such as the greatest whole number or the most perfect world); yet they may be capable of being cut up or recast in such arbitrary fashion that the gain will be very slight, if not illusory."

41. Ibid., 392: "I. *Ens reale,* the direct object of the intellect, does not imply actual existence. It is that which exists or *can exist* outside the mind, in the 'thing' (actual or possible). II. This *thing* can be considered either as something which exists or can exist for itself (a thing as thing), or as something that exists or can exist for the mind—something attained by it and made present to it (thing as object). III. The *object* is one with the thing and differs from it only by a virtual distinction of reason."

42. Ibid., 212: "The first intelligible 'formality' by which that which is becomes object, and which is attained in the concept of being, imbues everything real, is capable of everything that is."

43. Maritain, *Preface to Metaphysics,* 18.

of his own distinction between the grasp of an object in the rationale of the formal object as belonging to the thing, *ratio formalis objecti ut res,* and the grasp of the object in the mode of its objectivity, *ratio formalis objecti ut objectum.* While *ens ut primum cognitum* is, considered in terms of the "thing-from-which," certainly derived from the sensible-real, if considered in its mode of objectivity, what is communicated is not the mode of reality proper to a substantial existence as "that which exists independently of cognition." Rather, being as first known is that communication whereby all further objects of intellectual cognition are made capable of being grasped according to what they are in themselves, and not only what they are relative to the one cognizing. This communication is open to *entia rationis* and *entia realis* alike, and to whatever combination of the two might come to exist.

Thus, although Maritain correctly distinguishes the vague being of *ens ut primum cognitum* from the specific and determinate being of *ens inquantum ens,*[44] the subject of metaphysics, he nevertheless considers the two—being as first known and being as being—as related in a way which is problematic.[45] In sum, we must say that it is evidently a mistake based upon the aforementioned failure to take into account the distinction between the grasp of the formal object as thing and the formal object according to its mode of objectivity, that is, to consider the object to be one and the same thing grasped as differently, in an *abstractio totalis* or extensive visualisation in the case of the former, and in an *abstractio formalis* or intensive visualisation in the case of the latter.[46] Maritain makes this mistake in con-

44. Ibid., 30: "[B]eing as such is apprehended blindly at this level, in a sign, an object of thought, which is, as it were, a *surrogate* and a *mask of being as such, ens in quantum ens*.... Common sense will not explicitly conceive this being of which [the metaphysician] speaks otherwise than as the object of what Thomists call *abstractio totalis,* an abstraction is pre-scientific and infra-scientific."

45. Ibid., 29: "The knowledge of common sense is a natural and spontaneous growth, the product so to speak of rational instincts and has not yet attained the level of science.... It possesses a certain metaphysical value in as much as it attains the same objects as metaphysics attains in a different fashion. Common sense is therefore, as it were, a rough sketch of metaphysics, a vigorous and unreflective sketch drawn by the natural motion and spontaneous instincts of reason."

46. Maritain, *The Degrees of Knowledge,* 214–15: "As the first object grasped by the intellect, it is clear that being is not known in the mirror of some other previously known object. It is attained in sensible things by dianoetic intellection. Just as a generic or specific nature is known in itself by the property which reveals its essential difference, so an analogue (*analogum analogans*) is known in itself by that one of its analogates (*analogum analogata*) which first falls under the senses.... There is, therefore, an intellectual perception of being which, being involved in every

sidering the relationship between *ens ut primum cognitum* and *ens inquantum ens.*

---

act of our intelligence, in fact rules all our thought from the very beginning. And when this is disengaged for itself by the abstraction of the trans-sensible, it constitutes our primoridal philosophical intuition without which we can no more acquire the science of metaphysical realities than a man born blind acquires the science of colours. In this metaphysical intution the principle of identity: 'being is not non-being,' 'every being is what it is,' is not known merely *in actu exercito* and as an inescapable necessity for thought. Its ontological necessity is itself seen"; and ibid., 217: "Being, disengaged as such by *abstractio formalis,* being, with its transcendental properties and the cleavages it presents throughout the whole extent of things, constitutes the proper object of metaphysics.... The object of metaphysics is ... an entirely other world, the world of the superuniversal, the world of transcendental objects which, disengaged as such, do not demand, as genera do, to be completed by progressive differentiations coming as from outside, but offer a field of intelligibility which has in itself its own ultimate determinations. And those objects can be realized outside the mind in individual subjects which do not fall under the senses and so are outside the whole order of the genera and differentiations of the world of experience."

FRANCISCO EDUARDO PLAZA

Subjectivity and the *Prise de Conscience* in Jacques Maritain

I. Introduction

WHEN DISCUSSING THE "crisis of modernity," thinkers have frequently been tempted to focus exclusively on the problem without proposing a genuine solution. For many, indeed, the only way out of the modern crisis seems to be an impossible return to the past. Generally speaking, such a mistake is understandable, as it is easier to point out a problem than to come up with a solution. However, against this trend, some philosophers have sought to provide more than a purely negative critique. In particular, Jacques Maritain's analysis of modernity was able to capture the nature of the crisis itself while simultaneously unveiling the positive side of the modern era. For Maritain, we are living in the "reflective" or "reflex" age, one in which man is generally becoming more aware of and vested in his own subjectivity.[1] Maritain referred to this kind of self-awareness in various works as the *prise de conscience*, a beginning of awareness.[2] Karol Wojtyla (St. John Paul II) was another thinker who rec-

1. Maritain used this term in *Freedom in the Modern World*, translated by Richard O'Sullivan, in vol. 11 of *The Collected Works of Jacques Maritain*, edited by Otto Bird (Notre Dame, Indiana: University of Notre Dame Press, 1996), 65. He quoted this same passage of his in *Integral Humanism*, where he further elaborated on the point. See *Integral Humanism*, translated by Joseph W. Evans, in vol. 11 of *The Collected Works of Jacques Maritain*, edited by Otto Bird (Notre Dame, Indiana: University of Notre Dame Press, 1996), 226.

2. As noted, this term can be found in several of Maritain's works, more specifically in the following: "Creative Intuition and Poetic Knowledge," in *Challenges and Renewals* (Notre Dame, Indiana: University of Notre Dame Press, 1968), 276; *Integral Humanism*, 160, 168, 198, 201, 296–99; *On the Philosophy of History* (New York: Charles Scribner's Sons, 1957), 69; "Poetic Experi-

ognized this modern trend as a mark of genuine advancement in human thought. This emphasis on human subjectivity coincides with the "personalism" of both thinkers, that is, their insistence upon the intrinsic worth of each person. Although both Wojtyla and Maritain took a somewhat different approach to the matter, it is interesting to note that they nevertheless reached roughly the same conclusions with respect to their view on the person and his subjectivity. While Wojtyla had more confidence in what we may discover regarding man's subjectivity within philosophy, Maritain believed instead that much of the inquiry would fall within the domain of religion. We shall focus primarily on how Maritain presented subjectivity in the human person, and secondarily on the parallels between Maritain's thought and that of Wojtyla.

II. On Maritain's *Prise de Conscience* in the Modern Reflex Age

As Donald Gallagher summarizes in his introduction to Maritain's *Christianity and Democracy,* the French expression, "prise de conscience," as Maritain employed it, is "like an illumination on psychological, moral and historical progress."[3] Elaborating upon this in a footnote, Gallagher explains that Maritain has pointed to a "'growth in self-consciousness' in modern times" throughout several of his works, which he called "a widespread phenomenon of immense significance."[4] Bolstering this, Gallagher quotes *Integral Humanism,* where Maritain stated that "it is impossible to attach too much importance to this phenomenon of *prise de conscience,* for all the great advances in the modern age, in art, in science, in philosophy, in poetry, in the spiritual life itself, seem to belong principally to this order of growth in awareness."[5] Finally, Gallagher concludes his summary of the idea, explaining that "this acute sense of self often leads to extremes but it has given us a deeper appreciation of human subjectivity."[6]

Gallagher's summary serves as a good point of departure for explaining

ence," in *The Review of Politics* 6, no. 4 (1944): 390; *Religion et culture* (Paris: Desclée de Brouwer, 1946), 30–31.

3. Donald Gallagher, introduction to *Christianity and Democracy* and *The Rights of Man and Natural Law,* by Jacques Maritain (San Francisco: Ignatius, 1986), xvii.

4. Ibid., n. 6.

5. Maritain, *Integral Humanism,* 297.

6. Gallagher, "Introduction," xvii n. 6.

the *prise de conscience* in Maritain, as he brings together its three fundamental themes: self-consciousness (or consciousness-of-self), subjectivity, and progress in the modern age. The *prise de conscience* is a realization of the self which serves as a window into man's own subjectivity, as man reflexively considers his own internal dynamism. Man's subjectivity for Maritain is also his spirituality, and moreover, it cements the personhood of each individual by nature. The human being is essentially a spiritual being, which means, of course, that he is a person. As a person, he possesses his own particular subjective dimension, and he is free. All of these properties are intimately linked with one another, the culmination of which is to state that the human person is a universe unto himself, an intrinsic whole within the broader whole of creation.[7] Yet this is not the end of the matter, as Maritain followed St. Thomas Aquinas in stating that with respect to the community, man is a part within the whole.[8] This is the case, Maritain explained, because man is not a "pure" person (that is, a "divine" person), but an individual in a species. Within the society, "the human person as a member of society is a *part* of the latter as of a whole that is greater, but *not by reason of himself as a whole* and by reason of all that is in him! The core of his life as a person draws him beyond the temporal city, of which this life has nevertheless need."[9] Thus, there is a difficult balance that must exist between the person and the common good. Paradoxically, although the person in himself is a whole, he is also a part within a whole insofar as he is an individual.

Ultimately, this tension between the person and the temporal order illustrates to us that man is not his own end. Man is not put on this earth in isolation, and must therefore work with other persons to achieve the common good. Moreover, man's ultimate end lies beyond himself. However, as a person, man has dignity by nature, which in turn signifies that he cannot be completely submerged within the collective, for that would allow the individual person to be used purely as a means to establish the common good without consideration of his own end. Wojtyla made this very point with regard to the mean: "Thomistic Personalism maintains that the individual good of persons should be by nature subordinate to the common good at which the collectivity, or society, aims—but this subordina-

7. Jacques Maritain, *Existence and the Existent* (New York: Random House, 1948), 68. This is a recurring phrase throughout all of Maritain's work.

8. Maritain, *Integral Humanism*, 238.

9. Ibid. Italics in original.

tion may under no circumstances exclude and devalue the persons themselves."[10] This principle has clear political implications, as there are two possible extremes which adhere to one aspect but not the other: individualism and totalitarianism. Individualism comes to exist when the individual's dignity is over-exalted, pushing the common good aside completely. Here, man acts as an island, seeking his own good in isolation from anything or anyone else. On the other hand, totalitarianism has arisen from a desire to seek a common good at the expense of every individual. Under a totalitarian society, the individual is an obstacle; all that matters is the collective.

Now, the problem of individualism has been just as tempting as that of subjectivism in the modern age for the same reason according to Maritain: the anthropocentric character of modernity.[11] Thus, while the surging *prise de conscience* has borne great fruit (and indeed, is a good in and of itself), it has also been marred by the modern spiritual crisis of anthropocentric humanism. Here, man peers into himself, but due to his own pride loses sight of the world outside. Even though modern man has come to understand more about the human person as person, this knowledge has taken place within a void; without a proper understanding of spirituality or the true, final good, modern man knows himself as a person, but not how to live in light of it. Modern man wants to be free, but knows not for what purpose. Without a sense of the true good beyond oneself, modern man clings to his own personhood (or subjectivity) as the one good he can recognize, thereby hinging everything upon himself and his own fancies. Under this context, the *prise de conscience* may appear to encourage such individualism, as modern man becomes increasingly fascinated with himself alone. In Maritain's own words:

> A general progress of *prise de conscience* of self … characterizes the modern era. While the world turned away from spirituality par excellence and from that love which is our true end, to turn to exterior goods and the exploitation of sensible nature, the universe of immanence appeared on the scene, sometimes through sordid doors: a subjective deepening revealed their own peculiar spirituality to science, art, poetry, to the very passions of man and his vices, and the demand for freedom became all the more clamorous as men moved farther and farther away from the true conditions and the true notion of freedom. In short, in virtue of the

10. Karol Wojtyla, "Thomistic Personalism," in *Person and Community*, translated by Theresa Sandok (New York: Peter Lang, 1993), 174.

11. Maritain, *Integral Humanism*, 168

> ambivalence of history, the reflex age, with all the diminutions and losses which this word connotes, involved in other respects an undeniable enrichment, and one that we must hold for a definitive gain, in the knowledge of the creature and of human things, even if this knowledge was to empty into the interior hell of man a prey to himself. This murky way is not without issue, and the fruits that have been gathered while traversing it have been incorporated into our substance.[12]

Nevertheless, Maritain remained optimistic about the *prise de conscience* once placed within a modern evangelical context. When applied to the Christian laity, Maritain asserted that their *prise de conscience* has in turn revealed to them their "true cultural mission" in the temporal order.[13] This is what allows for the transition into the New Christendom of which Maritain spoke throughout his work, finally leaving behind the bankruptcy of anthropocentric humanism: "The injuries caused by the unhappy and divided conscience can be repaired only by a more perfect and fully spiritual *prise de conscience*. Only an evangelical consciousness-of-self can conquer the tragedy of the naturalist consciousness-of-self."[14]

III. Maritain and Wojtyla on the Subjectivity of the Person

With the exception of *Existence and the Existent*, Maritain's consideration of subjectivity is scattered in parts among many of his other works. While he had touched upon the subject briefly in his political writings, he also dealt with it in his meditations on poetry and art. Perhaps the reason behind this is that Maritain simply did not have much confidence in what philosophy may uncover about subjectivity as subjectivity, properly speaking. "This is the first point to which the consideration of subjectivity as subjectivity draws our attention; and it is a point of capital importance. Subjectivity marks the frontier which separates the world of philosophy from the world of religion," he wrote.[15] Maritain's justification for this was to say that philosophy only knows things in a reductive manner, that is, as objects; only religion can know a subject precisely as a subject. On this point, Maritain drew a parallel between our philosophical knowledge of

12. Maritain, *Religion et culture*, 31; quoted in, and translated by, Joseph Evans, "Jacques Maritain and the Problem of Pluralism in Political Life," *Review of Politics* 22, no. 3 (1960): 313.

13. Maritain, *Freedom in the Modern World*, 67.

14. Maritain, *Integral Humanism*, 198.

15. Maritain, *Existence and the Existent*, 72.

God and the experiential "knowledge" of God by way of our personal relationship with Him (using the term "know" analogously).

When God is known as the cause of being, the divine Self is rendered "an object of philosophical knowledge expressed in concepts."[16] This can only be accomplished by way of analogy.[17] However, these concepts cannot encompass the entire reality of God: "that divine reality infinitely overflows the banks of conceptual knowledge."[18] What philosophy can know is that "the reality thus objectised 'through a glass, darkly,' is the reality of a transcendent Self inscrutable in its being and its goodness, in its liberty and its glory."[19] Thus, in reducing God analogically to an object of conceptual knowledge, we can only capture a fragment of His ultimate reality. Nevertheless, we are simultaneously made aware that something lies beyond this concept, something transcendent and mysterious. Philosophy can only take us this far; if we wish to know more, we must approach God as one subject to another through religion. As Maritain explained, "religion is essentially that which no philosophy can be: a relation of person to person with all the risk, the mystery, the dread, the confidence, the delight, and the torment that lie in such a relationship."[20]

Just as there always remains a dimension of mystery in God with regards to our knowledge of Him, so too does subjectivity as subjectivity remain somewhat outside the scope of our intellect. This is precisely what Wojtyla called the "irreducible" in the human being.[21] Maritain formulated this irreducibility as a contrast between three vantage-points: our subjectivity as it presents itself to us via self-reflection, our subjectivity as seen through the eyes of another, and finally, our subjectivity as seen by God.[22]

We can understand each person to be at the center of the world if we consider this idea first from our own vantage point regarding our subjectivity. The objective reality of the world is not the same as each person's own subjective perception of it, even though the latter is certainly based upon the former. Nevertheless, with regard to subjectivity, I am at the cen-

16. Ibid.

17. Ibid. On "ana noetic knowledge," Maritain directs our attention to his *Degrees of Knowledge*.

18. Maritain, *Existence and the Existent*, 72.

19. Ibid.

20. Ibid., 73.

21. Karol Wojtyla, "Subjectivity and the Irreducible in the Human Being," in *Person and Community*, translated by Theresa Sandok (New York: Peter Lang, 1993), 211.

22. Maritain, *Existence and the Existent*, 74–75.

ter of this world as I experience it. Moreover, my own subjectivity is of the greatest significance to me, insofar as I am the only one who can control it; I alone am fully responsible for my actions. As Maritain put it: "My destiny is the most important of all destinies. Worthless as I know myself to be, I am more interesting than all the saints."[23] Yet, in spite of this, we cannot help but remain aware of the fact that we are also only one within the many of the world. This paradox exists for all other human persons as well, each of whom are also one within the many, even as they exist at the center of the world from their own individual perspectives. There is no way to reconcile this: If we ignore one aspect and focus on the other, we either fall into subjectivism or objectivism. Disregarding the world, if we are to concern ourselves exclusively with subjectivity, we absorb the world into ourselves, falling prey to hubris.[24] On the other hand, if we are to disregard ourselves in the face of objectivity, we are absorbed at once into the world, becoming lost within the collective, vulnerable to despair.[25]

As previously noted, it is through a realization brought about by self-reflection, a *prise de conscience*, that we gain an initial window into our own subjectivity. Maritain, following St. Thomas, held that, as a matter of "spontaneous reflection," we know by an "incommunicable" and "experimental" kind of knowledge that our soul exists, as well as the existence of our subjectivity which that entails.[26] However, this intuition of subjectivity does not disclose our essence to us; our subjectivity remains irreducible.[27] Regardless, this intuition is certainly some form of knowledge, given that we clearly understand what we refer to when saying "I." The issue is simply that this aforementioned "I" arises from an intuition that is felt rather than known (in the scientific sense).[28] Maritain once again relied upon St. Thomas to clarify this, stating that this intuition of self is a form of knowledge by way of "connaturality."[29] This was a crucial point for Maritain, as he continually referred back to it whenever he spoke of man's subjectivity. Returning then to the *prise de conscience* with respect to man's subjectivity, we may conclude that it is *a connatural form of knowledge whereby man experi-*

23. Ibid., 75.
24. Ibid.
25. Ibid.
26. Ibid., 69.
27. Ibid.
28. Ibid., 70.
29. Ibid., 71.

ences himself precisely as a self, intuiting his own subjectivity without reduction. It is important to emphasize this last point: "It is not rational knowledge, knowledge through the conceptual, logical and discursive exercise of Reason. But it is really and genuinely knowledge, though obscure and perhaps incapable of giving account of itself, or of being translated into words."[30]

The similarities between Wojtyla and Maritain are striking on these points. Wojtyla also began his analysis of personal subjectivity through self-reflection. As the person experiences herself, she can come to see her actions and inner happenings as they relate to her own subjectivity.[31] Wojtyla developed this point further, stating that our lived experience not only discloses the reality of our subjectivity (as Maritain held), but in addition reveals our own personal structures of self-possession, self-governance, and self-determination.[32] While Maritain would not disagree with this necessarily, it is nevertheless the case that Maritain did not devote much thought to what exactly we could come to know within our subjectivity through self-reflection. Maritain instead maintained a sense of mystery and caution in this respect, while still affirming the reality of man's inner structures: "It is a very simple-minded error to believe that subjectivity possesses no intelligible structure, on the ground that it is an inexhaustible depth; and to conceive of it as without any nature whatsoever for the purpose of making of it an absurd abyss of pure and formless liberty."[33]

Another similarity between Wojtyla and Maritain is that they both emphasized the role of love and action in coming to understand subjectivity. Human action lay at the heart of Wojtyla's analysis concerning human subjectivity: "I believe that the form of human *operari* that has the most basic and essential significance for grasping the subjectivity of the human being is *action*: conscious human activity, in which the freedom proper to the human person is simultaneously expressed and concretized."[34] As Maritain pointed out, human action flows through man's own subjectivity: "all vital productivity derives from subjectivity itself; subjectivity appears thus, according to its most profound properties, as a center of universe unto it-

30. Jacques Maritain, "On Knowledge through Connaturality" *The Review of Metaphysics* 4, no. 4 (1951): 474.

31. Karol Wojtyla, "Subjectivity and the Irreducible in the Human Being," 213.

32. Ibid., 214.

33. Maritain, *Existence and the Existent*, 81.

34. Karol Wojtyla, "The Person: Subject and Community," in *Person and Community*, translated by Theresa Sandok (New York: Peter Lang, 1993), 224.

self of productive vitality and spiritual emanation."[35] Moreover, Maritain made the same point as Wojtyla on the role of action in understanding subjectivity: "If subjectivity can be grasped *insofar as it is subjectivity,* this will happen only when it is grasped insofar as it is a center of productive vitality, as it is *productive,* not insofar as it is knowing by means of concepts and ideas."[36] Maritain likewise thought that love could unite us to the subjectivity of others. Wojtyla intensified this idea in his own work, arguing that the primary basis for community is a "we" relationship among persons.[37] We experience the other as "another I," and in so doing, incorporate the subjectivity of the other into our own through the common good.

Having briefly considered how the subjectivity of another presents itself to us, we can begin to investigate how our subjectivity is seen by others. Each person is unique and unrepeatable; the depth of one's subjectivity is infinite, expanding as the person matures through time. Thus, while we can come to know a great deal about a person by way of love and friendship, there will always be more to uncover. The same holds true, of course, for our friends and loved ones with respect to us. In contrast, the further we get from friendship and love, the more object-like we appear to others—though without completely losing our aspect of subjectivity. "Other men," Maritain wrote,

> know me as object, not as subject. They are unaware of my subjectivity as such; unaware not merely of its inexhaustible depth, but also of that presence of the whole in each of its operations, that existential complexity of inner circumstances, data of nature, free choice, attractions, weaknesses, virtues perhaps, loves, and pains; that atmosphere of immanent vitality which alone lends meaning to each of my acts.[38]

When we are known in this manner, Maritain explained, we are known "unjustly," for it is our subjectivity which truly renders meaning to who we really are. Still, if we reflect upon this, meditating upon *how* we are the *other* from another person's perspective, we can see other human beings as more than just another "object." After all, I know intimately of my own subjectivity, even if others do not share that same experience. Just as my own inner world is invisible to others, so too are theirs from my own perspective. The other person sees me just as I see them in my own subjectivity. We are all

35. Maritain, "Poetic Experience," 393.
36. Ibid.
37. Wojtyla, "The Person: Subject and Community," 249.
38. Maritain, *Existence and the Existent*, 76.

unique persons with our own inner worlds, therefore, yet at the same time, we all possess the same internal structures, the condition for the possibility of the shared experience of subjectivity.

We are thus faced with the following question: if others cannot know us fully, does this entail that we alone know ourselves? Maritain intensified the problem by arguing that not even *we* may arrive at such knowledge. Ultimately, he concluded, "Only God knows me in this wise; to Him alone am I uncovered. I am not uncovered to myself. The more I know of my subjectivity, the more it remains obscure to me. If I were not known to God, no one would know me. No one would know me in my truth, in my own existence."[39] We know our own subjectivity by way of connaturality, said Maritain, but this does not disclose our essence in its totality. Part of us remains uncovered—even to ourselves. Without God, therefore, our subjectivity would be doomed to fall into obscurity, never to be known fully by anyone at all: "If man is not known to God, and if he has the profound experience of his personal existence and his subjectivity, then he has also the experience of his desperate solitude; and the longing for death—more than this, the aspiration to total annihilation, is the sole spring that can rush forth within him."[40]

Maritain concluded this section by meditating religiously upon just what it means for God to be the only one who can know us fully. Such a thought may fill us with fear, as we come to grips with our own hidden evils.[41] If we continue along such lines, however, we also realize that our hidden goods must be understood as well: "how can we keep from thinking that God Who knows all these in their subjectivity, in the nakedness of their wounds and their secret evil, must know also the secret beauty of that nature which He has bestowed upon them, the slightest sparks of good and liberty they give forth."[42] Ultimately, while our initial observation brings us face to face with divine justice, it is the latter which shows to us divine mercy.[43] God's exhaustive knowledge of us, Maritain mused, is a "loving knowledge."[44]

39. Ibid., 77–8.
40. Ibid., 78.
41. Ibid.
42. Ibid.
43. Ibid., 79.
44. Ibid.

IV. Conclusion

The concepts of *personhood* and *subjectivity* were certainly known prior to the modern age, but they were not a focal point of philosophical reflection. When they assumed priority, however, reflection on subjectivity began as an overemphasis which sought to leave the objective, metaphysical realm behind. This hyper-modernism took modern idealism, nihilism, or skepticism to their logical extremes, leading to various dead ends in philosophy, culminating in the "absurd."[45] Our attempt to address the modern problem, however, does not need to be altogether negative. Wojtyla and Maritain responded not by abandoning subjectivity on account of this modernity, but to reconstruct our subjectivity with a metaphysical foundation. This move enables us to advance beyond modernity without regression, guiding the fruits of the modern age closer to truth. Maritain and Wojtyla's efforts in this regard thus render their thought truly "post-modern," in the fullest sense of the word.

45. This take on the term "post-modern" rests largely upon John Deely's critique primarily found throughout his *Four Ages of Understanding* (Toronto: University of Toronto, 2001). As he writes: "All the hoopla and pretensions surrounding literary postmodernism can be reduced to a single statement in the writings of their principal high-priest [Derrida]: 'the signified concept is never present in and of itself, in a sufficient presence that would refer only to itself'. We will leave to the next chapter the story of how these inheritors of modernity's idealism have tried to have it both ways: to revive the sign and yet leave epistemological matters to stand as they were when Kant left them; to revive the sign and yet maintain the illusion of Descartes that history counts for nothing and can be safely ignored" (611).

GREGORY KERR

Will the Real "Agents" Please Stand Up?

Jacques Maritain and David Bentley Hart on Science and Human Agency

Another source of conviction in the existence of God, connected with the reason and not with the feelings, impresses me as having much more weight. This follows from the extreme difficulty or rather impossibility of conceiving this immense and wonderful universe, including man with his capacity of looking far backwards and far into futurity, as the result of blind chance or necessity. When thus reflecting I feel compelled to look to a First Cause having an intelligent mind in some degree analogous to that of man; and I deserve to be called a Theist. But then arises the doubt—can the mind of man, which has, as I fully believe, been developed from a mind as low as that possessed by the lowest animal, be trusted when it draws such grand conclusions?

—*The Autobiography of Charles Darwin*[1]

I. Introduction

IN THE MUCH DEBATED section on "Religious Belief" in the epigraph above, we apparently see Darwin at first thinking metaphysically, then scientifically, and then losing all confidence in metaphysical thinking. Strangely, although he cannot trust his own mind when he thinks metaphysically, rather long-range scientific ideas inexplicably remain unscathed

1. Charles Darwin, *The Autobiography of Charles Darwin with Original Omissions Restored*, edited by Nora Barlow (New York: W. W. Norton, 1958), 92–93.

by similar doubts. *They,* apparently, do not need the assurance of a soundly working mind. For many today, the towering metaphysical speculation—as C. S. Lewis calls it[2]—that is philosophical naturalism does not need any justification at all. There seem to be no warning signs for the scientist who has left the very legitimate discipline of science and wandered, inadvertently, into philosophy.[3]

This is most apparent in contemporary treatments of human agency and consciousness (both of which are vital to personhood). According to Jacques Maritain in *Person and the Common Good* and *Education at the Crossroads,* a human being is one who "subsists and exercises existence for itself, holds itself in hand by his intelligence and will and is master of itself."[4] This notion of the human person as a real agent, one who is freely intelligent and intelligently free, is central to issues of human dignity, rights, and political freedom.[5] One of the greatest problems of our age, as it compares humans to apes, on the one hand, and to computers, on the other, is not only that we are misunderstanding human beings *as objects* that we know, but also that we are limiting our very capacity to even think in an authentically human way. Rather than seeing human beings as the principal agents in the human drama, they are now, at best, seen as secondary to the physical causes operating in their bodies and environment.

However, as I will argue below, human nature *as such* is simply not available to the sciences as they are practiced today. Indeed, as we read the results of science-based philosophies, we can actually "see" the human person begin to disappear and his agency dissolve. We will examine arguments that show that there are problems with physicalism when it treats of matters concerning human personhood, which we can see most convincingly when we look at the materialist attempt to explain consciousness itself. In the end, having been prepared by an examination of the limits of science in this area, we may be more willing to entertain the metaphysical notion of agency of a spiritual and active soul of the sort described above by Maritain.

2. C. S. Lewis, *Miracles: A Preliminary Study* (New York: Macmillan, 1947), 22.

3. In addition to the authors explored here in this paper, the reader might also profit from the discussions in Stephen J. Gould's *Rock of Ages* and Thomas Nagel's *Mind and Cosmos.*

4. Jacques Maritain, *The Person and the Common Good,* translated by John J. Fitzgerald (Notre Dame: University of Notre Dame Press, 1966), 40; *Education at the Crossroads* (New Haven, Connecticut: Yale University Press, 1943), 7–8.

5. Maritian was actively involved in the drafting of the *Universal Declaration of Human Rights* (1948). See William Sweet's entry in the Stanford Encyclopedia, http://plato.stanford.edu/entries/maritain/

II. On Human Nature

While the person *qua animal* or the person *qua matter* is available to science, the person *as such* is not. The principle of methodological naturalism binds and limits the knower to the physical, the measurable, and the testable. According to the National Academy of the Sciences, science is a unique way of knowing the world and explanations that are not observable and testable are not scientific. The Academy claims that,

> science is a particular way of knowing about the world. In science, explanations are restricted to those that can be inferred from the confirmable data—the results obtained through observations and experiments that can be substantiated by other scientists. Anything that can be observed or measured is amenable to scientific investigation. Explanations that cannot be based upon empirical evidence are not part of science.[6]

But what place does the *observer* have in a world in which only what is observable exists? In *Nature and the Greeks,* the great quantum physicist Erwin Schrödinger argues that while science provides us with an amazingly consistent and helpful picture of the universe, it leaves out all that is human, all that involves the person as such; man cuts himself out of the scientific picture he constructs of the world. As Schrödinger writes,

> we do not belong to this material word that science constructs for us. We are not in it, we are outside. We are only spectators. The reason why we believe that we are in it, that we belong to the picture, is that our bodies are in the picture. And the reason for this disconcerting situation is just this, that, for the purpose of constructing the picture of the external world, we have used the greatly simplifying device of cutting our own personality out, removing it; hence it is gone, it has evaporated, it is ostensibly not needed.[7]

6. *Teaching About Evolution and the Nature of Science* (Washington, D.C.: National Academy Press, 1998), 27. See http://www.nap.edu/read/5787/chapter/4. This excerpt was cited in the now famous Intelligent Design Trial (Tammy Kitzmiller, et al. v. *Dover Area School District,* et al., 04cv2688, *United States District Court for the Middle District of Pennsylvania,* Memorandum Opinion: Judge Jones, December 20, 2005, 66.) From http://files.findlaw.com/news.findlaw.com/hdocs/docs/educate/ktzmllrdvr122005opn.pdf.

7. Erwin Schrödinger, *Nature and the Greeks* in *Nature and the Greeks* and *Science and Humanism* (Cambridge: Cambridge University Press, 1964), 95–7, cited by Antony Flew, *There is a God,* 105ff. Schrödinger continues: "This is the reason I believe it to be true that I actually do cut out my mind when I construct the real world around me. And I am not aware of this cutting out. And then I am very astonished that the scientific picture of the real world around me is very deficient. It gives a lot of factual information, puts all our experience in a magnificently consistent order, but it is ghastly silent about all and sundry that is really near to our heart, that really

If Schrödinger is correct, we should be skeptical of claims that science has shown that there is no such thing as consciousness or free will. Strictly speaking, such claims are not the result of science, but presupposed by physicalism's overly narrow ontology. If we abide by the principle of methodological naturalism, in short, we know in advance that the "person" will have to go.

We can see the results of this methodological exclusion of personhood in the comments of those who ground their philosophical thinking in science. For instance, Richard Dawkins gives us a taste of this problem at the end of his book, *The God Delusion*. He tells us that a certain scientist, Steve Grand, pointed out that people are more like waves than permanent things. Recall a childhood experience, Grand asks us,

> [s]omething you remember clearly, something you can see, feel, maybe even smell, as if you were really there. After all, you really were there at the time, weren't you? How else would you remember it? But here is the bombshell: you weren't there. Not a single atom that is in your body today was there when that event took place.... Matter flows from place to place and momentarily comes together to be you. Whatever you are, therefore, you are not the stuff of which you are made.[8]

Similarly striking comments come from a leading author of noted Oxford University textbooks in the field of consciousness, Susan Blackmore. Most people assume that "experiences happen to someone; that there cannot be experiences without an experiencer," yet precisely this assumption, she argues, "has to be thrown out."[9] Blackmore concludes by claiming that a scientific method of studying consciousness "holds out the hope that science and personal practice might eventually come together to let us see clearly—dropping the delusions, penetrating the illusions of self and other, and leaving us with one world—no duality and no one asking the question."[10] Daniel Dennett would have told us that consciousness is like a magic trick, a "user illusion," that there is really no one home, no homunculus, no little man in the Cartesian theater of the mind. Still others, like Sam Harris in *On Free Will,* make the claim that since all of our supposed freely willed actions

matters to us. It cannot tell us a word about red and blue, bitter and sweet, physical pain and physical delight; it knows nothing of beautiful and ugly, good and bad, God and eternity. Science sometimes pretends to answer questions in these domains, but the answers are very often so silly that we are not inclined to take them seriously."

8. Richard Dawkins, *The God Delusion* (New York: Houghton Mifflin, 2006), 371.

9. Susan Blackmore, *Consciousness: A Very Short Introduction* (Oxford: Oxford University Press, 2005), 128.

10. Ibid., 133.

are preceded and caused by events occurring in our brain about which we are completely unaware, we have absolutely no free will. We are not responsible for our thoughts and decisions, for we had no role in their formation in our minds.

While justifying their positions, both Blackmore, Harris and many others point to experiments done by Benjamin Libet, who discovered in an experiment that there are electrical events—what Libet calls "readiness potentials"—that occur just before a person is conscious of deciding to do something, and which are clearly associated with subjects consciously choosing to do certain tasks. Harris and others conclude that since genuine free will requires that we know and have control over the sources/beginnings of our decisions, and since we apparently do not have this sort of control, we are not really free. However, Libet himself denies the validity of this conclusion. In "Do We Have Free Will?", an article written for the *Journal of Consciousness Studies,* he is outspoken about the fact that we do have free will of sorts. He suggests that we have something more akin to a conscious *censor* than a conscious *originator* of actions, and that eliminativist thinkers are wrong to draw determinist conclusions from his research. According to Libet, such thinkers illegitimately import their own deterministic philosophy into the discussion of the data. Science itself, Libet claims, supports no such conclusions.[11]

III. Responding to Eliminativism

To approach eliminativism in the spirit of a Thomist like Jacques Maritain would not entail a plea for the existence of something, some answer which could later be more satisfactorily provided by the physical sciences. We must not search for a kind of a "soul of the gaps." Not only would such an approach confuse the legitimate domains of metaphysics and empirical science, but even framing the problem in this way would beg the question against eliminitavism. Eliminativists themselves do not recognize that there is a deficit of scientific explanation in eliminitavism: there is no endpoint to cross the gap to! They do not hope for a future scientific explanation that would cover the phenomenon of the person, but simply deny its substantial reality.

11. Benjamin Libet, "Do We Have Free Will?" *Journal of Consciousness Studies* 6, nos. 8–9 (1999): 47–57.

As Roger Scruton has pointed out in *The Face of God*, Libet's experiments themselves even invite a "self of the gaps" approach. It is presumed that if there really is a free center of activity, it would appear as a break in, or as Scruton would say, be "an irruption in the stream of neural events."[12] This, of course, was never suggested by Thomistic metaphysicians. No one would claim that a substantial soul manifests itself as a unique physical thing, energy, or event appearing in the data. To further illuminate the difficulty, Scruton says that "sometimes, an intentional action is preceded by a decision or choice, certainly; but usually the action is the choice."[13] In that case, if we were to find a correlation between unconscious events in the neo-cortex and making decisions, as Benjamin Libet had discovered, we should not be surprised. For free will is not a spatio-temporal gap into which we insert *new* agency. It is, as David Bentley Hart writes in *The Experience of God*, a *formal* causality over a vast range of events. If it exists, the soul is the *form* of the body, not a piece of it. It animates the whole human being.

Yet, would a Thomistic metaphysician like Maritain have denied the unconscious irrational or arational beginnings to our thoughts and decisions? Surprisingly perhaps, he held that our decisions—when they were really free—actually do have deep preconscious and subconscious beginnings of which we are unaware. He developed quite an elaborate theory of the preconscious that he held was at the source of all concepts, decisions, and poetry. Then again, he was a Thomist; he did not define personality in terms of self-consciousness, as did Descartes. Nor did he believe, to borrow an idea from Bernard Lonergan, that you could just take a look and see it inside of you, as if consciousness were a piece of you. Maritain felt free to ask this question: what exactly are the metaphysical conditions of possibility for the arising of ideas and their frameworks in our minds with which we make free decisions? Maritain says it is enough to think about the times "in which our free decisions, when they are really free, are made, especially those decisions which commit our entire life—to realize that there exists a deep non-conscious world of activity."[14] For Maritain, all cognitive activity "is preceded by the hidden working or immense and primal preconscious life."[15]

12. Roger Scruton, *The Face of God* (London: Continuum International Publishing Group, 2013), 43.

13. Ibid.

14. Jacques Maritain, *Creative Intuition in Art and Poetry* (Princeton, New Jersey: Princeton University Press, 1953), 93–94.

15. Ibid., 94.

The stress on the origins, grounds, or conditions of possibility for consciousness have been insightfully taken up by David Bentley Hart in *The Experience of God*. Hart refers us back to scientific first principles and shows us that matter is not enough to explain consciousness. He refers us to what seem to be the working properties of "matter" as they are currently understood among physicalists. These thinkers insist that matter has no final causality inherent within it, no form, no purpose. Hart uses this fact to argue that

> nothing within the material constituents of those structures (in the brain) has the least innate tendency toward such order, any more than the material elements from which a watch is composed have any innate tendency toward horology. And, if complex rational order is extrinsic to what matter essentially is, how much more so must rationality itself be; for consciousness would appear to be everything that, according to the principles of mechanism, matter is not: directed, purposive, essentially rational. The notion that material causes could yield a result so apparently contrary to material nature is paradoxical enough that it ought to give even the most convinced of materialists pause.[16]

He continues:

> How could it be that, in this instance *alone*, the essential aimlessness of matter achieves so intense and intricate a concentration of its various random forces that, all at once, it is fantastically inverted into the virtual opposite of everything modern orthodoxy tells us matter is?[17]

Yet evolutionists like Richard Dawkins balk at the suggestion that the modern, non-teleological conception of matter cannot explain the intentional teleology evident in our own minds. In chapter four of *The God Delusion*, Dawkins agrees with advocates of intelligent design that chance, by itself, has no role in explaining the universe, but he denies that natural selection is simply chance. There are environmental laws and factors. Nature gets rid of the maladaptive. Further, life did not evolve all at once, he argues; that would be too improbable. Rather, evolution proceeded in small steps and increments, and *this* is what makes it plausible. He writes:

> What is it that makes natural selection succeed as a solution to the problem of improbability, where chance and design both fail at the starting gate? The answer is that natural selection is a cumulative process, which breaks the problem of improbability up into small pieces. Each of the small pieces is slightly improbable,

16. David Bentley Hart, *The Experience of God: Being, Consciousness, Bliss* (New Haven, Connecticut. Yale University Press, 2013), 154.

17. Ibid., 158; italics mine.

> but not prohibitively so. When large numbers of these slightly improbable events are stacked up in series, the end product of the accumulation is very, very improbable indeed, improbable enough to be far beyond the reach of chance. It is these end products that form the subjects of the creationist's wearisomely recycled argument. The creationist completely misses the point, because he (women should for once not mind being excluded by the pronoun) insists on treating the genesis of statistical improbability as a single, one-off event. He doesn't understand the power of accumulation.[18]

In other words, someone with a modern conception of matter, like Dawkins, would explain Hart's incredulity by arguing that his skepticism about the sufficiency of such a conception of matter to explain mentality is born of a failure to recognize that the change from unconscious matter to conscious matter did not occur "all at once," but gradually over the course of millions of years.

While it may be emotionally easier to swallow Dawkins' explanation, it nevertheless fails to provide a philosophically explanatory reason *why* such a change would happen or *what* powers the process. The assumption is this: if I can divide a phenomenon—including its coming into existence—into simpler parts, I have explained it. However, while this may work in biology, which *assumes* the existence of biological phenomena, the move to explain existence of the human mind itself in this way is unsatisfactory.[19] As Chesterton said decades earlier:

> this notion of [evolution being] something smooth and slow, like the ascent of a slope, is a great part of the illusion. It is an illogicality as well as an illusion; for slowness has really *nothing* to do with the question. An event is not any more intrinsically intelligible or unintelligible because of the pace at which it moves. For a

18. Dawkins, *The God Delusion*, 121–22.

19. Here we can see the difference between "explanation" for philosophy and for science. The traditional philosopher would balk at the following comments made by Dawkins. Right at the point where philosophy would demand an answer, the scientist seems to take the universe for granted. Dawkins says "a complicated thing is one whose existence we do not feel inclined to take for granted, because it is too 'improbable.' It could not have come into existence in a single act of chance. We shall explain its coming into existence as a consequence of gradual, cumulative, step-by-step transformations from simpler things, from primordial objects sufficiently simple to have come into being by chance.... I am a biologist. I take the facts of physics, the facts of the world of simplicity, for granted.... The biologist's problem is the problem of complexity. The biologist tries to explain the workings, and the coming into existence, of complex things, in terms of simpler things. He can regard his task as done when he has arrived at entities so simple that they can safely be handed over to physicists." Richard Dawkins, *The Blind Watchmaker* (New York: W. W. Norton, 1996), 22–24.

man who does not believe in a miracle, a slow miracle would be just as incredible as a swift one.[20]

In the end, Dawkins cannot in fact explain or eliminate intentionality, purposefulness, and human agency, and so must presuppose it in his account of the person by attributing these abilities and properties to human *parts*—say, genes—rather than to whole persons themselves. For instance, he describes genes as

> [swarming] in huge colonies, safe inside gigantic lumbering robots, sealed off from the outside world, communicating with it by tortuous indirect routes, manipulating it by remote control. They are in you and in me; they created us, body and mind; and their preservation is the ultimate rationale for our existence. They have come a long way, those replicators. Now they go by the name of genes, and we are their survival machines.[21]

Yet as Hart complains, "applying the imagery of agency—of hidden motives and purposes and designs—to what are, after all, only biochemical constituents of immeasurably more complex organic structures (many of which truly do possess the sort of real intentionality that genes do not)" is not scientific.[22] Genes cannot "seek" to survive; they cannot "program"; they cannot "guide" evolution.[23] They cannot do any of these things because they lack foresight to do so on Dawkins' view.

Once again, what drives such confusion is a mistaken understanding of what human agency is in the first place. It is not simply a part or a piece of the genetic or any other physical system. In that case it would be passive with respect to the human person; however, we can know our agency through our activity in the world. If Norris Clarke is right in insisting that "all knowledge is but an interpretation of action," and if it is true that our consciousness actually is our very own acting, then it would be absurd to think that we are mistaken about this most significant aspect of ourselves.[24]

20. Gilbert Keith Chesterton, *The Everlasting Man* (Garden City, New York: Image Books, 1955), 25.

21. Richard Dawkins, *The Selfish Gene*, 30th Anniversary Edition (Oxford: Oxford University Press, 2006), 19–20.

22. Hart, *The Experience of God*, 260. Even in the latest edition of *The Selfish Gene*, Dawkins continued to insist upon the metaphors. I might disagree with Hart here and entertain the idea that perhaps the imagery is fine as long as the scientific parameters are clear (the existence of the connections are assumed) and we are not making specifically philosophical and totalizing claims.

23. Ibid.

24. W. Norris Clarke, SJ, *The One and the Many: A Contemporary Thomistic Metaphysics* (Notre Dame, Indiana: University of Notre Dame Press, 2001).

As Hart notes:

Consciousness does not merely *passively* reflect the reality of the world; it is necessarily a dynamic movement of reason and will toward reality. If nothing else is to be concluded from the previous chapter, this much is absolutely certain: subjective consciousness becomes actual only through intentionality, and intentionality is a kind of agency, directed toward an end. We could never know the world from a purely receptive position. To know anything, the mind must be actively disposed toward things outside itself, always at work interpreting experience through concepts that only the mind itself can supply.[25]

This is very similar to what C. S. Lewis argued in *Miracles*. If naturalism were correct, then everything should in principle be explicable in terms of the whole system; however, reasoning itself cannot be explained in this way. Reasoning does not just simply *happen* according to the laws of physics or biology; *we* reason. *We* are the actors, the agents.[26] Moreover, if all our reasoning about morality were simply part of the whole physical system, moral judgments would simply be statements of fact about us and our states of mind. They would have no normative force. According to Lewis, "Evolution may (or may not) explain why men do in fact make moral judgments. It does not explain how they could be right in making them. It excludes, indeed, the very possibility of their being right. If Naturalism were true, 'I ought' is the same sort of statement as 'I itch.'"[27]

This is an old problem. As Socrates argued in the *Phaedo*, the physicalist explanation of Anaxagoras was not sufficient to explain why he was in prison. It could not explain why the Athenians thought it "fit" to "condemn" him or why he thought it "better and more right" to remain in prison. "There is surely a strange confusion of causes and conditions in all this," Socrates argues:

It may be said, indeed, that without bones and muscles and the other parts of the body I cannot execute my purposes. But to say that I do as I do because of them,

25. Ibid., 238; italics mine.

26. Dawkins himself seems to give us a hint of some of the problems with his system by saying—in a note in response to criticism by biologists about his original call for "rebellion" against the dictates of our genes at the very end of *The Selfish Gene* (pp. 200–201)—that we humans (by which he means "brains") "are separate and independent enough from our genes to rebel against them." Ibid., 332. Now, if we have the power of rebellion, one might ask where that power comes from. This is precisely the thing that many philosophers want explained. I am indebted to Alister McGrath's *Dawkins' God: Genes, Memes, and the Meaning of Life* (Oxford: Blackwell Publishing, 2005), 46–47.

27. Lewis, *Miracles*, 36.

and that this is the way in which mind acts, and not from the choice of the best, is a very careless and idle mode of speaking. I wonder that they cannot distinguish the cause from the condition, which the many, feeling about in the dark, are always mistaking and misnaming.[28]

Maritain himself put the point more formally in *The Degrees of Knowledge*. There are, he claimed, a "diversity of dimensions" in the world which a true epistemology must recognize.[29] The error motivating idealism and materialism alike is that they mistake part for whole, treating "a particular order of sciences as the univocal type of the world of knowing and constructs its whole philosophy of knowing with reference to that chosen type. Not only does it neglect vast areas of knowledge, but it also tends to reduce the diversities of the life of the mind to a noetic monism." The result is that such theories cannot "recognize that mind has any nature or any structure. [They] see it only as pure movement, a pure freedom. Hence, it never really gets beyond spreading it out, whole and entire, upon a single plane of intellection, like a two-dimensional world, infinitely flat."[30]

In this infinitely flat world, human agents do not exist. They never will. Monodimensional metaphysics, and the "sciences" built on them, never *prove* that human agency and consciousness do not exist; they preclude it at the beginning of inquiry. The materialist philosopher David Hume once asked, "What peculiar privilege has this little agitation of the rain which we call thought, that we must make it the model of the whole universe?"[31] There must have been something that caused Hume to say "Be a philosopher—[a Stratonician physicalist?]; but, amidst all your philosophy, be still a man."[32] He must have known that in his philosophy, there *are* no real men.

28. Plato, "Phaedo," in *Plato: The Trial and Death of Socrates: Four Dialogues*, translated by Benjamin Jowett (Mineola, New York: Dover Thrift Edition, 1992), 96–97.

29. Jacques Maritain, *Distinguish to Unite or The Degrees of Knowledge*, translated by Gerald B. Phelan (New York: Charles Scribner's Sons, 1959), 315–16.

30. Ibid., ix.

31. This question is voiced by the skeptical character Philo in Hume's *Dialogues Concerning Natural Religion* (New York: Macmillan Publishing Company, 1947), 148.

32. David Hume, *An Enquiry Concerning the Human Understanding* (London: Oxford University Press, 1975), 9.

FEDERICO TEDESCO

The Body's Justice

A Hylomorphic View of the Genesis of Virtue

"The bodily virtues such as health and a good state of body depend on a blending of hot and cold in due proportion."[1]

"Health, beauty, and the like [are goods] because are bodily virtues and [as such] are productive of many other goods."[2]

"Ad bonam autem complexionem corporis sequitur nobilitas animae."[3]

I. Introduction

THIS ESSAY WILL PROVIDE a synthetic and yet rather complete explanation of how justice must be conceived within an ethics consistent with the principles of hylomorphic theory as developed by the Aristotelian-Thomistic school. After having established the hylomorphic conception of justice, it will be possible to bring out the theoretical ground in virtue of which Jacques Maritain's *Pour la justice* is capable of going beyond *actualité,* despite the fact that its object falls within the domain of the historical contingency.

1. Aristotle, *Physics* 7.3, 246b4-6; my translation. All translations of Aristotle are mine unless otherwise noted.

2. Aristotle, *Rhetoric* 1.6, 1362b14-16.

3. Aquinas, *Sentencia De anima,* lib. II, lect. 19, n. 7; hereafter cited as *InDA.*

II. The Instrumental Conception of the Body

Let us begin by examining the thesis that Aristotle's ethical treatises *are not yet hylomorphic in character* such that it would be a mistake to search them for the principles of a fully hylomorphic ethic. This is not an entirely novel point. Several exegetes of eminent rank have argued for the pre-hylomorphic nature of Aristotle's ethical treatises.[4] We will provide further evidence of the pre-hylomorphic nature of Aristotelian ethics by examining its conception of the *soul-body relation* in the light of a triad of concepts, which then will be used to systematically determine the principles of a truly hylomorphic ethic. This triad of concepts is constituted by the notions of *koinonia* (community), *philia* (friendship), and *dikaiosyne* (justice).

As Aristotle rightly observes in *Eudemian Ethics,* these concepts must be conceived as *synora*, that is, as neighbouring notions.[5] This is because they have a common denominator, the concept of equality, *to ison*. In fact, *koinonia,* or community, can be defined as the set whose elements form a unity in virtue of a *koinon* (common end) in which they partake precisely on account of their equality. *Philia,* or friendship, is instead the specific relation that occurs among the elements of a given *koinonia. Dikaiosyne,* or justice, is the virtue that preserves the equality on the basis of which the friends share the end achieved thanks to their *koinonia.* Now it must be observed that Aristotle' ethics does not conceive the soul-body relation as a *koinonia* whose elements share a common end (*koinon*) on the basis of an equality

4. "Enfin, le livre VII [de l'Étique à Eudème] contient différent teste dans lesquels la conception mécaniciste-instrumentaliste se retrouve exprimée en termes fort nets.... Ici [dans l'Étique à Eudème], au contraire, on affirme que l'âme e le corps ne subsistent pas chacun pour sa part, parce que le corps est complètement subordonné à l'âme, à tel point même qu'il ne peut être question, entre eux, d'association ou de *koinonia*.... En fait, il y a donc contradiction flagrante entre les vues développées dans ces passages de l'Étique eudémienne et la conception de l'être vivant dépendant de la théorie hylémorphique." François Nuyens, *L'Évolution de la Psychologie d'Aristote* (Louvain-Paris: Vrain, 1948), 187–88; "En résumé, l'Étique à Eudème est la première ébauche et l'Étique à Nicomaque l'expression achevée de la morale qui repond à la nouvelle conception de l'homme qu'a élaborée l'Aristote de la période de transition ... une morale de cet vie, sans aucune ouverture sur un autre monde quel qu'il soit, et une morale qui sépare les valeurs corporelles et les valeurs psychiques bien au-delà de ce que pourrait se permettre une morale hylémorphiste." *L'Étique à Nicomaque,* vol. 1, edited by René A. Gauthier and Jean Y. Jolif (Louvain-Paris: Publications Universitaires, 1970), 54.

5. "Therefore, there are as many forms [*eide*] of friendship as there are of justice and of communities [*koinoniai*], and all these forms border on each other [*synora*]." Aristotle, *Eudemian Ethics* 7.8, 1241b15; hereafter cited as EE.

which must be preserved through justice.[6] This is due to the fact that in Aristotle's ethical treatises the body is conceived as an "organon," namely as a *tool* that the soul uses to carry out most of its vital functions.[7] For Aristotle, the "tool-artisan" relation is perfectly equivalent to the relation that occurs between the slave and the despot, as well as the subject and the tyrant.[8] In Aristotelian ethics, we therefore have, on the one hand, the set (α) "body, tool, slave, subject," and on the other, the set (β) "soul, artisan, despot, tyrant." The relation that links the elements of (α) with their counterpart in (β) cannot give rise to a *koinonia* for the simple reason that a common end (*koinon*) cannot be found in this case.[9] In fact, the ultimate end for the sake of which each member of (α) operates is the member of (β) that uses it rather than the goal which its user pursues.[10] Moreover, if the ultimate end of an instrument whatsoever coincides with its user, then the instrument must be conceived as something *belonging to its user*. Hence, if we assume that a community necessarily requires at least two distinct elements, it is evident that the relation "instrument-user" cannot give rise to any *koinonia* due to the fact that it does not occur between two different elements, but between an element and something that belongs to it.[11] This explains why Aristotle defines the slave as a part (*morion*) of the despot who uses him as a living instrument (*emphychon organon*) useful to achieve his own end.[12]

Let us call the *instrumental conception of the body* the thesis according to which the soul is the despot that uses tyrannically the body to achieve a good that the body does not share on account of its purely instrumental function.

This instrumental conception of the body, along with its main corol-

6. "But since the relation of soul and body, craftsman and instrument, and master and slave is the same [*homois echei*], between them there is no community [*koinonia*]." Aristotle, EE 7.8, 1241b17-19; "In tyranny there is in fact no friendship or it is very little [*mikron philias*]: in fact, where there is nothing common [*koinon*] to ruler and ruled, there is not friendship either, since there is no justice, as for instance between craftsman and instrument, soul and body, master and slave." Aristotle, *Nicomachean Ethics* 8.11, 1161a33-35; hereafter cited as NE.

7. "For the body is the soul's connate instrument [*organon symphyton*]." EE, 7.8, 1241b22; see also NE 8.13, 1161a33-35.

8. EE 7.8, 1241b17-19; NE 8.13, 1161a33-35.

9. "In a different way in fact the saw and the art that uses it are associated, namely not in view of some end common to both [*koinon*]—they are in fact like instrument and soul—but for the sake of the user." EE 7.10, 1242a13; see also *NE*, 8.13, 1161b3.

10. See EE 7.10, 1242a13-15.

11. See EE 7.9, 1241b19-20.

12. See EE 7.9, 1241b22-24.

laries, can be found also in some of Plato's dialogues. In fact, in the *Alcibiades*, Socrates precisely claims that the body is an instrument which the soul uses by way of command.[13] In this dialogue, Plato therefore maintains that the human being is nothing but an *anima utens corpore*, that is a soul which uses the body.[14] Consequently the *Alcibiades* comes to conceive the body precisely as an element belonging to the human being, rather than as a quidditative part of its own essence.[15]

III. Hylomorphic Theory and the Quidditative *Koinonia* between the Soul and the Body

Hylomorphic theory can thus be conceived as a systematic overthrow of the Platonic conception of the body, which Aristotle nevertheless retained in his ethical thought. In fact, the basic thesis of hylomorphic theory holds precisely that the psychosomatic composite underlies a *koinonia* whose existence can consequently be preserved only through justice.[16]

To understand in which sense the psychosomatic composite underlies a *koinonia*, it must be observed that the form and the matter of a hylomorphic compound are *incomplete quiddities*: "neither substantial form nor matter has a complete essence."[17] This is due to the fact that the principles of a hylomorphic substance have a quiddity whose definition can be provided only by the addition of something that is outside the genus in which form and matter respectively fall. The incompleteness of the principles of a hylomorphic substance thus generates a mutual transcendental relation *secundum dici* whereby form and matter unite.[18] In order to understand how deep the unity orig-

13. See *Alcibiades* 1, 129e.

14. See *Alcibiades* 1, 130c.

15. See *Alcibiades* 1, 131b.

16. "They all [Platonists and Pythagoreans] join the soul to a body, or place it in a body, without adding any specification of the cause of their union, or of the [bodily] dispositions required for it. Yet such explanation can scarcely be omitted; for it is in virtue of a community [*koinonia*] that one acts and the other is acted upon, one moves and the other is moved. No such correlations are to be found at random." *De Anima* 1.3, 407b17; hereafter cited as DA.

17. Aquinas, *De ente et essentia*, chap. 5.

18. "... nam in genere substantiae matteria et forma habent inter se veram et realem habitudinem essentialiter inclusam in proprio esse illarum, et ideo una definitur per habitudinem ad aliam." Francisco Suarez, *Disputationes metaphysucae* (Hildesheim: Olms, 1998), vol. II, sec. 3, n. 10, 798a; see also Cajetan, *Commentary on St. Thomas Aquinas' "On Being and Essence"* (Milwaukee, Wisconsin: Marquette University Press, 1964), 301; Joseph Grend, *Elementa philosophiae aristotelico-thomisticae* (Rome: SALER, 1935), 154 n. 190.

inated by a transcendental relation is, it is necessary to take into account that this kind of relation can be conceived as the ratio generated by a given quiddity, precisely on account of its incompleteness.[19] The *absolutum* of which the schoolmen talked in defining the transcendental relation is precisely the incomplete quiddity of the subject in which this relation is rooted.[20] A transcendental relation is thus *originated by the quiddity itself* of the subject of the relation, whereas a categorical ratio is a simple accident which has as its own cause (*fundamentum*) a property belonging to the subject: for example, a certain quality can give rise to the categorical relation of similarity. Being caused by the quiddity itself of the subject, the transcendental relation originates therefore an *essential unity* which Aristotle rightly defines *malista hen*, that is most of all one.[21] Thus between form and matter there exists an essential unity due to the mutual transcendental relation which they establish in virtue of their quidditative incompleteness. Now, the essential union of form and matter gives rise to a quidditative unity which is precisely the *complete essence* in which and by which the hylomorphic compound becomes apt to receive existence.

Having said that, the reason the hylomorphic composite has a quiddity that satisfies the notion of *koinonia* becomes clear: in virtue of their reciprocal transcendental relation *secundum dici*, form and matter give rise to a quidditative unity in order to achieve an act of being which precisely constitutes the good in which form and matter participate *as quidditative parts* of the complete essence. If the body and the soul are the hylomorphic principles of the living being, they must likewise give rise to a quidditative

19. On the vigorous debate among Thomists on the nature and the existence of the transcendental relation, see Anton Krempel, *La doctrine de la relation chez saint Thomas: Exposé historique est systématique* (Paris: Vrin, 1952). On the reaction provoked by Krempel's work among Thomists, it is interesting to read the review written by Adriaan Pattin in *Revue Philosophique de Louvain* 52, no. 33 (1954): 160–61.

20. "Ex quo etiam constat, quod relatio trascendentalis … non importat ex principali significato relationem, sed aliquid absolutum, ad quod sequitur vel sequi potest aliqua relatio. Nam si absolutum non importat, tascendentalis non erit … Unde relatio trascendentalis non est forma adveniens subiecto seu rei absolutae [= accident], sed [est forma] illi [subiecti] imbibita, connotans tamen aliquid extrinsecum, a quo pendet vel circa quo versatur, ut matteria ad formam", Ioannes a sancto Thoma, *Cursus Philosophicus Thomisticus*, (Paris: Vivès, 1883), tomus 1: *Logica*, II, q. 17, a. 2, 499 a.

21. "Two things are called [essentially] one, when the definition which states the [incomplete] essence of one is indivisible from another definition which shows us [the incomplete essence of] the other.… In general, those things the thought of whose essence is indivisible, and cannot separate them either in time or in place or in definition, are most of all one [*malista hen*]." Aristotle, *Metaphysics* 6.6, 1016a32-1016b3, translated by W. D. Ross.

koinonia that can be preserved only as long as the equality between its elements is accurately observed through justice.

Moreover, since friendship is the specific relation that occurs between the elements of a *koinonia*, the relation which the soul and its body establish at the level of their quidditative *koinonia* is a *friendship*. More precisely, the quidditative *koinonia* existing between the hylomorphic principles of the living being presupposes a friendship that can be defined as an *isotropic type*. A friendship is called "isotropic" if the members of the *koinonia* are arithmetically equal (*isoi*). The members of a *koinonia* are called arithmetically equal if they equally contribute to the achievement of the common end (*koinon*). Consequently, they share the good achieved thanks to their *koinonia* on the basis of a calculus that does not establish a proportion (*analoghia*) but rather an arithmetical equivalence. Therefore, since the members of the quidditative *koinonia* are parts of the complete essence to the same degree, it is necessary to grant them an arithmetical equality. Hence their relation within the quidditative *koinonia* must be conceived as an isotropic friendship.

That said, we must still establish that, from a hylomorphic point of view, the soul-body relation underlies an isotropic friendship that is based on virtue. A friendship is called "virtuous" if the ultimate end for the sake of which the members of the *koinonia* reciprocally act is the fulfilment of the goodness inherent in the other. Virtue is in fact nothing but the quality that fulfils the good inherent in a subject which acquires it. Hence, in order to prove that a virtuous friendship exists between the intellective soul and its body, it is necessary to show that they establish a *koinonia* in which each member acts in view of the virtues whereby the goodness inherent in the other achieves its perfect fulfilment.

IV. Bodily Justice

Let us consider first how the body exercises a virtuous friendship towards the soul that vivifies it. To understand in which sense the human body concurs with the virtues that the intellective soul can acquire, it is necessary to consider that the human body is able to possess a *somatic quality* that no other body is capable of developing. In fact, like all the physical substances of the sublunary region, the human body is a *quaternary compound*.[22] This

22. For the notion of "quaternary compound" see Harold H. Joachim, "Aristotle's Conception on Chemical Combination," *The Journal of Philology*, no. 29 (1904): 75.

simply means that the sublunary bodies result from the blending to which the elements give rise when they *reciprocally alter* their basic tactile qualities: hot, cold, dry, moist.[23] At the end of this process of multiple alterations, a homogeneous body is generated which possesses tactile qualities according to a degree it falls among one of the intermediate values included between hot and cold, dry and wet. These intermediate qualities inherent in the body of the sublunary substances constitute precisely their somatic complexion (*krasis*), which Aquinas later calls their *complexio corporis.*

The *complexio corporis* of the human body is made of tactile qualities which are *perfectly equidistant* from the contrary qualities inherent to their blended elements. Aquinas refers to this perfect equidistance when he points out that the human body is removed from contraries (*habet elongationem a contrariis*)[24] because its *complexio* can achieve in the fullest measure an intermediate state (*maxime reductum ad medium*).[25]

The human body can achieve a perfect equidistance from the contrary qualities due to the fact that its *complexio corporis* derives from a blending in which the elements can enjoy a *proportional equality*. This kind of equality is obtained by keeping constant the ratio existing between the elements' capacity of causing alterations (*virtus agendi*) and their amount in the blending. More exactly, the proportional equality that can occur among the elements of the human body is due to the fact that their amount in the mixture is *inversely proportional* to their *virtus agendi*; when this value increases, the amount decreases according to a given constant of proportionality.[26] The human body is therefore capable of possessing a perfect equidistance from contrary qualities in virtue of a formula of combination that establishes a proportional equality among the elements of the mixture. This explains why Aquinas holds that the human *complexio corporis* derives

23. Aristotle, *De Generatione et Corruptione*, 1.10.

24. "... as the heavenly bodies [made up of ether], the human being is removed from contraries [*habet elongationem a contrariis*] in virtue of a somatic complexion which is equable in the fullest measure [*per maximam aequalitatem complexionis*]." ST I, q. 91, a. 1; my translation. All translations of Aquinas are mine unless otherwise noted.

25. "Therefore, since the body to which the rational soul is united must be best disposed for the sense of touch, it must be brought in the fullest measure to an intermediate state [*maxime reductum ad medium*] by an equable complexion." Aquinas, *Quaestio de anima*, 8.

26. "Elementa quanto plus habent de specie et de qualitatibus activis [hot, cold], tanto plus habent de virtute agendi: unde non posset fieri adaequatio, nisi de elemento magis matteriali [earth] esset plus secundum quantitatem vel materiam. Ideo oportet corpus humanum secundum quantitatem habere plus de terrestri, quamvis non secundum qualitatem, quia in corpore vivo dominatur calidum." Aquinas, *In II Sent.*, d. 1, q. 2, a. 5, ad 4.

from the most perfect mode of combination.[27] Moreover, the fact that the human *complexio corporis* can be based upon a *perfectissimum commixtionis modum* explains why the body of the human being is considered the highest peak reached by nature in the sublunary region. The human body possesses a *complexio corporis* whose perfect equidistance from the contrary qualities of tactility allows it to be *supreme in the genus of body*, and to touch [*attingere*] consequently the lowest member in the genus of intellective substances—namely, the rational soul.[28]

However, affirming that the human *complexio corporis* can be based on a proportional equality is equivalent to saying that the human being has a body that can achieve a *distributive type of justice*. As Aquinas rightly observes in *II Super Sent.* 27, 1, 3, distributive justice consists in fact in keeping constant the proportional equality that occurs between two ratios whatsoever.[29] The human *complexio corporis* is marked precisely by the fact that it derives from a blending in which the ratio between the *virtus agendi* and the amount can remain proportionally equal for all the elements involved in the mixture. Hence, the proportional equality that the elements can enjoy in the human *complexio corporis*, confers upon the human body a somatic virtue that can be correctly called "bodily justice."

At this point we can begin to clearly appreciate how deeply the platonic conception of the body is overthrown in hylomorphic theory. In fact, according to the *Phaedo*, the body underlies by its very nature a kind of foolishness, *aphrosyne*, which brings about a contamination that prevents the soul from acquiring wisdom and the other virtues.[30] Hence, not to be contaminated by the madness of its body, the soul must necessarily crush the

27. "From what has been said, it is evident that the total operation of the inferior nature reaches its highest peak in [the body of] man as the most perfect being. For we see that the operation of nature ascends progressively from the simple elements, by blending them, until it reaches the most perfect mode of combination [*perfectissimum commixtionis modum*], which is [that underlying] the human body. Consequently, this disposition of the human body, to which the rational soul is united, must exist in order that the body may possess the most tempered complexion [*temperatissimae complexionis*]." Aquinas, *Quaestio de anima*, 8.

28. We have, therefore, to assume the existence of something supreme in the genus of bodies, namely, the human body that is endowed with an equable complexion [*aequaliter complexionatum*], which laps the lowest of the higher genus [*quod attingit ad infimum superioris generis*], namely, the human soul, which holds the lowest rank in the genus of intellectual substances." Aquinas, *Summa Contra Gentiles* II, chap. 68.

29. "Justitia vero distributiva aequalitatem respicit geometrica, quae est aequalitas proportionis." Aquinas, *In II Sent.*, d. 27, q. 1, a. 3.

30. "And in this way, freeing ourselves from the foolishness of the body [*tou somatos aphrosyne*] and being pure [*katharos*], we shall, I think, be with the pure." Plato, *Phaedo*, 67a.

koinonia with it.[31] In contrast, according the hylomorphic perspective, it turns out that the intellective soul can acquire virtuous habits only thanks to the somatic justice that its body is capable of possessing only as long as the soul preserves the body's proportional equality by respecting precisely their mutual *koinonia.*

V. The Friendship of the Body

To understand how this can occur, it is necessary to observe that the *complexio corporis* produces in the faculties of the intellective soul connate habits which are compatible or incompatible with the acquisition of the psychic virtues depending upon whether the *complexio corporis* is endowed with bodily justice. Let us consider first the function played by the *complexio corporis* in the genesis of the moral virtues whereby the intellective soul confers upon its emotional life a rational measure.

The so-called passions of the soul depend on a psychic faculty that is partially plunged into matter.[32] The appetitive faculty is in fact a potency of a bodily organ (the limbic brain) whose somatic dispositions produce connate habits that predispose the appetitive faculty to originate certain emotional behaviors. The inherent dispositions of the bodily organs depend directly on the *complexio corporis,* which is consequently the remote cause of the connate habits that predetermine the appetitive faculty.[33] If the *complexio corporis* is based on a proportional equality, then the body with which the soul is quidditatively united will be endowed with bodily justice. Consequently, the connate habits of the appetitive faculty will give rise to good emotional tendencies. This explains why Aristotle calls this kind of connate habit *physike arête,* namely "natural virtue."[34] If, on the contrary, the soul is incorporated in an unjust body, then the organ of the appetitive faculty produces in it connate habits that constitute natural vices.[35]

31. Ibid.

32. "Et ideo intellectus est forma subsistens, aliae potentiae [animae] sunt formae in materia." *InDA,* lib. 1, l. 2, n. 5.

33. "But on the part of the body, in respect of the individual nature, there are some appetitive habits by way of natural beginnings. For some are disposed by their somatic complexion [*ex propria corporis complexione*] to chastity or meekness or such like." ST I-II, q. 51, a. 1.

34. "... as practical wisdom [*phronesis*] is to cleverness [*deinotes*]—not the same, but like it—so is natural virtue [*physike arete*] to virtue in the strict sense [*kyria arête*]. For all men think that each type of character belongs to its possessors in some sense by nature." NE 6.13, 1144b2, translated by W. D. Ross.

35. Concerning the incorporation of the intellective soul see Federico Tedesco, "From Mar-

The vicious habits the *complexio corporis* produces in the appetite faculty through the inherent dispositions of its bodily organ prevent the soul from acquiring the moral virtues. This explains why Aquinas claims that the appetitive faculty (endowed with vicious habits) exercises a *ius contraddicendi* against the reason, namely the right to contradict the motions by means of which the reason generate the ethical virtues.[36] It is in fact altogether impossible that the appetite faculty could be simultaneously determined by contrary habits. Therefore, to acquire the moral virtues, the appetitive faculty must first lose the natural vices it possesses because of the somatic injustice to which the body is subject when it is endowed with a *complexio corporis* that lacks proportional equality. In other words, the appetitive faculty of the intellective soul cannot acquire the moral virtues unless the body with which it is united by the quidditative *koinonia* is endowed with such bodily justice. This explains why Aquinas holds that the moral virtues *presuppose* the natural virtues that the appetitive faculty possesses: its organ depends on a *complexio corporis* endowed with the somatic quality we have called "bodily justice."[37]

In order to understand that the intellect of the rational soul also possesses connate habits depending on the *complexio corporis*, it is sufficient to examine the role of the body in the genesis of noetic operations. Even though the human intellect is a faculty that operates independently of a bodily organ, it derives its object from the species produced by inner senses (imagination, cogitative power, memory) that do depend on bodily organs: "The faculty of thinking [*noetikon*] then thinks [*noei*] the forms [*eide*] in the images [*en tois phantasmasi*]."[38] The fact that the human intellect generates its cognitive species in virtue of bodily faculties explains why Aquinas holds that the body plays the role of *repraesentans obiectum*, namely, of a principle which pro-

itain to Aquinas: Beyond the Polarity between Individual and Person," in *Human Nature, Contemplation, and The Political Order*, edited by Peter Karl Koritansky (American Maritain Association Press, 2013; distributed by The Catholic University of America Press), 84–89.

36. See Aquinas, ST I-II, q. 58, a. 2.

37. "That there is a natural virtue, presupposed to moral, is obvious from the fact that individual virtuous or vicious practices seem to exist in some people naturally; immediately from birth certain men seem to be just or temperate or brave because of a natural disposition by which they are inclined to virtuous works.... This natural disposition can be considered from three viewpoints ... last, on the part of the sensitive appetite according as, by natural complexion [*ex natuali complexione*], some men are inclined to anger, others to concupiscence or passions of a different kind, either too much or too little, or with moderation in which moral virtue consists." Aquinas, *Sententia libri Ethicorum*, VI, lect. 11, translated by C. I. Litzinger.

38. See Aristotle, *De Anima*, 3. 7, 431b2-3, translated by J. A. Smith.

vides the object thanks to which the mind can form its own cognitive species.[39] The noetic operations of the human intellect therefore depends on inner senses upon which the *complexio corporis* confers connate dispositions, which in turn produce natural habits that can allow or prevent the mind's cognitive functions, depending upon whether the *complexio corporis* is endowed with or devoid of bodily justice.[40]

Moreover, it must be noted that the sensitive nature of a cognitive organism ultimately depends on the sense of touch.[41] Tactility requires the ability to perceive the tangible qualities of which an organ and the entire body to which it belongs are made up. Due to the *recipiens debet esse denudatum a recepto* principle ("the recipient must be deprived of the thing received"), any sense can perceive its object only if it does not possess it actually. Therefore, since an intermediate state is in potency to the contraries from whose blending it derives, the tangible qualities inherent in the organ of touch must necessarily be reduced to a mean. It follows that the more the human *complexio corporis* is reduced to a mean, the more the organ of touch will be well disposed for the sensory operation that lies at the ground of that refined sensitivity which a sovereign mind necessarily requires. There exists, therefore, a causal relationship between a *complexio corporis* endowed with bodily justice and the cognitive virtues that the intellective soul can acquire.[42] Aquinas can therefore link, in a unique sequence, all of the following: a *complexio corporis* based on proportional equality, a precise sense of touch, a good sensitivity, a sovereign mind, and a noble soul, the last of which consequently presupposes a body endowed with somatic justice.[43]

39. See Aquinas, *Quodlibet* VII, 5, 1, ad 3.

40. "But in respect of the individual nature, a cognitive habit is natural as to its beginning, in so far as one man, from the disposition of his organs, is more apt than another to understand well, since we need the sensitive powers for the operation of the intellect." ST I-II, q. 51, a. 1.

41. See *Quaestio de anima*, 8; *InDA*, II, lect. 19.

42. "While in respect of all the other senses we fall below many species of animals, in respect of touch we far excel all other species in exactness of discrimination. That is way man is the most intelligent of all animals. This is confirmed by the fact that it is to differences in the organ of touch and to nothing else that the differences between man and man in respect of natural endowment are due; men whose flesh is hard [due to a *complexion corporis* that lacks somatic justice] are ill-endowed by nature, men whose flesh is soft [in virtue of a *complexion corporis* based on somatic justice], well-endowed." Aristotle, *De Anima*, 2.9, 421a20-25, translated by J. A. Smith.

43. "The pre-eminence of touch in man is the reason why man is the wisest of the animals; moreover, among men it is in virtue of fineness of touch, and not of any other sense, that we discriminate the mentality gifted from the rest ... a fine touch is an effect of a good bodily complexion or temperament [*complexionis sive temperantiae*]. For as the organ of touch is itself necessarily

VI. Friendship of the Soul

Since friendship is a relation of reciprocal benevolence, there can be friendship between the soul and its body only if the soul corresponds to the virtuous benevolence of the body with an equal aptitude. From an hylomorphic standpoint it turns out that the soul does have a virtuous aptitude of benevolence toward its body. This is evident from the fact that the bodily justice cannot be maintained unless the soul preserves the proportional equality on which the *complexio corporis* of its body is based. The virtuous benevolence of the soul is still more evident when the body it vivifies lacks bodily justice. In fact, in this case, the intellective soul produces this somatic virtue by removing the lack of balance that prevents the *complexio corporis* from achieving proportional equality. Since a lack of balance is due to the fact that at least one element prevails against the others, and since the elements can transform into each other by altering their tactile qualities, the intellective soul produces in its body the somatic justice by increasing or decreasing the amount of the element that violates the proportional equality.[44]

In order to do so, however, the soul needs a diagnostic technique that allows it to detect what element prevails against the others. We know that the *complexio corporis* is the cause responsible for the connate habits that the appetitive faculty possesses because of the inherent dispositions of its bodily organ. This explains why Aquinas claims that the *complexio corporis* is the dispositive cause on which all the passions of the appetitive faculty depend.[45]

---

endowed with tangible qualities (being composed of the elements) it needs to be in a condition of potency to extremes of the tangible at least by itself constituting a mean between them. Now nobility of soul [*nobilitas animae*] follows upon a well-balanced physical complexion [*bonam complexionem corporis*]; because forms are proportionate to their matter. It follows that those whose touch is delicate are so much the nobler in nature and the more intelligent." *InDA*, II, lect. 19; translated by K. Foster and S. Humphries.

44. As for the transformation of the elements into each other see Aristotle, *De generatione et corruptione*, 2.4.

45. "For passions are ascribed to the bodily complexion [*complexioni*] as a dispositive cause in their regard, and as concerns that which is material in them, such as the heat of the blood [in anger] and the like." Aquinas, SCG II, chap. 63, no. 6. In distinguishing a material and a formal level of emotions, Aquinas has obviously in mind the thesis stated by Aristotle in *De anima* 403a25 according to which the passions experienced by the com-unity 'body-mind' are hylomorphic in character, since they are nothing but forms plunged into matter (*logoi enyloi*); "Whenever the physical complexion of the body [*complexio corporis*] contributes to a vital activity, the latter pertains to the body as well as the soul; but this happens in the case of all the passions of the soul, such as anger, meekness, fear, confidence, pity and so forth, hence all these passions would seem to belong partly to the body." *InDA*, I, 2; translated by K. Foster and S. Humphries.

Now if the ordinary passions of the soul causally depend on the *complexio corporis,* then the ordinary passions reveal the *complexio corporis.* Since they manifest the *complexio corporis,* the ordinary passions must be conceived as *signs* or symptoms whereby the intellective soul can understand the formula of combination of its own body. For example, let us suppose that fear is causally connected with the cooling of the body. A moral agent who has a *complexio corporis* wherein there exists an excess of cold will then be subject to this emotional behavior, as Aristotle points out in *De partibus animalium.*[46] The tendency towards fear is therefore what John Deely would call an "indexical sign," that is, a symptom that reveals a *complexio corporis* in which the excess of the tactile quality of water causes in the appetitive faculty a tendency to fear, thus predisposing the moral agent to feel this emotion.[47] Hence, considering its emotional life from a purely semiotic standpoint, the intellective soul can develop a *diagnostic technique* whereby it detects the element that mixes with the others according to a ratio which violates some proportional equality. The intellective soul can therefore exercise a virtuous benevolence toward its body either by preserving its somatic justice or by producing this bodily virtue through a physical process that corrects the *complexio corporis'* lack of balance on the basis of a diagnosis made possible by the semiotic of ordinary emotions.

In this case, the overthrow of Plato's conception of the body is complete. According to the *Phaedo,* there is in fact a sharp opposition between the *philosophos* and the *philosomatos,* namely, between the person who loves wisdom and the person who loves his own body.[48] From a hylomorphic point of view, however, it turns out that the philosopher acquires the virtues through which he or she achieves wisdom only thanks to the somatic justice that the human body gains precisely in virtue of the soul's friendship. Therefore, from a hylomorphic standpoint, the *philosophos* is necessarily a *philosomatos.*

46. See *De partibus animalium* 2.4, 650b27-30.

47. "Again, one thing can call another to mind by virtue of some causal connection between the two, as when a doctor diagnoses a certain disease from a series of spot or rash on the skin, or when a scout follows a trail of a fugitive seeking to flee, or a jungle cat seeks its prey from a spoor. In cases such as these, the traces in question provide an *index* or *indexical sign* of another than themselves." John Deely, *Logic as a Liberal Art: Rethinking Logic in the Perspective of Semiotics* (Kingston, Ontario: Queen's University Press, 1985), 21.

48. "It is a reliable sign [*tekmerion*], when you see a man troubled because he is going to die, that he was not a lover of wisdom [*philosophos*], but rather a lover of his own body [*philosomatos*]." *Phaedo* 68b; my translation.

VII. Conclusion

From what has been said, it is clear that an ethics based on hylomorphic theory recognizes three forms of justice: (a) *hylomorphic justice,* in virtue of which the body and the soul preserve the isotropic friendship that intervenes between them within the quidditative *koinonia;* (b) *bodily justice,* in virtue of which the human body maintains the proportional equality among the elements from whose blending its *complexio corporis* results; and (c) *ethical justice,* in virtue of which the members of the political *koinonia* share the common good on the basis of an equality that can assume an arithmetical or geometrical character.[49]

Ethical systems based upon an instrumental conception of the body necessarily violate all these forms of justice. By taking the soul to have a right to interact with its body according to a tyrannical aptitude, the instrumental conception of the body destroys hylomorphic justice whereby the hylomorphic principles of the human being preserve their isotropic friendship within the quidditative *koinonia.* In doing so, however, the instrumental conception of the body alters the proportional equality in virtue of which the human body enjoys somatic justice. Since the psychic virtues depend on bodily justice, the instrumental conception of the body therefore compromises the genesis of the moral virtues in the same moment in which it corrupts the proportional equality that lies at the ground of somatic justice.

It is important to note the effects generated by the instrumental conception of the body because most of the systems of thought that exercise an influence on the contemporary world are based precisely on this conception. Hinduism, Buddhism, and Platonism can only justify reincarnation by assuming that *homo anima utens corpore.* If we add to this belief the Protagorean thesis of the *homo mensura,* we obtain the assumptions by which transhumanism justifies the legitimacy of redesigning the human being by resorting to technological devices.[50] Likewise, the most important theses

49. From an hylomorphic standpoint there exists also a fourth kind of justice—which we can rightly call "theological"—that is the virtue which enables the human being to accept God's decision to incorporate his intellective soul in a body endowed with a specific *complexion corporis,* that confers upon his faculties certain connate habits.

50. As for the meaning of the Protagorean thesis, it is interesting to consider the explanation provided by Aristotle in *Metaphysics* 10.2, 1053a 35–1053b3.

of Aristotle's ethics depend ultimately on a Platonic understanding of the body, which were then transmitted to the Peripatetic School. Alexander of Aphrodisias, who is undoubtedly one of the most prominent of Aristotle's exegetes, claims that the Delphic precept to "know thyself" simply means to "know your soul," which is precisely the interpretation that Plato provides in the first *Alcibiades*.[51]

Within the Aristotelian School, Aquinas is thus one of the few thinkers who developed his thought on the basis of deep insight into hylomorphic theory. For example, Thomas explicitly holds that there is no vital function in human being in which the body does not communicate at least as *repraesentans objectum*: "Nec tamen est verum quod aliquis actus sit hominis in vita praesenti in quo corpus non communicet; quia, quamvis in actibus intellectivae partis non communicet corpus sicut instrumentum actus, communicat tamen sicut repraesentans obiectum ... et sic patet quod etiam intelligendo, et in aliis actibus animae, utimur aliquo modo corpore."[52] Interestingly enough, the verb that Thomas systematically employs in this text—*communicare*—is related to the term *communio*, which is precisely the Latin translation of the Greek word *koinonia*. Despite this, there remains in Aquinas' work a tendency to describe the soul-body relation using a language that is completely compromised by the instrumental conception of the body. For instance, commenting on Aristotle's *De anima*, Aquinas paradoxically continues to designate the body as the instrument of the soul.[53] Likewise, throughout the entire *Corupus Thomisticum*, Thomas says that the sensible faculties *use* their organs.[54] Now this manner of speaking is formally incorrect due to the fact that the faculties of a biological system whatsoever establish with their somatic counterpart the same hylomorphic relationship that occurs between the soul and the body that it vivifies.[55] In fact, a fac-

51. "Le Pythien prophétise et annonce que c'est par la connaissance de soi que chacun parviendra à vivre conformément à la nature. Or, la connaissance de soi réside dans la connaissance de ce en vertu de quoi l'on est soi-même. Et ce en vertu de son âme que l'home est home." Alexandre d'Aphrodise, *De l'âme* (Paris: Vrin, 2008), 67; Plato, *Alcibiades*, 130e.

52. *Quodlibet* VII, q. 5, a. 1, ad 3.

53. "For it should be realized that certain activities or modifications of the soul depend on the body both as an instrument and as an object." *InDA*, I, 2; translated by K. Foster and S. Humphries.

54. See for example ST I-II, q. 17, a. 7, where Thomas says that, "Omnis autem actus virtutis utentis organo corporali, dependet non solum ex potential animae, sed etiam ex corporali organi dispositione."

55. "Suppose that the eye were an animal, sight would have been its soul, for sight is the substance [*ousia*] of the eye as its form [*kata ton logon*], whereas the eye is the matter of seeing....

ulty of a living being is just the *hylomorphic form* in virtue of which a given matter is able to carry out a specific vital functions. Unfortunately, this use of pre-hylomorphic language to convey hylomorphic thought led many Thomists to develop a theory in which assumptions based on the instrumental conception of the body contradictorily coexist with hylomorphic principles.

Let us consider for instance Evangeline Anderson's *The Human Body in The Philosophy of St. Thomas Aquinas*. In this work, the author rightly admits a mutual transcendental relation between the soul and the body which it vivifies as its hylomorphic form.[56] Consequently, she comes to conceive the body as a quidditative part of the human essence, which consequently plays the role of co-principle of man's quiddity.[57] At this point however Anderson claims that the human body is just a servant that the intellective soul uses as the instrument whereby it carries out the biological functions of which it is the first root.[58] Now, it must be noted that this assumption is altogether incompatible with the hylomorphic principles on the ground of which Anderson bases her account of human nature. In fact, as we already know, the instrumental conception of the body exactly denies what the hylomorphic affirms, namely, that the soul-body relation gives rise to a quidditative *koinonia*. Hence it is pretty clear that it is impossible to assume an instrumental conception of the body within an hylomorphic framework without generating *ipso facto* a contradiction that collapses the entire theory.

Moreover, it must be noted that Anderson's instrumental conclusion is based on a premise that underlies a deep misunderstanding of Aquinas' hylomorphic theory that seems to be shared by some other Thomists. In fact, behind Anderson's notion that the body acts only by means of the soul,

---

We must now extend our consideration from the part to the whole living being; for what a specific sense is to the bodily part which is its organ, that the whole faculty of sense [namely the soul] is to the whole sensitive body as such" Aristotle, *De Anima*, 2.1, 412b19-25.

56. "The soul, disunited from the body, is no longer a person. Its natural affinity and transcendental relation to the body remains." M. Evangeline Anderson, *The Human Body in the Philosophy of St. Thomas Aquinas* (Washington, D.C.: The Catholic University of America Press, 1953), 5–6; concerning the role played by the body in the genesis of the human person see Tedesco "From Maritain to Aquinas," 76–84.

57. "An investigation of the nature of the body reveals that it is the co-principle in a human essence, united substantially, immediately [namely in virtue of a transcendental relation], personally, and naturally to the human form which gives it being and life." Anderson, *The Human Body*, ix.

58. "Because the body acts only by means of the soul, the body's role is that of servant and instrument in the attainment of any and all additional and secondary acts of perfection." Ibid., 7.

there seems to be Thomas' hylomorphic principle that states that *forma dat esse materiae* (the form causes the existence of the matter of a physical substance): "Talis autem invenitur habitudo matteriae et formae quod forma dat esse matterie."[59] The way in which this basic principle of the hylomorphic theory is formulated is particularly misleading. In fact, it seems to convey the erroneous idea that the form is the *efficient cause* of existence. This explains why Aquinas feels the need to clarify that the hylomorphic form is the *principium essendi* not as an efficient cause, but rather from a formal standpoint: "Esse comparatur ad formam sicut per se consequens ipasam, non autem sicut effectus ad virtus agendi."[60] What is meant by the form being the *causa essendi* only in the formal order? It simply means that the form can bring about existence only insofar as *it is united to matter* in order to constitute the complete quiddity of a physical substance: "Per hoc enim in compositis ex matteria et forma, dicitur forma esse principium essendi, quia est complementum substantiae [= quidditatis substantialis] cuius actus est ipusm esse."[61]

Properly speaking, therefore, the *causa essendi* of the physical being is not the form alone, but the form insofar as it is quidditatively united to matter by means of the mutual transcendental relation which occurs between them. Briefly it can be said that the proper principle of the existence of a physical substance is the *complete essence* that it acquires in virtue of the quidditative union of its hylomophic principles, form and matter: "Esse est in re, et est actus resultans ex principiis rei [= form and matter]."[62] This follows from the existence being the act of the complete quiddity of a substance. In the case of a physical substance, the complete quiddity always results from the essential unity that form and matter establish in virtue of their mutual transcendental relation. Having said that, it becomes pretty clear why Aquinas, in describing hylomorphic substances, claims that their (complete) essence is simultaneously the subject of existence and the principle which allows them to receive *esse*: "Essentia dicitur secundum quod per eam et in ea ens habet esse."[63] Being a quidditative part of the complete

59. Aquinas, *De ente et essentia*, chap. 4.

60. Aquinas, *Quaestio de anima*, q. 14, ad 4.

61. Aquinas, SCG II, chap. 54; "... haec est ratio quare forma est causa [essendi], quia perficit rationem quidditatis rei." John of Saint Thomas, *Cursus philosophicus*, tomus II: *Philosophia naturalis*, I, q. 11, a. 1, 206b; see also Étienne Gilson, *L'être et l'essence* (Paris: Vrin, 1972), chap. 3.

62. Aquinas, *In III Sent.*, III, d. 6, q. 2, a. 2.

63. Aquinas, *De ente et essentia*, chap. 1.

essence of the hylomorphic substance, matter cannot therefore be conceived as an instrument of its formal counterpart. More generally, matter is involved in three types of causal relations, none of which can be reduced to instrumental causality. First of all, hylomorphic matter is such as to *receive* its proper form in virtue of its quidditative incompleteness. Consequently, it contributes to the generation of the complete essence of the hylomorphic substance by uniting to the substance's form on the basis of a transcendental relation. Moreover, being the subject of the becoming, matter is the inner cause on which depends all types of generation.[64] At the origin of Anderson's instrumental conception of the body there is, therefore, on the one hand, an erroneous understanding of the *forma dat esse* principle and, on the other, a wrong theory of matter's causality.

Being severely compromised with the instrumental conception of the body, the current version of hylomophism underlies several assumptions that are not hylomorphic in character.[65] If this analysis is correct, then it must be admitted that the Thomistic school has not developed yet a fully hylomorphic ethics, one entirely consistent and in the light of which human beings can project a world wherein their hylomorphic nature can fully flourish. An entirely hylomorphic humankind is therefore a reality that has yet to be realized, one perfectly capable of projecting a world entirely conceived according to all the exigencies of justice.

64. "Tres possunt enumerare effectus, circa quos versatur matteria.... Versatur enim matteria circa forma recipiendo, compositum constituendo, generationem patiendo ab agente." John of Saint Thomas, *Philosophia naturalis*, I, q. 11, a. 1, 204b.

65. As far as I know, the first attempt to rethink the current version of the hylomorphic theory was made by Pedro Descoqs in *Essay critique sur l'hylémorphisme* (Paris: Beauchesne, 1924).

IV

ETHICS AND AESTHETICS

JAMES JACOBS

The Corrosive Effect of Doubt on the Natural Law

1. Introduction

In the essays collected in *Pour la justice*, Jacques Maritain surveys the causes, and hoped for resolution, of the "world trial" and "crisis of civilization" of the 1940s.[1] Maritain argues that the root of Europe's devolution toward barbarism lies in the secularization of the Christian idea of man and the anthropocentric humanism that goes with it. This, in turn, points to what is required to solve the crisis: a renewal of true humanism reflecting a proper estimation of man based on both the certainties of metaphysics and the wisdom of religious faith.[2]

This secularized anthropology is, for Maritain, the result of a confluence of forces in modernity, from the Reformation to the Enlightenment, which casts doubt upon man's natural community in the natural law, as well as his innate ordination to the transcendent as the source of ultimate value.[3] While he acknowledges that modernity has had positive insights,

1. These descriptive phrases are taken from the titles to two of the more significant essays in the collection. See Jacques Maritain, *Pour la justice: Articles et discours (1940–1945)* (New York: Éditions de la Maison Française, 1945); "The Crisis of Civilization," 136–54, and, "World Trial: Its Meaning for the Future," 231–42.

2. See "The Crisis of Civilization," 139.

3. One enumeration of these forces is from "World Trial," in *Pour la justice*, 235: "We are looking on at the liquidation of that world which Machiavelli's pessimism has made to take unjust force for the essence of politics, which Luther's secession has thrown off balance by cutting Germany off from the European community, wherein the absolutism of the Ancient Regime has little by little changed the Christian order into an order of compulsion which was increasingly separated from the Christian sources of life, which the rationalism of Descartes and the

including an emphasis on human dignity and the utility of technology, it is equally true that its anthropocentrism had led to the irrationalism which has engulfed the world; thus, he offers the judgment that "the modern world has pursued good things down wrong pathways."[4] The paths of modernity have proved to be fatal because they neither begin nor end in transcendence: the pessimism of the Reformation views human nature as depraved, thereby severing human nature from God. This existential isolation is compounded by the ungrounded philosophical optimism of the Enlightenment which assumes that salvation is not from God, but rather is wholly immanent and attainable by reason alone. Maritain concludes: "Having given up God so as to be self-sufficient, man has lost track of his soul."[5] This loss of the soul's transcendence carries over into human society, for man now lacks a natural basis for community: he has common life but no common good, freedom without responsibility, and equality in place of justice.[6] With these changes, modern man is left to seek individual happiness without knowing his true end, and without the help of God's grace, thus perpetuating a pursuit destined to induce despair, for it is a search that can never be consummated.[7] Yet man nonetheless *seeks*: the futility of that search is manifested in the irrationalism asserting itself in the world trial that is its inevitable result.

This essay will consider why modern man's search for happiness led to a civilizational crisis, and will show that we are still in the grip of that crisis inasmuch as contemporary America embodies the same foundational assumption that led to the conflagration of the 1940s. This problematic assumption is, as Maritain points out, the denial of transcendence; but this

---

Encyclopedists has thrown into an illusory optimism, which the pseudo-Christian naturalism of Jean-Jacques Rousseau has led to confuse the sacred desires of man's heart with the expectation of a kingdom of God on earth procured by the State or by the Revolution.... Its error, in a word, was in believing that man works out his own salvation, only by his own power and that human history is made without God." See the parallel argument that elucidates this at greater length in Jacques Maritain, "Christian Humanism," in *The Range of Reason* (New York: Charles Scribner's Sons, 1942), 187–88. (A French version of this essay is in *Pour la justice*, 97–112.)

4. Maritain, "World Trial," 236.

5. Maritain, "Christian Humanism," 191.

6. Maritain, "The Crisis of Civilization," 140.

7. Maritain makes this point strongly in "Christian Humanism," 188: "The most significant political improvement of modern times, the concept of, and the devotion to, the rights of the human person and the rights of the people, was thus warped by the same loss of the concept and the sense of purpose or finality, and by the repudiation of the evangelical ferment acting in human history."

is not the ultimate cause, for there must be a reason why modernity has come to reject human transcendence.[8] In fact, the ultimate cause is an atmosphere of doubt which distorts the way man pursues the primary precepts of the natural law. The natural law cannot be ignored, yet doubt leads modern man to assume that he cannot fulfill it, that he can neither know Truth nor enjoy a truly common Good. This doubt of attaining happiness inculcates, in place of a hope for ultimate achievement, an existential fear, and as a consequence, man seeks only to avoid harm, thereby denying the greatness of soul which is realized only in striving to attain civic friendship and eternal beatitude. Thus, it is, ironically, man's inclination to fulfill the precepts of the natural law—albeit vitiated by an atmosphere of doubt—that lies at the explanatory heart of the crisis of civilization which continues to be one of the great global challenges confronting Thomism.

II. Natural Law in an Atmosphere of Doubt

While the natural law itself cannot change, the way its precepts are understood is ineluctably shaped by the intellectual milieu into which we are born; we are often not masters, but subjects, to the times in which we live. Charles Taylor elaborates on this point to explain the ascendency of secularism in the twentieth century: "The complex environing backgrounds of our thought and action ... impinge on our lives in a host of ways.... We are in fact all acting, thinking, and feeling out of backgrounds and frameworks which we do not fully understand."[9]

8. Maritain intuits that there is a deeper unity behind the many modern errors when he says, "Every great period of civilization is dominated by a certain peculiar idea that man fashions out of man. Our behavior depends on this image as much as on our very nature.... [This image is] strong enough to mold after its own pattern the social and political formations that are characteristic of a given cultural epoch." "Christian Humanism," 185.

9. Charles Taylor, *A Secular Age* (Cambridge, Massacheusetts: The Belknap Press of Harvard University Press, 2007), 387. The notion that our worldview acts as an interpretive framework to specific practices and understandings is, of course, the recurrent theme of Alasdair MacIntyre's critique of modern ethics in terms of the necessity of ethical traditions. As he recently described his project: "But it is of course not in such abstract terms [as are used in philosophical ethics] that particular agents in particular times and places understand themselves or that we as observers understand them. It is always in and through the particularities of the social, economic, and cultural relationships of their own time and place that individuals and groups pursue their individual and common goods." From MacIntyre's "Epilogue" to *What Happened in and to Moral Philosophy in the Twentieth Century? Philosophical Essays in Honor of Alasdair MacIntyre*, edited by Fran O'Rourke (Notre Dame, Indiana: University of Notre Dame Press, 2013), 477–78. I believe that the approach I outline in this essay—to assert that the first principles of natural

However, the most universal enframing principle underlying modernity is, as Josef Pieper argues, the attitude of *doubt.* This doubt, descended from both nominalism's rejection of the intelligibility of being,[10] as well as the Reformation's rejection of free participation in divine grace,[11] and made emblematic of modernity with Descartes' reorientation of philosophy toward the supposed certainties of purely mundane concerns, stands in marked contrast to the *wonder* which lay at the root of ancient philosophy.[12] The ancients were impressed by the exuberant intelligibility of the world, its gratuitous beauty and goodness, and so, "astounded by the deeper aspect of the world," fell into wonder. Thus, for the ancients, to "find the truly unusual and extraordinary, the real *mirandum, within* the usual and the ordinary, is the beginning of philosophy."[13]

However, as Pieper notes, "it is curious that in modern philosophy, especially, the aspect of the wonderful has taken on a different appearance so that the old doctrine of wonder as the beginning of philosophy has acquired the meaning, '*Doubt* is the beginning of philosophy.'"[14] Whereas wonder invites man to revel in mystery and to uncover the knowable, doubt replaces mystery with unknowability, and darkens the intellect by celebrating the adamantine limits of rationality. Thus, not only is the transcendent utterly

law are indeed universal, but are pursued under a distorting worldview—can explain the plurality of traditions while still adhering to the insight that there are self-evident principles of the natural law, thereby integrating MacIntyre's ideas with more traditional approaches to natural law. For example, MacIntyre writes at great length of the idea of virtue in warrior culture. But even our understanding of how to worship God can be seriously distorted by that tradition, as is evidenced in, for example, the Book of Joshua, chapters 6–10. The Israelites know that they must order all things to God; and yet, since that which is received is received according to the mode of the receiver, the primitive warrior culture of Israel can conceive of fulfilling this goal only in terms of submitting their enemies to the ban. While we understand this is the wrong way to implement that principle of the natural law, it nonetheless illustrates how it is pursued in an inadequate and ultimately futile way because of the cultural context of the society.

10. See Jacques Maritain, *Distinguish to Unite, or The Degrees of Knowledge,* translated by Gerald B. Phelan (Notre Dame, Indiana: University of Notre Dame Press, 1995), 1: "A deep vice besets the philosophers of our day.... It is the ancient error of the *nominalists....* The reason [for their pervasive skepticism] is that while having a taste for the real indeed, they nevertheless have no sense of being. Being as such ... for them is only a word."

11. See Charles Morerod, OP, *Ecumenism and Philosophy: Philosophical Questions for a Renewal of Dialogue,* translated by Therese C. Scarpelli (Ann Arbor, Michigan: Sapientia Press, 2006), 59–102.

12. Josef Pieper, *Leisure, The Basis of Culture,* translated by Gerald Malsbary (South Bend, Indiana: St. Augustine's Press, 1998), 100–105. For the ancient sources, see Plato, *Theaetetus* 155d1-4, and Aristotle, *Metaphysics* 1.2, 982b12-28.

13. Pieper, *Leisure,* 102.

14. Ibid., 104.

incomprehensible, but the intentions, nature, and even existence of my fellow man falls victim to skepticism. This doubt is the background pessimism which permeates modernity.

This atmosphere of doubt exercises a corrosive effect on every human endeavor, but it has an especially perverse effect on the way in which man understands the precepts of the natural law. Thomas Aquinas argues that the precepts of the natural law follow from man's natural teleological inclinations. The two most fundamental precepts are self-evident derivations from the fact that man "has a natural inclination to know the truth about God, and to live in society."[15] These are self-evident and primary because they follow directly from man's rationality: man, by nature, desires to know the highest truth as the ultimate explanation of all that is, and, in order to attain this wisdom, he seeks friendship so that through social intercourse he can develop virtue to grow in knowledge and love. Thus, the temporal order of society exists for man's perfection toward wisdom and love, yet this perfection of the intellect and will lead inexorably to man's ascent to transcendent Being, which alone satisfies the soul's thirst for universal truth and goodness.[16]

Thomas's argument here clearly presumes the philosophical condition of wonder. The assumed intelligibility of the universe opens man to the possibility of attaining transcendent truth; the assumed sociability of man naturally opens him to his fellow man as an inexhaustible source of growth, giving life breath to a vibrant and mutually supportive society. These represent common goods of mutual perfection, inspired by a hopefulness that drives human aspirations.

What happens to these same natural inclinations when considered under the influence of the doubt characteristic of modernity? Man cannot help but continue to pursue those ends that are connatural to his rationality; however, this doubt obscures the intelligibility of God, making faith a subjective and irrational act; and ignorance of our common nature and

15. *Summa Theologica* I-II, q. 94, a. 2; all citations to the *Summa Theologica* (ST) are taken from the translation by the Fathers of the English Dominican Province (New York: Benzinger, 1948). It might be noted that Nicanor Austriaco, OP, has demonstrated that man's teleology toward society and God are principles borne out by the findings of contemporary science; see "Substantial Forms, Living Networks, and Natural Ends: Recovering the Teleology of St. Thomas Aquinas in Biology" (unpublished manuscript).

16. On this understanding of man's twofold teleological order, see Jacques Maritain, *The Person and the Common Good*, translated by John J. Fitzgerald (Notre Dame, Indiana: University of Notre Dame Press, 1966).

common good inculcates a primeval distrust of other men. The natural law, instead of being predicated on an optimism toward fulfilling our sense of wonder in communion with others, is now predicated on fear born of doubt and distrust. An inscrutable God is no longer constrained by truth and goodness, but is a capricious God before whom we can only bow in blind faith. Society is no longer people bound in love for common perfection, but a contract for mutual protection. Given the context of modernity, we approach other men not with an eagerness to find communion, but in the suspicion of fear; we approach God not with joy, but in craven submission since He cannot be known, and man cannot be made worthy in any case.

In short, for both fundamental ends of the natural law, attaining the *summum bonum*, knowledge of God and love of neighbor, is replaced by avoiding the *summum malum*, divine punishment and temporal violence. Maritain recognizes it is these distorted impulses of an inverted natural law that lie at the root of modernity, inherited from the Reformation and the failed rationalism of the Enlightenment. It is this skepticism and fear that leads to a modern culture in which order can only be achieved by feats of self-assertion. Yet even this is in vain, for there can be no tranquil order where human transcendence is not recognized. As Maritain puts it, "the general paganization of our civilization has resulted in man's placing his hope in force alone and in the efficacy of hate.... Our natural love for God and for the human being is fragile; charity alone received from God as a participation in His own life, makes man efficaciously love God above everything, and each human person in God."[17]

III. The American Experiment

At the same time that Maritain was exploring the crisis in European civilization, Ralph Barton Perry was analyzing the genealogy of American exceptionalism in his aptly-titled study, *Puritanism and Democracy*.[18] It is unlikely that Perry realized it, but this dyadic paternity nicely embodies the two fundamental ends of the natural law, both temporal community and eternal sanctification. Now, as has been argued by John Courtney Murray

17. "Christian Humanism," 195–96.

18. Ralph Barton Perry, *Puritanism and Democracy* (New York: Vanguard Press, 1944), esp. 1–61.

and others, America was founded on *some* notion of natural law.[19] The critical question, however, is whether this natural law foundation reflects the optimistic order grounded in wonder, or the pessimistic order grounded in doubt. A consideration of Perry's analysis of the American character in conjunction with evidence drawn from a variety of contemporary analyses shows that America is now living through the same crisis of modernity which Maritain describes. This is so because the puritanism and democracy that define America are themselves exemplars of the corrosive doubt that poisons her appreciation of the natural law.

The two characteristics which Perry highlights reflect the circumstances of America's founding: the Puritan's search for a New Jerusalem, coinciding with an Enlightenment rationalism that establishes democracy as the ultimate arbiter of value. These are "ideals embraced within the social heritage of Americans ... [that are] charged with emotional appeal and provide incentives to actions ... reaching not only through the length of American history, but breadthwise from center to extremities, touching American experience and behavior at every point."[20] That this is an uneasy alliance should be evident; indeed, Perry's book documents that the complication of making peace between these divergent muses accounts for much of the drama of our national history.

However, that both puritanism and democracy embody the pessimistic doubt of modernity is evident when Perry points out the one thing that unites these two fonts of American identity: individualism.[21] While individualism undoubtedly has good aspects, it nevertheless requires the same

19. See John Courtney Murray, SJ, *We Hold These Truths* (New York: Sheed and Ward, 1960), 27–44. For a more recent iteration of this argument, see Robert P. George, "Natural Law, God, and Human Dignity" in *Conscience and Its Enemies: Confronting the Dogmas of Liberal Secularism* (Wilmington, Delaware: ISI Books, 2013), 71–90.

20. Perry, *Puritanism and Democracy*, 33.

21. Ibid., 192: "The deepest bond between puritanism and democracy was their common respect for the human individual." Perry also emphasizes that the relationship between these two sources is not purely contingent. First, by arguing that all man are equal in the order of grace, Puritanism helped prepare the way for the democratic idea that all men are equal in the order of nature (ibid., 358). Second, both were understood to be *salvific*, for they gave moral purpose to the new nation and were a condition of its liberty: Democracy atoned for the abuses of institutional authority, and allowed for the free exercise of reason and individual conscience by which man is saved; Puritanism atoned for the sins of the flesh and human pride, and found freedom by finding refuge from all troubles in God (ibid., 196). For a penetrating analysis of how the Puritan settlement was attempt to "immanentize the eschaton" by domesticating salvation and creating paradise on earth, see Eric Voegelin, *New Science of Politics* (Chicago: University of Chicago Press, 1952), 133–61.

anthropocentrism Maritain decries as being at fault in the European crisis. The critical problem is that individualism denies the reality of anything beyond self-interest which justifies the natural community binding man to neighbor and God. On the contrary, as Perry explains, in both cases, this individualism means community is founded on nothing more than the expediency of a contract:

> The democratic state was conceived as a contract among human individuals by which they created a temporal authority and agreed to obey it; the puritan theocracy was a contract among believers by which they agreed to obey God.... The contract theory in both of its forms implied that obedience is based upon a quid pro quo. It commended itself to the individual's reason because he, *qua* individual, could translate it into terms of his own consequent happiness or salvation.[22]

If man pursues the ends of the natural law, both temporal society and eternal union with God, for personal benefit, this reflects not an extroverted wonder at the intelligibility of being and the goodness of man, but an introverted fear, an anxiety that is discernible at the heart of democracy and religion. This attitude, woven into the DNA of our national identity, continues to be an intellectual and moral impediment to the happiness of the American people. This sad truth, however, is not often recognized because those baleful effects are obscured by the abundant goods which characterize America: the benefits of democratic processes, and the plentiful rights that go with it; the fact that these benefits are often justified as being simply "self-evident" to reason; and finally, the fact of the nation's religious founding is often taken as a sign of Providential blessing. Nevertheless, it is arguably the case that behind each of these apparent virtues hides a profound sense of doubt and fear, and this is manifest in the social disorder we observe today.

IV. Democratic Individualism

As Aquinas says, the proximate end of the natural law is that social union whereby man is taught the virtue necessary to perfect himself in wisdom and love. Let us first consider whether the American tradition of democracy is capable of achieving this end of intellectual and affective union,

22. Perry, *Puritanism and Democracy*, 194. As Perry points out, this ideology becomes the foundation for the unique American sense of opportunity in the economic transformation of the environment; see ibid., 206 and 568–72.

and whether the rights guaranteed by democracy are conducive to a life of virtue.

The Declaration of Independence, as Perry persuasively argues, springs from a philosophy of radical individualism.[23] Jefferson, of course, invokes the "Laws of Nature and of Nature's God," which can be read as an affirmation of natural law, but this is an Enlightenment version of natural law derived from Hobbes and Locke and tied to the social contract.[24] This social contract is not ordered to the common good of shared virtue, but is rather founded on the idea of individual benefit; as Perry notes, "political obedience is a contractual obligation which rests upon the keeping of promises, or the payment of what one 'owes'; and which rests, more fundamentally, upon the profitableness of a bargain to both parties, and their voluntary agreement upon it for the sake of the profit."[25]

Now it is obvious that contracting for the sake of individual benefit is very far from a moral dedication to the common good, for while I may benefit materially from a certain arrangement, it is not necessarily the case that that material benefit will encourage the growth in virtue characteristic of human perfection. Indeed, the American tradition, following that "American Socrates"[26] Benjamin Franklin, will even reinterpret virtue as that which leads to material benefit, which is then (mis)understood as definitive of the common good.[27] The inability to understand virtue in terms of shared wisdom and love illustrates that this individualism rejects the wonder of objective truth and goodness in favor of a relativistic pragmatism, as if material benefit were the only good available to us.

More fundamentally, even democracy itself, when viewed in terms of

23. Ibid., 118.

24. Ibid., 147.

25. Ibid., 171–72.

26. See Paul K. Conkin, *Puritans and Pragmatists: Eight Eminent American Thinkers* (New York: Dodd, Mead, and Co., 1968), 74: "To even partially understand Franklin is inevitably to learn something about America, for there seems to be much of Franklin in many Americans. Yet, the various interpretations of Franklin have borne witness to the diversity of American thought and, less clearly, to the major shifts of basic concern from generation to generation.... He may be the American Socrates. And who knows whether this is a compliment to America, or a horrible indictment of it?"

27. Consider, for example, Franklin's addition of this marginal note to his *Autobiography*: "Nothing so likely to make a man's fortune as virtue." Excerpted in *American Thought Before 1900*, edited by Paul Kurtz (New York: Macmillan, 1966), 134. Franklin also wrote in a letter: "Be industrious and frugal, and you will be rich. Be sober and temperate, and you will be healthy. Be in general virtuous, and you will be happy." Cited in Conkin, *Puritans and Pragmatists*, 99.

the social contract, is based not on a true appreciation of a common good, but on fear of other men. It has long been recognized that fear of the *summum malum* underlies the social contract for both Hobbes (fear of death or physical injury) and Locke (fear of loss of property).[28] But as John Wild argues, even the movement to accept democratic processes is grounded not on enlightenment optimism, but on a fear of oppression.[29] On his analysis, democracy emerges from the struggle against feudalism and class tyranny. This begins by abolishing hereditary office, then by asserting the right to remove public officials from office, and finally ends in the formal separation of powers. He comments: "When thus defended, democracy is represented as a wholly negative doctrine, its aim being exhausted in the avoidance of tyranny. All common actions and government are viewed as evil, though perhaps necessary in minimal degrees." And this justification of democracy—to limit the authority others may exercise over the sovereign individual—is very much the currency of contemporary politics, both liberal and conservative, for today, any claim to objective moral truth is summarily dismissed as discriminatory and oppressive.[30]

If democratic processes reflect doubt of true community, that same doubt is even more evident in the kinds of rights to be protected by democracy. These rights concern not the development of cooperative virtues, but an asocial individualistic license. This Enlightenment theory of individualistic rights, Perry shows, develops as a corollary to Enlightenment atheism. In a society ordered by theism, there are universally binding laws directing man to an objective good; but the atheism of the *philosophes* obliterates the transcendent lawmaker, and so law can only be a self-imposed command. However, since there can no longer be any transcendent justification, this self-imposed law is justified by the bald assertion that it is "self-evident,"

28. For Hobbes, see *Leviathan,* chapters 13–14; for Locke, see *Second Treatise of Government,* sections 57 and 124.

29. John Wild, *Plato's Modern Enemies and the Theory of Natural Law* (Chicago: University of Chicago Press, 1953), 44.

30. The importance James Madison laid on the separation of powers in the Constitution manifests the fact that his main goal was to limit power to avoid tyranny; see *Federalist* 51: "A dependence on the people is, no doubt, the primary control on the government; but experience has taught mankind the necessity of auxiliary precautions. This policy of supplying, by opposite and rival interests, the defect of better motives, might be traced through the whole system of human affairs, private as well as public. We see it particularly displayed in all the subordinate distributions of power, where the constant aim is to divide and arrange the several offices in such a manner as that each may be a check on the other that the private interest of every individual may be a sentinel over the public rights."

obviously necessary for human happiness. However, what now constitutes happiness is the subject of individual whim. Thus, the Enlightenment's exaggerated confidence in human reason ends up with a natural law based not on objective principles, but a "credulous intuitionism which multiplies unchallenged axioms" and rights.[31] If rights are so arbitrarily asserted, with no more justification than an airy insistence on their self-evidence, then we can wholly agree with Alasdair MacIntyre's judgment that rights as conceived in liberalism are no more than fictions.[32] It follows, then, that the fictitious and unjustified rights protected in our democracy are not those necessary for the development of virtue, but instead are sentimental claims encouraging license. "The maximum rights of the individual involve not merely the satisfaction of his desires, but also the realization of his prerogatives."[33] Clearly, our relation to neighbor is not based upon the common good of wisdom and love; it is rather based on a radical individualism motivated solely by subjective desire, and by a resentful fear of those who would resist that claim.[34] One need only point to Justice Kennedy's travesty of logic in his re-

31. See Perry, *Puritanism and Democracy*, 415–17. It is well to compare what Thomas claimed as self-evident—the general fact of man's social nature with a transcendent end, both of which are inherent in the discursive drive of rationality—with the much more specific claims of later eras. Thomas would argue that specific rights would not be self-evident, but would have to be derived from the self-evident principles in light of actual human nature; Enlightenment thinkers, having blotted out specific human nature, make rights directly discernible from some sort of Platonic realm of rational truths, without reference to the concrete conditions of human existence.

32. Alasdair MacIntyre, *After Virtue: A Study in Moral Theory*, second edition (Notre Dame, Indiana: University of Notre Dame Press, 1984), 69–70.

33. Perry, *Puritanism and Democracy*, 450. As Yves Simon points out, America's foundation in fact inherited some the of the objective moral force of traditional natural law, which would limit the indulgence of license, but this was exhausted by the time of Andrew Jackson; see *Philosophy of Democratic Government* (Chicago: University of Chicago Press, 1951), 149. Remarkably, Perry agrees with this assessment: "[Jacksonian democracy] revealed the inherent and besetting evils of democracy: the envy of superiority, and the compensatory pride of inferiority; the loss of standards of excellence; the transfer of political authority from the higher faculties of man to his based passions; the arts of the demagogue by which ambitious men acquire power through flattery." *Puritanism and Democracy*, 139. Maritain, too, agrees with this judgment about the devolution of democracy in general: "Democracy tended to become an embodiment of the sovereign will of the people in the machinery of a bureaucratic state more and more irresponsible and more and more asleep." "Christian Humanism," 188.

34. This is in fact part of the English common law tradition, if we are to believe Blackstone: "The only true and natural foundations of society are the wants and the fears of individuals.... [I]t is the sense of their weakness and imperfection that keeps mankind together; that demonstrates the necessity of this union; and that therefore is the solid and natural foundation, as well as the cement, of society." Cited in Perry, *Puritanism and Democracy*, 420; from *Commentaries on the Laws of England*, Introduction, Section the Second.

fusal to defend marriage on the assumption that opposition to homosexual marriage can only be based on animus denying someone a right to personal fulfillment.

V. The Pessimism of Puritanism

If doubts can be raised about our political tradition, one might be tempted to take comfort in the idea that the religious strand of the American tradition must reflect truly the natural law's ordering of man to God as his eternal end. However, this would only be wise if Puritanism were an adequate expression of the Christian faith—which it is not.

Perry presents Puritanism as an intensification of the basic elements of Protestantism, all of which focus on a radical individualism: "the elimination or reduction of intermediaries between man and God, the alleged priesthood of all believers, the exaltation of the elect, the emphasis on the self-validating force of religious experience, the substitution of Biblical for institutional authority, and the acknowledgement of the right of private judgment."[35] This individualism becomes the de facto common creed ordering Americans to the transcendent.[36] This individualism of Puritanism is again a manifestation of a corrosive pessimism, one that is in fact discernible at the roots of Protestantism itself. To illustrate this, I will consider the arguments of Michael Allen Gillespie's *The Theological Origins of Modernity*.[37]

Gillespie argues that modernity has two goals: "to make man master and

35. Perry, *Puritanism and Democracy*, 106.

36. Ibid., 111. The Presbyterian and congregational roots of puritanism coincide with the individualistic tendencies of democratic politics, especially the extreme suspicion of authority. Chesterton recognized this aspect, writing in the *New York Times* on July 12, 1931: "America had a great political idea, but it had a small religious idea. The spiritual vision was not wide enough for the breadth and variety of brotherhood that was to be established among men.... The nation arose not with unity of philosophy but with variety in fanaticism; with sects built on special dogmas or on the denial of special dogmas, on something that was not merely private judgment but particular judgment." In *Ecumenism and Philosophy*, 103–115, Morerod has argued that Protestant anti-rationalism is actually the foundation for political social contract theories characteristic of modernity because there is a direct connection between Luther's voluntarist idea of divine causality and the Hobbesian view in which every man is for himself alone, creating a war of all against all. Although Luther wants to protect the absolute nature of divine sovereignty, this backfires: "For Luther, 'God can only be everything, if man is nothing.' But man does not feel like nothing, and later would think it necessary to affirm himself against God" (ibid., 114). But to affirm oneself against God also implies affirming one's prerogative against one's neighbor.

37. Michael Allen Gillespie, *The Theological Origins of Modernity* (Chicago: University of Chicago Press, 2008), esp. 19–43.

possessor of nature and to make human freedom possible."[38] He shows that these are realized in both the temporal and religious spheres because of modernity's reaction to late medieval nominalism. Nominalism undermines ontological realism; consequently, there is no objective intelligible order of causes in the world. The only available alternative is that God's will alone determines worldly events. God's will is, however, utterly inscrutable. This "capricious God, fearsome in his power, unknowable, unpredictable," is not a God who can be worshipped with confidence.[39] Rather, God can now only be approached with an obsequious fear.[40] The Protestant reaction to this is, famously, that the simple act of individual belief becomes adequate for salvation. This, then, gives us the rather paradoxical conclusion: because the transcendent is unintelligible, each person is now wholly in charge of his own eternal destiny. This doctrine is perfectly embodied by the Puritan founders of our nation, as can be seen in Jonathan Edwards' pointed statement of unpleasant premise followed by the unlikely conclusion: "There is nothing that keeps wicked men at any one moment out of hell, but the mere pleasure of God.... Therefore, let everyone that is out of Christ, now awake and fly from the wrath to come."[41] For religion in the American tradition, in the face of an unknowable God, fideism assures individual salvation.

A similar analysis of the Protestant ethic is offered by Brad Gregory in *The Unintended Reformation*.[42] Gregory argues that the nominalism of late

38. Ibid., 42.

39. Ibid., 29.

40. It may be objected that, as Isaiah 11:3 insists in listing the gifts of the Holy Spirit, the righteous man will "delight in the fear of the LORD." But it is crucial that we distinguish servile from filial fear in this case (see ST II-II, q. 19, a. 2). Servile fear of God is a fear of the evil of punishment, and so it is this that is really self-centered. On the other hand, filial fear is fear of offending a beloved Father (a fear of the evil of fault), and so has as its referent objective goodness itself. Mature faith is motivated by the latter, not the former. If, however, objective value is unknowable, then only servile fear can motivate the believer.

41. Jonathan Edwards, *Sinners in the Hands of an Angry God*, available at http://www.ccel.org/ ccel/edwards/sermons.sinners.html. Gillespie also argues (*The Theological Origins*, 273) that this fideism assuring individual salvation also gives rise to a secular backlash, one which marginalizes religious truth claims, thereby reinforcing the subjectivism of faith. Since man cannot really worship a capricious and cruel God, man attempts to take control of his temporal destiny; this is evidenced in the rise of Renaissance humanism and the Enlightenment, in which human reason declares its independence from God. This displacement of God transfers divine attributes to the human will: man alone now is in control of the natural world, and man alone determines his own existence.

42. Brad S. Gregory, *The Unintended Reformation: How a Religious Revolution Secularized Society* (Cambridge, Massachusetts: Belknap Press of Harvard University Press, 2012).

medieval philosophy also explains *why* God becomes largely irrelevant for the secularists in contemporary America. The univocal idea of being they upheld means that all causes—both natural and supernatural—must operate in the same fashion; as a consequence, if science can explain some causal relation, there is no longer any role for God to play. However, if science explains everything, Ockham's razor would lead us to drop the theistic hypothesis completely.[43] This is of great importance, for it makes religious belief a purely subjective act, one with no relation to the strictures of objective truth. This loss of a common transcendent reference desacramentalizes the world, giving man the complete freedom and dominion modernity sought. Such an attitude continues to exercise a corrosive power on American society today, as Gregory elaborates in great detail, for it dissolves all persuasive foundations for understanding human rights: "The intellectual foundations of modernity are failing because its governing metaphysical assumptions in combination with the findings of the natural sciences offer no warrant for believing its most basic moral, political, and legal claims."[44]

Taken together, these attitudes subordinate religious truth to an individual's own sense of what God and salvation ought to be. All the critical details of salvation are relegated to private faith.[45] This religious voluntarism embodies not a real appreciation of the transcendent, but is rather a skepticism born from the unknowability of God. This is made clear by Ross Douthat's assessment of religion in America in *Bad Religion: How We Became a Nation of Heretics*.[46] His survey is the *reductio ad absurdum* of the individualism and puritanical fear that motivates man to create a God in his own fallible image. Douthat comments: "the American public [is] disillusioned with traditional Christianity but still religious enough to be eager for alternative portrayals of Jesus.... You [also] have a host of scholars, journalists, novelists, and provocateurs eager to supply them—even to the point of fantasy and folly."[47] While the natural law's inclination to know God is clearly acknowledged in American culture, it has been domesticated in accordance with the demands of individual freedom, especially freedom

43. Ibid., 25–73.

44. Ibid., 381.

45. Perry points out that for all its religiosity, the public piety of America is based on Enlightenment natural theology, not any revealed religion; see *Puritanism and Democracy*, 152.

46. Ross Douthat, *Bad Religion: How We Became a Nation of Heretics* (New York: Free Press, 2012), esp. 149–293.

47. Ibid., 152.

from objective values of a truly transcendent God. Thus, we make of God whatever our personal predilections demand.[48] All of this suggests that in religion, as within the temporal sphere, the natural law's ordering of man to the transcendent is characterized by doubt, which leads to not to faith, but to the heresy in which every man makes of God whatever brings him comfort.[49]

VI. Democracy and Religion

Perhaps the most revealing illustration of doubt's corrosive influence on the ends of the natural law is that which concerns the intersection of America's founding principles, democracy and puritanism, as embodied in America's vaunted legal protections for freedom of religion. But even here, as legal scholar Steven Smith has shown in his book *The Rise and Decline of American Religious Freedom*, recent court decisions against religious freedom demonstrate the fragility of our situation.[50] In particular, these decisions expose the inherent problems of a democracy based not on corporate virtue but individual desire, as well as the objective irrelevance of religion that eschews the transcendent in favor of subjective comfort.

Smith begins by showing that, like America herself, the doctrine of religious freedom has a dual paternity, one religious and one secular. From the Christian tradition, religious freedom is grounded in Augustine's doctrine

48. See ibid., 232–33, where Douthat cites the research of Christian Smith, who claims the American Creed (which he calls "moralistic therapeutic deism") has five main premises, none of which has any substantive content or challenging claims: (1) A God exists who created and orders the world and watches over human life on earth; (2) God wants people to be good, nice, and fair to each other, as taught in the Bible and by most world religions; (3) The central goal of life is to be happy and to feel good about oneself; (4) God does not need to be particularly involved in one's life except when he is needed to resolve a problem; (5) Good people go to heaven when they die. Douthat concludes that Americans' attitude to traditional religion "promote[s] a hermeneutic of suspicion ... a way of looking at faith that inspires searching rather than settling, a highly individualistic theology rather than submission to authority, and a skepticism that makes any sort of enthusiastic joining seem like a mug's game;" ibid., 176.

49. Indeed, as Robert George argues (in *Conscience and Its Enemies*, 122), even the notion of freedom of religion itself can be seen to be an expression of a "liberalism of fear," since it is founded not on a fulsome appreciation of the transcendent good of religion, but on the presumed necessity for a "mutual non-aggression pact with other faiths." George contrasts this liberal defense of freedom with the positive understanding of religious freedom emerging from Vatican II in *Nostra Aetate* and *Dignitatis Humanae*.

50. Steven D. Smith, *The Rise and Decline of American Religious Freedom* (Cambridge, Massacheusetts: Harvard University Press, 2014).

of two cities and the concomitant independence of the Church, which is reinforced by the Christian insistence on the sincerity of belief which militates against government coercion.[51] These ideas fall into a coincidental agreement with the secularism emerging from the Enlightenment, which insists that the government not concern itself with, or legislate on the basis of, the irrational subjective belief of individuals.[52]

The critical point for Smith is that this dual paternity allowed for the uniquely open and flexible "American Settlement" in which one can understand America either from a religiously inspired Providentialist position, as is evident from the invocations of public religion from the likes of Washington and Lincoln, or, on the other hand, from a Secularist position in which America has no state religion, a position closer to Jefferson, Madison, and prominently stated in the famous 1797 Treaty with Tripoli: "The government of the United States of America is not, in any sense, founded on the Christian religion."[53] These contradictory interpretations can exist side by side because, Smith argues, there is a distinction between the Constitution, a legal positivist document which is officially secular, and what might be called popular constitutionalism, the living tradition of custom and precedent, which is in fact profoundly religious. Thus, the Providentialists lean on popular constitutionalism, while the Secularists lean on the legal Constitution, and the result is freedom of conscience for all citizens inasmuch as all religions are equal before the law.

Smith shows, however, that in the twentieth century there were two key changes to this amicable settlement.[54] First, instead of separation of *Church* and state, the courts illicitly substitute *religion* for Church. This radically alters the meaning of the non-establishment clause of the First Amendment, which now appears to regulate relations between government and religion in general. The state must now be protected not from any one church, but all religion. Rather than viewing religions as equally good before the law (which fosters religious freedom and mutual respect), the Court denigrates

51. Ibid., 38.

52. Ibid., 81–82.

53. Cited in Smith, *The Rise and Decline*, 97. It should be noted that this claim is limited to the *government* of the United States. Of course, a nation is not the same as the government, and it is clear that historically (as Perry shows) the *nation* is founded on Christian principles. The only way to reject this distinction is to identify the nation with the government, which is the premise of fascism.

54. Ibid., 111ff.

all religious expression as being inconsistent with the common good.[55] Moreover, we would add that the Supreme Court's dismissive attitude toward religion is ultimately a consequence of the fact that in the American tradition, religion itself is framed by the doubt of modernity which destroys its objective significance: religion had long ceased to order man to a transcendent end, instead (as we have seen) becoming a subjective invention to assuage existential fear in the face of an inscrutable divinity. Since democratic government exists to protect men from one-another, the Court's only recourse is to limit these subjective beliefs as much as possible.

The second change in the twentieth century reflects the corrosive doubt at the basis of democracy. This is the decisive rejection of popular constitutionalism in favor of the positivistic notion of Constitutional law. This change is the natural culmination of the assumption that there can be no real community, no common good among people on the basis of nature. Lacking a natural inclination to community, the corollary to be drawn is that all public acts must be dictated by the government. As a result, the letter of the Constitution is the only thing holding the nation together. Accordingly, the Supreme Court must now enforce a single reading of the constitution on citizens, and ensure compliance with that reading on all levels of society.[56] The loss of popular constitutionalism results in the triumph of the Secularist interpretation of America in which religion deserves no special consideration. This, in turn, transmutes freedom of conscience, which becomes untethered from religion completely, so that it is now being understood as *any* deeply held belief. Thus, the transcendent end of man is obliterated in favor of blind preference; religion and perversion are made equal before the law.[57]

These two changes demonstrate clearly that the ultimate grounding for both polity and religion in the American tradition were destined to fail because that grounding was based on doubt, which inculcated fear of neighbor and a craven fear of God. To gain control of temporal society, we institute democracy, but deprive ourselves of civic amity, true community in a

55. On the Court's peculiar view that religion is an evil to be avoided, see Russell Hittinger, "The Supreme Court v. Religion," in *First Grace: Rediscovering the Natural Law in a Post-Christian World* (Wilmington, Delaware: ISI Books, 2003), 163–82

56. This, of course, is an innovative understanding of the Fourteenth Amendment.

57. Smith, *The Rise and Decline*, 126. This is the background for Judge Walker's inexplicable judgment overruling Proposition 8 on basis that the prohibition was based on religion alone; since a moral judgment is a personal belief, the state has no interest in enforcing private religious beliefs, and so it cannot legislate any position with respect to marriage.

common good. To gain control of the eternal, we deny the objective truth of religion and make God in our own image, even though this deprives life of any common transcendent meaning. This does not lead to true fulfillment; rather, it harms society, for as Smith concludes, this "elevation of secularism to an official constitutional position … [created] a dynamic of suspicion, resentment, and bewilderment" between citizens leading to the culture wars.[58]

VII. Conclusion

It is obvious, now, that we are living out the same crisis and trial which Maritain decried in the 1940s. We have fortunately (as yet) been spared the violence; but to live in resistance to the precepts of the natural law is to constantly invite the violence that is sin's inexorable recompense. Virtue is rejected in favor of tolerance; God is rejected in favor of anthropocentric narcissism. The unavoidable result is precisely what Hobbes saw in man's war of all against all, with no objective value by which to adjudicate conflict.[59] All that is left is self-assertion in which one demands his desires be treated as equal to any other claim. Smith sees this as the primary characteristic of contemporary American politics: "In this equality oriented framework, traditional virtues and vices get re-ordered. Previously 'deadly sins' like pride, lust, and sloth are displaced on the list of evils by more currently loathsome traits—bigotry and intolerance—that are thought to violate the 'equal respect' axiom. Consequently, a good deal of political polemics (and, for the matter, constitutional jurisprudence) consists of efforts to show that one's opponents are acting from bigotry or prejudice."[60] But without objective criteria of good and evil, there is no way to determine the value of any desire, so all claims are "equal" and all things must be allowed. Thus, any discrimination based on value is invidious, and to despise vice is itself only an act of "animus."

What we see, then, is exactly what Maritain could not see in the heat of the War, but something he recognized shortly thereafter. This is that although Communism and Fascism are true challenges to human flourish-

58. Ibid., 127.

59. Hobbes, *Leviathan,* chap. 13: "To this war of every man against every man, this also is consequent; that nothing can be unjust. The notions of right and wrong, justice and injustice, have there no place."

60. Smith, *The Rise and Decline,* 149–50.

ing, the greatest challenge comes from bourgeois individualism.[61] America is now living through the triumph of that ideology and the tragedy of its consequences: because its individualism is based on doubt, we shun a true common political good, and we reject the objective truths about a transcendent God. The solution is still the one Maritain implored: we Thomists must persevere in the renewal of true humanism, based on a proper estimation of man, reflecting both the certainties of metaphysics and the wisdom of religious faith.[62] Therefore, while Taylor is certainly correct in asserting the historical contextualization of our beliefs, we are nevertheless able to overcome this for, as Chesterton discovered, the Catholic Church "is the only thing that frees a man from the degrading slavery of being a child of his age."[63] The principles of the natural law may be distorted by the doubt of modernity, but this distortion will inevitably lead to an epistemic and moral crisis in which the true meaning of those principles will be rediscovered in philosophy and in faith.[64] This is how Thomists must continue to engage the world: we thus have to reject the doubt of modernity and the false comforts of bourgeois individualism; we must recover the faith that is the well-spring of the love and wisdom that alone can erase the barriers which stand between men in society and between this world and God.[65]

61. See Jacques Maritain, *The Person and the Common Good*, 90–105.

62. See "The Crisis of Civilization," in *Pour la justice*, 139. Maritain insists that the key is to open man up to the suprarational, which "means the discovery of a more profound and real sense of the dignity of the human person. As a consequence, man would rediscover himself in a rediscovered God and would direct social work towards a heroic idea of fraternal love conceived ... as a difficult and painful conquest of the spirit, as a work of grace and virtue." "World Trial," 237.

63. From "Why I Am a Catholic," available at http://www.chesterton.org/why-i-am-a-catholic/.

64. This, of course, is a reference to MacIntyre's description of how moral traditions continue to develop and to remain adequate expressions of man's natural teleological drives; see Alasdair MacIntyre, *Whose Justice? Which Rationality?* (Notre Dame, Indiana: University of Notre Dame Press, 1988), 349–69. Also, as emphasized by both St. John Paul II (in *Fides et Ratio*) and Benedict XVI (the Regensberg speech), faith and reason must work together in guiding man to the truth of these principles.

65. Maritain, "World Trial," 238. In the essay "Religion and Peace," 306–307, Maritain specifies that this means a rejuvenation of democracy itself: instead of the value neutral bourgeois democracy in which truth emerges spontaneously from public debate of individual opinion, a new personalist democracy must be committed to natural law and the concomitant flourishing of religious life.

ANNE FRANCES AI LE, OP

"It is Right and Just"

Ontological Poverty and the Duty of Religion

I. Introduction

THE OLD ADVICE NOT TO discuss religion or politics often harbors the assertion that it is impossible to have a fruitful discussion concerning such topics. The assumption is that one's religion or politics is a matter of personal taste, of no real consequence, and more importantly, that no governing principle can influence one's views or demand allegiance to a particular code of conduct. In a number of essays in *Pour la justice,* however, Jacques Maritain brings precisely such topics to the forefront of his discussions, insisting on a proper relation between religion and politics as the solution for the crises of civilization. Following his lead, this essay will argue for the significance of the duty of religion in the Thomistic tradition against the popular claim that religion is but a matter of personal preference and thus should be relegated to the personal, subjective sphere.

II. The Nature of Religion

In considering the nature of religion, Saint Thomas discusses three possible meanings of the term *religio* derived from various sources: *religare, relegere, reeligere.*[1] Thomas identifies the common denominator of these

1. ST II-II, q. 81, a. 1: "[S]icut Isidorus dicit, in libro Etymol., *religiosus, ut ait Cicero, a religione appellatus, qui retractat et tanquam relegit ea quae ad cultum divinum pertinent.* Et sic religio videtur dicta a religendo ea quae sunt divini cultus, quia huiusmodi sunt frequenter in corde revolvenda, secundum illud Prov. III, *in omnibus viis tuis cogita illum.* Quamvis etiam possit intelligi

meanings as being in relation to God who is the object of those actions, whether *religare, relegere,* or *reeligere.* He explains, "For it is He to Whom we ought to be bound [*religare*] as to our unfailing principle; to Whom also our choice should be resolutely directed [*reeligere*] as to our last end; and Whom we lose when we neglect Him by sin, and should recover [*relegere*] by believing in Him and confessing our faith."[2] Moreover, Saint Thomas not only acknowledges the relation of religion to God but also categorizes it as a virtue in relation to God. As a virtue makes its possessor good and one's acts likewise good, it follows that every good act must belong to a virtue. The act of rendering anyone his due has the aspect of good, Thomas explains, since by rendering a person his due, one becomes suitably proportioned to him by being ordered to him in a becoming manner, and order comes under the aspect of good. Thus, since religion pertains to the good of paying due honor to God, it is evident that religion is a virtue.[3] Lest one believe that the notion of paying what is due, that is, of duty, diminishes the voluntariness of an act of virtue, Thomas offers the analogy of a slave who makes a virtue of necessity by doing his duty voluntarily. In the same way, due service to God may be an act of virtue, insofar as man does so voluntarily.[4] Moreover, Thomas affirms that it belongs to the dictate of natural reason that man should do something with respect to reverence for God.[5] In other words, man's natural reason makes him aware of his duty towards God, namely, to worship God. Since religion is giving due honor to God and honor is due to someone under the aspect of excellence, honor belongs by a singular excellence to God insofar as God surpasses all things

religio ex hoc dicta quod *Deum reeligere debemus, quem amiseramus negligentes,* sicut Augustinus dicit, X de Civ. Dei. Vel potest intelligi religio a religando dicta, unde Augustinus dicit, in libro de vera Relig., *religet nos religio uni omnipotenti Deo.*" All Latin texts of *Summa theologiae* are from *Summa theologiae,* vols. 4–12 of *Opera Omnia* (Rome: The Leonine Edition, 1882–). All English translations are from *Summa Theologica,* translated by Fathers of the English Dominican Province, 5 vols. (New York: Benziger Brothers, 1948).

2. Ibid.: "Ipse enim est cui principaliter alligari debemus, tanquam indeficienti principio; ad quem etiam nostra electio assidue dirigi debet, sicut in ultimum finem; quem etiam negligenter peccando amittimus, et credendo et fidem protestando recuperare debemus."

3. ST II-II, q. 81, a. 2: "Cum igitur ad religionem pertineat reddere honorem debitum alicui, scilicet Deo, manifestum est quod religio virtus est."

4. ST II-II, q. 81, a. 2, ad 2: "etiam servus potest voluntarie domino suo exhibere quod debet, et sic facit de necessitate virtutem, debitum voluntarie reddens. Et similiter etiam exhibere Deo debitam servitutem potest esse actus virtutis, secundum quod homo voluntarie hoc facit."

5. ST II-II, q. 81, a. 2, ad 3: "de dictamine rationis naturalis est quod homo aliqua faciat ad reverentiam divinam, sed quod haec determinate faciat vel illa, istud non est de dictamine rationis naturalis, sed de institutione iuris divini vel humani."

and exceeds them in every way.[6] Giving due honor to another is the formal character of the cardinal virtue of justice. Religion, therefore, is a distinct virtue categorized under the virtue of justice.

III. Religion and Justice

We can make the manner of this relationship more evident with a closer examination of the virtue of justice. Using Aristotelian and Roman juridical sources, Thomas defines justice as "a habit whereby a man renders to each one his due by a constant and perpetual will."[7] As a virtue that directs man in his relations with others, however, justice implies a certain equality (*aequalitatem quandam*) between giver and receiver.[8] How, then, can an equality be established between man and God so as to render religion a part of justice? The answer is simply that no such equality can be found *per se*. Instead, a solution can be found in the nature of justice as a cardinal virtue or principal virtue. Each of the four cardinal virtues consists of subjective, integral, and potential parts, each in turn consisting of various virtues related to the cardinal virtue.[9] The potential parts of justice in particular consist of certain virtues that are annexed to it and as such do not strictly observe the requirement of equality. Religion is among such annexed virtues.

In his discussion of the potential parts (*partes potentiales*) of justice,

6. ST II-II, q. 81, a. 4: "Unde ei debetur specialis honor, sicut in rebus humanis videmus quod diversis excellentiis personarum diversus honor debetur, alius quidem patri, alius regi, et sic de aliis. Unde manifestum est quod religio est specialis virtus."

7. ST II-II, q. 58, a. 1, c.: -Et ideo praedicta definitio est completa definitio iustitiae, nisi quod actus ponitur pro habitu, qui per actum specificatur, habitus enim ad actum dicitur. Et si quis vellet in debitam formam definitionis reducere, posset sic dicere, quod iustitia est habitus secundum quem aliquis constanti et perpetua voluntate ius suum unicuique tribuit. Et quasi est eadem definitio cum ea quam philosophus ponit, in V *Ethic.*, dicens quod *iustitia est habitus secundum quem aliquis dicitur operativus secundum electionem iusti.*"

8. ST II-II, q. 57, a. 1: "ustitiae proprium est inter alias virtutes ut ordinet hominem in his quae sunt ad alterum. Importat enim aequalitatem quandam, ut ipsum nomen demonstrat, dicuntur enim vulgariter ea quae adaequantur iustari. Aequalitas autem ad alterum est."sIn ST II-II, q. 58, a. 2, St. Thomas argues that justice is always towards another: "iustitiae aequalitatem importet, ex sua ratione iustitia habet quod sit ad alterum, nihil enim est sibi aequale, sed alteri."

9. In ST II-II, q. 48, a. 1, Aquinas describes the three kinds of parts of a virtue. Integral parts are those things which are necessary for the perfect act of a virtue as "wall, roof, and foundations are parts of a house"; subjective parts are the various species of a virtue as "ox and lion are parts of animal"; and potential parts of a virtue are the virtues connected with it, which lack in some way the whole power of the principal virtue, as "the nutritive and sensitive powers are parts of the soul."

Thomas articulates two criteria which must be met in order for a virtue to be "annexed" to a principal virtue: (1) it must agree or share something in common (*conveniant*) with the principal virtue; and (2) it must in some respect fall short (*deficiant*) of the perfection of the principal virtue. Consider the first criterion. Since justice is of one individual to another, all the virtues that are directed to another person may by reason of this agreement or common aspect (*ratione convenientiae*) be annexed to justice. The common aspect of being a relation of one individual to another provides an extensive list of virtues that can be annexed to justice.[10] Such virtues can be further categorized according to the second criterion concerning how they fall short of justice, either by falling short of equality (*a ratione aequalis*), or by falling short regarding what is due (*a ratione debiti*), which are the integral parts of justice.[11]

From such parameters, then, Thomas categorizes virtues annexed to justice into three groups and distinguishes them from one another according to the particular way in which they fall short of justice. The first group consists of virtues which fall short of the aspect of equality, while the others fall short regarding what is due.[12] Within the first group, therefore, certain virtues exist which indeed pertain to rendering another his due, but not according to *equal* due or due *measure*, and the foremost among these

10. ST II-II, q. 80, a .1: "in virtutibus quae adiunguntur alicui principali virtuti duo sunt consideranda, primo quidem, quod virtutes illae in aliquo cum principali virtute conveniant; secundo, quod in aliquo deficiant a perfecta ratione ipsius. Quia vero iustitia ad alterum est, ut ex supradictis patet, omnes virtutes quae ad alterum sunt possunt ratione convenientiae iustitiae annecti."

11. ST II-II, q. 80, a. 1: "Ratio vero iustitiae consistit in hoc quod alteri reddatur quod ei debetur secundum aequalitatem, ut ex supradictis patet. Dupliciter igitur aliqua virtus ad alterum existens a ratione iustitiae deficit, uno quidem modo, inquantum deficit a ratione aequalis; alio modo, inquantum deficit a ratione debiti. Sunt enim quaedam virtutes quae debitum quidem alteri reddunt, sed non possunt reddere aequale." See also ST II-II, q. 58, a. 11: "Materia iustitiae est operatio exterior secundum quod ipsa, vel res qua per eam utimur, proportionatur alteri personae, ad quam per iustitiam ordinamur. Hoc autem dicitur esse suum uniuscuiusque personae quod ei secundum proportionis aequalitatem debetur. Et ideo proprius actus iustitiae nihil est aliud quam reddere unicuique quod suum est."

12. In ST II-II, q. 80, a. 1, Thomas similarly discusses the second two groups of virtues that fall short of just due either morally or legally. Since legal due is that by which one is bound to render by reason of legal obligation, it pertains chiefly to justice. The moral due is that to which one is bound to render to with regard to moral rectitude, and is of two kinds. The first of the virtues fall short of rendering the moral due necessary for moral rectitude, and includes truth, gratitude, and vindication, while the second falls short of the moral due that conduces to greater moral rectitude, and includes honesty, liberality, affability, and friendship, and the like.

is religion.[13] Whatever man renders to God, Thomas explains, is due, yet cannot equal what is due, as though man were ever able to render to God as much as he owes Him. One can only exclaim with the Psalmist, "What shall I render to the Lord for all the things that He hath rendered to me?" (*Ps* 115.12). Even if one were to love God with one's whole heart, mind, and soul, the love rendered can never equal what God deserves, since God is infinitely great. Cicero likewise recognized the lack of equality that marks religion as a virtue annexed to justice in defining religion as "offering service and ceremonial rites and worship to 'some superior nature that men call divine.'"[14] Religion, therefore, is related to justice as potential part to principal virtue by observing the two requirements for this relationship. First, understood as paying due worship to God, religion shares something in common with justice, namely, the aspect of being in relation to another. Second, religion falls short of the perfection of justice regarding rendering what is due to another by not being able to meet what is owed to another.

IV. Ontological Poverty and the Duty of Religion

The relationship between religion and justice is intimately linked to the ontological poverty of man, which describes our dependence on others and ultimately on God.[15] Who of us can claim self-sufficiency? Who of us does not require something from another on an everyday basis? Who of us can claim to bring ourselves into existence? Many thinkers have discussed how an awareness or recognition of this ontological poverty is capable of uncovering our utter dependence on God for what we have and are. For instance, Mennessier observes that Rudolph Otto speaks of this experience as awakening in man in the face of the "mysterium tremendum," what Otto refers to

13. The other two virtues also annexed to justice in this regard are piety, which is directed to onelso annexed to justice in this regard are piety, excel in honor. See ST II-II, q. 80, a. 1: "Secundo, parentibus non potest secundum aequalitatem recompensari quod eis debetur, ut patet per philosophum, in VIII *Ethic.* Et sic adiungitur iustitiae pietas, per quam, ut Tullius dicit, *sanguine iunctis patriaeque benevolis officium et diligens tribuitur cultus.* Tertio, non potest secundum aequale praemium recompensari ab homine virtuti, ut patet per philosophum, in IV *Ethic.* Et sic adiungitur iustitiae observantia, per quam, ut Tullius dicit, *homines aliqua dignitate antecedentes quodam cultu et honore dignantur.*"

14. ST II-II, q. 80, a. 1: "Et secundum hoc adiungitur iustitiae religio, quae, ut Tullius dicit, *superioris cuiusdam naturae, quam divinam vocant, curam caeremoniamque vel cultum affert.*"up

15. For a more detailed discussion on ontological poverty and the counsels, see Christopher A. Franks, *He Became Poor: The Poverty of Christ and Aquinas' Economic Teachings* (Grand Rapids: Eerdmans Publishing, 2009), especially chap. 3.

as "Kreaturgefül," the "awareness of being a creature." Mennessier also points to Saint Thomas's "reverential" as similarly describing "this awareness of the creature before the inimitable transcendence" (*quando in consideratione tantae altitudinis homo in propriam resilit parvitatem*).[16] In such expressions, one can recognize not only an awareness of an ontological poverty but also simultaneously an experience of God as the Supreme Being on whom all things depend.

Yet how is this recognition of God attained or characterized? Fulton Sheen, in his consideration of what is generally referred to as "a religious experience," acknowledges that the expression can refer to one of two things: on the one hand, a non-intellectual approach to God in which feeling is primary; on the other, an intellectual approach where reasoning, even though confused, is primary, followed by an affective or emotional response and a reflex intellectual state. Sheen provides a number of brief examples of the former and rejects it as based upon "bad psychology, i.e., that the emotion about, precedes the idea of, God."[17] Quoting Saint Thomas' *De Veritate* q.10, a.11, ad 6, Sheen points out the right psychology, so to speak: "The affective state begins when the intellectual operation is finished." In other words, emotions follow upon knowledge, not vice versa, as proponents of an emotional and non-intellectual view of religious experience maintain.

Sheen maintains that though the term "religious experience" has generally been applied to the affective approach to God, any such experience devoid of the intellectual element "must necessarily be illusory."[18] In brief, Sheen maintains that the valid type of religious experience must involve three elements: a *confused* intellectual knowledge, an emotional response, and a *reflex* or distinct intellectual knowledge. Paraphrasing John of St. Thomas, Sheen explains the distinction between confused and reflex intellectual knowledge:

> Confused intellectual knowledge is that by which something is known without discernment and of its parts or predicates and in which it is not always easy to distinguish one object from another. Reflex or distinct knowledge, on the contrary, discerns parts and predicates and differentiates one object from another.[19]

16. A. I. Mennessier, "Christian Perfection," *The Virtues and States of Life*, vol. 4 in Theology Library, edited by A.M. Henry (Chicago: Fides Publishers, 1923), 397, citing Rudolph Otto, *The Idea of the Holy*, (Oxford: Oxford University Press, 1923).

17. Fulton J. Sheen, *Philosophy of Religion: The Impact of Modern Knowledge on Religion* (New York: Appleton-Century Crofts, 1948). Sheen names Otto's view as among the non-intellectual views he rejects.

18. Ibid., 239.

19. Ibid., 239.

As the wording itself suggests, confused knowledge is simply the knowledge of something in a general, undifferentiated way, while reflex knowledge is attained through reflection and thus is knowledge of something well and in all its parts. Sheen is so convinced of the naturalness of "this rational, confused, spontaneous approach to God" that he affirms such an approach "almost happens in spite of ourselves."[20] Natural though it may be, Sheen acknowledges that this confused intellectual knowledge of God is not perfect, but requires reflex knowledge "to bring determination and completeness, and to lift the undeveloped knowledge into a knowledge which will stand analysis and criticism."[21] For Thomas, confused knowledge only allows man to come to some knowledge of God as creator and governor of the universe; the analysis of the nature of this Creator, including His Unity, and His Perfection, as well as other attributes, is done through a more refined reasoning process, such as Saint Thomas's celebrated Five Ways. Thomas's arguments in the Five Ways demonstrate the capability of unaided reason—that is, unaided by revelation, but not without the help and guidance of others—to attain to the knowledge of the existence of a supreme being on whom depends all of creation. In his cosmological argument for the existence of God, Thomas identifies in man the faculty that is ordered to God, since it is able to know God, and consequently has a natural desire for God according to his intellect.

Prior to formulating these famous ways of knowing God by reason alone, Thomas had similarly argued in the *Summa Contra Gentiles* on the basis of Aristotle's dictum that *all men by nature desire to know* and added that man has a natural desire to know God as first cause:

> Besides, there is naturally present in all men the desire to know the causes of whatever things are observed. Hence, because of wondering about things that were seen but whose causes were hidden, men first began to think philosophically; when they found the cause, they were satisfied. But the search did not stop until it reached the first cause, for 'then do we think that we know perfectly, when we know the first cause.' Therefore, man naturally desires, as his ultimate end, to know the first cause. But the first cause of all things is God. Therefore, the ultimate end of man is to know God.[22]

20. Ibid., 240.

21. Ibid. Such a distinction calls to mind Saint Paul's teaching of man's ability in this life to know divine things only in a glass darkly (1 Cor 13:12), or about mysteries made known to human reason and likewise those knowable by human reason on its own, to which Saint Thomas refers in his own explanation of man's knowledge of God as self-evident, which Sheen likewise adduces as examples.

22. *Summa contra gentiles*, book III, chap. 25, translated by Vernon J. Bourke (New York: Ha-

This intellectual inclination of man toward God reflects Sheen's intellectual explanation of our awareness of God's existence.

The awareness of our ontological poverty, then, simultaneously awakens our intellectual awareness or recognition of God, on Whom our entire being depends. Admittedly, the simultaneous recognition of one's ontological poverty and God's existence and providence can draw a twofold response from us, either fear and despair, or love and trust. Since the concern here is with religion, our present focus will only be on our positive response to this double awareness. Mennessier speaks positively of this response as "a sense of the sacred, the instinct of reverence which is evoked in those who have an insight of the majesty of God."[23] An awareness of the majesty of God cannot but deepen the recognition of one's littleness, or poverty. When this is acknowledged, an awareness of one's ontological poverty in turn breeds a recognition of God's providence, which in turn generates recognition of a duty to honor God for His providential care.

Being capable of knowing God and of God's relation to man as the greatest of benefactors—one responsible for one's existence and sustenance—would justly require us to give some expression of gratitude and reverence to God. Showing God gratitude and reverence for His abundant goodness is nothing other than fulfilling the duty of religion.

V. Religion and Politics

The argument we have traced from man's natural capacity for knowledge of God to a duty to worship God may serve to explain Maritain's insistence on the need for a proper relation between religion and politics, particularly between Christianity and democracy. Maritain identifies the problem ultimately as a spiritual one, resulting from a rejection of the evangelical inspiration of true democracy. The "principal reason" for the failure to realize Christianity in the social order, he writes,

nover House, 1955–57). "Naturaliter inest omnibus hominibus desiderium cognoscendi causas eorum quae videntur: unde propter admirationem eorum quae videbantur, quorum causae latebant, homines primo philosophari coeperunt, invenientes autem causam quiescebant. Nec sistit inquisitio quousque perveniatur ad primam causam: et tunc perfecte nos scire arbitramur quando primam causam cognoscimus. Desiderat igitur homo naturaliter cognoscere primam causam quasi ultimum finem. Prima autem omnium causa Deus est. Est igitur ultimus finis hominis cognoscere Deum." From the Leonine *Opera Omnia* edition of the SCG.

23. Mennessier, "Christian Perfection," 397.

is one of a spiritual nature. It lies in the inner contradiction and tragic misunderstanding of which the modern democracies, particularly in Europe, have been the victims. This form and ideal of the common life which we call democracy springs in its essentials from the inspiration of the Gospel and cannot subsist without it.[24]

According to Maritain, democracy is so deeply rooted in Christianity that a rejection of Christian principles would bring about the destruction of democracy. Moreover, when the proper relation between religion and politics is not maintained, one opposes the other, each trying to gain the upper hand, stifling the other, resulting in a strained relationship between them, to say the least. Maritain notes the mutual harm in this relationship:

[W]e saw for a century the directing forces in the modern democracies repudiating the Gospel and Christianity in the name of human liberty, while the directing forces in the Christian social strata were combating democratic aspirations in the name of religion.[25]

In such a case, the duty of religion would not only not be acknowledged and therefore become neglected but might even be forbidden altogether, to the detriment of society. Maritain, moreover, holds that a false understanding of religion can also negatively affect democratic flourishment, imposing fideistic tendencies on political discussions that can only bring about confusion rather than clarity. Maritain is clear that in order for civilization to flourish, both religion and politics must be allowed to exercise their respective authority in the public, social sphere, while respecting the parameters of one another. In modernity, however, the problem lies more so with the denial of religion, particularly Christianity, its place and role in shaping society.

Indisputably, the end of politics, on the whole, is the pursuit of the common good. This pursuit, however, would be sorely lacking were religious aspirations arising from the very nature of human beings neglected. The pursuit of the common good without any consideration of religion leads inevitably to a diminishment of human life, since the highest aspirations of the human spirit is ignored or repressed. As something discernible by human reason, religion belongs in the public arena to inform politics for the betterment of society in pursuit of the common good. Religious principles and values should not be left out of political forums simply because they are religious. Chris-

24. Jacques Maritain, "Religion and Peace," in *Pour la justice: Articles et discours (1940–1945)* (New York: Éditions de la Maison Française, 1945), 303; also stated almost verbatim in "Christianity and Democracy," in *Pour la justice*, 244.

25. Maritain, "Religion and Peace," 303.

tian principles and values in particular can help to shape politics to achieve the good of society in a more complete way. With a proper understanding of religion and politics put into practice, each exercising its authority in public discussions, religion along with politics would be rescued from the personal, subjective sphere. No longer would religion and politics be but matters of personal taste. Since they are about essential, human concerns, they express common values and principles that rightly deserve their place in public discussions and social influences.

VI. Conclusion

It is my contention that based on our ontological poverty, an understanding and acceptance of religion as a duty of all human beings and thus observed communally can serve to better explain and strengthen the need for the proper relationship that Maritain promotes between religion and politics in general and in particular between Christianity and democracy, which is especially relevant to our times. In sum, man's knowledge of God simultaneously reveals his total dependence on God, resulting in a deepened awareness of his ontological poverty, which imposes on him a sense of duty to render to God what is owed to Him in fulfillment of the demands of justice. This fulfillment of justice to render to God what is owed Him is specifically the virtue of religion. Contrary to popular opinion, then, religion is not merely a matter of taste and therefore to be relegated to the personal, subjective sphere. Instead religion is a matter of duty, to be rightly and justly carried out by all human beings if we are to find fulfillment as rational beings, that is, in being fully human.

JUSTIN C. GABLE, OP

Revisionism or Within the Roman Catholic Ethical Tradition?

Pope John Paul II on Assisted Nutrition and Hydration

I. Introduction

On March 20, 2004, at the conclusion of an international congress sponsored jointly by the Pontifical Academy for Life and the International Federation of Catholic Medical Associations entitled "Life-Sustaining Treatments and the Vegetative State: Scientific Advances and Ethical Dilemmas," Pope John Paul II gave a concluding allocution. The pope restated many aspects of the Church's teaching over the past several decades, including the human dignity of those in a persistent vegetative state (PVS), the right of such persons to basic health care, and the correlative moral duties of doctors and healthcare professionals. Pope John Paul II also made a pronouncement regarding the care of PVS patients that seemed both definitive and new, namely, that "the obligation to provide the normal care due to the sick in such cases includes, in fact, the use of nutrition and hydration."[1]

This statement by the pope regarding the obligatory character of nutri-

1. Pope John Paul II, "Care for Patients in a 'Permanent' Vegetative State," *Origins* 33 (April 8, 2004): 737, 739–40; reprinted in *Artificial Nutrition and the Permanently Unconscious Patients,* edited by Ronald P. Hamel and James J. Walter (Washington, D.C.: Georgetown University Press, 2007), 203–206. This allocution can also be found on the Vatican City website: http://w2.vatican.va/content/john-paul-ii/en/speeches/2004/march/documents/hf_jp-ii_spe_20040320_congress-fiamc.html

tion and hydration in the care of PVS patients has caused some consternation. There was an immediate negative response to the pope's address by many prominent bioethicists. Within the next year and a half, entire issues of major bioethics journals, including *Christian Bioethics* and the *National Catholic Bioethics Quarterly*, were devoted to the question of PVS patient care, the moral implications of assisted nutrition and hydration (ANH), and an evaluation of the pope's remarks. In 2009, the Consortium of Jesuit Bioethics Programs challenged the allocution,[2] questioning the papal insistence that ANH "should be considered, in principle, ordinary and proportionate and, as such, morally obligatory."[3] Nearly ten years later, the debate surrounding the pope's remarks still continues.

Two of the most articulate critics of the pope's statement have been Thomas Shannon and James Walter, who have charged Pope John Paul II with "revisionism." According to Shannon and Walter, the papal allocution on March 20, 2004 represents "a significant departure from the Roman Catholic bioethical tradition with respect to both the method and the basis upon which decisions are made."[4] They charge that the pope's approach to the issue of PVS patient care has moved away from the traditional method of determining the use of a medical intervention by weighing its potential benefits against the likely harm, pain, or burden it will impose upon an individual patient, his or her family, and community. Instead, they allege, the pope has had recourse to a deontological approach to the care of PVS patients and a "determination of principles by definition or stipulation."[5]

2. Cf. "Undue Burden? The Vatican and Artificial Nutrition and Hydration," *Commonweal* 136, no. 3 (February 13, 2009): 13–15. This critique of Pope John Paul II's 2004 allocution and the Vatican's position on PVS patient care met with its own critique: Cf. The Catholic Medical Association, "Response to the Consortium of Jesuit Bioethics Programs' Statement 'Undue Burden?'" *Linacre Quarterly* 76, no. 3 (2009): 296–303; and William E. May, "The Vatican and Artificial Nutrition and Hydration," *Commonweal* 136, no. 8 (April 20, 2009): 9–11.

3. Cf. Pope John Paul II, "Care for Patients in a 'Permanent' Vegetative State": §4.

4. See Thomas A. Shannon and James J. Walter, "Assisted Nutrition and Hydration and the Catholic Tradition," *Theological Studies* 66 (2005): 655; reprinted in *Contemporary Issues in Bioethics: A Catholic Perspective*, edited by Thomas A. Shannon and James J. Walter (Lanham, Maryland: Rowman and Littlefield, 2005), 269–80. Cf. also Thomas A. Shannon, "Nutrition and Hydration: An Analysis of the Recent Papal Statement in the Light of the Roman Catholic Bioethical Tradition," *Christian Bioethics* 12 (2006): 29–41. Shannon and Walter reiterated their allegation of revisionism several years later in "The PVS Patient and the Foregoing/Withdrawing of Medical Nutrition and Hydration," in *Artificial Nutrition and Hydration and the Permanently Unconscious Patient: The Catholic Debate*, ed. Ronald P. Hamel and James J. Walter (Washington, D.C.: Georgetown University Press, 2007): 143–70.

5. Ibid. The charge of revisionism has been taken up by other bioethicists. Cf., for example,

Does Pope John Paul II's allocution represent a new direction in Catholic moral teaching and a break with the traditional understanding of patient care and end-of-life decision-making? In what follows, I will examine the charge of revisionism and the substance of Shannon and Walter's critique of Pope John Paul II's allocution. While at first glance the papal allocution does seem to confirm Shannon and Walter's analysis, a closer look reveals other interpretive possibilities. The pope's remarks would seem to allow some instances where ANH is not morally obligatory, but open to the kind of concrete moral evaluation espoused by the Catholic moral tradition and described by Shannon and Walter. However, the pope's statement on the obligation to provide ANH to PVS patients should not, as some scholars argue, be interpreted merely as a presumption in favor of ANH. I will argue that the essential connection between the deprivation of nutrition and hydration and death, even in healthy human bodies, underlies the pope's insistence that ANH is not medical care, but basic comfort care that is in principle ordinary. Given this, I will conclude that the pope's allocution articulates an understanding of ANH as morally obligatory for the care of PVS patients and, further, that this is in accord with the fundamental tenets of the Catholic bioethical tradition.

II. Ordinary vs. Extraordinary: Balancing Benefits and Burdens

Shannon and Walter allege that Pope John Paul II's 2004 allocution on the care of PVS patients constitutes a shift away from the traditional moral teaching of the Roman Catholic Church. In support of their claim, Shannon and Walter cite the "Declaration on Euthanasia" issued by the Congregation for the Doctrine of the Faith on May 5, 1980, Pope Pius XII's 1957 address on "The Prolongation of Life," and two pastoral letters issued by the United States Catholic Conference of Bishops, "The Challenge of Peace" (1983)

Janette Blandford, "An Examination of the Revisionist Challenge to the Catholic Tradition on Providing Artificial Nutrition and Hydration to Patients in a Persistent Vegetative State," *Christian Bioethics* 17, no. 2 (2011): 153–64. The arguments of Kevin O'Rourke tend to support the charge of revisionism, although his position is not identical to that of Shannon and Walter. O'Rourke argues that Pope John Paul II's allocution bears little resemblance to the Church teaching that precedes or follows it, thus calling into question its magisterial authority. Cf. Kevin O'Rourke, OP, "Reflections on the Papal Allocution Concerning Care for Persistent Vegetative State Patients," *Christian Bioethics* 12 (2006): 83–97. As we shall see, a close look at official Church documents do not support such a conclusion.

and "Economic Justice for All" (1986) as examples. These documents, according to Shannon and Walter, draw only provisional conclusions and acknowledge the possibility that other judgments could be made using the same principles. This presents a marked contrast to the pope's remarks on the obligatory nature of ANH for the care of PVS patients.

Perhaps even more troubling for Shannon and Walter, however, is the apparent absence in Pope John Paul II's allocution of any role for the weighing of potential benefits and burdens that traditionally determines the appropriateness of any medical treatment for a given patient. While the pope's remarks use the vocabulary of "ordinary" and "proportionate," Shannon and Walter see a shift in the meaning of these terms: "What may be *medically* ordinary or routine may not in fact be *morally* ordinary because of a disproportion of the benefit-burden ratio for the patient. We must avoid the common equivocation on the word 'ordinary.'"[6] In traditional Catholic moral thought, "ordinary" in the moral sense is not a universal categorization, nor is it equivalent to what might be thought of as medically common, but is the conclusion of an assessment of the benefits and burdens relative to a particular patient in a particular set of circumstances.[7] However, argue Shannon and Walter, it is precisely on an understanding of "ordinary" or "extraordinary" as universal classifications, if not a more egregious confusion with what is medically routine, that Pope John Paul II's pronouncement on ANH rests. It is in this sense that Shannon and Walter can characterize Pope John Paul II's approach to PVS patient care as "deontological," and as relying on "definition and stipulation."[8]

III. Presumption in Favor of Assisted Nutrition and Hydration

Shannon and Walter have made a reasonably good case for the charge of "revisionism," but there is considerable disagreement with their position. Many scholars have argued that, far from ignoring the traditional

6. Shannon and Walter, "Assisted Nutrition and Hydration and the Catholic Tradition," 657. The emphasis is Shannon and Walter's.

7. Cf. Ibid., 658: "[T]he tradition does not use the terms ordinary and extraordinary as a means of abstract classification, but as the conclusion of an argument about the proportion and disproportion of benefits and burdens, as the CDF phrases it.... [T]he equivocation on the term ordinary and the use of the terms as means of categorizing interventions set the context for the presumption of the use of assisted nutrition and hydration."

8. Cf. note 5 above.

Catholic understanding of the term "ordinary," the pope's allocution takes into consideration the limits of what can be considered morally obligatory, and acknowledges the necessity of weighing the benefits and burdens of ANH. Some of Pope John Paul II's defenders emphasize that ANH is, in the words of the allocution, only considered ordinary and proportionate "in principle" and "insofar as and until it is seen to have attained its proper finality, which in the present case consists in providing nourishment to the patient and alleviation of his suffering."[9] As William May puts it, "the pope recognized that ANH can rightly be withheld if judged either ineffective or unduly burdensome."[10]

Jeffrey Bishop and Elliot Bedford have also argued that the papal allocution has been overinterpreted by some bioethicists.[11] Critics of the pope have tended to assume that the pope's remarks imply that the wishes of the patient or the judgment of family members are irrelevant. Bedford and Bishop argue that, to the contrary, the pope's address is directed to physicians and care personnel, and not to patients or their families. His remarks ought to be interpreted, then, as an anthropological teaching, affirming the dignity of the human person even in a vegetative state, and his or her right to assisted nutrition and hydration. Such an interpretation allows Bishop and Bedford to hold that the pope's position "does not entail that nutrition and hydration must be provided in all circumstances—even over the patient's refusal—only that it is a matter of justice that human beings be provided with the means which, according to human nature, are necessary for responsible stewardship of their lives."[12] This would allow for the possibility of a PVS patient or his or her family to determine in any particular case whether or not ANH is either ordinary or extraordinary care.

Read in this way, the pope's allocution can be interpreted as merely a presumption in favor of ANH. Just as in civil law a defendant can be tried and convicted, but is presumed innocent until proven guilty, so ANH might be said to be presupposed ordinary and proportionate care until shown otherwise. This is the interpretation suggested by Bedford and Bishop, May, and others, and it is not implausible.[13] It is also similar to a position articulated

9. Pope John Paul II, "Care for Patients in a 'Permanent' Vegetative State," §4.

10. William E. May, "The Vatican and Artificial Nutrition and Hydration," 9.

11. Cf. Jeffrey P. Bishop and Elliot Louis Bedford, "Medically Assisted Nutrition and Hydration: The Vegetative State and Beyond," *Christian Bioethics* 17, no. 2 (2011): 100.

12. Ibid.

13. This interpretation is not, however, sufficient for refuting the charge of revisionism in the

by the New Jersey Catholic Conference of Bishops in 1987,[14] and the United States Catholic Conference of Bishop's Third Revised Edition of the *Ethical and Religious Directives for Catholic Health Care Services* issued in 1994.

Despite the merits of this interpretation, however, there is good reason to suspect that it is not entirely satisfactory. Returning to the papal allocution itself, Pope John Paul II does not speak of a "presumption" in favor of ANH, nor do his remarks indicate that ANH can be considered extraordinary care if the judgment of the patient or family members deem it to be so. Pope John Paul II's wording suggests something stronger:

> The obligation to provide the normal care due to the sick in such a case [PVS] includes, in fact, the use of nutrition and hydration. The evaluation of probabilities, founding on waning hopes for recovery when the vegetative state is prolonged beyond a year, cannot ethically justify the cessation or interruption of minimal care for the patient, including nutrition and hydration. Death by starvation or dehydration is, in fact, the only possible outcome as a result of their withdrawal. In this sense it ends up becoming, if done knowingly and willingly, true and proper euthanasia by omission.[15]

The pope's statement seems quite definitive. In the case of PVS patients, a low probability of recovery cannot justify the denial or interruption of ANH. The only qualification mentioned in the pope's statement is in those circumstances where ANH cannot attain "its proper finality." Put another way, ANH is morally obligatory as long as and until it is no longer effective in providing nourishment to the patient, either because the patient is unable to absorb nutrients or because she is too sick to derive any benefit from nutrition.[16]

On August 1, 2007, the Congregation for the Doctrine of the Faith (CDF) formulated responses to questions presented by Bishop William S. Skylstad, then President of the USCCB, regarding assisted nutrition and hydration.[17] The responses to Bishop Skylstad's questions, together with

---

eyes of Shannon and Walter. Cf. Shannon and Walter, "Assisted Nutrition and Hydration and the Catholic Tradition," 659.

14. Cf. New Jersey Catholic Conference of Bishops, "Providing Food and Fluids to Severely Brain Damaged Patients," *Origins* 16 (January 22, 1987): 582–84.

15. Pope John Paul II, "Care for Patients in a 'Permanent' Vegetative State," §4.

16. Cf. ibid.

17. Congregation for the Doctrine of the Faith, "Responses to Certain Questions of the United States Catholic Conference of Bishops Concerning Artificial Nutrition and Hydration," *National Catholic Bioethics Quarterly* 8, no. 1 (2008): 123. This document from the CDF can also

the explanatory commentary, provide definitive answers to questions of the role of ANH in PVS patient care. These answers not only reflect the language of Pope John Paul II's allocution, they also leave little doubt as to the impossibility that the morally obligatory character of ANH could simply be interpreted as a presumption in favor of ANH: "It [ANH in the case of PVS patients] is obligatory to the extent which, and for as long as, it is shown to accomplish its proper finality, which is the hydration and nourishment of the patient. In this way suffering and death by starvation and dehydration are prevented."[18] When asked whether ANH might be discontinued when qualified physicians agree that the PVS patient will never regain consciousness, the CDF's response is clearly and definitively in the negative.

The language of presumption in favor of assisted nutrition and hydration found in the Third Revised Edition of the *Ethical and Religious Directives for Catholic Health Care Services* (1994) has given way to the language of obligation in the Fifth Edition (2009): "In principle, there is an obligation to provide patients with food and water, including medically assisted nutrition and hydration for those who cannot take food orally."[19] The same paragraph (Directive #58) goes on to explain that ANH becomes morally optional for any kind of patient only when it causes "significant physical discomfort" or when it cannot "reasonably be expected to prolong life."[20]

The actual verbiage of Pope John Paul II's allocution, together with the statements issued by the CDF and the ethical directives published by the USCCB, would seem to indicate that an interpretation of the pope's allocution as advocating for a mere presumption in favor of ANH for PVS patients is not faithful to the sense of the address. Whether or not we can acquit the allocution of Shannon and Walter's charge of revisionism, the idea that it was intended only to emphasize the dignity of the PVS patient and present ANH as the generally preferred course of care no longer seems defensible.

---

be found online at http://www.vatican.va/roman_curia/congregations/cfaith/document/ rc_con_cfaith_doc_20070801_riposte-usa_en.html.

18. Ibid.

19. USCCB, *Ethical and Religious Directives for Catholic Health Care Services* (Washington, D.C.: USCCB, 2009), Directive #58.

20. Ibid.

IV. Assisted Nutrition and Hydration and the Catholic Moral Tradition

Shannon and Walter point to the weighing of the benefits and burdens involved in the use of a treatment for a particular patient as the essential criteria for determining whether any given medical intervention is ordinary (and thus morally obligatory) or extraordinary (and therefore morally optional). In contrast, Pope John Paul II's allocution on the care of PVS patients states that ANH is morally obligatory, except in cases where ANH is ineffective. It would seem that the pope is either revising Catholic moral teaching by excluding the traditional process of moral discernment—this is Shannon and Walter's thesis—or that there is something quite unique about ANH and, in particular, ANH with regard to PVS patients. So we might begin by asking: Is ANH different from other treatments, and what makes it so?

In contrast to medical interventions which respond to diseases or specific conditions of an ailing human body, ANH does not provide a particular course of treatment designed to counteract a specific illness or injury. Rather, ANH is a method for providing the nutrients which any human body as such requires to live. This means that the deprivation of nutrition and hydration has a direct causal link to death, even in healthy human bodies: "Death by starvation or dehydration is, in fact, the only possible outcome as a result of their withdrawal."[21] This means that the choice to deprive a patient of ANH is not simply a case of "foregoing treatment" and letting a disease or the effects of a bodily injury run their course. It is to cause death. If we appreciate this fact, we can see not only how ANH is different from other kinds of medical treatments, but why ANH must, as a result, have a different moral status. This would help to explain why the papal allocution characterizes ANH as "a natural means of preserving life, not a medical act" and why it insists that ANH "should be considered, in principle, ordinary and proportionate, and as such morally obligatory."[22]

Shannon and Walter are right to see the determination of medical treatments as ordinary and extraordinary, along with the concrete weighing of

21. Pope John Paul II, "Care for Patients in a 'Permanent' Vegetative State," §4.

22. Ibid. Thus this characterization of ANH is not meant to deny that it is most commonly administered by medical personnel, nor that ANH employs an artificial means of delivery to provide nutrition and hydration.

benefits and burdens that underlies such a determination, as essential to the Catholic moral tradition. However, also essential to the tradition is the distinction between killing and letting die. It is immoral to directly intend evil, including the death of an innocent person.[23] In the context of medical care, it is not permissible to choose an intervention in order to cause or hasten death, although it is morally acceptable to forego medical treatments which are judged to be excessively burdensome. In the absence of a condition which prevents ANH from being effective, depriving a patient of nutrition and hydration, whether administered through normal eating, manual feeding, or via a PEG (percutaneous endoscopic gastrostomy) feeding tube,[24] means to cause their death. Such deprivation "ends up becoming, if done knowingly and willingly, true and proper euthanasia by omission."[25]

Shannon and Walter charged that the papal allocution, among other pronouncements issued by the Vatican in the last several decades, have constituted a shift. Part of this shift has been methodological, a turn to "deontology and a determination of principles by definition or stipulation."[26]

23. It is this absolute prohibition against directly intending evil, along with the insight that we live in an imperfect world where there are almost always unintended negative consequences to our actions, that has given rise to the doctrine of double effect. This doctrine distinguishes between actions which include unintended evil consequences, even if these are foreseen, and actions which directly intend evil or necessarily include the commission of evil to achieve their aim. For more on the tradition of double-effect reasoning and the many moral questions which surround it, cf. John Berkman, "How Important is the Doctrine of Double Effect for Moral Theology? Contextualizing the Controversy," *Christian Bioethics* 3, no. 2 (1997): 89–114; James F. Keenan, SJ, "The Function of the Principle of Double Effect," *Theological Studies* 54 (1993): 294–315; and Christopher Kaczor, "Double-Effect Reasoning from Jean Pierre Gury to Peter Knauer," *Theological Studies* 59 (1998): 297–316. For an application of double-effect reasoning to end-of-life decisions, cf. J. Andrew Billings, "Double Effect: A Useful Rule that Alone Cannot Justify Hastening Death," *Journal of Medical Ethics* 37, no. 7 (2011): 437–40; and Rita L. Marker, "End-of-Life Decisions and Double Effect: How Can This Be Wrong When It Feels So Right?" *National Catholic Bioethics Quarterly* 11 (2011): 99–119.

24. PEG, or percutaneous endoscopic gastrostomy, is a minimally invasive procedure that uses endoscopy to insert a feeding tube directly into the stomach or lower intestine, and is the most common way ANH is administered. There is an extensive literature on the benefits and potential complications for a PEG tube feeding. Cf., for instance, R. Y. Haddad and D. R. Thomas, "Enteral Nutrition and Enteral Tube Feeding: Review of the Evidence," *Clinics in Geriatric Medicine* 18, no. 4 (2002): 867–81; Erik J. Meidl, MD, "A Case Studies Approach to Assisted Nutrition and Hydration," *National Catholic Bioethics Quarterly* 6 (2006): 319–36; William Plonk, "To PEG or Not to PEG," *Practical Gastroenterology* 29, no. 7 (July 2005): 16–31; and Ephraim Rimon, et al., "Percutaneous Gastrostomy: Evidence of Different Prognosis in Various Patient Subgroups," *Age and Aging* 34, no. 4 (July 2005): 352–65.

25. Pope John Paul II, "Care for Patients in a 'Permanent' Vegetative State," §4.

26. Shannon and Walter, "Assisted Nutrition and Hydration and the Catholic Tradition," 655.

It is clear, however, that the papal allocution has not simply arbitrarily redefined ANH as ordinary and proportionate. Rather, the pope is identifying something essential in the nature of ANH itself and, in particular, ANH relative to PVS patient care. Further, to characterize the pope's procedure as deontological is at best misleading, for it implies that teleological reasoning (or other non-deontological approaches) cannot disclose universal practical principles. This is simply not the case. In addition, to argue that a principled approach necessarily constitutes a turn from the Catholic tradition of moral reasoning fails to appreciate that the tradition has always included universal moral precepts, even those of an exceptionless nature:

> In the context of the Catholic moral tradition, "teleological" is not synonymous with consequentialist. Rather, as we understand it, the teleological framework found within the Catholic tradition recognizes the moral relevance both of rules of right conduct and of consequences. In other words, the Catholic moral tradition has always recognized some negative obligations of a fundamentally deontological nature, including of course the obligation never to directly intend the destruction of innocent human life.[27]

Contrary to Shannon and Walter, the mere presence of universal principles in the papal allocution does not, in and of itself, constitute a new direction in Catholic moral thinking. Quite the opposite. One could argue that the absence of universal moral principles and a reduction of the Catholic moral tradition to a case-by-case discernment of benefits and burdens would be the innovation. Although Shannon and Walter frequently speak as if the weighing of burdens and benefits were the whole of the Catholic moral tradition's contribution to discerning biomedical moral obligations, the tradition has also relied on the key distinction between killing and letting die, based on the principle that no evil can be directly intended. The tradition has always acknowledged that in addition to the circumstances and consequences of an action, an agent's intention (i.e., the end or purpose of the action) and the nature of the act must also be considered. The

27. Mark Repenshak and John Paul Slosar, "Medically Assisted Nutrition and Hydration: A Contribution to the Dialogue," in *Artificial Nutrition and Hydration and the Permanently Unconscious Patient: The Catholic Debate,* edited by Ronald P. Hamel and James J. Walter (Washington, D.C.: Georgetown University Press, 2007): 216. For a detailed exposition of the existence of universal and even exceptionless moral norms in the Catholic tradition, cf. Christopher Kaczor, "Exceptionless Norms in Aristotle? Thomas Aquinas and the Twentieth-Century Interpreters of the *Nicomachean Ethics,*" *Thomist* 61, no. 1 (1997): 33–62; cf. also Kaczor, *Proportionalism and the Natural Law Tradition* (Washington, D.C.: The Catholic University of America Press, 2002), especially chapter seven.

papal allocution, I would argue, attends to these other facets of the moral tradition, facets that are either ignored or at least not explicitly considered by Shannon and Walter in this context.

Pope John Paul II's remarks are confined to PVS patients and, as such, cannot be extrapolated to all cases without qualification. The circumstances of other patients who might require PVS, such as persons with advanced dementia or end-stage cancer, alters the effectiveness and burdensomeness of ANH.[28] In dying patients, ANH can prove not only useless, but excessively burdensome: dying patients' bodies are often unable to absorb nutrients at all. In such cases, PEG feeding tube insertion can result in additional medical complications and physical pain, or simply be the source of significant psychological discomfort. With PVS patients, however, the circumstances which might render ANH excessively burdensome do not seem applicable: psychological discomfort is not a factor; the PEG feeding tube insertion is not prone to complications as a result of the patient's PVS status; even the cost of ANH and maintenance of a PEG feeding tube is relatively affordable.[29] All these factors are considered by the papal allocution. Although the conclusions of the papal allocution are framed as a universal precept, it is clear that a consideration of the circumstances in which ANH is provided to PVS patients is, along with the intention and nature of the medical intervention, also present in the pope's thought.

28. This is due, in large part, to the different situation confronting the administration of ANH in other types of patients. For a lucid exposition of the benefits and burdens of ANH posed to patients with advanced dementia, cf. John S. Howland, MD, "A Defense of Assisted Nutrition and Hydration in Patients with Dementia," *National Catholic Bioethics Quarterly* 9 (2009): 697–710. Cf. also Patrick Guinan, MD, "Is Assisted Nutrition and Hydration Always Mandated? The Persistent Vegetative State Differs from Dementia and Frailty," *National Catholic Bioethics Quarterly* 10 (2010): 481–88.

29. A certain confusion tends to set in when the potential burdensomeness of ANH is considered. We must carefully ask whether we are determining the burdens involved in ANH, which are relatively minimal, or the potential burdensomeness of continued existence in the condition of PVS. In the same vein, we must distinguish between the cost of ANH and the overall cost of caring for a loved one. The cost and burden of ANH for PVS patients is relatively minimal, although the pain caused by the PVS condition and the cost of the continued care of a loved one can be much greater. Ultimately it is the burdens of the procedure, not the value of "quality of life" (the burdens of continued existence versus non-existence) that is to be weighed in determining whether a given intervention is ordinary or extraordinary, according to the Catholic moral tradition. As Mark Latkovic puts it, "Quality of life judgments focus not so much on the objective usefulness of the *treatment*, but on the value of the *life* that is to be preserved or not preserved; not on whether the treatment is burdensome, but on whether the person's life is burdensome." Cf. Mark Latkovic, "The Morality of Tube Feeding PVS Patients: A Critique of the View of Kevin O'Rourke, OP," *National Catholic Bioethics Quarterly* 5 (2005): 509.

The heart of the matter, however, is the direct causal link between nutrition and hydration and a patient's death. Depriving a PVS patient of nutrition and hydration would be an instance of directly intending death. The physician or family member refusing ANH on behalf of the patient would no longer be merely foregoing treatment or letting die, but killing the patient. Death would not, in this instance, be the outcome of the underlying condition, but the direct result of dehydration and starvation.

Yet is this not to confuse nutrition and hydration with ordinary food and water? It is true that to deprive a person of food and water would be a clear instance of killing. In the case of PVS patients, however, they are unable to eat and drink for themselves. In this case, it could be argued, the decision to forego ANH on their behalf is a decision not to deprive them of food and drink, but of artificially delivered nutrition and hydration. It does not constitute a decision to kill a patient by starvation or dehydration, but the declining of a medical intervention. It is, one could argue, analogous to the decision to forego the use of a ventilator once a person is unable to breathe on their own.[30] To decline artificial respiration is not the same as killing by suffocation. The moral difference between the decision to forego or terminate mechanical ventilation and suffocation is highlighted by Pius XII in his 1957 Address on "The Prolongation of Life."[31] Here the pope clearly establishes that a physician may, but is not obligated to use, artificial respiration when there is little hope of the patient's survival, or when resuscitation and ventilation would constitute an excessive burden for the patient's family:

> Consequently, if it appears that the attempt at resuscitation constitutes in reality such a burden for the family that one cannot in all conscience impose it upon them, they can lawfully insist that the doctor should discontinue these attempts, and the doctor can lawfully comply. There is not involved here a case of direct disposal of the life of the patient, nor of euthanasia in any way: This would never be licit. Even when it causes the arrest of circulation, the interruption of attempts at resuscitation is never more than an indirect cause of the cessation of life.[32]

30. For the use of this analogy as an argument against the type of moral reasoning presented in the papal allocution, cf. Benedict Ashley, OP, and Kevin O'Rourke, OP, *Health Care Ethics: A Theological Analysis,* fourth edition (Washington, D.C.: Georgetown University Press, 1997), 422. For a more sustained argument against this analogy, cf. Mark S. Latkovic, "The Morality of Tube Feeding PVS Patients: A Critique of the View of Kevin O'Rourke, OP," 508.

31. Pope Pius XII, "The Prolongation of Life: Address to the International Congress of Anesthesiologists," (November 24, 1957), *The Pope Speaks* 4 (1958): 395–98; reprinted in *Catholic Health Care Ethics: A Manual for Practitioners,* edited by E. J. Furton, P. J. Cataldo, and A. S. Moraczweski (Philadelphia: National Catholic Bioethics Center, 2009): 299–301.

32. Ibid., 396.

If this analogy between ANH and artificial respiration holds, Pope Pius XII's remarks would seem to confirm Shannon and Walter's charge of revisionism, and stand in direct opposition to the teaching of Pope John Paul II. If ANH for PVS patients and artificial respiration for those with critical injuries are analogous to one another, Pope John Paul II's insistence that ANH is morally obligatory would constitute a shift from the ethically optional character attributed to such interventions by Pope Pius XII and the Catholic moral tradition.

In the end, however, the analogy is suspect. Artificial respiration is used when a patient cannot breathe by herself. The ordinary functionality of her lungs and pulmonary system are not sufficient to provide her oxygen. By contrast, in the vast majority of cases, PVS patients are not only able to digest the nutrition provided them through ANH, they are able to swallow, and thus can even be manually fed. Manual feedings are, however, inconvenient and time consuming, and thus a feeding tube (PEG) is typically used to increase the efficiency and quality of care.[33] Even in those PVS patients who could not be manually fed, their stomach and digestive tract are still functioning, able to process nutrients and maintain the patient's bodily health. Despite the apparent similarities between patients who need artificial ventilation for survival and PVS patients who require ANH, then, the medical differences are vast and morally significant: while removing artificial ventilation may result in the death of a patient, the cause of that death is ultimately the injury or condition which has caused the pulmonary system to cease functioning properly. On the other hand, depriving PVS patients of ANH inevitably results in the death of these patients by starvation and dehydration, a death unrelated to PVS or its underlying condition.

The case of forgoing or removing artificial ventilation is far more similar to those cases in which a patient's body is no longer able to absorb nutrition, and it is precisely in these cases that the papal allocution explicitly allows for the foregoing of ANH. In those cases which do strongly resemble the situation of reliance on artificial respiration, there is no moral obligation to ANH. Indeed, in such situations, it would be considered extraordinary and burdensome. If this is the case, then it would seem that, despite

33. Cf. Mark Latkovic, "The Morality of Tube Feeding PVS Patients," 507. Latkovic cites the work of Eugene F. Diamond as well as studies presented in the *British Medical Journal*. Cf., for instance, Eugene F. Diamond, MD, "Medical Issues When Discontinuing ANH," *Ethics and Medics* 24, no. 9 (1999): 1–2.

the *prima facie* difference, there is a fundamental agreement between the statements of Pope Pius XII in his address on "The Prolongation of Life" and the remarks of Pope John Paul II in his papal allocution. In contrast to the charge of revisionism, there would seem to be a strong case for a continuity of Catholic moral teaching.

V. Conclusion

Pope John Paul II's allocution, "Care for Patients in a 'Permanent' Vegetative State," raises many difficult issues. I do not claim to have adequately addressed these issues, nor have I attempted to provide a thoroughgoing justification of the pope's statements, particularly for those who stand outside the Catholic moral tradition. Nevertheless, I believe the charge of revisionism has been shown to be relatively empty. Shannon and Walter have argued that a substantial change of methodology and emphasis has taken place. I would argue, however, that such a characterization relies too heavily on one aspect of the tradition, the determination of a medical treatment as ordinary or extraordinary by a prudential weighing of concrete benefits and burdens, while overlooking other aspects of the tradition. In particular, Shannon and Walter have neglected the essential distinction between killing and letting die, a distinction founded in the intention of the agent or decision maker, as well as the nature of the act. Since the tradition is clear that no evil can be directly intended, the latter is licit, while the former is prohibited. It is only within the parameters of "letting die" that the judgment regarding whether a medical intervention is ordinary or extraordinary can be made at all. Given the universal human need for nutrition and hydration, as well as the nature of the persistent vegetative state, the decision to forego ANH is not morally optional, except in cases where it cannot achieve its proper end. Such an analysis is firmly in keeping with the Catholic moral tradition, whose teleological approach and respect for the concrete has never excluded the articulation of universal principles.

MEGAN FURMAN

Art and Morality

Nuancing Maritain's Divide through Creative Intuition

I. Introduction

IN ACCEPTING THE SCHOLASTIC definition of art as a virtue of the practical intellect (*recta ratio factibilium*), Jacques Maritain formally distinguishes the realm of art from that of morality, the realm of human action (*recta ratio agibilium*). Maritain insists on this separation for a number of reasons, including the fact that in most cases good artists are not saints and saints rarely make good artists. Nevertheless, Maritain does not seem to want to posit a strict division. In various works, he takes up the issue of art and morality, suggesting that they are somehow—if unclearly—related. However, his statements can appear to be ambivalent or even contradictory. For example, in *The Responsibility of the Artist,* he seems to maintain that morality is antagonistic to art, and that art is, in fact, fed by immorality:

> To sum up, on the ground that art reflects morality, one insists that art exacts a life which is morally dangerous, and new experiments in morality as in aesthetics—that is to say experiments to render innocent, thanks to the sorcery of poetry, the very things God forbids. This means, if you like, subordinating art to morality, but to a morality that art has violated.[1]

Other excerpts, meanwhile, offer a different sentiment, prompting Ralph McInerny to assert that Maritain seems "attracted by the view that the mor-

1. Jacques Maritain, *The Responsibility of the Artist* (New York: Charles Scribner's Sons, 1960), 96.

ally good person will be a better artist for that very fact."[2] After all, a chapter of *Art and Scholasticism* is devoted to Christian Art. Such preoccupation suggests that the state of one's soul—a moral concern—has some bearing upon one's art. How can these various positions be reconciled?

The purpose of this essay is to nuance Maritain's divide between art and morality in order to show in what way Maritain's vision for the artist does involve moral virtue. This will require, first, that one understand the ways in which art is both amoral and moral, and second, that one assemble a picture of Maritain's vision for artists. Therefore, in order to demonstrate what has been proposed as a twofold aspect of art, the first part of this essay will examine the root of all artistic activity, namely, creative intuition. Then, by turning to the paradigm of Dante, the second part will illustrate Maritain's vision of the integrated artist. This interpretation draws from a range of Maritain's works in aesthetics, including *Art and Scholasticism, Creative Intuition in Art and Poetry, The Responsibility of the Artist,* and *Situation de la poésie,* but also works in other areas of philosophy, from *The Range of Reason* and *The Degrees of Knowledge* to *Liturgy and Contemplation, Approaches to God,* and *Moral Philosophy*. Contemporary criticism includes the work of John G. Trapani Jr. and John W. Hanke.

A few fundamental assumptions are needed. The first is that one understands that Maritain is dealing not with art as such, but with a particular species of art—*fine art*—which, according to Maritain, is born from "creative intuition," the immediate, affective, connatural intuition of beauty in the things of the world. A second assumption is that one is basically familiar with Maritain's notion of the relationship between the artist and the work. In an "Essay on Art," we are told that every work "bears the mark of the artist; it is the offspring of his soul and spirit."[3] The work is the manifestation of things in the world as they resonate within the subjectivity of the artist.[4] A third assumption is that when one speaks of a beautiful work, one takes as a measure Maritain's notion that beautiful art shines forth the "splendor, the mystery of a *form*, in the metaphysical sense of this word."[5]

2. Ralph McInerny, "Maritain and Poetic Knowledge," in *Being and Predication* (Washington, D.C.: The Catholic University of America Press, 1986), 312.

3. Jacques Maritain, "An Essay on Art," in *Art and Scholasticism and the Frontiers of Poetry* (New York: Charles Scribner's Sons, 1962), 87.

4. Without going into detail here, Maritain's is a unique "ontology" of art—one that is more thoroughly examined by John W. Hanke in *Maritain's Ontology of the Work of Art* (The Hague: Martinus Nijhoff, 1973).

5. Maritain, "An Essay on Art," 86.

II. The Amorality of Creative Intuition

In *Creative Intuition in Art and Poetry,* Maritain explores the peculiar nature of that moment of insight from which all artistic creativity flows. One of its most important characteristics is what Maritain calls "creative innocence," which he describes in a baptismal analogy. In creative intuition, he says, all things pass through a "night;" they "touch the deep waters over which it reigns."[6] There, they are transformed and, as it were, reborn with new natures. It is worth quoting Maritain here at length:

> The inner world in the midst of which such a place exists may be filled with impurity; the moral experience of a poet may be rotten; his thought and his passion may be stimulated by energies of illusion or perversity. When the things he has nourished in himself enter his earthly paradise of creative innocence, they keep their moral impurity—if they have any—which will also pass into the work. But they bathe in the ontologic purity of this place. In the waters of poetic knowledge they are dehumanized . . . transmuted into forms of the revelation of being through creative emotion; they receive a new nature, a poetic nature, a new principle of existence, which replaces in them the human one, and causes their moral impact and moral qualities, as well as the marks and stains upon them of a man's tics or vices, to become henceforth accidental and secondary in the particular sphere of this new state of existence, where only poetry and beauty are essential. . . . Thus it is that a great poet can be corrupt, while his creative intuition never is.[7]

Maritain describes this place of creative innocence as a "kind of earthly paradise," a sacred place, "the only one that is not wounded" by original sin.[8] But the purity of this place is of an ontologic, not a moral, nature. It has only to do with the intuition of the poet and with what Maritain identifies as poetic *naivete* and *integrity*. The naive poet believes in the world, in his experience, and in the correlation between the two; he believes in his feeling, in his own work, and in his ability to speak something true.[9] The poet of integrity possesses disinterestedness.[10] He is honest. To his creative intuition, he adds no agendas, morals, or meanings.

While for Maritain, it is possible for moral impurities to work their

6. Jacques Maritain, *Creative Intuition in Art and Poetry* (New York: Pantheon Books, 1953), 372.

7. Ibid., 375.

8. Ibid., 374.

9. Ibid., 370.

10. Ibid., 372.

ways into a work, creative innocence renders them impotent. All things pass through this purifying "bath." The work presents its subject matter simply for contemplation. As proof, Maritain points to the test of time. By time, says Maritain, "the moral impact through which human souls may possibly be wounded is blurred and extinguished." Only "some deeper revelation of the heart of man"—only beauty—remains.[11] While time has no impact on the poet's soul, it is "the redeemer of the poet's work."[12]

To the extent that it renders a work simple testimony to *what is,* creative innocence represents the amoral aspect of creative intuition, and—so it follows—of art. Creative innocence gives art domain over all things under the sun. It is this amoral aspect that accounts for the fact that beautiful works of art can be produced by immoral artists; it also accounts for the amoral nature of the work itself. To the extent that a work testifies to a poet's experience of reality, it can be honest, true, and good. The creatively innocent work can be beautiful.

III. The Morality of Creative Intuition

Having established an amoral aspect to creative intuition, it is now necessary to show wherein a moral aspect is included. This is to suggest that in the realm of the fine arts, there is indeed a moral aspect to the virtue of art. Often overlooked, this moral aspect is attributed to the *dispositional* aspect of creative intuition. Through material causality, Maritain allows for—and at times is preoccupied with—the influence of moral virtue not within, but *upon,* creative intuition.

While creative intuition can neither be learned nor taught, Maritain insists that it can be guarded, protected, and nurtured. By its connatural character, creative intuition is contingent upon "intact dynamic integrity ... the temperament of each individual, his natural inclinations, and his capacity for and fidelity to spiritual repose."[13] All of these features point to a dispositional aspect. Maritain affirms that certain virtues can dispose one for creative intuition. Primary among these is self-awareness; others include soberness, chastity, respect, fortitude, renouncement, obedience, order, humility, prudence and strength, temperance, and ingenuity. However,

11. Maritain, *Responsibility of the Artist,* 87.
12. Ibid., 86.
13. Maritain, *Creative Intuition,* 244.

Maritain calls these "aesthetic virtues." They are only parallel to—not identical with—their moral counterparts, for their purpose or end is the work of art, not the good of man. Nevertheless, while formally distinguished, these virtues may in reality be identical to their moral counterparts. For example, contemplative recollection may open one with the habit of art to creative insight. Thus, one's behavior can enhance one's art by, for example, "removing obstacles and noise" to prepare the senses and the mind for creative intuition, and subsequently, in the practice of the virtue itself, by refusing to betray the creative intuition at its source, but rather, subordinating to it (i.e., the creative intuition) all external influences. The latter practice, especially—Maritain explicitly states—requires a "school" in discipline and sacrifice.[14] Thus it is clear that the realm of human action plays at least a material role in creative intuition and art.

But does morality in its proper meaning—as concerned with the ultimate good of man—have any bearing on creative intuition? In this context, it is worth turning to Maritain's special treatment of the Christian artist. If morality has no bearing upon art, then why would Maritain be preoccupied with the vocation of the Christian artist?

IV. Maritain's Vision for the Artist

In *Art and Scholasticism,* Maritain identifies the general rule of the fine arts merely to produce a work of beauty. To even conceive of such a work, reason is not enough; the artist must be connatured to beauty, he must be in love with beauty:

> If every faculty of desire and emotion in the artist is not fundamentally rectified and exalted in the line of beauty, whose transcendence and immateriality are superhuman, human life, the humdrum activity of the senses, and the routine of art itself, will degrade his conception. The artist must be in love, must be in love with *what he is doing,* so that his virtue becomes in truth, St. Augustine's phrase, *ordo amoris.* [sic] so that beauty becomes connatural to him, bedded in his being through affection, and his work proceeds from his heart and bowels as from his lucid mind.[15]

But what happens with the addition of grace? In other words, what is distinctive to the Christian artist?

14. Ibid., 139.

15. Jacques Maritain, *Art and Scholasticism with Other Essays,* translated by J. F. Scanlan, 3rd revised edition (New York: Kessinger, 2006), 38.

In Maritain's theology, grace entirely transforms human nature, elevating all the virtues to their supernatural end. But grace builds on nature: Maritain's insistence upon this point requires that Christian artists be, first and foremost, artists. They must cultivate the virtue of art in order for their art to be disposed to animation by grace. But the soul of the Christian artist, who is in love with beauty, will first and foremost be directed to the supernatural end by the supernatural love of charity. And, according to Maritain's Thomistic inheritance, charity orders all lesser loves in an architectonic way.

Here, then, lies the most prominent link between morality and art. If charity orders what one loves, then it will order what one perceives as beautiful. Maritain writes:

> If the artist loves truth and his fellowmen, anything in the work which might distort the truth or deteriorate the human soul will displease him, and *lose for him that delight which beauty affords.* Respect for truth and for the human soul will become an objective condition or requirement affecting his virtue of art itself.[16]

One's appetites, one's moral character, have real—if indirect—roles within the very perception of reality that is equally the font of creative intuition. Since all of one's activities—whether philosophy, medicine, or art—spring from a single source, the state of the source will affect all the activities that flow from it. As in the previous section, this causality can likewise be described as material.[17] Importantly, it pertains to both graced and natural virtue:

> Are not the inner inclinations of the artist the very channel through which things are revealed to him? Is it not in and through himself, through his own emotion and subjectivity, that the poet, in so far as poetic intuition is concerned, knows everything he knows? What is most real in the world thus escapes the notice of a darkened soul.[18]

What, then, is one to do with the excerpts in which Maritain states that immorality fuels art? In *Responsibility of the Artist,* he affirms that "moral

16. Maritain, *Responsibility of the Artist,* 61; italics mine. In order to underscore the proper order of things, Maritain clarifies that the aforementioned "objective conditions," which are in essence moral, here can be likened to a rule of prosody for the classical poet, or to the necessity of having doors and windows in a house. These parameters, he adds, "have never obliged an artist to bend or force down his art." Instead, "They oblige him to make his art more straight, and more powerful."

17. Ibid., 93.

18. Ibid.

poison" may in fact "have stimulated or sensitized" the "power of vision"—but this only in the short term. In the long run, Maritain states that moral poison will warp the power of vision and, "through an indirect reprecission … artistic creativity."[19] Nevertheless, he is careful to avoid swinging the pendulum too far in the opposite direction. A moral man, Maritain insists, may in fact produce worse art *by that very fact,* if he allows moral sense to censor or alter creative intuition. Moral influence, he summarizes, "is … subject to any kind of contingency, and it can be at play in various, even opposite directions."[20] The goal, it seems, is to order and integrate art and morality by beginning with an accurate disposition towards reality. Such a disposition, which requires that one's appetites are properly ordered, begins at the very core of the poet, in that ontological place from which all the soul's activities spring.

V. Dante, the Exemplar

In chapter nine of *Creative Intuition,* Maritain provides a paradigm for the way in which morality and art can be properly integrated, yielding their fullest potential. Such integration is the unique achievement of Dante, held up by Maritain as one of the greatest poets. According to Maritain, Dante's greatest asset is his profound depth of insight. To what can one attribute this? To artistic genius? To genetic disposition? Loyal to the principle that grace animates nature, Maritain attributes Dante's greatness to a fruitful partnership among natural and supernatural influences. Among these are certain external factors afforded by his particularly Christian socio-historical context, which include: first, existential certitude; second, maturity in subjectivity (which Maritain claims was not achieved until the Middle Ages); and, third, a depth of knowledge. According to Maritain, Dante's Christian heritage contributed the metaphysical material, while the Christian context of the Middle Ages furnished the security and freedom needed to probe its depths in a non-didactic way:

> Because he was so perfectly sure of his faith, his poetry was able freely to play even with its tenets, and to fancy, without deceiving anybody, that condition of the "neither rebellious nor faithful," rejected by both heaven and hell, which theology

19. The poison will not "prevent the work from being great and treasurable," but because the work "always *avows,*" it will reveal "some soft spot in this progress." Ibid., 92–93.

20. Ibid., 92.

does not know. . . . He was eager for knowledge, whose consonance with his faith was for him divinely unquestionable.[21]

On the one hand, the factors named above shape Dante the man, not the artist; on the other, insofar as Dante is one man, all action springs from his core. Thus Maritain describes the causality of these factors as "*extrinsic* and *indirect*" to art.[22] Nevertheless, it is significant. He states: "I do not believe that the creative innocence of Dante, and the transparency of his poetic experience, could have been so deep, had not the innocence of his heart established his entire soul in genuine connaturality with them."[23] Dante's moral character influences his vision, which in turn lies at the root of his poetry.

In Dante, Maritain presents a paradigm artist in whom the proper integration of art and morality is achieved. Dante's success is attributed to the fact that Dante ordered things rightly; he allowed neither morality nor faith to filter his art, but rather, integrated both into creative intuition. Maritain clearly states his vision for such fruitful integration in the following:

> Beauty and Poetry are an inexorable absolute which requires a total gift of oneself and which suffers no division. Only with God can a man give himself totally *twice at the same time,* first to his God and second to something which is a reflection of his God.

When the love on which the perfection of human life depends, and which tends to the self-subsisting Absolute, is integrated in the creative source itself, it brings no division in creative activity, because it penetrates and activates everything, and the very love of an artist for the particular absolute he serves.[24]

With this, one can begin to order Maritain's apparently ambivalent remarks on art and morality. His vision is one in which the virtue of art benefits from the insight made possible by aspects of a moral nature, and which is ultimately animated by grace. Of course, to say this is to leave aside the more complex issue of who is disposed to grace—a topic far too expansive for this essay.

But Maritain's nuanced perspectives need not be problematic. Rather, they can serve as a challenge to his fellow Christians, and especially to art-

21. Maritain, *Creative Intuition,* 380.
22. Maritain, *Responsibility of the Artist,* 93. Italics in original.
23. Maritain, *Creative Intuition,* 380.
24. Maritain, *Responsibility of the Artist,* 114–115. Italics are Maritain's.

ists. Towards the end of *The Range of Reason,* Maritain states that supernatural virtue will only take effect in a soul depending on how deeply it has been penetrated by the Gospel. The goal, then, is to achieve the unity afforded by cooperation with grace. A Christian work, says Maritain, "would have the artist, as man, a saint."[25] While creative intuition may be a special gift, the poet whose heart is united to Christ's and whose eyes are trained on the things of this world is perhaps uniquely positioned to discern the living Gospel, and therefore, to produce the most beautiful work in which heaven and earth unite.

25. Maritain, *Art and Scholasticism with Other Essays,* 55.

KAREN CHAN

Mothers, Children, and Their Common Good

I. Introduction

SOME OF THE GREATEST challenges facing contemporary society are the attacks against traditional conceptions of the family, and relatedly, the dignity of the vocation of motherhood. Attacks on the family are widespread, ranging from debates about what constitutes a family, what marriage is, the importance of the presence of a father and mother in the household, issues concerning sexual freedom, reproductive health and technological solutions to infertility, as well as abortion and beyond. The Synods of Bishops on Family, the 2015 World Meeting of Families in Philadelphia, and the ongoing debates in the secular sphere testify to the timeliness and importance of ongoing discussion about these issues of the family and motherhood. This essay will bring Maritain's important insights about the nature of the political common good and the distinction between the person and the individual to bear upon the common good of the family and the personality and individuality of mothers in relation to this domestic common good.

II. Review of Maritain on the Common Good

In *The Person and the Common Good,* Martiain famously writes:

The common good of the city is neither the mere collection of private goods, nor the proper good of a whole which, like the species with respect to its individuals or the hive with respect to its bees, relates the parts of itself alone and sacrifices them to itself. It is the good *human* life of the multitude, of a multitude of persons;

it is their communion in good living. It is therefore common to both *the whole and the parts* into which it flows back and which, in turn, must benefit them.[1]

Thus, the common good, or end, of political society is the shared life of virtue of citizens. In order to achieve this common good as end, the structure of the political society—including the laws and the type of political regime—must be set up in order to enable all citizens to live virtuous lives in communion with others. Further, this goal will require a certain level of material wealth and security so that persons can effectively pursue the life of virtue rather than simply struggle for survival, and it may necessitate that certain goods be held in common, such as public utilities, roadways, libraries, etc.[2] This notion of the common good is formal insofar as it specifies that all citizens live a common life of virtue; however, what exactly this common life of virtue looks like is undetermined, as "the common good of society" is flexible enough to accommodate a variety of political structures, vocations, and lifestyles.

In sum, there are two important points to note about the nature of the common good. The first is that the common good is the end or goal of the social unit, just as beatitude is the end of each particular person. This common good will guide the relationships that constitute the political society: the relationship between the ruler and the citizens must aim at the common good of society, as must the relationships between the citizens themselves. The second point is that the common good is not only the good of the entire community as a whole, but is also the good of each particular person—each particular person must benefit from the common good. Hence, no particular citizen can be sacrificed against his will for the sake of the common good. Maritain clearly rejects the "tendency to enslave and diminish the person in the measure that society considers the person as a part and as a mere material individual."[3]

III. The Common Good of the Family

These two aspects of the common good of the political society will apply to the common good at any level. Whenever two or more persons are

1. Jacques Martiain, *The Person and the Common Good* (Notre Dame, Indiana: University of Notre Dame Press, 1973), 51; italics in original.

2. Ibid., 52.

3. Ibid., 77.

united in some relationship or community, there will be some good common to the unity, some end that all members seek to achieve together. The family unit, the basic social unit that makes up the political society, is such a community. Thus, because the family is a community of persons with a basis distinct from that of the state, there must be a common good, or end, of the family (also called the "domestic society") that is distinct from (though certainly related to) the common good of the political society.

We can extract St. Thomas's teaching about the common good of the family from his definition of marriage. In marriage, the husband and wife are united in the conjugal relationship, which is constitutive of domestic society. Thus, the conjugal relationship must be directed to the good of the domestic society as a whole. In his *Summa Contra Gentiles,* he writes that, "Matrimony, then, in that it consists in the union of a husband and wife purposing to generate and educate offspring for the worship of God, is a sacrament of the Church."[4] Concerning the end of marriage, Question 44 of the *Supplementum* to the *Summa* reads:

> A joining denotes a kind of uniting, and so wherever things are united there must be a joining. Now things directed to one purpose are said to be united in their direction thereto, thus many men are united in following one military calling or in pursuing one business, in relation to which they are called fellow-soldiers or business partners. Hence, since by marriage certain persons are directed to one begetting and upbringing of children, and again to one family life, it is clear that in matrimony there is a joining in respect of which we speak of husband and wife; and this joining, through being directed to some one thing, is matrimony; while the joining together of bodies and minds is a result of matrimony.[5]

Just as the common good of the political society is the shared life of virtue lived in common by the citizens, so in parallel manner the common good of the family is the shared domestic life of virtue lived in common by the members of the family organized around the generation and education of offspring.

As the conjugal relationship derives its end from the end of the domestic society as a whole, so also do parental relationships—that is, the relationships between father and child, and mother and child. Each of these

4. Thomas Aquinas, *Summa Contra Gentiles* [SCG] IV, chap. 78, translated by Charles J. O'Neil (Notre Dame, Indiana: University of Notre Dame Press, 1975).

5. Thomas Aquinas, *Summa Theologica* Suppl. III, q. 44, a. 1, second revised edition, translated by the Fathers of the English Dominican Province (Westminster, Maryland: Benzinger Brothers, 1948).

relationships exists for the sake of the common good of the domestic society. Thus, the subordinate society formed by the parent and child, as a constitutive part of the domestic society, must be derived from the common good of the family. The common good of the parental society, then, is clearly the shared domestic life of virtue lived in common by the parents and children, specifically organized around the education of the children. For the parental duty of raising children does not extend only to providing material necessities, but as St. Thomas explains:

> Again, we must consider that in the human species offspring require not only nourishment for the body, as in the case of other animals, but also education for the soul. For other animals naturally possess their own kinds of prudence whereby they are enabled to take care of themselves. But a man lives by reason, which he must develop by lengthy, temporal experience so that he may achieve prudence. Hence, children must be instructed by parents who are already experienced people.[6]

IV. The Common Good Must Flow Back to Its Parts

Thus far, we have established that just as there is an end of the political society that is its common good, so there must be an end to the domestic society that is its common good. This domestic common good must guide all the constitutive domestic relationships, including the mother-child relationship. We now turn our attention to the second aspect of the common good: namely, the good of the whole and also each of its parts. The question is: does the common good of the domestic society, that is the generating and educating of offspring, benefit both children and parents (and specifically for the purposes of this essay, mothers) as parts of the whole? Does the domestic common good flow back to each particular member?

The ways in which the mother-child relationship benefits the child are obvious: after all, the end of the parental society is the education of children. The child receives life, care and affection, food, shelter, academic education, moral formation, the faith, etc. *Prima facie,* it seems that the children are the immediate—and only—beneficiaries of this parental society.

Moreover, common rhetoric and popular conceptions typically paint motherhood as inherently sacrificial, that mothers receive no benefit from their children. Mothers sacrifice many things for their children: careers,

6. SCG III, chap. 122.

sleep, even their lives when necessary. With young children at home, parents cannot go to nice restaurants or movies spontaneously; they may need to stop listening to certain radio stations to avoid exposing children to inappropriate topics or lyrics; they may need to play chauffeur instead of reading a good book. It is precisely this charge of motherhood as sacrifice that gives pro-choice advocates the strongest and most attractive ammunition: why should women be called to sacrifice so much (their individual goals, careers, bodies, etc.) for the sake of a child who will demand continuous sacrifice for at least eighteen years? Why should women have to put their lives on hold for such a long time? On the other side, pro-life advocates oftentimes accept and embrace the characterization of mothers as sacrificial victims and advocate that women ought to be willing to sacrifice all for their children, that motherhood is essentially a sacrifice, and a good one at that.

However, if we accept the view that motherhood is essentially a sacrifice for the sake of the children, then in what sense does the common good flow back to each and every member of the society? Or is the common good of the parental relationship substantially different from the common good of all other societies such that it is not redistributed to every member of the society, but rather only to the children?

V. Perfective Motherhood

To answer this challenge, we must be precise about what we mean by "sacrifice." There are two notions of sacrifice that commonly are used when people talk about motherhood: (1) sacrifice as limiting choices; (2) sacrifice as giving something up for the sake of another.[7] In which of these two senses, if any, is motherhood a sacrifice?

Consider the first option, that motherhood is a sacrifice because it limits a woman's choices. Once a woman has a child and devotes herself to raising this child, there are many things she cannot (or at least should not) do. When she is pregnant, she cannot go on certain rides at Disneyland. She cannot drink alcohol. She cannot sleep through the night without waking up a few times. When eight months pregnant and perhaps for a period after giving

7. Of course, there may be sacrificial aspects to motherhood in the theological sense. However, a discussion of the theological definition of sacrifice is outside of the scope of this present paper. Rather, this paper discusses the notion of sacrifice that underlies most contemporary—and oftentimes secular—attitudes toward motherhood.

birth, she cannot wear her favorite pair of skinny jeans. When she is in the hospital giving birth, she certainly cannot be at work. When she raises her children, she must use money to send her children to school or to clothe her children instead of using this money for a spa vacation. Once she becomes a mother, certain doors close—there arise limits as to what she can do.

However, it must be stated, motherhood is not unique in limiting the choices of a person. Any path or action a person chooses will limit his or her present and future options—this is simply a fact about the finiteness of human life. We cannot do or be all things at once. If a person decides to become a professor of philosophy, he must go to graduate school for some number of years. While he is in graduate school, it will be impossible for him to be a full-time NBA basketball player. If a person decides to go to the movies, she will be unable to go to the beach at one and the same time. Thus it is not *motherhood* specifically that limits one's choices, but the nature of finite human life that limits the range of possibilities for us. Therefore, the fact that motherhood limits choices (and is thereby sacrificial) is not an objection to motherhood qua motherhood at all.

Now consider the second option, in which sacrifice is understood as giving something up for another. In this sense, the common good of the family for which the mother sacrifices also benefits her as a member of the domestic society. On the one hand, it is likely that a mother will receive love and affection from her children, homemade ornaments and drawings as gifts, and will be cared for in her old age. Yet the mother also benefits in a deeper, ontological sense—motherhood *perfects* her as a woman. According to Thomistic metaphysics, perfection refers to the actualization of a natural potency. For example, when the intellect is actualized and a human being actively knows something, he is perfected insofar as his potentiality for knowing is actualized. Females have the natural potency to reproduce and become mothers, so in an obvious sense, when females actualize this potency and become pregnant and raise their children, they become perfected by motherhood. A natural potency is actualized.

Of course, women have a wide variety of natural potencies. The realization of any of these potencies—not just the potency for reproduction—can be considered perfections for the female. Entering the profession of medicine actualizes certain natural potencies, as does devoting one's life to the study of ancient texts. In order to be a non-trivial claim, then, we must further establish that motherhood is an especially significant mode of perfection for females qua females. Maritain's insightful distinction between *personality* and *individuality* is extremely helpful in this regard.

According to Maritain, "the human being is caught between two poles; a material pole, which, in reality, does not concern the true person but rather the shadow of personality or what, in the strict sense, is called *individuality*, and a spiritual pole, which does concern *true personality*."[8] We are hylomorphic unities of soul and body, form and matter. Individuality refers to our materiality as the principle of distinction, separateness, self-enclosedness: "In each of us, individuality, being that which excludes from oneself all that other men are, could be described as the narrowness of the ego, forever threatened and forever eager *to grasp for itself*."[9] Personality, on the other hand, refers to our spiritual nature, to the fact that all human souls are universal insofar as they share specifically the same kind of soul as all other humans. Maritain explains:

> Metaphysically considered, personality is, as the Thomistic School rightly asserts, "subsistence," the ultimate achievement by which the creative influx seals, within itself, a nature face to face with the whole order of existence so that the existence which it receives is *its own* existence and *its own* perfection. Personality is the subsistence of the spiritual soul communicated to the human composite. Because, in our substance, it is an imprint or seal which enables it to possess its existence, to perfect and give itself freely, personality testifies to the generosity or expansiveness in being which an incarnate spirit derives from its spiritual nature and which constitutes, within the secret depths of our ontological structure, a source of dynamic unity, of unification from within.[10]

Whereas individuality limits and yearns to pull everything into itself, then, personality communicates and gives of itself to others in generosity and abundance. Nevertheless, Maritain reminds us,

> in order to avoid misunderstandings and nonsense, we must emphasize that [the person and the individual] are not two separate things. There is not in me one reality, called my individual, and another reality, called my person. One and the same reality is, in a certain sense an individual, and, in another sense, a person. Our whole being is an individual by reason of that in us which derives from matter, and a person by reason of that in us which derives from spirit.[11]

8. Ibid., 33; italics in original.
9. Ibid., 37; italics in original.
10. Ibid., 41; italics in original.
11. Maritain, *The Person and the Common Good*, 43.

The integrated and perfected human is the one who successfully integrates his/her personality and individuality, expressing her personality *through* her individuality.

We are claiming that a unique and significant expression of this perfection or integration for the female is motherhood. If we consider the mother as an individual, we can see how motherhood becomes sacrificial insofar as she is seen as an individual in conflict with all others; distinction is emphasized. However, if we consider the mother as a person, motherhood is an expression of abundance, a generous overflowing of act. As such, this generosity is perfective of the woman, metaphysically speaking. Can there be any more generous act than that of a mother giving of her own body to conceive a child, protecting and nourishing this child in her womb, and then giving her time, love, faith, and knowledge to raising this child? In having a child, the female fully expresses herself not only as a generously communicating person, but also as an individual. Motherhood unites personality and individuality: from a woman's own material body (which is her aspect of individuality), she expresses her personality by generating another from herself, multiplying from her own individuality.

The generosity with which the mother gives life and nurturing to her child is therefore not so much *sacrificial* generosity, but rather *overabundant* generosity. The former would give something to another such that the giver no longer has it. The good is limited and scarce. Overabundant generosity, in contrast, is a sharing or communicating with another such that both the giver and receiver share the gift. In most cases, the mother shares life with her child in overabundant generosity—she herself does not lose her life in order to give it to her child. Her sharing of knowledge, of love, and of care are also acts of overabundant generosity. These goods are not limited, but rather multiply when they are shared with another. Thus, what is essential to motherhood is not sacrificial generosity, but overabundant generosity.

VI. Perfection and the *Imago Dei*

Finally, we shall consider the idea that motherhood is a uniquely female way of participating in the *imago dei*. As Aquinas affirms repeatedly, men and women participate in the *imago dei* insofar as they are rational: "Since man is said to be in the image of God by reason of his intellectual nature, he is the most perfectly like God according to that in which he can best imitate God in his intellectual nature."[12] Both men and women participate in the *imago dei* through reason since they have the same kind of soul. Nevertheless, the way in which they lead their lives according to reason will differ according to the type of body they have. Reason as exercised in a female body will be different from reason as manifested in a male body.

The intentional generation and education of children on the part of the mother is the way in which a woman can participate in the *imago dei* in a way that is not open to men, and thereby wholly different from the way in which a man can participate in the *imago dei*. To bring even closer together motherhood and the *imago dei*, we can turn to St. Thomas's epistemology. Here we can ascertain a direct parallel between the conception of children and the intellectual act. Aquinas writes: "[I]t should be noted that our intellectual word, which enables us to speak about the divine Word by a kind of resemblance, is that at which our intellectual operation terminates. This is the object of understanding, which is called the conception of the intellect."[13] The human act of knowledge reaches perfection when the human forms the mental word, or idea, or concept (*conceptus*). Regarding this generation of the mental word, St. Thomas also writes: "[W]e may say that in rational creatures wherein we find a procession of the word in the intellect ... there exists an image of the uncreated Trinity."[14] In the act of knowledge, the human *conceives* an idea. This language is revealing, because the word "conceptus" directly ties intellection to procreation. As the intellect conceives the *conceptus* or idea, the woman conceives the *conceptus* or child. As the concept perfects the intellect and is the result of the intellect (which is man's highest faculty) in its highest action, so the child perfects a woman and is the result of the woman's most unique faculty in full act.

The parallel between the *conceptus* of the intellect and the *conceptus* of the female signals that reproduction is the way in which women most perfectly mirror the productive reason of God, and is thereby a uniquely female way of participating in the *imago dei*. As St. Thomas explains: "[I]t is manifest that God causes things by His intellect, since His being is His act of understanding; and hence His knowledge must be the cause of things, in so far as His will is joined to it."[15] Further, God gives of his own exis-

12. ST I, q. 93, a. 4.

13. Thomas Aquinas, *Questiones Disputate de Veritate*, q. 1, a. 2, translated by Robert W. Mulligan Jr. (Chicago: Henry Regnery, 1952).

14. ST I, q. 93, a. 6.

15. ST I, q. 14, a. 8.

tence to creatures when he creates *ex nihilo,* and women who intentionally generate and educate children mirror God's creative thought. They give their own bodies to their children. In having and raising children, women are able to mirror and participate in the fecundity of God in a way wholly unique to females.

Reflection upon the nature of motherhood reveals how intellectual an enterprise it is. After all, women have children through the interplay of will and reason. As they gestate a child in their wombs, they are constantly deliberating about practical matters: what diapers to buy, how to decorate the nursery, what foods to avoid, etc. It is, in addition, an occasion for speculative thought: women can be led to contemplate the wonders and marvels of existence, the wonders of the human body, the possibility of creation, and the rapidity of change. As she educates her child, the mother not only shares her own knowledge and experience with her child, but is in return challenged by him. Through the questions of her child, who his a natural philosopher filled with wonder, the mother is called to contemplate the cosmos and to answer all of the "Why?" questions her child poses. Mothers exercises their reason in a uniquely female way in raising their children.

VII. Conclusion

We have argued that the common good of the domestic society is the shared life of virtue of the family members, organized around the generation and education of children, and this common good must flow back over each member of the domestic society, including mothers. We then made the further claim that motherhood offers an ontologically significant level of perfection for females *qua* females, and that motherhood allows females qua females a unique avenue of participation in the *imago dei.* The hierarchy we are suggesting is an ontological hierarchy, one based on perfection or actuality. This ontological hierarchy does not mean that those who are not mothers have less dignity or are less fully human or female. After all, St. Thomas teaches that according to an ontological hierarchy of perfection, angels are ontologically more perfect than humans because angels, as immaterial substances, have less potency, and also that the contemplative life is more perfect than the active life because it is more self-sufficient and most fully actualizes man's highest faculties. Yet, considered another way, humans are higher than angels. Writes Aquinas:

> [W]e may consider the image of God as regards its accidental qualities, so far as to observe in man a certain imitation of God, consisting in the fact that man proceeds from man, as God from God; and also in the fact that the whole human soul is in the whole body, as God from God; and also in the fact that the whole human soul is in the whole body, and again, in every part, as God is in regard to the whole world. In these and the like things the image of God is more perfect in man than it is in the angels.[16]

Likewise, the active life can be considered to be higher than the contemplative life because it is necessary for the contemplative life. The popular misconception of motherhood as sacrificial and damaging to females is therefore a dangerous mistake that begs the question about the value of motherhood. We must learn from St. Thomas and Maritain and avoid thinking of motherhood as uniquely and inherently sacrificial so that we can properly locate motherhood on the hierarchy of ontological perfection and thus properly defend the vocation of motherhood.

16. ST I, q. 93, a. 3.

About the Authors

NOEL ADAMS has written mostly on Kierkegaard and the philosophy of religion. His interests in the boundaries of rational discourse and thought are reflected in his research projects concerning paradox, ambiguity, and indirect communication. These general interests naturally led him to the study of the writings of Søren Kierkegaard. His research on Kierkegaard is informed by both historical sources and analytical methods. He is currently working on the historical sources of influence on Kierkegaard during the early part of Kierkegaard's authorship, as well as providing a philosophically suitable framework for approaching Kierkegaard's "Concluding Unscientific Postscript to Philosophical Fragments." His fluency in Danish has permitted him to spend extended periods of study at the Søren Kierkegaard Research Center in Copenhagen, Denmark, as well as the Søren Kierkegaard Library in Northfield, Minnesota.

STEPHEN CHAMBERLAIN is Associate Professor of Philosophy at Rockhurst University in Kansas City, Missouri. He received his PhD in philosophy from Fordham University and his Master's Degree in Philosophy from Boston College. His areas of specialty are medieval philosophy, epistemology, metaphysics, and aesthetics. He has published numerous articles, essays, and reviews in these areas.

KAREN C. CHAN currently serves as Academic Dean and Associate Professor of Philosophy at St. Patrick's Seminary and University of the Archdiocese of San Francisco. She received her undergraduate degree from the University of San Francisco and her doctorate in philosophy from the University of Notre Dame. Her research interests center on Aristotelian-Thomistic moral philosophy and its application to contemporary issues such as medical ethics and motherhood.

JOHN MARSON DUNAWAY is Professor Emeritus of French and Interdisciplinary Studies at Mercer University in Macon, Georgia. Author, editor, or translator of ten books on modern French religious writers, his latest include translations of Vladimir Volkoff's last two novels: *L'Hôte du Pape/The Pope's Guest* and *Le Tortionnaire/The Torturer* (Mercer University Press, 2013 and 2016), and Jean-Louis Chrétien's *Sous le regard de la Bible/ Under the Gaze of the Bible* (Fordham University Press, 2014). In retirement he is involved in racial reconciliation work in Macon.

MEGAN FURMAN is a doctoral candidate in philosophy at the University of Dallas. A graduate of the University of Notre Dame (BA English), Oxford University (MSt English), and The Dominican School of Philosophy and Theology in Berkeley (MA Philosophy and MA Theology), Furman's work has focused on the philosophy of beauty, aesthetics, moral philosophy, and the philosophy of language. She has worked for ten years in international and foreign affairs authoring three books, editing three academic volumes, and contributing to three documentary films, including two for *National Geographic.*

JUSTIN C. GABLE, OP, received his PhD from Fordham University. He is Assistant Professor of Philosophy at the Dominican School of Philosophy and Theology in Berkeley, California and a friar of the Province of the Most Holy Name of Jesus (Western Dominican Province, USA). He teaches courses in Thomistic philosophy, ethics, phenomenology, and postmodernism, and his research interests include issues in bioethics, philosophy of mind, and the intersection between phenomenology and cognitive science.

ANNE FRANCES AI LE, OP, is a member of the Dominican Sisters of Mary Immaculate Province. She holds a doctorate in philosophy from the University of St. Thomas in Houston, Texas. She has had several publications through the American Maritain Association in the recent past. Presently, she teaches philosophy and theology at St. Mark's and Corpus Christi Colleges in Vancouver, British Columbia.

BRIAN KEMPLE received his PhD in philosophy from the University of St. Thomas, in Houston, Texas, with the Center for Thomistic Studies. His dissertation, *Ens Primum Cognitum in Thomas Aquinas and the Tradition,* was written under the direction of John Deely. His work focuses on the relationship between traditional metaphysical thought and the philosophy of knowledge developed within phenomenology, seeking a coherent approach to the whole of human experience, grounded in the nature of the human person. In 2015 he published "Examining Étienne Gilson's Metaphysical Realism" in *Studia Gilsoniana,* and "Wojtyla: Nature, Person, and Teleology" in *Thomas Aquinas: Teacher of Humanity.* His other research interests include the dissemination of philosophical thought to the public sphere at large, the nature of socially-constituted reality, and the dynamics of interpersonal relationships.

GREGORY J. KERR is currently Associate Professor of Philosophy at DeSales University in Center Valley, Pennsylvania. He received his BA and MA in philosophy from Boston College and his PhD from Fordham University, where he did his dissertation on *Maritain's Receptive Intuition and the Benefits of Art.* He is a former editor of the *Maritain Notebook,* the official newsletter of the American Maritain Association. He has published articles on Maritain's views on aesthetics, epistemology, ethics, love, and education in volumes in the AMA's series and elsewhere. He has a special interest in exploring the very different and conflicting ways humans know. He is married to Cindy and they have four sons and two grandchildren.

JAMES M. JACOBS is Professor of Philosophy and Assistant Academic Dean at Notre Dame Seminary in New Orleans, Louisiana, where he has taught since 2003. He holds a BA from Harvard University and a PhD from Fordham University. His major area of research is Thomistic metaphysics and ethics, and more generally the need for a philosophical realism as a response to modern nominalism and skepticism. His most recent articles have appeared in the journals *International Philosophical Quarterly, Lex Naturalis,* and *Logos.* He edited the American Maritain Association volume, *A Piercing Light: Beauty, Faith, and Human Transcendence* (2014), and is currently the Vice President of the association.

FLORIAN MICHEL is Associate Professor of Modern History at the University of Paris 1 Panthéon Sorbonne; Vice President of the "Cercle d'études Jacques et Raïssa Maritain" (France); author of *La pensée catholique en Amérique du Nord. Réseaux intellectuels et échanges culturels entre l'Europe, le Canada et les États-Unis (années 1920–1960)* (Paris: Desclée de Brouwer, 2010); editor of the integral Jacques Maritain-Yves Simon correspondence

(800 letters, published in two volumes, by Éditions CLD, Paris, 2008 and 2012); author of an intellectual biography of Étienne Gilson (Vrin, 2017). Michel is now working on the publication of the complete works of Étienne Gilson and on the integral notebooks of Jacques Maritain.

FRANCISCO EDUARDO PLAZA is a doctoral candidate in philosophy at the Center for Thomistic Studies at the University of St. Thomas, in Houston, Texas. Under the direction of John Hittinger, his dissertation focuses upon Jacques Maritain's philosophy of culture, and how it can be used with the work of Karol Wojtyla (St. John Paul II), Eric Voegelin, and others to addresses the crisis of modernity. His research interests are primarily the study of ethics and political theory, their metaphysical foundation, Thomistic personalism, and the philosophy of culture and human subjectivity. A large component of his work is centered on the relationship between Thomism and contemporary philosophy, particularly personalism and phenomenology, and how this may aid us in our understanding of modernity.

GREGORY M. REICHBERG is a Research Professor at the Peace Research Institute Oslo (PRIO). He heads the Research School on Peace and Conflict, a consortium for doctoral students that is based at the University of Oslo. His most recent book is *Thomas Aquinas on War and Peace* (Cambridge University Press, 2017). A member of the Pontifical Academy of Social Sciences, he has been a professor at Fordham University and The Catholic University of America.

RICHARD SCHENK, OP, is a Dominican priest of the Province of the Most Holy Name of Jesus (Western Dominican Province, USA), currently in the chaplaincy to the University of Freiburg im Breisgau. He held the rank of Professor of Philosophy and Theology at the Graduate Theological Union in Berkeley from 1990 to 2011, was Director of the Hannover Institute of Philosophical Research from 1991 to 2000, and Director of the Intercultural Forum for Studies in Faith and Culture (Washington, D.C.) from 2004 to 2006. Most recently, he was President of The Catholic University of Eichstaett-Ingolstadt from 2011 to 2014. He is the founding president (2007-2008) of the Academy of Catholic Theology and a Member of the European Academy of Sciences and Arts.

JOSHUA SCHULZ is Associate Professor of Philosophy at DeSales University in Center Valley, Pennsylvania, and the editor of the American Maritain Association's *Maritain Notebook*. He holds a PhD from Marquette University, and a BA from the University of Nebraska at Kearney. Working in the Aristotelian-Thomistic tradition, he has recently published papers on the ethics of humor, technology, hypocrisy, and religious belief, and the capability approach to human development. He teaches courses on Alasdair MacIntyre, ethics and economics, medical ethics, and Thomistic virtue ethics.

WALTER SCHULTZ is Auxiliary Professor in the Faculty of Philosophy at the Dominican University College in Ottawa, Canada. He received his PhD in Western Religious Thought from McMaster University. For many years, he was a teacher and worked in Program Design for the Dufferin Peel Roman Catholic Separate School Board, Mississauga, Ontario, developing and implementing throughout the board a senior level philosophy program based on the work of Jacques Maritain. His publications are primarily concerned with education and the relevance of Maritain's thought for contemporary society and politics. He is currently President of the Canadian Jacques Maritain Association and Editor of the journal *Études maritainiennes/Maritain Studies*.

FEDERICO TEDESCO is Professor of Hylomorphic Ethics and Thomistic Philosophy of the Body at the Istituto Veritatis Splendor of Bologna. He received his PhD in 2013 from the University of Verona. He has several essays in the American Maritain Association book series. He is also one of the founders of SOMA: Center for the Development and the Practice of Body-Mind Unity.

MICHAEL D. TORRE has been Associate Professor of Philosophy at the University of San Francisco for the last twenty-two years and recently completed a term as President of the American Maritain Association (2012-2016). He edited for it *Freedom in the Modern World: Jacques Maritain, Yves R. Simon, and Mortimer J. Adler,* (1989; second printing, 1990), which assembled the first collection of essays published on Yves R. Simon. As the General Editor of the AMA Book Series from 2009-2013, he oversaw the publication of eight of its volumes. He has published two books dealing with man's responsibility for sin: *God's Permission of Sin* (Fribourg Univer sity Press, 2009) and *Do Not Resist the Spirit's Call* (The Catholic University of American Press, 2013). He has also published numerous articles in the AMA Book Series, as well as further articles on Yves R. Simon: "Yves R. Simon: The Merit and Limit of Federalism" (*Notes et Documents*, 1992), and "Jacques Maritain and Yves R. Simon on Freedom of Choice" (in the AMA volume *Human Nature, Contemplation, and the Political Order*, 2014). His editing of the *Yves R. Simon Reader* is presently being considered for publication by the University of Notre Dame Press.

Index

PUBLICATIONS OF THE AMERICAN MARITAIN ASSOCIATION

1. *Jacques Maritain: The Man and His Metaphysics*
Edited by John F. X. Knasas, 1988
ISBN 978-0-268-01205-2, (out of print)
Distributed by the University of Notre Dame Press

2. *Freedom in the Modern World: Jacques Maritain, Yves R. Simon, Mortimer J. Adler*
Edited by Michael D. Torre, 1989, Second Printing, 1990
ISBN 978-0-268-00978-6
Distributed by the University of Notre Dame Press

3. *From Twilight to Dawn: The Cultural Vision of Jacques Maritain*
Edited by Peter A. Redpath, 1990
ISBN 978-0-268-00979-3
Distributed by the University of Notre Dame Press

4. *The Future of Thomism*
Edited by Deal W. Hudson and Dennis Wm. Moran, 1992
ISBN 978-0-268-00986-1
Distributed by the University of Notre Dame Press

5. *Jacques Maritain and the Jews*
Edited by Robert Royal, 1994
ISBN 978-0-268-01193-2
Distributed by the University of Notre Dame Press

6. *Freedom, Virtue, and the Common Good*
Edited by Curtis L. Hancock and Anthony O. Simon, 1995
ISBN 978-0-268-00991-0
Distributed by the University of Notre Dame Press

7. *Postmodernism and Christian Philosophy*
Edited by Roman T. Ciapolo, 1997
ISBN 978-0-8132-0881-7
Distributed by the Catholic University of America Press

8. *The Common Things: Essays on Thomism and Education*
Edited by Daniel McInerny, 1999
ISBN 978-0-9669226-0-8
Distributed by the Catholic University of America Press

The Failure of Modernism:
9. *The Cartesian Legacy and Contemporary Pluralism*
Edited by Brendan Sweetman, 1999
ISBN 978-0-9669226-1-5
Distributed by the Catholic University of America Press

10. *Beauty, Art, and the Polis*
Edited by Alice Ramos, 2000
ISBN 978-0-9669226-2-2
Distributed by the Catholic University of America Press

11. *Reassessing the Liberal State: Reading Maritain's Man and the State*
Edited by Timothy Fuller and John P. Hittinger, 2001
ISBN 978-0-9669226-3-9
Distributed by the Catholic University of America Press

12. *Faith, Scholarship, and Culture in the 21st Century*
Edited by Alice Ramos and Marie I. George, 2002
ISBN 978-0-9669226-5-3
Distributed by the Catholic University of America Press

13. *Jacques Maritain and the Many Ways of Knowing*
Edited by Douglas A. Ollivant, 2002
ISBN 978-0-9669226-4-6
Distributed by the Catholic University of America Press

14. *Truth Matters: Essays in Honor of Jacques Maritain*
Edited by John G. Trapani, Jr., 2004
ISBN 978-0-9669226-6-0
Distributed by the Catholic University of America Press

15. *The Human Person and a Culture of Freedom*
Edited by Peter A. Pagan Aguiar and Terese Auer, OP, 2009
ISBN 978-0-9669226-7-7
Distributed by the Catholic University of America Press

16. *Maritain and America*
Edited by Christopher M. Cullen, SJ and Joseph Allan Clair, 2009
ISBN 978-0-9669226-8-4
Distributed by the Catholic University of America Press

17. *The Renewal of Civilization: Essays in Honor of Jacques Maritain*
Edited by Gavin T. Colvert, 2010
ISBN 978-0-9669226-9-1
Distributed by the Catholic University of America Press

18. *The Vocation of the Catholic Philosopher: From Maritain to John Paul II*
Edited by John P. Hittinger, 2010
ISBN 978-0-9827119-0-3
Distributed by the Catholic University of America Press

19. *Reading the Cosmos: Nature, Science, and Wisdom*
Edited by Giuseppe Butera, 2011
ISBN 978-0-9827119-1-0
Distributed by the Catholic University of America Press

20. *Distinctions of Being: Philosophical Approaches to Reality*
Edited by Nikolaj Zunic, 2013
ISBN 978-0-9827119-2-7
Distributed by the Catholic University of America Press

21. *Love and Friendship: Maritain and the Tradition*
Edited by Montague Brown, 2013
ISBN 978-0-9827119-3-4
Distributed by the Catholic University of America Press

22. *Aquinas and Maritain on Evil: Mystery and Metaphysics*
Edited by James G. Hanink, 2013
ISBN 978-0-9827119-4-1
Distributed by the Catholic University of America Press

23. *Human Nature, Contemplation, and the Political Order: Essays Inspired by Jacques Maritain's* Scholasticism and Politics
Edited by Peter Karl Koritansky, 2014
ISBN 978-0-9827119-5-8
Distributed by the Catholic University of America Press

24. *Redeeming Philosophy: From Metaphysics to Aesthetics*
Edited by John J. Conley, SJ, 2014
ISBN 978-0-9827119-6-5
Distributed by the Catholic University of America Press

25. *A Piercing Light: Beauty, Faith, and Human Transcendence*
Edited by James M. Jacobs, 2015
ISBN 978-0-9827-1197-2
Distributed by the Catholic University of America Press

26. *The Wisdom of Youth: Essays Inspired by the Early Work of Jacques and Raïssa Maritain*
Edited by Travis Dumsday, 2016
ISBN 978-0-9827119-8-9
Distributed by the Catholic University of America Press